Studies in African Literature

African Writers on African Writing
Edited by G. D. KILLAM

The Writings of Chinua Achebe
G. D. KILLAM

The Writing of Wole Soyinka
ELDRED JONES

The Poetry of L. S. Senghor
S. O. MEZU

The Poetry of Okot p'Bitek
G. A. HERON

The Novels and Plays of Ngugi
G. D. KILLAM

The Novels of Ayi Kwei Armah
ROBERT FRASER

Critical Perspectives

Critical Perspectives on Chinua Achebe
Edited by CATHERINE INNES and BERNTH LINDFORS

Critical Perspectives on Amos Tutuola
Edited by BERNTH LINDFORS

Critical Perspectives on V. S. Naipaul
Edited by ROBERT HAMNER

Critical Perspectives on Nigerian Literatures
Edited by BERNTH LINDFORS

African Literature Today
Edited by ELDRED JONES

Omnibus edition, volumes 1–4
The Novel in Africa 5
Poetry in Africa 6
Focus on Criticism 7
Drama in Africa 8
Africa, America and the Caribbean 9
Retrospect and Prospect 10

The Growth of the African Novel

Studies in African Literature

The Growth of the African Novel

EUSTACE PALMER

Associate Professor
English Department, Fourah Bay College,
University of Sierra Leone

LONDON
HEINEMANN
IBADAN · NAIROBI

Heinemann Educational Books Ltd
22 Bedford Square, London WC1B 3HH
P.M.B. 5205, Ibadan · P.O. Box 45314, Nairobi

EDINBURGH   MELBOURNE   AUCKLAND
HONG KONG   SINGAPORE   KUALA LUMPUR   NEW DELHI
KINGSTON   PORT OF SPAIN

Heinemann Educational Books Inc.
4 Front Street, Exeter, New Hampshire 03833, U.S.A.

ISBN 0 435 91801 X (cased)   79-23244
ISBN 0 435 91802 8 (paper)

Filmset in Monophoto Plantin by
Northumberland Press Ltd, Gateshead, Tyne and Wear
Printed in Great Britain by
Richard Clay (The Chaucer Press) Ltd, Bungay, Suffolk

To my mother and father

Contents

▼▼▼▼▼▼▼▼▼▼▼▼▼▼▼▼▼▼▼▼▼▼▼▼▼▼▼▼▼▼▼▼▼▼▼▼▼▼▼

Introduction

▼▼

A quarter of a century after the publication of the first African novels worth the name a substantial body of criticism has emerged which in its range and erudition indisputably matches the volume and importance of the new literature. For all its brilliance, however, this criticism displays a certain amount of disarray among the critics about the criteria to be used in the evaluation of African fiction. This has been particularly evident in the publication of a number of critical works such as Charles Larson's *The Emergence of African Fiction*, Christopher Heywood's (ed.) *Perspectives on African Literature*, Eldred Jones's *The Writings of Wole Soyinka*, Bruce King's (ed.) *An Introduction to Nigerian Literature*, the present writer's *An Introduction to the African Novel* and several articles in numbers 5, 6 and 7 of *African Literature Today* edited by Eldred Jones. It seems necessary, therefore, that in the introduction to yet another critical work on African fiction one should set out one's criteria for evaluation.

The view is gaining ground in African literary circles that African literature should not be judged by the criteria which have so far been used in the evaluation of western literature. The reasons for the objection to the use of western criteria are not always literary or cultural; to a very large extent they are complicated by nationalistic and ideological considerations. Having shaken off the imperialistic yoke there is a tendency in some quarters to reject everything associated with the imperialists. In the colonial days African culture was adversely affected by the imperialist experience since everything was judged by western cultural standards and there was a tendency, in fact, to suppress those aspects of African culture which could not be reconciled with western culture. It therefore seems unthinkable to a number of African intellectuals that even after liberation African culture should continue to be dominated by western standards. This would seem, to them, to be a form of cultural neo-imperialism. For most African countries the experience of actually having writers in print is new and exciting and therefore a source of national pride. They can at last take their places alongside other nations who boast a written literature. Their writers therefore become national heroes almost overnight. That the works of some of these writers should be denigrated by foreign critics using foreign criteria must be a source of great annoyance. Inevitably, therefore, there is the call for indigenous criteria, and behind it is the barely concealed assumption that these indigenous criteria will be slightly more relaxed and flexible.

The nationalistic and ideological objections to the use of western criteria are not very valid. If the purpose of criticism is to display as accurately as possible the genuine quality of a work, then our aim should be to use or evolve criteria which will be the most helpful in bringing out that genuine quality, whether those criteria have been used by the West or not. Our considerations must be literary and cultural rather than ideological, nationalistic or political. Nevertheless, there are some genuine cultural and literary reasons for the objection to western criteria. Literature generally evolves out of a people's historical and cultural experience. In the case of African literature this experience was completely different from the western. Inevitably, the attitudes of African writers to certain subjects are likely to differ from those of western writers. Since, it is argued, the African writer goes to traditional culture for the sources of his inspiration and occasionally for his techniques, the form of the works he produces will not be western, or they will at least involve a considerable modification of western forms. It will therefore be a literary crime to measure what is after all an indigenous African form, putting across an indigenous African point of view, by an alien standard. This is a weighty argument which ought to be considered seriously. It is reasonable to assume that the formal aspects of African poetry and drama, while making concessions to the influence of the western tradition, derive largely from indigenous forms of these genres. A legitimate case can therefore be made for the use of indigenous criteria in the evaluation of African poetry and drama, although in practice most critics of African poetry have discussed it in western critical terms. We are concerned here, however, with prose, and there the matter is not so clear-cut. If it can be demonstrated that the African novel is entirely different in form from the western and that it derives from indigenous African traditions, then the case for the rejection of western criteria in its evaluation will be incontestable.

There are important differences between African and western

novels. The most important is likely to be the use of language. African novelists writing in English will use the language differently from English novelists, either because of inadequate control of a linguistic medium which is not native to them, or through the realization that the frontiers of the language have to be extended to accommodate their insights. In the majority of cases, therefore, an African novel written in English is unlikely to read like an English one. Yet one must discriminate between the attempts of novelists like Achebe, Ngugi and Soyinka who, having acquired mastery over the language, modify it consciously to achieve their purposes, and less skilled craftsmen who merely manifest inadequate control. One cannot simply talk of 'difference'. In any case, one should also bear in mind that various English novelists use English differently, some of them, like Defoe, even incompetently. One must also realize that some English novelists, too, are engaged in pushing back the limits of the language. Joyce is a good example of a writer from the British Isles whose practice with words demands that the reader adjust his mode of apprehension slightly. And yet Joyce can be conveniently discussed within the English literary tradition and with the same critical principles that would be applied to Virginia Woolf, for instance. The difference in the use of language does not by itself justify the use of different criteria. Some critics do suggest, however, that allowances should be made for African novelists who use the language incompetently. The usual argument offered in support of this is that the author has a burning message to deliver to his people and the world. If it had been possible for him to write in his own language and still have a large audience he would have done so readily and competently. But he is forced to write in a language not of his own choosing and in which he is not at home. Should we not be grateful that the message has been conveyed? Is not the message the important thing? Should we cavil about linguistic mistakes? One would agree that it is important that the message be communicated. But surely the message and its communication cannot be divorced from the language in which it is communicated. One should only make allowances for inadequate control if it does not impair the reader's overall satisfaction from the work.

It is also conceivable that, given the difference in cultural and historical background, the themes of African novels might be different from western ones. This also applies, of course, to setting, which is perhaps the most obvious indicator of the 'Africanness' of a novel. But difference of theme and setting, like difference in the use of language, does not justify the deployment of different criteria. After all, there are signs that the younger generation of African novelists, like Kole Omotoso, are now concerning themselves with new themes, and that the preoccupation with certain stock themes was only a passing phase. In any case, even within the corpus of the western novel itself we find a wide variety of themes. It is also to be expected that because of the difference in background the African novelist's point of view will be different from that of his western counterpart. Indeed, in the very vexed exercise of defining African literature, this question of point of view, or spirit, or attitude is the one definite factor that can reliably be referred to as distinguishing African literature from other literatures. But will difference in point of view justify the use of different criteria for evaluation?

The tenor of the argument so far has been to the effect that the African novel is not widely different from the western and we therefore do not need very different criteria for evaluation. If it could be proved, however, that the African novel emerged from traditional African sources quite independent of western influences, then there might be some justification for the use of purely African critical terms of reference in keeping with the sources and the indigenous development of African fiction. The view that the African novel evolved, not from the western novel, but from the well-established tradition of African prose writing and the even more ancient tradition of oral literature, has gained wide currency, and needs to be considered seriously. It is incontestable that African prose writing did not start with Amos Tutuola and Cyprian Ekwensi, as Lalage Bown has demonstrated. She shows that the range and wealth of African prose writing from the eighteenth-century figures Equiano, Ignatius Sancho and Cuguano, through Africanus Beale Horton, Samuel Crowther and Edward Blyden I to comparatively modern writers like Casely-Hayford.[1] But while it is easy to demonstrate the growth of the English novel in the eighteenth century out of Bunyan's tracts, the essays in the *De Coverley Papers*, the Rogue Biographies and the Travelogue, it is difficult to see any direct link between the prose works discussed by Lalage Bown and the rise of the African novel. It is probably more rewarding to try to trace the development of the African novel from the African oral tradition. Africa has always been extremely rich in oral literature, and the tradition of story telling is well established, probably more so than in many other cultures. Generally speaking, also, there is some continuity between the oral and written traditions of a literature. This is just as true of English as of other literatures. Must we therefore suppose that the same phenomenon was at work in the development of the African novel? Tutuola was the first significant writer of fiction in Africa to make elaborate use of traditional tales. He was largely influenced by the works of D. O. Fagunwa who wrote his tales in Yoruba.[2] Can it be said that the African novel grew out of the efforts of Tutuola and Fagunwa (whose works in a sense look like Romances) in the same way as the western novel developed from the prose Romance, but essentially as a reaction to it? A detailed examination of the forms and structures of the earliest African novels like Achebe's *Things Fall Apart*, Laye's *The Radiance of the King* or Ekwensi's *People of the City* would reveal that they could not possibly be outgrowths of the oral tale. The African novel was neither a continuation of the Tutuola tradition nor a reaction to it. Tutuola's practice was not followed by later novelists.[3] Ekwensi, who comes next to him in chronological importance, goes for inspiration, not to the traditional world, or the world of fantasy, but to the world of the city. *Burning Grass*, his only novel resembling a folk tale, was his third. A number of African novelists incorporate elements of the oral tradition into their novels, but these are not therefore outgrowths of the oral tale. Much as we would like to think so, for nationalistic and other reasons, the novel, unlike poetry and drama, is not an indigenous African genre. To say this is not to be un-African or a fifth columnist; it is to strive after the true position which after all is the object of all research. The African novel grew out of the western novel, and writers like Achebe, Laye and Ekwensi were much more influenced by Conrad, Hardy, Dickens, Kafka and George Eliot than by the African oral tale. They had all of them been exposed to western literature during their student days. Indeed, some of them have furnished us with lists of the western writers who left a profound impact on them. Many critics of the African novel have recognized its debt to the western novel. J. P. Clark has stated that the novel is the only genre of art that Nigerians have really borrowed;[4] Povey mentions the orthodoxy of Achebe's handling of the novel form, suggesting that his work can be conveniently set within the wider context of the field of English language writing;[5] and Killam recognizes that the modern Nigerian novel follows the main historical development of the English novel, making additions of its own, the additions being largely in the way of themes.[6] A reasonably fair statement of the position would seem to be that the African novel grew out of the western novel, but that African novelists have modified the genre largely in the direction of themes, language, setting and point of view. But this does not suggest that it is basically different from the western and that entirely different criteria should therefore be used in its evaluation.

If we are to display clearly the genuine quality of a work, then our criticism should be descriptive, analytic and evaluative. In order to ensure this we must pay attention to the meaning, the author's intention, the subject matter and the relevance of the work for its immediate community and for humanity as a whole; but we must also evaluate the author's treatment of his subject and his success in general, which means paying attention to technique. This surely suggests that our criticism cannot be purely sociological, as some critics have recently recommended. It cannot merely confine itself to a discussion of the work's relevance. Irele, for instance, declares that we must approach African works

> with an insight into, and a feeling for, those aspects of African life which stand beyond the work itself, its extension into the African experience, and its foundation into the very substance of African existence... This approach, in its fullest and widest meaning, implies that our criticism should take into account everything that has gone into the work, and specifically for our literature; everything within our society which has informed the work, as Leavis would put it.[7]

He feels that this would help demonstrate to African readers the relevance of the work for them.

In spite of his awareness of the need for literary evaluation, Irele is arguing for an essentially sociological criticism. No one will deny the importance of a sociological approach, especially in cases where the literature is being read by a foreign audience who will need to be aware of all the various forces impinging on the consciousness of the writer as he wrote the work, in order to appreciate his attitude and treatment of his subject fully. It will also help to highlight immediately the significance of the work for its own African nationals. Nor would a sociological approach be peculiar to the criticism of African literature. One thinks immediately of Arnold Kettle's brilliant essay on Defoe's *Moll Flanders* in *On Books and Humankind* in which he tries to make a convincing case for Defoe and his heroine by analysing the social forces with which Defoe and Moll were confronted. In concentrating on the sociological, therefore, we would not necessarily be applying an African criterion. But a purely sociological criticism poses serious problems and involves grave dangers. The first of these is that a number of inexpert critics would feel that all that is required for evaluation is to discuss themes and subject matter and point out the work's social or historical relevance, documenting in detail its social references. Indeed, some of the advocates for a sociological criticism seem to imply that there would not be any point in evaluation at all. Criticism would then degenerate into sterile sociological and historical commentaries and there would be no essential difference between this and the debased anthropological criticism by the earliest critics of the African novel. In all probability the work would be buried under a welter of notes and references and the author's essential achievement obscured. In any case, does the African reader, for whom all this referential information is presumably intended, need all of it? Does he not know about most of it already? In possibly a majority of cases the necessary sociological information would probably be provided by the author in the work itself. If it is not, and it is essential for our understanding, we would then be right to go outside the work to get it. But we must move from the work outwards. We must have come across a situation in the work which is not quite clear from the context and which is essential for our understanding of the whole; then we would be justified in going outside. This is the value of a sociological approach. Surely in order to demonstrate the relevance of a novel for its African readers one need not point out 'everything within the society which has informed the work'. A novel, while being a realistic work of fiction, is not a photographic copy of everything that has gone on in society. It is the result of a scrupulous process of selection during which the author assembles his materials from within the social or historical situation, transforming them into a satisfying work of art which gives his own interpretation of the situation, an interpretation which might be quite different from the historian's or the sociologist's. The literary critic must concern himself not just with the social or historical details, but precisely with this process of selection; with the work of art, in fact.

Another danger inherent in the sociological approach is that works of a dubious literary value would be treated with respect because of their sociological relevance. Indeed, the main reason for Irele's call for a sociological criticism as the best way of approaching African literature is his feeling that western literary criteria which show at least equal concern for coherence and artistry as for social realism might not see much value in some African works which have a certain social relevance but do not rate very highly as works of art. Hence his complaint that the critical apparatus sometimes brought to bear on the works of African writers is too heavy and well above the level of what the writer himself is offering.[8] But if these writers are to be taken seriously as both artists and analysts of their societies, and not merely as popular entertainers, then in what sense could the critical apparatus applied to them be called too heavy, and what alternative apparatus should be used to bring out their importance as both social analysts and artists? The sociological approach in the hands of inexpert critics might even lead easily to the dogma that the only African works worth considering are those dealing with social or historical reality. Novels, therefore, which explore themes like love or relations between the sexes might tend to be devalued.

We must never forget that in the business of criticism we are primarily concerned with the work in front of us, not with its background. In the final analysis our attitude will depend on whether we regard the novel as a work of art which demands evaluation, or as a sociological or historical document whose main function is to act as a handmaid of sociology or history and teach us about our societies. Put in these terms it might almost seem as if one were stating the opposition between the concept of literature as mimesis, as an imitation or reflection of real life, and as an autonomous aesthetic form obeying its own laws. It might also seem that one were stating the opposition between sociological and artistic criticism, or between a realistic and a formalist view of fiction. There need not, of course, be any such opposition. If my comments so far have suggested that I feel that the sociological kind of criticism is inadequate, I also feel that purely artistic criticism, or a preoccupation with art for art's sake, is equally inadequate. We must demand that an African novel demonstrates some relevance. It follows that novels which do not show this relevance cannot be highly rated and, correspondingly, criticism which merely concerns itself with pointing out the beauties is inadequate. But the alternative to artistic criticism is not sociological criticism, nor is the alternative to sociological criticism artistic criticism. The alternative to both is a criticism which evaluates the literary quality of the work and also discusses the novelist's concern with and treatment of real issues that are relevant to the lives of the people. The considerations influencing critical judgement should be human, literary and social. There should be no opposition between them.

This surely means that in the evaluation of the African novel, if we cannot afford to neglect subject matter, reality of themes, and so on, we cannot afford to neglect technique either. We must remind ourselves that throughout the history of African culture, if there has always been a concern for reality, there has also always been a concern for artistry, for technique. We can see this, surely, in the formal elements of African sculpture and in the traditional story teller's concern with his craft. How can we then be expected in the criticism of African fiction to ignore coherence, artistry and technique? I quote here an excerpt from an article by Mark Schorer which talks of the importance of technique.

> . . . technique is the means by which the writer's experience, which is his subject matter, compels him to attend to it; technique is the only means he has of discovering, exploring, developing his subject, for conveying its meaning, and, finally, of evaluating it. And surely it follows that certain techniques are sharper tools than others, and will discover more; that the writer capable of the most exacting scrutiny of his subject matter will produce works with the most satisfying content, works with thickness and resonance, works which reverberate, works with maximum meaning.[9]

Schorer's emphasis on technique has led to the mistaken impression in some quarters that he is given an extreme statement of the formalist position. This is to do him an injustice. He is talking about the relationship between subject matter, content, experience and technique. Surely he implies that we must concern ourselves with the writer's experience, with his presentation of reality (hence his reference to works with thickness, resonance, maximum meaning and satisfying content), but in order to apprehend this fully we must look at the way in which he has used techniques to shape this experience.

In sum, then, I am suggesting that criticism of African fiction should take into account both the relevance of the work to the human condition (the sociological, if one prefers that term) and the novelist's artistry. And artistry should include coherence of plot and structure, language (making suitable allowances for any necessary and deliberate modifications the writer may have made in order to accommodate his insights), setting, presentation of character, descriptive power, and so on. Only by the successful deployment of such techniques will the writer be able to give his works the semblance of realism. The list is by no means exhaustive; there will always be innovations and experiments, and novelists will use some or all of these techniques in varying combinations. We must be prepared to be flexible and respond to the use of new tools. All that we must ask is that the author's technique be suited to his subject matter and that he uses it well.

These two main criteria I have suggested – social relevance and artistry – might superficially seem to be western; but it is a distortion to describe them as such. If they have grown up alongside the development of the western novel it is most probably because the western novel was the first to be discussed seriously. They are probably the qualities that readers everywhere will take into consideration in order to account for the impact of serious novels on their minds. And they are so generalized, in any case, that they allow for a tremendous amount of flexibility and can be applied to divers kinds of novels and novelists.

NOTES

1 Lalage Bown, 'The development of African prose writing in English: a perspective', in *Perspectives on African Literature*, ed. Christopher Heywood (Heinemann, London, 1971), pp. 33–48.
2 For Tutuola's debt to Fagunwa, see especially Bernth Lindfors, 'Amos Tutuola and D. O. Fagunwa', *Journal of Commonwealth Literature*, no. 9 (1970), pp. 57–65.
3 See Chapters 1, 2 and 3 below for a more thorough examination of this issue.
4 J. P. Clark, 'Our literary critics', *Nigeria Magazine*, no. 74 (December 1962), p. 80.
5 John Povey, 'The novels of Chinua Achebe', in *Introduction to Nigerian Literature*, ed. Bruce King (University of Lagos and Evans, Lagos and London, 1971), p. 97.
6 G. D. Killam, 'Cyprian Ekwensi', in *Introduction to Nigerian Literature*, op. cit., p. 77.
7 Abiola Irele, 'The criticism of modern African literature', in *Perspectives on African Literature*, op. cit., pp. 16 and 19.
8 ibid, p. 13.
9 Mark Schorer, 'Technique as discovery', in *The Novel: Modern Essays in Criticism*, ed. Robert Murray Davis (Prentice-Hall, Englewood Cliffs, NJ, 1969), p. 75; originally published in *The Hudson Review*, I (1948).

1. Amos Tutuola

▼▼▼

It is now over twenty-five years since the Nigerian writer Amos Tutuola made his explosive debut on the world literary scene with *The Palm-Wine Drinkard* (1952). He was the first West African writer to be published by a major British company and to be extensively reviewed and acclaimed by the western world. It is now a matter of common knowledge in literary circles that the tone of the metropolitan readers' response was set by Dylan Thomas's wildly enthusiastic review in *The Observer*; he saw the work as a brief, thronged, grisly, bewitching, tall, devilish story, in which nothing is too prodigious or trivial to be put down.[1] Following in the wake of Dylan Thomas, the reactions of western critics like Gerald Moore, Dr G. Parrinder and Harold Collins, in books, reviews, articles and introductions, continued to be largely favourable, although the enthusiasm declined slightly with the publication of Tutuola's other works. On the other hand, the first reactions of Nigerians and other West Africans were almost uniformly hostile. They raised objection to two aspects of Tutuola's art: his use of the English language and his originality. On the whole these critics got to the heart of the Tutuola problem and their diagnosis was largely correct, although they were wrong in concluding that Tutuola's work should be dismissed on these grounds. The metropolitan critics were equally misguided in praising Tutuola for the wrong reasons, though their general conclusion that Tutuola was a writer of genius was not far off the mark. The western critics generally claimed that Tutuola's work was written in 'West African English' and that in the process he had injected new life into the moribund English language. This drew scorn from most West Africans who realized that it is simply untrue to say that Tutuola's English is typical of West Africa or acceptable in those circles. Similarly, the metropolitan critics' enthusiasm over Tutuola's originality and fertile, inventive imagination is likely to sound hollow in the ears of Africans who have heard similar tales told on countless occasions in the village square or round the family hearth.

In their haste to reject the western critics' view, however, the African critics blind themselves to the fact that Tutuola's claim to greatness lies, not in the originality of his imagination, but in his skilful remodelling of old tales.

The truth about Tutuola surely lies between these two extreme views. In order to establish his position in African literature and to estimate him properly, it is essential to be clear about the genre in which he wrote. It has been too facilely assumed, particularly in the western world, that he wrote novels. Yet, however flexible we may be in our definition of the novel or in the choice of criteria for its evaluation, it will be difficult, if not impossible, to find a definition or set of criteria which will enable us to describe the works of Tutuola as novels. To attempt to make a serious evaluation of Tutuola as a novelist is to apply to his works a body of assumptions to which they are incapable of rising and to do a grave disservice to his reputation. For Tutuola is not a novelist, but a brilliant teller of folk tales. In order to answer the objections of most African readers we have to concede that his language is not quite up to standard, and not just deliberately so; but we can then go on to suggest that within the genre of the folk tale this deficiency does not matter – in fact, it is, in a sense, a positive asset. Similarly, we have to agree with most African readers that Tutuola is not strikingly original, but we can then go on to assert that whereas realism and originality are expected of the formal novel, the teller of folk tales is expected to take his subject matter and the framework of his tales from the corpus of his people's traditional lore.

The most useful approach to Tutuola, then, is to regard him as working within the African oral tradition.[2] The folk tale is common property belonging to the people as a whole; it is an expression of their culture and their social circumstances. The teller of folk tales knows that the framework of the story he is about to tell is already known to a majority of his hearers; but he knows equally that his reputation as a teller will depend on the inventiveness with which he modifies and adds to the basic framework of the tale. For within the basic framework the teller is allowed considerable room for manoeuvre. His audience, knowing the details of the tale already, will look forward, not to his accuracy, but to the extent and effectiveness of his improvisations and modifications, to the skill with which he makes use of facial expressions, gestures, pauses and rhetorical devices and creates suspense and excitement. While using the inherited framework, the brilliant teller of folk tales transforms them into something uniquely his own.

Tutuola is precisely such an author. Taking his stories direct from his people's traditional lore, he uses his inexhaustible imagination and inventive power to embellish them, to add to them or alter them, and generally transform them into his own stories conveying his own message. It is obvious that most of the stories in his works come direct from the oral tradition. Several readers have identified many of them as belonging to their tradition, others bear a marked resemblance to folk tales in various collections and all of them manifest the characteristics of the folk tale. A very good example is the story of the girl who marries the 'complete gentleman' in *The Palm-Wine Drinkard*. This story is to be found in the oral tradition of many African peoples. So too is the story of the baby who, having been born miraculously from its mother's thumb, proceeds to perform the most stupendous feats. In *My Life in the Bush of Ghosts*, the story of the struggle between the gate-keeper with the seven jujus who is able to change night into day, and the ghost-thief with the eight jujus who is capable of changing day into night, obviously comes from the oral tradition, as does the story of the ghost-magician who discovers where 'the ground has head and eyes', only to be executed when the discovery turns out to be false. In *Simbi and the Satyr of the Dark Jungle*, Simbi's encounter with the hunter and the three miraculous animals – the rat, the snake and the tiger – comes from oral lore, and in *The Brave African Huntress* the story of the king of the Ibembe town whose head sprouts two horns is obviously from the oral tradition.

Several of the stories still retain the stamp of the oral tradition even in written form. This is seen, for instance, in the insistence on the moral at the end, involving either retribution, punishment or the idea of 'the tables turned'. Thus the girl in the 'complete gentleman' story is punished for her disobedience when her handsome gallant turns out to be a skull, and in the same work the prince-killer who had hoped to get the Drinkard and his wife executed for a murder he himself had committed is justifiably killed instead. And of course, Simbi is punished for her obstinacy in persevering with her desire to discover 'the poverties and punishments', and she at the end vows never to disobey her mother in future.

In most of the stories the accents of the story teller are clearly discernible. For instance, at the end of the entire story of the Palm-Wine Drinkard, Tutuola, reverting to the third-person omniscient, says: 'That was how the story of the Palm-Wine Drinkard and his dead palm-wine tapster went.' It has been generally recognized that this is the way in which most folk tales are concluded. It is also to the oral tradition that we owe the apparently unnecessary repetitiveness at certain points in Tutuola's stories. Is this not typical of the practice of the story teller who wants to make sure that his audience do not forget certain important points in the story and therefore feels obliged to recapitulate?

The world of Tutuola's stories is the world of traditional lore where human beings mingle freely with beings from the spirit world. It is a world in which animals, vegetation and spirits are frequently given human attributes and human paraphernalia, whereas human beings are endowed with miraculous supernatural powers. It is a world of fantasy where the human being is apparently at the mercy of the incomprehensible forces of the universe. Indeed, it can be said that the creation of the Tutuolan world is an attempt to come to terms with those hidden forces lurking in nature – the forbidding forces associated with the forest and the depth of streams which have always haunted the African imagination. The Tutuola story usually takes the form of a quest from which the hero or the heroine emerges stronger and wiser. By the very nature of his quest the human hero is forced into contact with these forces who regard his irruption into their midst with great hostility; he is automatically branded as a suspect who must therefore be destroyed at all costs. The Drinkard, Simbi, Adebisi, the hero of *My Life in the Bush of Ghosts* are all engaged in confrontation with the seemingly insuperable forces of the spirit world. At the centre of the Tutuolan world is man, but he is a man who is out of his element since he has journeyed from the normal world, and has to put up a desperate struggle for his very survival against beings who tower over him. But although man seems physically weaker than the forces of the spirit world he is not entirely helpless; he possesses tremendous resilience and courage and can always rely on his superb intelligence and the efficacy of his magical powers to see him through. With the aid of these he ultimately baffles and outwits the apparently superior spirit forces. The Tutuolan works are therefore a saga demonstrating man's capacity for struggling successfully with the dark, unreclaimed forces of nature.

A look at some of the Tutuolan stories derived from the oral tradition will demonstrate how he transforms them into something uniquely his own. First, the story of the headstrong girl and the 'complete gentleman'. In the Tutuola version, the extraordinarily beautiful girl originally rejects all offers of marriage. However, on seeing this 'complete gentleman' at the market who is so beautiful that 'if he had been an article or an animal for sale, he would be sold for at least £2000 (two thousand pounds)', the girl is instantly infatuated and makes advances to him. He ignores her, but she follows him nevertheless at the end of the market day, although the gentleman repeatedly urges her to return home. Eventually they enter an 'endless forest' and the 'beautiful gentleman' begins to return parts of his body which he has apparently hired from the rightful owners. The girl naturally becomes alarmed and now wants to return home, but the 'complete gentleman' refuses to allow her. Eventually he returns his belly, ribs and chest leaving only his head, arms and neck. Within a short time this 'complete gentleman' is reduced to a mere skull, but it possesses extraordinary powers. On arrival at the gentleman's home, a hole inhabited by several other skulls, the girl is prevented from escaping by means of a cowrie-alarm tied to her neck and a skull with a whistle acting as guard. The cowrie also has the effect of making the girl dumb.

It is one of the Drinkard's tasks to rescue the girl. Having set out on his journey, he eventually identifies the 'complete gentleman' at the market, watches him go through the motions of returning the hired parts of his body, and trails him to his hole where he finds the girl. By using his magical powers and changing himself into air he is finally able to rescue the girl, but not before he has had once more to change himself into a bird and the girl into a kitten. Later he restores the girl's power of speech by cleverly discovering from the 'complete gentleman' the specific leaf which will cure her dumbness; and as a reward for his success he is allowed to marry the girl himself.

Several variants of this story are to be found in the traditional lore of numerous African countries. In a Yoruba version published in Ogumefu's collection of legends, the complete gentleman is originally a head, not a skull, belonging to a country entirely peopled by heads.[3] He comes to the human world because he has a longing to see it and he borrows (there is no mention of renting) his parts from humans. On arrival at the town it is actually he himself who is initially attracted to a group of dancing girls, one of whom he persuades to marry him and return with him to his own country. When the bride eventually realizes that her husband is nothing but a head she runs away, horrified, to her home, and since the head now has neither body, arms nor legs, he is unable to pursue her and thus loses her. In another version the girl is saved by a wind which her mother causes to blow her home,[4] and in the Sierra Leonean version the gentleman sheds only his clothes, not the parts of his body.

It should be perfectly obvious that Tutuola's adaptations and additions are considerable and they are generally of three kinds: there are the additions he makes to draw attention to the Drinkard's power and skill in rescuing the lady; there are those which deepen the moral dimension of the tale; and finally there are those which increase the suspense and fascination that the audience of an oral tale would naturally expect. At the start Tutuola makes the skull hire his clothes and the other parts of his body, thus conferring on him a certain dignity and independence; he is clearly a force for the Drinkard to reckon with. Then the girl does not merely escape because the head is rendered powerless or because some wind blows her home, for it is essential that the Drinkard should be the agent of rescue in order to call attention to his tremendous powers of resilience and courage from the start of the tale. In line with this purpose, Tutuola does not merely strip the 'complete gentleman' down to a mere skull or head, thus emphasizing the deceptiveness of appearances; he makes the skull a most formidable character and adds the paraphernalia of the other skulls and the entire episode of the Drinkard's ingenious and successful rescue bid. If the skull is a formidable character, he meets an equally formidable opponent in the Drinkard. Tutuola also adds the detail of the girl's disobedience of her father, her wilful rejection of other suitors and her insistence on following the skull in spite of his warnings, in order to make the girl herself ultimately responsible for the disaster that almost overtakes her, and thus to sharpen the moral point. Then he heightens the girl's fascination with the gentleman for the benefit of his audience and colours the gentleman's description in such terms that the audience's interest is aroused. One can almost hear the accents of the story teller emphasizing and exaggerating the details of his beauty: 'if this gentleman went to the battle field, surely, enemy would not kill him or capture him and if bombers saw him in a town which was to be bombed, they would not throw bombs on his presence, and if they did throw it, the bomb itself would not explode until this gentleman would leave that town, because of his beauty'.[5] But although Tutuola has a moral intention he is a good enough artist to realize that the moral point should not be made overtly; consequently he tones down the overt moralizing found in the other versions where the girl is virtually asked what lessons she has learned from her experiences.

Another story which Tutuola similarly modifies to his own advantage is that of the extraordinary child born out of its mother's thumb. This story, which is commonly known as the legend of the Child-Wiser-Than-His-Father, is included in Iyatemi and Currey's *Folk Tales and Fables*.[6] In this Yoruba version the child is born out of the big toe of a previously childless woman who had begged a god to give her a child. He is called Mogbonjubaba (Omo-gbon-ju-baba), or child-wiser-than-his-father, and although he is tiny at birth he walks and talks immediately and grows with astonishing rapidity. In the morning he asks his father to take him to the farm, but the latter refuses on the grounds that the child is too young and inexperienced. However, Mogbonjubaba trails his father by putting ashes into his bag and drilling a hole in it. When he arrives at the farm he asks his astonished father to play a game with him which involves covering himself with a basket and getting his father to throw a bunch of palm-kernels on top of the basket. The father does so, but Mogbonjubaba cleverly escapes from under the basket before the bunch of palm-kernels can harm him. Pretending that he has been under the basket all the time and has been miraculously unhurt, he asks his father to take his turn. The father does so, and the bunch of palm-kernels comes crashing down, killing him. Mogbonjubaba then cuts out his father's liver, takes it to his mother and tells her that it is from an animal they have killed on the farm. When the mother cooks and eats it, Mogbonjubaba triumphantly tells her that she has eaten her husband's liver.

Although in Tutuola's version the mother does not actually pray to the gods for a child and the child is born out of her thumb and not out of her big toe, the circumstances of his birth are still extraordinary. The thumb swells out as in the Yoruba version, and the child is born when the mother accidentally pricks it on a palm-tree thorn. As in the Yoruba version, he walks and talks immediately and grows at a rapid rate. But Tutuola does not place the emphasis on his low cunning; in fact his name is 'Zurrjir', which means a son who will change himself into another thing very soon, and his distinctive characteristics are his strength and his gluttony – he drinks five kegs of palm-wine in five minutes, eats everything in the village that he can lay hands on and mercilessly beats up anyone who tries to prevent him. In the end the villagers are forced to get rid of him by setting fire to the house in which he sleeps. Significantly, Tutuola does not make Zurrjir kill his father, since the Drinkard is required for the laborious quest that lies ahead of him; rather it is the child who is killed, although he is resurrected again in the form of a 'half-bodied' baby who has to be carried about until Drum, Song and Dance mercifully take him off his parents' hands. The child becomes merely one of the many trials that the Drinkard must undergo, and Tutuola skilfully weaves his story into his theme by giving him the same quality of gluttony as his father. He is thus an externalization of his father's worst quality. He forces the Drinkard to realize what his own father must have experienced – the difficulty of supporting a lazy and gluttonous son.

It is in ways such as these that Tutuola cleverly adapts and transforms the inherited stories, welding them into the framework of the themes of his own books. Skilful story teller that he is, the additions not only add depth of meaning, but also heighten suspense, create humour and fascination, and generally attempt to capture the spirit of folk tales as they are actually told.

It is an integral part of Tutuola's handling of the traditional that he quite unashamedly incorporates into it elements from the modern technological world, thus imparting new vitality and interest. Moving with perfect ease within the imaginary fantastic world of the traditional, he is yet able to endow his creatures with modernistic trappings, thus attuning them to modern sensibilities. At times he merely takes images from the modern world into the traditional to give colour and vividness to his stories, as when he says, for instance, that the baby resurrected from the ashes of Zurrjir 'speaks with a lower voice like a telephone', or when he compares the throbbing of the hero's heart in *My Life in the Bush of Ghosts* to a telegraphist sending telegraph messages. But often he actually transfers phenomena from the modern into the traditional. On their way to the Faithful Mother's domain, for instance, the Drinkard and his wife are photographed. In the 'Lost or Gain Valley' in *My Life in the Bush of Ghosts*, the hero and his wife turn out to have been wearing the most modern clothes: shirt, tie, socks, golden ring, costly wristwatch, underwear, gown, golden beads, hat, shoes and 'lofty handbag';[7] the hero's cousin's capital looks like a modern city with medical facilities, modern schools, modern churches and a police system; and, of course, as every critic has remarked, the ghostess who finally shows the hero his way home has hands with television sets on them. Even in *The Brave African Huntress*, which seems to be the most traditional of the tales and the least influenced by western technological ideas, there is a suggestion that the inhabitants of the pigmies' town use tumblers, and the liberated prisoners sing a song about chocolate and ice-cream.

This transfer of the modern and technological into the world of the traditional is, of course, anachronistic. A small detail in *My Life in the Bush of Ghosts*, where the hero informs us that his brother is a slave dealer who indulges in human sacrifice, suggests that the imaginative period of the tale and presumably of the others is sometime preceding this century. Perfectly equipped hospitals, schools and an adequately staffed judicial system must therefore be anachronistic. But there are mercifully few instances when the anachronisms call attention to themselves. Generally, the modernistic additions make Tutuola's stories more colourful.

Tutuola also transforms the traditional by means of exaggeration. Fantasy and exaggeration are hallmarks of his art. They are also, of course, hallmarks of the folk tale, though Tutuola's details are perhaps the most fantastic and exaggerated that will be found anywhere in the world of the folk tale. His monstrous creatures, particularly the wicked ones, always perform the most extraordinary feats. When the 'complete gentleman' becomes a skull his voice can be heard 2 miles off and he jumps a mile to the second; soon after they leave the 'greedy bush' the Drinkard and his wife see some monstrous birds, only 2 feet long, who are nevertheless capable of making fifty holes per second in the bodies of large animals, and devouring them in two minutes. In *My Life in the Bush of Ghosts* the hero, now turned into a cow, springs a distance of 90 yards, and the Flash-eyed Mother's body has millions of heads which sound like the striking of iron or church bells when talking together, while the Flash-eyed Mother's own laugh is like an exploding bomb. These extraordinary details of time and distance have nothing to do with 'good time' and 'bad time' as Larson suggests;[8] they are simply in line with Tutuola's flair for fantasy and are perfectly acceptable in the world of the folk tale.

Although a large number of Tutuola's stories come from the oral tradition, there is no doubt that many others have been concocted by his own fertile imagination. Having been steeped in the wonders of traditional lore, he shows himself quite adept at inventing his own mythology and so colouring it that it looks even more fantastic than folklore. We think of the sheer fantasy of the 'spirit of prey' who kills an animal each time he closes his eyes, of the strange inhabitants of the 'Unreturnable Heavens Town' who climb a ladder before leaning it

against a tree, and wash their domestic animals but leave themselves
dirty. In *My Life in the Bush of Ghosts* there is the monstrous figure of
the Flash-eyed Mother – so obviously the product of Tutuola's
fantastic imagination – who alone fills the town like a vast hill.

> . . . The hair on her head was just as bush, all could weigh more than
> a ton if cut and put on a scale, each was thicker than a quarter of an
> inch and almost covered her head, except her face. All these hairs
> were giving shelter to her whenever it was raining and whenever the
> sun was scorching her as she was not walking to anywhere. Both her
> hands were used in stirring soup on the fire like spoons as she did not
> feel the pain of fire or heat, her finger nails were just like shovels and
> she had two very short feet under her body, she sat on them as a
> stool, these feet were as thick as a pillar. She never bathed at all. (pp.
> 98-9)

One must admit that some of the products of Tutuola's imagination
are nauseating.

Although tribute must be paid to Tutuola's inventiveness, the point
must still be made that his imagination is essentially almost childlike.
These fantastic creatures appear at times like the bugbears conjured up
by the child's imagination which is haunted or delighted by stories of
the monstrous, the fantastic and the incredible. The description of the
repulsive-smelling ghost in *My Life in the Bush of Ghosts* is surely the
product of a childlike imagination. When the hero marries a ghostess
in a ceremony which looks very much like an imitation of a church
wedding, the total effect seems rather like childlike daydreaming. Only
a childlike imagination could make the Faithful Mother inspect a
guard of honour specially arranged for her by the Flash-eyed Mother.
Take the references to killing away, and the Big Bird's ranting in *The
Brave African Huntress* looks rather like two boys bragging about their
physical prowess. The impression of simple-mindedness it creates is
reinforced by the style in which it is couched.

> 'I am a wonderful bad creature who is half human and half bird. I am
> so bad, bold, cruel and so brave that I am eating together with
> witches! I am one of the fears of the Jungle of the Pigmies! I am a bad
> semi-bird who has long sharp thorns on both my wings! My beak
> was so long and sharp that I have pierced several people to death
> with it! I am quite sure that there is no another living creature or
> human being in this world who is so brave and cruel enough to
> challenge me in the night!'[9]

It is now time to discuss Tutuola's language in some detail. While
his style has proved objectionable to many West African readers,

Tutuola has had many stout defenders from the western world. Ulli Beier talks about the vigour and freshness he brings to the language by his refusal to be merely correct; Harold Collins, endorsing Beier's further claim that Tutuola's innocent approach allows him to distort the language to suit his own purposes, goes on to suggest himself that 'Tutuola's innocent manhandling of our language gives results that are extremely interesting for language study; they suggest the malleability of the language, the possibilities in the language for creative expansion, for freshness and the assimilation of alien ideas';[10] and Ronald Dathorne asserts that 'Tutuola's English is a sensible compromise between raw pidgin (which would be unintelligible to European readers) and standard English ... He is a conscious craftsman, who knows where his own talents lie'.[11] All these views suggest that Tutuola has perfect control of the language and chooses to manipulate it in his own way for very laudable reasons. Nevertheless, we still have to make certain discriminations if our criticism is to be valuable, however great our admiration for Tutuola. It is now generally recognized that the West African writer, forced to write in a language which is not his own, and which is often inadequate to accommodate his insights, will bend it to suit his own purposes. But no less a person than Chinua Achebe has warned that this kind of manipulation of the language can only be done from a position of strength by writers who are competent in its use, not from a position of weakness. It is idle to pretend that Tutuola deliberately distorts the language to suit his own purposes or that he consciously fashions a sensible compromise between raw pidgin and standard English to meet the predilections of his European readers. Tutuola does not 'refuse to be merely correct'; he would have found it difficult to be correct, given his standard of education which did not proceed beyond the elementary stage. We must make a distinction between his practice and that of, say, Okara or James Joyce, who quite consciously put the English language through interesting hoops precisely because they are at home in it. It should be possible to admit that Tutuola breaks most of the rules of the language without necessarily denigrating the value of his art, for one can also surely point out that this kind of language is perfectly suitable for the genre in which he has chosen to write. Let us look at some specimens of Tutuola's English in action. First, his treatment of clauses:

As I was waiting for him to bring the palm-wine, when I saw that he did not return in time, because he was not keeping me long like that before, then I called two of my friends to accompany me to the farm. (*PWD*, p. 8)

But immediately he heard from me that I had brought Death and when he saw him on my head, he was greatly terrified and raised alarm that he thought nobody could go and bring Death from his house, then he told me to carry him (Death) back to his house at once, and he (old man) hastily went back to his room and started to close all his doors and windows, but before he could close two or three of his windows, I threw down Death before his door and at the same time that I threw him down, the net cut into pieces and Death found his way out. (*PWD*, p. 15)

As we entered the bush, when we had travelled for about 2 miles inside the bush, then we began to notice that there were many trees without withered leaves, dried sticks and refuse on the ground of this bush as was usual in other bushes ... (*PWD*, p. 51)

The second extract in particular demonstrates Tutuola's habit of piling up clauses, thus constructing extremely long and awkward sentences. In fact, all the extracts show his inability to combine clauses properly, subordinating them to a main clause. The first and third examples reveal an unnecessary reliance on the temporal clause when another main clause would have been more appropriate. In fact, Tutuola cuts down the use of main clauses to a minimum, putting almost everything into subordinate clauses, whether appropriate or inappropriate, as though he wished to keep the reader in a state of suspended animation until the main event.

Tutuola's sentence construction is another interesting aspect of his use of language. Harold Collins himself mentions the tautologies, syncopations, sentence fragments and strange idioms, although he sees these as a virtue.[12] Here are some examples:

As we were going in this bush, we saw a pond and we branched there, then we started to drink the water from it, but as the water dried away at our presence and also as we were thirsty all the time, and there we saw that there was not a single living creature. (*PWD*, p. 52)

Although she was a wonderful singer whose beautiful voice could wake deads and she was only the most beautiful girl in the village. (*Simbi*, p. 7)

All these horns were faced its front accurately. (*BAH*, p. 16)

The first two sentences are obviously incomplete; the second consists, in fact, of three subordinate clauses without a main clause. Tutuola often seems unaware that a sentence is not just a conglomeration of clauses but needs a main clause to be complete. In the final example there is obscurity resulting from poor construction, possibly due to the confusion of active and passive ('faced' and 'were faced') and a wrong choice of word in 'accurately'.

It is, of course, to Tutuola's grammar that many readers take exception. Here are some examples:

(1) They saw me lied down (*PWD*, p. 11)
(2) We saw a male child came out (*PWD*, p. 31)
(3) But I lied down there awoke (*PWD*, p. 14)
(4) The next thing that which she was doing (*Simbi*, p. 7)
(5) To safe your life (*Simbi*, p. 12)
(6) He wore several oversize garments for her (*Simbi*, p. 22)
(7) But all her efforts were failed (*Simbi*, p. 29)
(8) But when I rose up my head and looked at the top of them ... (*PWD*, p. 52)

In (1) Tutuola has attempted to use a past definite form when he should have used a participial form or the past continuous, but he has got the past of this particular verb wrong. In (2) he is wrong again in using the past definite form, but this time at least he does not get the past tense of 'come' wrong. In (3) we see an inability to distinguish between the past tenses of 'lie' meaning to say a falsehood, and 'lie' in the sense of reclining. There is ignorance also of the fact that 'awake' in this expression is not a verb but an adjective. Tutuola was probably misled by the analogy with expressions such as 'he lay there vanquished' where 'vanquished' is, in fact, not a past tense but a past participle doing the work of an adjective. Confusing the past participle with the simple past, he thought he needed the past tense of 'awake' in the sentence quoted. The fourth example shows confusion about the use of the relative pronoun, and the fifth an inability to distinguish between the verb 'save' and the adjective 'safe'. In (6) Tutuola writes 'for her' instead of 'on her' which suggests the intrusion of pidgin and in (7) there is confusion between the active and passive voices and ignorance of the past tense of intransitive verbs. In the last example Tutuola seems unaware of the difference between the verbs 'rise' and 'raise', one an intransitive and the other a transitive verb.

Most significantly, however, Tutuola is uncertain about the use of past tenses. We often find expressions like 'I was seriously sat down' (*PWD*, p. 8), 'I saw the lady sat' (*PWD*, p. 26), 'she was nearly to faint'

(*Simbi*, p. 8), 'She . . . did not happy' (*Simbi*, p. 8), 'She met him sat' (*Simbi*, p. 11), 'as if she had already dead' (*Simbi*, p. 17) and 'She should had died' (*Simbi*, p. 29). The past continuous, in particular, and the use of a participial phrase describing a noun which is the object of a past verb, as in the second example, continually baffle him. Quite often he uses a preterite form when a past continuous is needed and vice versa.

There are hosts of examples in Tutuola's works of the wrong use of idioms, vocabulary, prepositions and comparatives. For example, in 'I had no other work more than to drink palm-wine', he fails to see that the use of 'other' precludes the use of 'more'. He almost always misuses 'but' as in 'Immediately this man told or promised me so, I went away, but after I had travelled one mile away then I used one of my juju . . .' (*PWD*, p. 10) and 'I went to the place that he threw both leaves, then I picked them up and I went home at once. But at the same time that I reached home I cooked both leaves separately . . .' (*PWD*, p. 30). Tutuola frequently punctuates badly, putting full stops where there should be commas and vice versa.

In defence of Tutuola, Afolayan, in an extremely valuable essay, suggests that Tutuola's English is Yoruba English representing the interaction between Yoruba deep grammar and English surface grammar. The unusual lexical items, the strange idioms, the wordy repetitive style and the grammatical confusion are often the result of Yoruba interference.[13] When Tutuola says 'the whole people' instead of 'all the people' he is probably reflecting Yoruba usage of the one word in both contexts. Similarly, it is probably Yoruba influence which makes him use the definite article with 'poverty' and 'punishment' in situations where normal English would not. However, this offers an explanation rather than a justification for Tutuola's practice, and it still amounts to saying that his control of the language is far from complete, for interference is often a sign of inadequate control. Afolayan is surely right when he says that a lot of the vigour and freshness that Gerald Moore and others see in Tutuola's language derives from his original Yoruba and the subsequent interplay between the two languages, Yoruba and English, and not so much from Tutuola's 'refusal to be merely correct'.[14]

But Tutuola shows himself quite capable of inventing his own words. The word 'drinkard' itself must not be hastily dismissed as bad English – a corruption of 'drunkard' – but as a personal invention deriving from the realization that 'drunkard' would not quite convey the sense of what Tutuola intends, that is, a man who is addicted to palm-wine drinking as opposed to being habitually drunk. Then there is the vivid word 'uncountable' which is much stronger than the usual 'innumerable' and suggests the folk tale teller's capacity for exaggeration and his actual striving after a word which would convey this sense of exaggeration. When Tutuola says 'this old man was not a really man' he probably wants a word which is much stronger than 'real' and which suggests that the old man possesses much more than the essence of humanity.

Tutuola's English is demonstrably poor; this is due partly to his ignorance of the more complicated rules of English syntax and partly to interference from Yoruba. But it would be a serious mistake to deprecate this as a weakness in his art or to use it as an excuse for invalidating it completely. For by one of those strange accidents of fate, the language ideally suits the genre of the oral tale. It is the language of the speaking voice telling a tale in a particular situation, exaggerating, elaborating, repeating, explaining and inevitably making numerous errors; but all these add to the vigour and colour of the tales. In reading Tutuola's works we are aware of a voice talking and we unconsciously make the same allowances that we would make for a normal speaker. The mistakes then do not seem to matter, particularly as we are carried on breathlessly by the tale. Indeed, the errors only become immediately obvious in those works like *The Brave African Huntress* where Tutuola relies less on the resources of the oral tradition than on his own fantastic imagination.

The Palm-Wine Drinkard is indisputably Tutuola's most accomplished work. The achievement here lies in the skilful welding of several tales from the oral tradition into one extended folk tale, subordinating all of them to his main theme. Characteristically the hero of the work sets out on a quest to find his dead palm-wine tapster. The Drinkard is a lazy glutton addicted to palm-wine, and just as modern doctors compassionately prescribe drugs for drug addicts, so the Drinkard's father, on realizing that he does nothing but drink palm-wine from morning till night and from night till morning, engages an expert palm-wine tapster for him and gives him a palm-wine plantation with 560 000 palm trees. For the Drinkard, therefore, the death of his tapster means the loss of one on whom he is dependent for his very existence and his social relations. Tutuola skilfully sketches in the Drinkard's sense of loss and loneliness on the death of the tapster.

When it was early in the morning of the next day, I had no palm-wine to drink at all, and throughout that day I felt not so happy as before; I was seriously sat down in my parlour, but when it was the third day that I had no palm-wine at all, all my friends did not come to my house again, they left me there alone, because there was no palm-wine for them to drink.

But when I completed a week in my house without palm-wine, then I went out and, I saw one of them in the town, so I saluted him, he answered but he did not approach me at all, he hastily went away. (pp. 8–9).

It is therefore essential that, like Eurydice, the tapster must be brought back from the clutches of death. The Drinkard's quest is no less than an attempt to discover the meaning of life and death, to explore the boundaries between them, to see whether the distinction can be blurred, whether death can be baffled and the dead reclaimed for the world of ordinary humanity. This is why the binding of Death is such an important part of the Drinkard's quest.

The binding of Death is the first task imposed on the Drinkard by the old man from whom he asks the whereabouts of his tapster, and several critics have recognized the similarity between this and many other figures in the tale to the taskmasters of heroic myth who impose various labours on the hero. The second task is that of rescuing the old man's beautiful daughter from the 'complete gentleman'. The successful completion of these two tasks proves the Drinkard's competence and earns him the title 'Father of gods'. He has proved himself more than a match for the terrible spirits and monsters he is going to encounter on his quest and is thus a fitting person to explore the realms of the dead. As 'Father of gods' he is equipped with powerful juju which puts him on a par with these supernatural creatures and enables him to hold his own and to demonstrate man's capacity for survival even when faced with overwhelming supernatural odds.

The consequence of his success in these first two tasks is that the Drinkard also acquires a wife – the very girl he rescues from the 'complete gentleman'. Critics like Gerald Moore have also pointed out this girl's similarity to the female helpmates who partner mythological heroes – Theseus' Ariadne and Jasons' Medea.[15] Subsequently the wife's role changes from being merely a wife to a mysterious creature who is capable of reading the future and is consequently more helpful to her husband. As they pursue their quest the Drinkard and his wife encounter several adventures, some pleasant, but most of them distinctly unpleasant. On the one hand they have a lyrically happy interlude with the Faithful Mother in the White Tree which they are consequently reluctant to leave until the Faithful Mother informs them that they may not, according to unalterable laws, stay for more than a fixed period. On the other hand, on leaving the White Tree they meet the monstrous Red Bird and Red Fish who demand human sacrifice. The tortures and perils to which they are subjected are all properly part of the quest theme, for in overcoming and surviving them the Drinkard continues to prove his worth as a fitting penetrator of the land of the dead and he grows spiritually and intellectually. The Red Bird and the Red Fish are reminiscent of the many man-devouring monsters of heroic myth, and the Drinkard's delivery of the Red Town from their menace and from the doom of human sacrifice is a significant advance. It is the last major obstacle he and his wife have to surmount before arrival at the 'deads town'.

On arrival at the 'deads town' the Drinkard learns the important lesson that the living are not allowed to enter the land of the dead and that little contact is allowed between them. Although he does not enter the town, his tapster comes out to meet him and in conversation with him teaches him about the difference between life and death. The Drinkard has thus gained in knowledge and experience although he has not been entirely successful in his quest, and he is ready for ascent into the human world again.

On his return home, the Drinkard, like Galahad and other quest heroes, is called upon to save his land from a curse – a famine caused by a quarrel between Earth and Sky which has resulted in the sky withholding rain from the earth. Using the magic egg which his tapster had given him as a consolation prize, he is able to feed his people and alleviate the effects of the famine. But the egg is broken through the people's gluttony and, when patched together, produces whips instead of food and scourges the people. Eventually it is the Drinkard, now a much wiser man than he was before setting out on his quest, who shows the people how to settle the quarrel between Earth and Sky and bring back plenty to the starving land. This story of the conflict between Earth and Sky which might at first sight appear an irrelevant interpolation, is actually very relevant; it is needed to show the Drinkard's growth and his role as the purger of his stricken land. The story of the conflict centres on the theme of gluttony and greed, and if we recall that the Drinkard's own story started with his personal gluttony and addiction to drink, we realize that his story has now come full circle. The Drinkard's consolation prize, the magic egg, is lost through the people's gluttony, with several of them dying in the process. It seems as if Tutuola is saying that death and loss are the price we have to pay for greed.

It has been generally recognized that several of the creatures the Drinkard and his wife encounter have counterparts in the folk mythology of several non-African peoples. The child born out of its mother's thumb recalls the legend of the English 'Tom Thumb' or the archetypal child of mysterious origin; the 'Faithful Mother' could be the 'archetypal mother' or the 'Mother Goddess'; the interior of the White Tree has associations with the Garden of Eden; the White Tree itself could be the tree of knowledge in the Garden of Eden, or a very similar tree, the golden apple tree in the Garden of the Hesperides; the hungry creature recalls the story of Jonah and the Whale. This appearance in Tutuola's work of a number of figures apparently taken from international mythology has suggested to some critics that Tutuola was well-read in mythological lore. To make this assumption, however, is to commit a terrible mistake. From what we know of his level of education it is highly unlikely that Tutuola could have been able to read so widely in world mythology. As the researches of Professor Northrop Frye and others have shown us, there are certain archetypal mythical patterns running through most mytho-logies. It should therefore not be a matter of surprise if Yoruba mythology (from which Tutuola clearly derived most of these figures) shares a number of archetypes in common with European mythology.[16]

After the spectacular success of *The Palm-Wine Drinkard*, Tutuola's work shows a distinct falling off in power. In the other works the pace of the narrative slackens, the language is much less captivating and the readers' imagination less enthralled. Little attempt is made to fuse the numerous episodes to suit the purposes of a single overriding theme. Tutuola's second tale, *My Life in the Bush of Ghosts*, shows this falling off in intensity. The incidents, though haunting and gripping for the most part, lack a single unifying purpose. The quest idea recurs, since the hero is searching for his lost home and parents, although his quest is of a slightly different nature from those of the other Tutuola heroes and heroines who deliberately set out with a moral or material purpose in mind. Nevertheless, he also goes through a process of moral and spiritual growth during his wanderings. His experiences make him aware of the nature, existence and consequence of jealousy and hatred, and he comes to understand the meaning of good and evil.

Having blundered into the Bush of Ghosts in his quest for his lost parents, the hero receives more than his fair share of adventures involving the most bizarre monsters. It soon becomes obvious that Tutuola's conception of 'ghosts' refers not just to the spirits of the dead, but generally to all the inhabitants of the spirit world. The hero is all the more unfortunate since, unlike the other Tutuola heroes, he is not initially aided by any powerful juju in his struggle against these spirits. This is man absolutely on his own and apparently defenceless in the face of terrible and venomous forces. The hero is eventually able to be reunited with his people, but Tutuola allows the story to drift on unchecked for too long. He is so carried away by his fantastic imagination that he seems to forget the theme of the work and his hero's original purpose, which was to find his way back home as quickly as possible. By inventing some more fantastic but pointless adventures, thus postponing the hero's return home for no plausible reason, Tutuola damages the unity of the story and taxes the reader's attention.

Simbi and the Satyr of the Dark Jungle is much more unified and much less dependent on Tutuola's own imagination than *My Life in the Bush of Ghosts*, although it falls short of the power of *The Palm-Wine Drinkard*. Here all the episodes are subordinated to the main theme which is Simbi's quest for experience. Right from the start Simbi deliberately sets out to find out what she calls 'the poverties and the punishments'. She is a highly privileged and accomplished girl who has been accustomed to a sheltered life and has been pampered by her wealthy mother. Realizing, however, that a whole area of experience has been blocked to her and that she must toughen her character by being exposed to a wider world of suffering and poverty, Simbi leaves home deliberately against all advice, to broaden her horizons. Some stress is laid on her obstinacy; and in the first encounter with Dogo, Tutuola brings out her arrogance and awareness of the superiority that wealth and position confer; but the reader is captivated by her boldness, her sense of independence and adventure and even by her rebelliousness. Though a woman, Simbi is far from being helpless; she has tremendous courage and presence of mind, a most captivating voice with magical powers and, from time to time, some powerful juju.

As the work's title implies, the centre of interest is Simbi's confrontation with the Satyr who seems to be a concentrate of all those mysterious forbidding forces with which the African imagination invests the jungle. She actually confronts him on three occasions, the first being a grimly comic scene in which the Satyr indulges in the most grotesque boasting and the courageous Simbi matches him word for word: 'Woe unto you, the Satyr, the noxious guard of the Dark Jungle! Woe unto you! I am ready now to fight with you' (p. 78); and she does. Eventually escaping from him, she is exposed to the most gruesome experiences, one of which involves pounding her first baby in a mortar to placate an angry god. In the end, aided by her courage and intelligence, she is able to surmount her troubles and kill the Satyr by changing herself into an insect and biting him to death. Simbi has thus experienced suffering and poverty and she returns home much wiser, less obstinate and determined to be obedient to her mother.

The Brave African Huntress is probably the least successful of these four works. It consists merely of a string of fantastic adventures most of which have come, not from the oral tradition, but from Tutuola's own imagination. The basic framework is once more that of the quest, since the heroine Adebisi sets out to find her four lost brothers in the Jungle of the Pigmies, but the quest here lacks the moral and spiritual dimensions of those in *The Palm-Wine Drinkard* and *Simbi*. There are no signs of any moral and spiritual development in Adebisi, even though she emerges a physically tougher character at the end. It is likely that Tutuola wanted to present Adebisi as a feminist out to demonstrate the woman's ability to hold her own in an otherwise exclusively man's world, and it is significant that the sphere in which she attempts to prove it is that of hunting which, in the African context especially, is a masculine preserve. Adebisi, scorning convention, purposefully trains as a hunter and boldly announces her intention of going to the dreaded jungle to kill all the terrible creatures and rescue her brothers, a task at which all other hunters have failed. She also realizes that in the absence of her brothers there is no one to continue her father's line, and she therefore wishes to be the agent whereby that line will be continued. In other words, she adopts an increasingly masculine role.

Appropriately, she leaves on the 'day of the new creation' which suggests hope and regeneration. It is in the Jungle of the Pigmies that the most monstrous creatures in the whole of Tutuola's works are to be found. But Adebisi is able to defeat all of them by a combination of sheer pluck and powerful juju with which she is much more plentifully supplied than the other Tutuola protagonists. The story goes on, however, for much too long, and as with *My Life in the Bush of Ghosts*, Adebisi often forgets her original purpose and remains in the Jungle of the Pigmies much longer than is necessary. Once more Tutuola does not seem to be able to stop himself inventing more fantastic adventures for his heroine, some of which are not relevant to the work's themes.

It is not too difficult to demonstrate that Tutuola's works cannot be regarded as novels in the normal sense since they are so glaringly deficient in some qualities that have come to be associated with the genre. Without being dogmatic or prescriptive, it is safe to say that we expect most novels to demonstrate some measure of psychological plausibility and consistency, thus revealing the author's control over the materials of his story. But the inconsistencies and psychological implausibilities in Tutuola are legion. In *The Brave African Huntress*, for instance, it is surely strange that Adebisi is able to kill the 'Obstacle' with her gun even though we have been told that guns are powerless against him, and that the skull of the 'super-animal' fits Adebisi's head exactly although Tutuola has informed us that its head is as big as an elephant's. In *The Palm-Wine Drinkard* the hero, during his sojourn in the Red Town, first kills the Red Fish and is then confronted by another creature (which we are made to understand is the Red Bird). But we are then told that this new creature first swallows the Red Bird which the Drinkard had killed. Surely, it is the Red Fish which the Drinkard had killed and it is this latter creature (not the Red Bird) which is now swallowed by the Red Bird that confronts the hero. In *My Life in the Bush of Ghosts* the hero has a gruelling contest with a magician during which the former turns himself into a stick and starts beating the latter. The magician then turns himself into fire, thus burning the stick to ashes. But we soon find that the hero is able to change himself into rain although he was the one who had presumably been changed into a stick and should logically have been burnt to ashes. In *Simbi* we are told that the Satyr killed Simbi's friends Kadara and Sala, although we had earlier been informed that it was the Phoenix who had stoned them to death.

There are also, in Tutuola's works, several examples of people possessing information which they could not possibly have been in a position to acquire. For instance, even before meeting the 'complete gentleman', the Drinkard seems to know somehow that he is in reality only a skull, although no one apart from the reader and the girl should have discovered this fact. In *Simbi* a reward is offered for the head of a hunter who is also a liar, and the people seem to sense somehow that the wanted hunter is the particular one who betrayed Simbi although they could not have known about the betrayal. Where a novelist would have had to ensure that such inconsistencies and implausibilities were smoothed over, the teller of tales is right to ignore them, for they do not matter in a world of fantasy which is where they belong.

Tutuola does not also seem to have that overriding concern for unity of plot and structure which most novelists consider essential. *Simbi* is probably the most unified of his tales. Even in *The Palm-Wine Drinkard* he gets so carried away that he includes a tale or two not strictly relevant to his central theme. The irrelevancies and superfluities in *My Life in The Bush of Ghosts* and *The Brave African Huntress* are legion. Tutuola also repeats several details time and time again; two examples here are the references to the powerful eyes of the 'super-animal' and the pigmies' probable lack of teeth in *The Brave African Huntress*.

As might be expected from the oral tale, conversation in the works of Tutuola is limited, and what there is is stylized. Only in *Simbi* do we have something approaching meaningful dialogue in the various exchanges between Simbi and her friends, or between her and Dogo. The few passages of introspection in the tales are usually very unconvincing, as in this example from *My Life in the Bush of Ghosts*.

'Ah! the earthly person is running away, how can I catch him now, oh! what can I ride on to the conference today, as all the ghosts who invited me are waiting to see me on a horse. Oh! if I had known I should have changed him to a horse before I left home. But if my head helps me and I catch him now I will change him from today to a permanent horse for ever. Ah! how can I catch him now?' (p. 41)

Three of the four works dealt with here – *The Palm-Wine Drinkard, My Life in the Bush of Ghosts* and *The Brave African Huntress* – are related in the first person by the protagonists themselves, while *Simbi* is told by the omniscient narrator. In the first three of these tales, however, Tutuola occasionally takes over unconsciously from the narrators, consequently getting the point of view confused. It is surely Tutuola himself, not Adebisi, who says in *The Brave African Huntress*: 'But there were many wonderful things in the days gone by' (p. 44). It cannot be Adebisi since she is herself existing 'in the days gone by'.

While these shortcomings might have mattered greatly in the conventional novel, they do not matter in the least in the tradition of the oral tale. Indeed, in this genre, we expect some measure of inconsistency, psychological implausibility and fantasy. Similarly, we do not expect highly developed dialogue or convincing passages of introspection. Looked at as examples of oral literature, Tutuola's stories are excellent in their way, but they will fall down disastrously if analysed as novels.

One of the most striking aspects of Tutuola's art is his insistence on details. He shows a particular concern for the exact details of measurement. He quotes the exact sums involved in certain transactions and the exact distances to be traversed in getting to certain places. The Drinkard and his wife enter the 'Greedy Bush' at precisely half-past one in the morning; a creature they see in one of the bushes is a quarter of a mile long and 6 feet in diameter, and they live with the Faithful Mother for a year and two weeks. The Methodist Church of the Bush of Ghosts is 90 feet by 70, and the number of people who attend service one Sunday is 133 exactly. This insistence on details is one of the ways in which Tutuola attempts to tone down the incredibility and impart some measure of realism to his work.

There is a certain element of wish-fulfilment in Tutuola's works, particularly in *My Life in the Bush of Ghosts*, which often gives the impression of a child's yearning after what is basically unattainable in life but could be realized in the world of the imagination. The Tenth Town of Ghosts, where the hero meets his cousin, is every pioneer's dream of the model town he is going to build. It is the narrator's cousin who introduces Christianity to the town, builds a church, starts the practice of holding synods and establishes schools, hospitals and a judiciary. This element of wish-fulfilment reinforces the impression that Tutuola's imagination has its childlike side.

If Tutuola's monsters repel us, it is not so much because they are frightening as because they are nauseating. Although Obiechina suggests that they are always built on a gigantic scale and imbued with supernatural power in the same way as Milton builds up Satan, the comparison is really very tenuous.[17] Where Satan is an awe-inspiring figure of great dignity and stature, Tutuola's monsters, though gigantic, are too grotesque and ridiculous to be awe-inspiring and dignified. In practice the monsters turn out to be remarkably inefficient, stupid and easy to defeat. Death turns out to be a very tame person whose cleverest ruse is to offer the Drinkard a bed of bones in the hope that when the latter is sound alseep, he will club him to death; and he allows himself to be captured in a net like any ordinary animal.

The Satyr in *Simbi* and Odara in *The Brave African Huntress* seem to be morons who are only capable of boasting, and they are comparatively easily defeated by Simbi and Adebisi. It is partly in order to ensure the survival of his protagonists that Tutuola makes their opponents so moronic and inefficient; but in doing so he robs them of their power as frightening monsters.

Grim though Tutuola's world is, it is also often a humorous one, though one doubts whether the comedy is always deliberately intended. And it is usually the monsters who contribute to the humour by their grotesque behaviour. The Satyr, for instance, tells Simbi and the other girls: 'Come along, my meat, I am ready to eat both of you now! Come along, and don't waste my time' (p. 73). In their preposterous conceited blustering, the monsters always appear comic. The Ibembe Bird in *The Brave African Huntress* is childish and comic even as he revels in his wickedness, and the Gate-keeper is surely comic when he says: 'All right, come and lay your head on this rock and let me cut it off. I do not need yourself or the rest part of your body but your head' (p. 50).

Tutuola's world is a morally neutral one, even though there are scraps of moralization in some of the tales. For instance, it does not seem to bother Tutuola or the Drinkard much that the whips produced by the altered magic egg cause a stampede leading to the deaths of several people including children and the elderly. Nevertheless, his work has a religious dimension. In the midst of adventures involving pagan gods and human sacrifice there are suddenly references to the Christian God such as 'God was so good ...' or 'It was only the God Almighty helped me to conquer this Satyr'. In *My Life in the Bush of Ghosts* the ghosts attend church service, worship God and have to wait for the judgement day. Of course, in the African situation, belief in the existence of spirits and monsters is not incompatible with belief in the Christian God. Tutuola is known to be a devout Christian; it is his very Christian devotion that makes him so powerfully aware of the unseen forces lurking in the universe, waiting to pounce on man.

Where, then, does Tutuola stand in the history of African literature? His place in African letters is assured because he represents the transition from an oral to a written literature. He has put down his tales on paper, but he has captured as brilliantly as anyone could the nuances, the techniques and effects of the oral tale. Few other writers of fiction have followed his example and it will be a very brave critic indeed who will say categorically that his work leads in a straight line to the novel. These and related questions will be considered in the next few chapters.

NOTES

1 Dylan Thomas, review, *Observer*, 6 June 1952.
2 This is the main virtue of E. N. Obiechina's excellent article 'Amos Tutuola and the oral tradition', *Présence Africaine*, vol. 65 (1968), pp. 85–106.
3 M. I. Ogumefu, *Yoruba Legends* (Sheldon Press, London, 1951).
4 Elphinstone Dayrell, *Folk Stories of Southern Nigeria* (Longman, Greene, London, 1910).
5 Amos Tutuola, *The Palm-Wine Drinkard* (Faber, London, 1961 edn), p. 25. All further page references are to this edition.
6 P. Iyatemi and P. Currey, eds. *Folk Tales and Fables* (Penguin, Harmondsworth, 1953).
7 Amos Tutuola, *My Life in the Bush of Ghosts* (Faber, London, 1964), p. 132. All further page references are to this edition. The references to *Simbi and the Satyr of the Dark Jungle* are to the Faber 1955 edition.
8 Charles Larson, *The Emergence of African Fiction* (Indiana University Press, Bloomington, Ind., and London, 1971), p. 103.
9 Amos Tutuola, *The Brave African Huntress* (Faber, London, 1958), p. 38. All further page references are to this edition.
10 Harold Collins, *Amos Tutuola* (Twayne, New York, 1969), pp. 102–3.
11 Ronald Dathorne, in *Introduction to Nigerian Literature*, ed. Bruce King (University of Lagos and Evans, Lagos and London, 1971), p. 72.
12 Collins, op. cit., pp. 101–3.
13 A. Afolayan, 'Language and sources of Amos Tutuola', in *Perspectives on African Literature*, ed. Christopher Heywood (Heinemann, London, 1971), pp. 49–63.
14 ibid., p. 61.
15 Gerald Moore, *Seven African Writers* (Oxford University Press, London, 1962), p. 46.
16 See Northrop Frye, *Anatomy of Criticism* (Princeton University Press, Princeton, NJ, 1957).
17 Obiechina, op. cit., p. 96.

2. Cyprian Ekwensi

▼▼▼▼▼▼▼▼▼▼▼▼▼▼▼▼▼▼▼▼▼▼▼▼▼▼▼▼▼▼▼▼▼▼▼▼▼

Cyprian Ekwensi's historical importance in the development of the African novel is assured. He belongs to the very first wave of African novelists, his *People of the City* (1954) being the first West African novel worth the name to be published in English. After a period of almost unanimous denigration by the professional critics, his reputation seems to be enjoying a much-needed revival.[1] This was probably inevitable, given the present preoccupation among most critics of African literature with the development of an African aesthetic which is not manifestly derived from the European literary tradition. That tradition, it has often been mistakenly supposed, has paid too much attention to the purely literary aspects of fictional works, and African writers who are primarily concerned with the social, political, cultural and historical aspects of their environment cannot be adequately discussed and evaluated on this basis. Much more weight, the view goes, should therefore be given to the writers' exploration of the forces at work in their society. Cyprian Ekwensi's concern is nothing if not social, and his reputation was therefore bound to rise.

Indeed, in the drive to found an African aesthetic and in the debate about the relevance and purpose of literature in an African environment, Cyprian Ekwensi must inevitably feature prominently. It would not be too difficult to dismiss his works from a purely artistic point of view; but his serious social concern makes his novels highly attractive to those who feel that the purpose of literature in Africa is to highlight the African predicament. Current discussion of his work often ends, therefore, in attackers and defenders adopting extreme positions and in heated argument tinged at times with nationalistic feelings. The interchange between Bernth Lindfors and Ernest Emenyonu is typical of this. Lindfors, who is primarily concerned in his article with the formal aspects of Ekwensi's art, points out that the author vitiates his insights by a reliance on the worst possible kinds of influences and models – 'third-rate American movies and fourth-rate British and American paperback novels' – and the more sensational works of Stevenson and Rider Haggard.[2] This provoked a vehement retort from Emenyonu.[3] Although Lindfors probably understressed the social relevance of Ekwensi's work, the fact remains that his article represents honest literary criticism; he does not merely make unproved assertions, but goes to extreme lengths to demonstrate his points by a detailed reference to Ekwensi's works, and he succeeds in highlighting the artistic deficiencies of the novelist. Emenyonu's rejoinder, on the other hand, makes greater use of rhetoric and assertion than of detailed, logical demonstration. It soon becomes obvious that he is interested, not in answering Lindfors' strictures about the shortcomings of Ekwensi's art, but in asserting the latter's importance as a novelist because of his preoccupation with the problems of 'African cities undergoing the tremors of transition'.

John Povey's article is a much more serious attempt to make a credible case for Ekwensi.[4] He recognizes the artistic flaws and admits that many of the condemnations made by the critics have been just; but he also realizes that Ekwensi is a serious writer with an important social concern. The implications of this point, however, lead Povey into rather troubled waters. It is easy to see the source of his difficulty. An avowedly rigorous critic with an undoubted concern for the maintenance of the highest standards, Povey finds himself in a position in which he has to assert that Ekwensi's social preoccupation should induce us to play down his artistic weaknesses: 'There must be some concern for the sociological and cultural aspects of writing that would be of considerably less interest and significance when discussing more established literatures.'[5] It is important to make certain points clear: Povey is not merely suggesting that the criticism of African literature should show some concern for the sociological and cultural aspects of writing, but that these factors should assume a much greater importance in the overall evaluation than they do in the criticism of more established literatures. Since the criticism of more established literatures has, in fact, always taken into account cultural and sociological aspects, John Povey, in arguing that these should count for much more in the evaluation of African literature, could only logically be suggesting, not just that there should be sociological and cultural concern, but that this should considerably outweigh purely literary considerations. This is rather condescending to African literature and may, in fact, be a dangerous critical doctrine. Povey then goes on to suggest that Ekwensi's work must be evaluated in terms of what he creates and what he attempts, and that he should not be belaboured for the lack of qualities he quite deliberately avoids. The key to any appreciation of Ekwensi, he continues, resides in the fact that he is a writer for the masses and his position lies somewhere between popular paperbacks and the middlebrow Book-of-the-Month.[6] This surely amounts to asserting that Ekwensi does not deserve discussion as a serious writer in such a work as *The Critical Evaluation of African Literature*. Surely it is pertinent to make a distinction, as Lindfors does, between those of Ekwensi's works like *When Love Whispers* and *The Passport of Mallam Ilia* which are obviously directed at an adolescent or semi-literate audience and which no serious critic would attempt to discuss in high critical terms, and more sophisticated works like *Jagua Nana* and *People of the City*. It is also idle to pretend that a writer who concerns himself with the sociological problems of his day is not addressing himself to 'intellectuals' and does not intend to be discussed seriously. We cannot eat our cake and have it too. If we are to discuss Ekwensi as a serious novelist 'with important and influential qualities', then we must pay as much attention to his art as to his social concern. It is interesting to note that when Povey really gets down to discussing Ekwensi seriously he pays considerable attention to his artistry and makes strictures which are as damaging as Lindfors': 'Ekwensi seems incapable of distinguishing true style from rubbish: his intention is serious, but he seems unable to see how his intentions are blighted by the literary means he employs.'[7]

It is one of the virtues of Killam in his modest essay on Ekwensi that he does not allow himself to fall into Povey's pitfalls.[8] His balanced article shows equal awareness of both the artistic deficiencies and the social concern. And surely this balance is right.

Since Ekwensi comes next to Tutuola in chronological order it will be interesting to see how much he owes to oral literature and whether the tradition started by the earlier author continues in an unbroken line through him. If this can be established it will be possible to argue plausibly that the African novel grew out of purely indigenous sources. But one's task here is made very difficult by the near-impossibility of establishing the order in which Ekwensi wrote his works. Dates of publication do not help, because it has been fairly well established that some works published late in the sixties had actually been in existence either in finished or rudimentary forms as early as the mid-1940s. *Juju*

Rock, published in 1966, and *The Passport of Mallam Ilia* (1960) were probably written twenty years earlier; [9] and although *People of the City* was written in 1953 and published in 1954, it probably existed in note form as far back as 1947. [10] It is safe to assume, however, that the first works conceived and given some shape by Ekwensi included *Juju Rock*, *The Passport of Mallam Ilia*, *The Leopard's Claw* and *When Love Whispers*. None of these works can be said to derive from the oral tradition. Whatever Ekwensi is doing here, he is not reworking an oral tale into the more sophisticated form of the novel. The most obvious and the most dominant influence on all these works, as Lindfors has conclusively proved, is a certain kind of western fiction. They are all deliberately directed at an adolescent audience and in both form and content they have obviously grown out of Ekwensi's memories of works like *King Solomon's Mines* and *Treasure Island*.

This is not to say that Ekwensi was not interested in the oral tradition. He had shown interest in it from the earliest stages of his writing career when he collected and translated folk tales. His *An African Night's Entertainment*, published in 1962, had been collected as early as 1947. However, an interest in folk tales does not necessarily suggest that the novels derived from them, especially as there is not much internal evidence to support this. Ekwensi published his folk tales as folk tales and went to other sources for his novels. The only exception seems to be *Burning Grass* which could conceivably have been modelled on a folk tale; but this work was conceived and written later than the others. (It was probably written around 1950 though not published until 1962.) And even here the influence of the traditional tale seems to be competing for paramountcy with non-indigenous influences. Certain features of Ekwensi's work, such as the heavy-handed moralizing, resemble aspects of the oral tradition. But Ekwensi could have got them from other sources, since they are not, in fact, unique either to the oral tradition or to African literature. Ekwensi does not follow in the footsteps of Amos Tutuola and without denigrating his originality it seems fair to conclude that he owes little to the oral tradition, and that the inspiration of this first major West African novelist is distinctly non-African so far as form is concerned.

Many of the weaknesses usually detected in Ekwensi's works stem from these early influences. Starting his literary career as a writer for the masses, interested in giving hordes of semi-literate Nigerians 'words' they would be capable of understanding, he chose to go back to those works he had himself read in his younger days which were similarly directed at a popular audience – novels of adventure, magazine pulp fiction, cheap American sex-and-crime paperbacks and Wild West stories. But this choice of models inevitably leads to sensationalism, melodrama, embarrassing cliché-ridden descriptions of the female anatomy and of torrid sex, and the contrived fairy-tale conclusion in which the villain is punished and the hero is miraculously rescued from his misfortunes. While these features may have been perfectly suited to the needs of a readership desiring little more than to be entertained in the crude sense of the term, they are most unfortunate in works whose audience would inevitably include more mature people. But Ekwensi shows little stylistic development, the errors made in the earliest works being repeated right through, even in the thematically more serious ones. Ekwensi's work also abounds in inconsistencies, indicating a failure to keep a proper grip over all the materials of the story. There are psychological implausibilities with characters' actions not stemming logically from the situations depicted, and a certain inability to present these characters convincingly when they are operating under extreme emotional or mental tension. But it is probably to Ekwensi's inadequate control of his linguistic medium that most critics would raise objection. He certainly does not manifest that sensitivity towards language and that ability to manipulate it to convey his insights that we find in writers of the stature of Achebe, Ngugi and Soyinka, to name a few. His awkward English style degenerates often to eighteenth-century archaisms and is full of clichés such as 'her firm bosom heaved against the clinging blouse' (*People of the City*, p. 7) and 'there was a new and wicked glint to her eye' (*People of the City*, p. 27).[11] There are occasional grammatical lapses and, most important, an inconsistency in his extensive use of pidgin, particularly in *Jagua Nana*.

The catalogue of weaknesses seems depressing. What redeems Ekwensi's work, however, is his concern with the problems of the city. When he started writing in the late 1940s and early 1950s the problems of urbanization in African states were only just beginning to make themselves felt. Today they are taken for granted as being among the facts of life in Africa, but at that time it was left to only a few people with remarkable foresight to point out the dangers for the future. It is to Ekwensi's credit that he was one of these. Any visitor to Nigeria will realize that the problems he analysed, far from having been solved, have multiplied a thousandfold, and his books, far from dating, now have a relevance to the social situation much greater than they had twenty years ago. The rapid expansion of cities and the population explosion which accompanied this is one aspect of the adjustment that African societies have had to make after the traumatic experiences of the clash with an alien colonial civilization. The breakdown of traditional societies and culture, the introduction of a cash-based economy, the growth of education and the centralization of administration have all inevitably led to a drift from the countryside to the growing cities which were seen as the only centres of advancement. Hence arose the now-familiar social problems like juvenile delinquency, prostitution, organized crime, housing rackets, filth and squalor. The rural innocent, in particular, who is ignorant of the qualities needed to survive in the hot-house that is the city, and who is quite often inadequately equipped, as far as education is concerned, to qualify for the more lucrative jobs the city offers, easily becomes a prey for the smart boys, the pimps, the politicians in need of thugs or mistresses, and the housing racketeers.

Ekwensi prefixes *People of the City* with a statement, which though uncomfortably reminiscent of the chapter headings of the works of the eighteenth-century English novelist Henry Fielding, is yet effective in highlighting the destructiveness of the city: 'how the city attracts all types and how the unwary must suffer from ignorance of its ways'. In particular, the housing racket is ruthlessly exposed. A man thrown out of his lodgings becomes succulent meat for the financiers in a situation where a reasonably decent house goes for £1000 a year, five years' rent in advance, and an ordinary room is not really much less expensive. The author, in fact, consistently uses the recurrent image of eating to suggest the voraciousness with which the city devours its unwary victims.

Inevitably, Ekwensi contrasts life in the country with life in the city and proceeds to idealize the former. Since the traditional taboos still largely obtain in the country, values such as honesty, industry, and respect for the elders, ancestors and God are held in high regard; the countryside is consequently seen as the repository of virtue while the city thrives on vice. It is for this reason that Ekwensi's harassed protagonists always return to the country at some stage or other of their experiences, usually after a period of slow moral and physical decay. The effect of the countryside on their parched souls is restorative, refreshing and spiritually uplifting.

People of the City is concerned precisely with this problem of a bludgeoning urban environment. The hero, Amusa Sango, is ideally placed to be an observer of life in the city; as a dance-band leader he moves among the new 'jet-set', the sleek fast youngsters, the frequenters of night-clubs and pleasure seekers; as a journalist he is in a position to observe life in the raw and to be abreast of the latest gossip. The events of the novel are narrated almost entirely through his eyes and with his point of view, there being an almost complete identification between Ekwensi and his hero. Indeed, only twice during the novel does the point of view switch to someone other than Sango – on page 90 to Aina and on page 117 to Lajide. This concentration of the focus on Sango's point of view leads at times to idealization and has unfortunate consequences for Ekwensi's overall vision in the novel.

Like most of Ekwensi's leading characters, Sango is originally attracted to the city from his native countryside and his traditional values by the desire for advancement. He himself expresses a basic desire for peace; but both desires are continually frustrated by the exigencies of life in the city. His part-time profession exposes him to the attention and lusts of women of all kinds. Far from leading to peace and advancement, a whole-hearted immersion in the social life of Lagos can only tend towards gradual moral, and in some cases material, deterioration. Sango's story is, in fact, one of progressive degradation. However, this cannot be entirely attributed to the destructive nature of the city. As with all Ekwensi's heroes and heroines, he possesses major weaknesses, although it is far from certain whether the author sees all of them clearly. There is a strong streak of callousness in him, manifested particularly in his relations with women, whom he sees merely as objects of pleasure to be discarded after enjoyment. From the very first chapter of the novel the reader gets the impression that Sango's ruthless drive to achieve his ambitions has left him absolutely without feeling. Furthermore, he is flippant, egoistic and condescending, and although he is sometimes aware of his own shortcomings, particularly his aimless drifting through Lagos society, he does not always realize that the criticisms he levels at others apply to himself. He is also shown to be irresponsible and simple-minded in getting involved in some shady quasi-criminal affairs which his professional experience as a man-of-the-world should have warned him are dangerous and hare-brained.

The portrait of the city is inevitably one of this novel's claims to attention. It emerges as a place of violence, crime, filth, unspeakable cruelty, lust and the ugliest of passions; a place where a husband drags his wife home by the hair, where the Lagos crowd almost lynch a young girl thief to death although most of them are burning with desire for her, where the jealous wives of a tycoon attack and beat up his mistress and pour red pepper into her eyes, nostrils, mouth and private parts, and where the mistress later dies in the most abject poverty and has to be buried as a pauper. There are macabre reports of murder, sorcery and black magic with the spotlight turned on the sinister Ufemfe society to which the unfortunate turn in their desperate scramble for respectability and prosperity.

We also see the poverty and squalor which are both a cause and an effect of the city's problems.

> He tried to move, but something caught his step and he staggered. Then he realized that the entire floor was covered with sleeping bodies. He was in a kind of bedless open dormitory. Everyone but the old woman slept on the floor. Old, young, lovers, enemies, fathers, mothers, they all shared this hall. From early childhood Aina had listened to talks about sex, seen bitter quarrels, heard and perhaps seen adults bare their passions shamelessly like animals . . . from early childhood she had learned the facts of life without being taught. (p. 34)

The young girl Aina is only one of the victims of the city. A girl who was initially capable of demonstrating warm feelings, she becomes inevitably conditioned by the city's callousness into a hardened thief and blackmailer. Nothing could demonstrate more convincingly than her harsh sentence and subsequent brutalization in prison that the problem of crime will not be solved until the root causes are attacked. Another such victim is Beatrice, whose career and fortune further demonstrate the ways in which the city can lure the innocent from the country only to destroy them in the end. One of Ekwensi's vivacious women, she already demonstrates, on our first acquaintance with her, the restlessness and the yearning for excitement, activity and freedom which usually impel those who are destined to be the city's victims; but she is also showing signs of degradation and disintegration – she already suffers from the deadly disease which is eventually to claim her life. It is a supreme irony that she never gets the freedom she was looking for when she left her husband, and although she left home because she could not be content with poverty, she dies utterly destitute. However, in the portrayal of Beatrice, Ekwensi glosses over her moral failings and comes very close to idealizing her. He sees nothing wrong in her infidelity as a wife and heartlessness as a mother.

Indeed, Ekwensi's presentation involves some inconsistencies and psychological implausibilities. It does not seem very plausible, for instance, that Beatrice would leave her husband so easily in spite of the fact that, according to Ekwensi, she doted on him. Very often Ekwensi's comments on his characters are quite unrelated to what has preceded or what succeeds.

The city also houses the agents of destruction, like Lajide who exploits the grim situation he sees around him for his material aggrandizement or sexual satisfaction, and Bayo the delinquent who refuses to settle down to any serious occupation, although he is not averse to using dishonest means to amass wealth. In the midst of this vice and squalor the innocence of Elina and the idealism of Beatrice II are remarkably refreshing. Beatrice II is an exemplary girl who is conscious of her national heritage and of the best things in her society, like the nationalist Pereira's devotion to his cause, and who is prepared to stand up against the dictates of her family and marry the man she loves. She is also prepared to reject the allurements of the city for a life of service in the country.

However, the outcome of the novel in which Sango marries Beatrice II is a tasteless melodramatic contrivance which flagrantly conflicts with what has been demonstrated. It is engineered in order to bring Sango, who has reached the nadir of his fortunes, to a happy end. But in order to bring this about, Beatrice's fiancé, who was a medical student in London, is conveniently killed. Such a fairy-tale conclusion is irrelevant to the story that has been demonstrated. Sango does not deserve such good luck, which never happens in real life in any case, and, as far as we can see, never happens to the people of the city. This is one of those instances demonstrating that Ekwensi has derived a warped notion of what a novel ought to be from rather poor sources.

People of the City is generally marred by this recourse to the melodramatic and the sensational in order to get the story moving. For instance, there is the chaos created by Aina's arrest at the start, and the 'dramatic' attempt to rescue Beatrice I from imminent death under the feet of the crowd towards the end. The inconsistencies, psychological implausibilities and deliberate contrivances suggest that the novel's artistry could have been more expertly managed. Although it is clear, for instance, that Sango met and made love to Aina only the day before she was arrested and taken to prison, almost everyone, including Bayo and Aina's mother, seems to regard Aina as Sango's girlfriend and talks about the affair as though it has been going on for some time. Ekwensi has obviously not got the materials of this novel firmly under control. It is difficult to account for the actions of some of the characters, such as Kekure's deliberate revelation of Lajide's plans regarding stolen motor vehicles to the real policemen, thus plunging him into deep trouble. Loyal wives, whatever might be their moral fervour, do not leak out their husbands' secrets like that. Is it also credible that the now-hardened Aina would attend Sango's wedding to Beatrice? Is it likely that the Aina we know would prove such a 'good sport' and 'good loser'? A few episodes such as the exchanges in the offices of the *West African Sensation* between Lajide and his debtor Layemi are quite irrelevant, and the plot is much too clumsily contrived to ensure that most of the characters turn out to be connected with each other.

The novel ends inconclusively with Sango and his bride deciding to go to the Gold Coast, but the question of what Sango will do with his life still remains, for after the spinelessness we have observed in him, we can have no assurance for the future.

There are certainly some passages of powerful description and vivid realization in this novel. Particularly impressive is the scene between Sango and his first fiancée, Elina, when they meet for the first time in the convent, and Sango realizes that this girl cannot possibly inspire him. But all in all, *People of the City*, though an interesting presentation of certain social evils, must be rated an indifferent whole.

Ekwensi's second novel, *Jagua Nana* (1961), is for many readers his best. It is, in fact, a considerable advance on *People of the City*. Though not entirely free of irrelevancies and amateurish contrivances, the plot is more tightly knit, the characterization is surer and the inconsistencies and implausibilities are mercifully fewer. But not even this novel is free from what Lindfors calls 'amateurish blots and blunders'.

The heroine Jagua herself is at the centre of the story – a central consciousness through whose eyes and with whose point of view we see all the events. The use of Jagua as a reflector is probably more necessary for Ekwensi than the similar use of Sango in *People of the City*, since Jagua, for all her captivating charm, is a much more immoral character, and a certain amount of built-in sympathy therefore has to be ensured. The first few pages of the novel are very impressive; they present Jagua as an essentially lonely figure, conscious of advancing age, trying strenuously to push back the years and clinging on to her young man Freddie as security for the future. The inevitable clichés are, of course, used in her description, but Ekwensi does convey the feeling of her sensuality. We are told that they called her 'Jagua' after the prestigious British car because of her good looks and stunning fashions; in fact, when she is dressed to kill and in her element, she is not merely Jagua but 'Jagwa'.

> The mirror which she had placed in that position in the room, gave her an exciting view of her own feet and of the feet of the men as they made love to her. And when she rose she would turn first to the left, and pat her wide buttocks and turn to the right and pat her tummy. She never failed to revel in the beauty of her body. The superb breasts, God's own milk to humanity, the lovely shoulders, and the skin, olive-orange, in the manner of the best Eastern Nigerian women. (p. 54)[12]

Jagua's situation is often compared to Moll's in Defoe's *Moll Flanders*. There is, of course, a certain similarity; both are extremely highly sexed women operating in the dubious underworld of the city, first as prostitutes and then as thieves or the accomplices of thieves. But there the similarity really ends. Defoe's purpose is to demonstrate that Moll has been largely conditioned by her social circumstances and is forced into prostitution and crime out of dire necessity in the struggle to acquire an economic competence in a materialistic man's world. If it was also Ekwensi's intention to present Jagua as the victim of social circumstances – a woman whose immoral conduct is necessitated by the forces in her society – then he has not achieved this in the novel that we have. A comparison of the background of the two women will make the point clear. Moll was in many ways an underprivileged child who had to be brought up in an orphanage and then by foster parents, and was subsequently seduced. Society is to blame, at least initially, for Moll's disasters. On the other hand, Jagua was well brought up by a clergyman father and a devoted mother in the traditional rural environment where the old values still survived. Unlike Moll who had to accept the first offer of marriage that came her way, Jagua turned down several offers, persistently refusing to marry, in the hope that some eminent stranger would come along and marry her. Jagua is looking away from the traditional world of the village to wider horizons; she is also looking for superior sexual experience. When she does marry, it is to a man from the city, the coal city. But since he lacks the glamour and glitter that Jagua desires, she absconds to Lagos. The two dominant drives in Jagua's life are therefore the need for the adventurous and exciting life of the city and the need for superior sexual experience.

Even after leaving her husband several alternatives for earning a respectable living present themselves to Jagua. She takes to trade, commuting between Lagos and Ghana, and while she gives her business maximum concentration, she is moderately successful. After the visit to Bagana she temporarily heeds her brother's plea and turns to trade again, but having this compulsive urge to be near the bright lights of the city, she devotes less application to the business than it demands, it inevitably fails and she returns to the city. Unlike other girls who go to the *Tropicana* out of dire necessity, Jagua goes because it has become a part of her; it is 'in her blood'. These cardinal points about Jagua must be appreciated at the outset. To suggest, as some critics do, that she is more sinned against than sinning, or that she is the victim of circumstances, is to propound a view which has no justification in the text. It will not do either to try to present Jagua as the elderly prostitute with a good heart. True, she can be generous – to Freddie and Rosa for instance – but her nastier qualities predominate. Forceful, wilful and relentless, she attempts to drag the sober-minded Freddie into the sordid world of the *Tropicana*. She is really a most unscrupulous woman who at one moment protests her love for Freddie and clearly hopes that he will return home after his studies to marry her, and at the next tries to force the young man to accept that she must continue to be a prostitute and go to bed with other men each night in order to earn money to keep herself. In pursuit of this she has no compunction in humiliating the young man in the face of her elderly Lebanese and Nigerian clients. She is a woman of absurd moods, fierce emotionalism and the wildest, most irrational anger. Her fits of jealousy can also lead to great vindictiveness. When Freddie, now married to Nancy, returns from his studies, she begins quite irresponsibly to plot his downfall out of a desire for revenge, although she continues to make love to him.

Now she was determined to turn Freddie against his wife, to make him loath the very sight of her, to break up his home if only to repay Nancy's humiliation of her. She would show Nancy that a harlot can wield great power over men's homes. Uncle Taiwo she had already worked up into such a state of anger against Freddie that he could easily waylay and fight him. She had told him that Freddie was pestering her life, that she had warned him often never to come to her but obstinately he still came to worry her in her home. Also that Freddie was resorting to subterfuge to snatch Obanla constituency from him. All this made Uncle Taiwo determined to get even with Freddie. (p. 149)

In a very real sense it is Jagua who signs Freddie's death warrant.

Like Sango's, Jagua's history in Lagos is one of progressive deterioration. She drifts into crime and becomes an accomplice of thieves, for a life of prostitution inevitably leads to association with thieves. Whatever spark of decency she once possessed has now disappeared, for she is prepared to take her role as disposer of stolen goods seriously. It is only when she comes face to face with death as a consequence of a life of crime and vice that she begins to have second thoughts; it is now that she urges Dennis Udoma to give up such a life. Clearly the author intends this as a point in Jagua's favour. It is from passages such as the following that the view of Jagua as the elderly prostitute with a good heart derives: 'With her elderly woman's heart, she could not bear to see this young boy who could well be her son sacrificed on the altar of recklessness.' If Jagua had proffered her advice before the taxi-driver's death, before she herself had started to relish her role as disposer of stolen goods, then this view of her would have been more tenable.

Eventually Jagua becomes the mistress of the unscrupulous Uncle Taiwo and drifts into the world of politics which in the Lagos context is as repulsive as the world of crime. When Uncle Taiwo loses the election and disappears, she reaches the nadir of her fortunes, losing all her possessions in the reprisals which follow. But then, in one of those crude contrivances which mar even Ekwensi's best effects, Uncle Taiwo's suitcase which he had entrusted to Jagua before his disappearance and death turns out to contain five thousand pounds. Although the money unquestionably belongs to Uncle Taiwo's party and creditors, Jagua sees absolutely nothing wrong in taking possession of all of it. Indeed, she sees it as just compensation for her sufferings in this world; this is Divine Providence making provision for her at last, and her conscience is salved by the decision to give a part of the money to the church. Nor does it seem to have occurred to Jagua's creator that what she has done amounts to felony.

Jagua is not like Moll Flanders, whose goodness is inseparable from her badness, or who is nasty and marvellous at the same time. Apart from her splendid looks and figure there is nothing that is marvellous or good about Jagua. It is her creator's deliberately chosen method of narration, which narrows the focus down to her point of view, that ensures a certain kind of sympathy for her and gives the erroneous impression that she is more sinned against than sinning.

The portrayal of Jagua's young lover, Freddie, is one of the book's grave weaknesses. At the start we are impressed by his idealism and desire for material and intellectual improvement. But it is never made convincingly clear why this handsome young man who could have had many beautiful young girls at his beck and call allows himself to be captivated by an ageing prostitute, even though Ekwensi does his best to demonstrate the possessive hold Jagua has on him. This Freddie, who was supposed to have been enslaved body and soul by Jagua, starts an affair with the first beautiful young girl that turns up and he is immediately aware of the differences between age and youth: 'The pleasure he had found in Nancy's youthfulness, her sensitivity, came as from a fable. He could not help contrasting her skin which was firm and elastic, with Jagua's flabby and soggy for all the artifice' (p. 29). How then do we explain the fact that Freddie has hitherto yielded to Jagua's possessiveness? Freddie is not impecunious, and he soon realizes that life with the prostitute Jagua must inevitably mean progressive degradation which conflicts with his desire for intellectual, social and material exaltation. Jagua is a blight on Freddie's life, and only by breaking completely free will he be able to realize his ambitions. This he finally does.

The change in Freddie's character towards the end of the novel when, on his return from England as a qualified barrister, he immediately plunges into the dirty political fray through a desire for material aggrandizement, is far from convincing. Ekwensi cannot really convince us that the Freddie we have come to know would have been so completely changed and hardened by his education as to become a cynical and callous self-seeker.

Ekwensi's presentation of the city in *Jagua Nana* is more thoroughgoing than in any of his other works. Here we are plunged deep into the seamy side of Lagos life, into the world of prostitutes, murderers and thieves; we see the dirty viciousness of a real Lagos election campaign and the corruption of a clogged bureaucratic system. This insight into the lower reaches of Lagos life where everyone is involved in the eternal struggle to live is particularly revealing.

A young woman in the corner of the smelly room seemed to be making a statement which Freddie had interrupted. She stood away from the counter which ran across the room and began bawling

swear words at the young police constable, who ignored her and kept
on writing steadily. Freddie observed at once that other constables
were deriving some lecherous satisfaction from the young woman's
behaviour. She had a defiant twinkle in her eye, her breath smelled
of alcohol and her blouse – one arm of which had been torn in some
scuffle – slouched over a naked young breast with a dare-devil
abandon that could not but be comical. She seemed by her manner
to be conscious of the power of her femaleness over the males in
the khaki uniforms.

Freddie stared at this ragged woman who confronted him with the
eternal struggle to live, so tragic in the lower reaches of Lagos life.
(p. 22)

The squalor and filth are also powerfully portrayed.

> She stored away the food, then took out her towel and went to the
> bathroom, but when she knocked a man answered her from the
> inside and she went instead to the lavatory. The same old bucket,
> piled high; the floor messed about, so she could see nowhere to put
> her silver sandals. It was all done by those wretched children
> upstairs. Why blame them when their mothers did not know any
> better. Where was the landlord? Where was the Town Council
> Health Inspector? This Inspector was supposed to come here once
> in a while, and whenever he came he made notes in his black book
> but nothing ever happened. She would talk seriously to him the next
> time. The unpleasant side of Lagos life: the flies in the lavatory – big
> and blue and stubborn – settled on breakfast yam and lunch-time
> stew (they were invisible in a stew with greens). But Jagua closed her
> eyes and shut her nostrils with her towel. (p. 108)

The case of the young prostitutes is pathetic; they go to the *Tropicana*
daily out of desperation, hoping that something will happen which will
put an end to poverty and starvation. *Jagua Nana* is a uniquely detailed
presentation of the causes and consequences of urban crime and
prostitution.

The inevitable contrast between the innocence of the country and
the viciousness of the city features in this novel. This is why Ekwensi
makes Jagua take that most unrealistic and unnecessary trip to Ogabu
and Bagana in the middle of the novel. There would otherwise seem to
be no point in her visiting Bagana, Freddie's home, since she and the
latter have quarrelled, and Freddie has gone to England estranged. It is
significant, however, that Jagua goes to Bagana at a time when she is
beginning to be disenchanted with Lagos. There is no mistaking the
lyricism which characterizes Ekwensi's presentation of the village of

Ogabu. Here there is fellow-feeling, co-operation and even a desire for progress. By implication, Jagua's city ways stand condemned by rural values. On her arrival she breathes the air of the countryside into her system and basks in its luxuriance and naturalness. In Bagana she responds to the rhythm of the drums and the dancing, thus demonstrating that in spite of her sojourn in the city, traditional life is still capable of appealing to all that is basic in her.

The Bagana scenes are unrealistic in many ways. The leading male characters – Uncle Namme and Chief Ofubara – are grotesque Victorian caricatures who are not presented with any depth, subtlety or conviction. There are also a number of melodramatic and sensational incidents uncomfortably reminiscent of some of the worst films on Africa. Finally, it is hard to believe that the politically innocent Jagua would have been able to solve such a delicate and complicated issue as the dynastic struggle between Chief Ofubara and his cousins across the creek by merely using her feminine charms.

The reconciliation is meant to show Jagua in the best possible light, so that she wins the admiration and sympathy of the Baganans and the reader. This is indeed the purpose of the entire countryside episode. Ekwensi must show that Jagua endears herself to and is at home in this idealized rural environment. But a closer examination of the rest of the novel shows that Jagua does not really prefer the country to the city. Even before leaving Bagana for Lagos she is highly conscious of the fact that she is losing 'her chic', becoming more provincial and less 'Jagua-ful'. She accordingly returns to Lagos. It is only when she disastrously loses everything in the end that she feels a sudden urge to go back to the country. And when she does go she is unable to stay for more than six months although someone is needed at home, on the death of her father, to look after her ageing mother. In the end she arrives at a compromise: she will live out of Lagos, since she now has money – Uncle Taiwo's money – but she will live in Onitsha, not in Ogabu, and she will try to become one of the merchant princesses of the city. But Onitsha, though less vicious than Lagos, is not the countryside. The return-to-the-country idea is therefore undermined by the reluctance of the novel's major character to settle there.

The political scenes are more skilfully handled, although Uncle Taiwo is another caricature.[13] His behaviour, which borders at times on clownishness, suggests that he also derives from those tenth-rate films on Africa where the 'bad man' makes the most frivolous boasts and ends every threat with guffaws of 'ha-ha'. The art here appears naive and crude. It seems as if Ekwensi is incapable of creating genuinely bad characters without making caricatures of them.

Nevertheless, the presentation of political life in Lagos is thorough and frightening. Nowhere do we get a better statement of the chicanery, lies, intrigue and inequalities which lead to the political battle than in Jagua's electioneering speech.

'You see the sort of people you will be voting for, if you vote for O.P.1. You will be voting for people who will build their private houses with your own money. But if you vote for O.P.2, the party that does the job, you will see that you women will never pay tax. Don't forget that. O.P.2 will educate your children properly. But those rogues in O.P.1? They will send their children to Oxford and Cambridge, while your children will only go to school in Obanla. No: Oblana is still too good for your children, because – oh! – how can your children find the space to be educated in Lagos schools, if O.P.1 ever comes into power? No, your children will be sent to the slummy suburbs.' (p. 145)

Uncle Taiwo's grim death, Freddie's murder and Jagua's loss of all her property are timely reminders of the fate that awaits those who play the dirty game of politics.

A few scenes in the novel demonstrate that Ekwensi possesses powers of invention and imagination. Apart from the telling description of Uncle Taiwo's death, there is the vivid realization of the Dennis Udoma scenes and those between Jagua and Freddie; also, Jagua's discovery of Freddie and Nancy in bed together will never be forgotten by readers of this novel. But these brilliantly executed passages are continually being marred by the tendency towards melodrama and sensationalism which dominates the whole work.

The greatest weakness of this novel, however, is the almost total absence of any overall moral vision or unifying moral idea. It seems as if it is fashionable these days to regard the idea of an overall moral vision as an extra-literary quality. An overall moral pattern need not be anything religious or even overtly moralistic. It could, in fact, be equated with the general significance which the author expects the reader to extract from his work. To bring out this significance the author must surely evaluate his situations and characters and communicate to the reader what he feels about them. In insisting on moral evaluation, one is not crudely suggesting that the good should be rewarded and the bad punished. It might indeed be part of the author's purpose to demonstrate that in our world the good often suffer and the bad are often successful; but then both the good and the bad must have been convincingly presented as good and bad. This implies that the author must have evaluated them and shown us the differences between them and the logical consequences of their personalities. Even though vice may triumph in the end, he must have clearly indicated where his sympathy lies. Whether in the evaluation of his characters and situations an author outrages our normal moral human values or not is properly part of the aesthetic satisfaction we derive from such a work, and an insistence on moral evaluation or an overall moral pattern is not, therefore, non-literary.

There is little doubt about the quality of Ekwensi's moral evaluation in this novel; it is almost complete endorsement of, and sympathy for, Jagua. He expects the reader also to sympathize with his heroine, to see that Jagua is a victim of circumstances, that she has suffered in the world and is entitled to her £5000 and happiness at the end. But in doing this he completely blinds himself to her nastier qualities. In the face of all the evidence in the novel he does seem to believe with Jagua that she has been a pawn in the hands of 'criminals, Senior Service men, contractors, thieves, detectives, liars, cheats, the rabble, the scum of the country's grasping hands and headlong rush to "civilization", "sophistication", and all the falsehood it implied'. She has been a pawn in the hands of everyone, in fact, except Jagua. Even in that terrible scene where Jagua's brother Fonso tries to plead with her to return to the bedside of her dying father, that scene where we are so strongly aware of Jagua's lack of feeling, Ekwensi still tries to force the reader to endorse her by putting forward the plea of poverty. So strong is his sympathy that he comes pretty near to endorsing crime and criminals.

Ekwensi has taken it upon himself to analyse one of the most pressing problems facing Africa today. We look to him for words of wisdom and for insight, but he has no insight to convey. If a writer shows so much sympathy for a character who brings all these social evils on herself because of her initial and subsequent conduct, and makes her triumphant in the end, then he is not only being unrealistic, he is showing a lack of real understanding of these complex social forces and of their possible consequences, and he can have no words of wisdom for us as to how we should reorder our society. *Jagua Nana* would have been a great work if its author, in yearning after the sensational and in identifying himself with his heroine, had not so glaringly missed his opportunities.

Ekwensi's next novel, *Burning Grass*, is of an entirely different stamp. From the world of the city, he takes his readers to purely traditional life, for the novel is set, not in Lagos, but among the nomadic Fulani of northern Nigeria. This is the Ekwensi novel which most clearly bears the stamp of the oral tradition. It often reads like an extended folk tale. From the very start we are aware of the element of folk tale in the episode of the beautiful young damsel who, on being rescued from her captors, plunges the family of her rescuer into an endless vendetta. It is also to the folk tale tradition that the novel owes the element of fantasy which predominates towards the end. Certain features such as the lack of psychological plausibility, and the absence of any detailed demonstration of thought processes leading to crucial actions, consequently seem excusable here, since they could not be expected of the folk tale.

It might seem on a first reading that there is no serious meaning to this tale of an old man who must continually wander from place to place because he has been struck by the *Sokugo* or wandering disease. However, its significance lies in the valiant attempt by Mai Sunsaye to stave off the threat of disintegration which Fatimeh's rescue introduces into his family. The apparently casual nature of relationships, the very nomadic nature of the society, and the constant threat of violence, all suggest the difficulty of keeping families together. A further theme is the old man's eventual discovery of areas of experience hitherto closed to him. As in all picaresque novels, the hero gains in experience during his travels. His journey takes him away from the traditional world of the countryside with which he has been familiar all his life, to the wider world of urban experience where the white man has consolidated his influence and brought significant changes to the society.

The novel's two themes are linked by the fact that during the journey Mai Sunsaye sees all his sons prospering in the various areas they have chosen, whether it be in traditional life like Jalla, or in the new world of the city like Hodio; and even the youngest, Rikku, is full of promise for the future as a cattleman like his ancestors. The threat of disintegration is thus staved off, the tensions between the various sons are resolved, and the old man finally able to gather together the broken remnants of his family and die content.

In this work traditional life inevitably looms much larger than it does in *People of the City*, *Jagua Nana* and *Beautiful Feathers*. Whereas the movement in these latter is from the city to the country and back again to the city, the movement in *Burning Grass* is from the country to the city and back again to the country. The setting is essentially rural and traditional; it is a world where the old folk tales and folk tunes abound. Here we come face to face with the use of charms and talismans, with riddles and proverbs and with the various rites of passage, such as the shango where the young man must prove his manhood before taking a wife.

There is, however, an uneasy sense of the impending thrust of modern ideas on this impressive traditional life. At the beginning of the novel one of Sunsaye's sons, Hodio, decides against traditional rules and values, to run away with Fatimeh to the town where no one cares about such values. We therefore sense a radical fervour among the young who are in favour of change because of the liberation it brings them, while the old, like the quaint old man Sunsaye meets in Old Chanka, are determined to resist. Like the old man, Sunsaye also voices his preference for traditional life with all its drawbacks, and his antagonism towards a monotonous and mechanical modernity.

Of Sunsaye's three sons, Jalla makes an early decision to stick to the traditional nomadic life, taking to the traditional occupation of cattle rearing, marrying his wife in the traditional way and participating in the traditional rituals. Inevitably he is the son for whom his father has the greatest respect. Hodio scorns tradition in favour of modern ways, moves from the country to the town of New Chanka, and tries to make his way in the modern sugar-producing industry. The third son, Rikku, is torn for most of the novel between tradition and modernism. Like his father, he wanders from place to place, experiencing good and evil, seeing the horrors of life and growing in consequence. In the episodes with Kantuma, Rikku's devotion to the countryside and traditional life is severely tested, for Kantuma offers strong temptation to him to remain in the city. The confrontation between Ligu and Kantuma can be regarded as a struggle between the traditional and the modern for the soul of Rikku. Ligu is the embodiment of the traditional – a woman who is yet the most famous cattle rearer of them all – and Kantuma is so obviously the unfaithful, scheming, urbanized, modern woman. It is the traditional that wins in Ligu, and at the end, Rikku, who has now outgrown his calf-love for Fatimeh and wishes to be a man in the clan, chooses to be a cattleman like his father before him.

Burning Grass probably has a greater share of the sensational than the other novels. If Ekwensi seems to have incorporated elements from the fantastic world of the fairy tale (*The Arabian Nights* perhaps), he has also incorporated details from the world of the western film. This is suggested by the rustlings, stampedes, ambushes, kidnappings and pitched battles. There is a marked resemblance between Shehu, one of the bad characters, and the stock villain of the western thriller. Of course, there are the usual inconsistencies (Mai Sunsaye mentions Rikku's journey to the border country at a time when he could not possibly have heard of it), and certain incidents (like the fuss about the white vulture and the evil portents associated with it) are given a distinctly anti-climactic conclusion. However, the plot and structure are more compact than in the other novels and there are signs of a definite advance in the use of language. The prose is quite often elegant, and a deliberate attempt has been made to impart an African flavour to the characters' speech by the use of proverbs and by direct translations from the forms of the indigenous language. There is some justification for the view that artistically *Burning Grass* is perhaps Ekwensi's most satisfying work.[14]

Beautiful Feathers is the most overtly didactic of the novels. It deals with the relationship between private and public life. The hero, Wilson Iyari, apparently respected because of his political activities, cannot wield authority in his home. And at every possible opportunity Ekwensi drives home the moral that 'however famous a man is outside, if he is not respected inside his own house he is like a bird with *beautiful feathers*, wonderful on the outside but ordinary within'. This heavy-handed insistence on the moral is one of the factors which seriously weaken the effect of this novel.

Beautiful Feathers is probably Ekwensi's least impressive novel, possessing in large measure all the characteristic weaknesses of his art. First, it lacks thematic unity and clarity. The two themes – political fame and involvement and domestic unhappiness – are not successfully blended, since it is not clearly shown that Wilson's domestic troubles are caused by his political involvement (the domestic problems had commenced long before the start of his political career); nor is the contrast between the unsuccessful husband and the famous public figure convincingly enacted, since Wilson does not emerge from the novel as a powerful public figure in any case.

The problem probably lies partly in Ekwensi's choice of a political movement. Unlike someone like Uncle Taiwo, Iyari is the leader, not of a national political party dedicated to the achievement of independence or the raising of the people's standard of living, but of the National Movement of African and Malagasy Solidarity whose aim is to achieve African unity. Without minimizing the importance of African unity, it is still fair to say that such a movement can hardly be calculated to set the imagination of the mass of the people alight. It certainly is not obvious that a political party is needed to bring the idea of African unity to the people and their leaders. The NMFAMS is simply not weighty or dignified enough to confer importance on its leader or to generate the sense of urgency which would make its demonstrations and other activities seem necessary in such apparently unfavourable circumstances. Moreover, the activities of the NMFAMS are so disreputable as to suggest that it belongs almost to the lunatic fringe. The reader wonders how the leader of a movement whose members are so childish and amateurish ever managed to become respected. Its activities are much more disorganized and seem much less justified than an ordinary student demonstration, and in planning these its members prove both incompetent and dishonest. It is not surprising, therefore, that some of these demonstrations degenerate into hooliganism, and xenophobist, anti-white, anti-colonialist riots in which the 'respectable' and 'famous' Wilson, who had himself preached the message of 'peaceful demonstration', throws stones at the car of an American diplomat. Must we attribute such silly episodes to the tendency towards sensationalism, or does the author seriously intend these activities to be regarded as justifiable? One certain consequence of such conduct, which the author ought to have seen, is that it does considerable damage to the reputation and credibility of the movement and its leader.

In the light of all this, it is surprising that the prime minister selects the now discredited Wilson Iyari (whom he had scarcely heard about before the demonstration) to lead the country's delegation to a conference on African unity at Dakar. Ekwensi is surely sufficiently experienced in the ways of the world to know that African rulers do not select leaders of fringe parties to lead delegations to conferences on African unity. However, it turns out that the 'famous' and 'respected' leader of the movement has hitherto never given any serious thought to the implications of the whole concept of African unity; he has never really considered whether it is practicable or possible, and it is only now that he is forced to think about such matters. The conference itself goes rather well, but at the end there is a big-game hunt during which the delegates kill a huge beast 'shaped like a rhino, but infinitely more elegant'. An argument now arises among these supposedly mature and important delegates about the means of disposing of the dead animal. This leads even more incredibly to a gun-fight in which Wilson is seriously injured; but what is most incredible is that during the fight among the black delegates the white observers run away with the dead beast. One wonders why Ekwensi makes his important characters in this novel behave like children in a kindergarten. The symbolism of the episode is clear, but it is crude and obvious and becomes simple-minded when the Senegalese president hammers home the moral point: 'You know ... it is like the struggle for African unity. While Africa burns, interested parties carry away the loot.' Small wonder that on his return to Nigeria, Wilson, now properly educated about the problems of African unity and savouring his new found relationship with the prime minister, has no qualms about killing off the NMFAMS.

Perhaps the problem of the novel lies partly with Iyari himself. Like most other Ekwensi heroes he is a spineless character who, in spite of his often-mentioned fame and respectability, lacks foresight, imagination and intelligence. As far as the reader can see, he is unimpressive in both his home and his public life. On the other hand, his wife Yaniya is a much more forceful character, obviously the dominant personality in the household, and she is much more effectively realized. She can be unfaithful, proud and decadent, but also intelligent and in a sense realistic. Essentially, Yaniya is a spoilt child who refuses to accept the responsibilities of married life and longs to go back to the scenes of her childhood. The marriage begins to flounder because it represents a clash of intentions and personalities. Yaniya looks to Wilson to give her comfort after a number of disastrous affairs with other men, and Wilson, for his part, had been blind to Yaniya's uglier faults during the courtship. When the problems begin both demonstrate their irresponsibility.

Beautiful Feathers also has the usual idealization of the countryside to which Yaniya returns as a haven from the ordeals of her married life. Correspondingly there is a presentation of the city's decadence and immorality. But since the virtuous countryside is represented here by the quaint, unrealistic 'kingdom' of Yaniya's eccentric father, and since little Lumumba dies there for want of proper medical attention, it is hardly possible to sustain the myth of the country as the repository of all that is good and admirable. The novel is redeemed, as far as it can be redeemed, by some very effective satire at the expense of the Ministry of Consolation, one of whose officials, Gadson Salifas, is for a while Yaniya's paramour. The title of the ministry indicates the mockery. The minister himself is presented as vain, incompetent and indifferent to the welfare of his staff. He looks little better than a clown.

> The Minister of Consolation was standing before the mirror admiring his own image. He turned his face to the left and smiled. He turned his face to the right and smiled. He watched the mirror to see the effect of smiling with his teeth shut tight, with his lips parted and his tongue lolling out. (p. 74)

There could be no better exposure of incompetence than this.

> 'All right, then. I want you to write me a speech, quickly'. He glanced at the mirror. 'Don't make it too long. Any speech!' The Perennial Secretary was prepared. He sat in a corner of the lounge and drafted a speech which he took along to the Minister, who was still standing before the mirror . . . 'Write me another speech at once. The first one is not strong. I want a strong one this time'. 'What about, may I ask, Mr. Minister?' 'Just write me a speech.' 'Yes, sir.' (pp. 75–6)

The comedy here is worthy of Soyinka.

Ekwensi, then, does certain things well in this novel. But the overall impression must be that the art is shoddy. It is in this novel that we have the greatest reliance on the melodramatic and sensational to get the story moving or to tie up the plot. Apart from the big-game hunt and the demonstration, there are the terrible final scenes where Yaniya, determined to sacrifice herself as a penance for Lumumba's death, receives the knife blow that was intended for Wilson at the NMFAMS final rally, and the equally grotesque Dickensian death-bed scene in which Yaniya urges Wilson to marry another girl, Chini, who would make him a better wife. However, Chini is never called upon to make the sacrifice, for Yaniya miraculously recovers, and Chini is conveniently bundled off to a United Nations job in Geneva. There are psychological implausibilities such as the unconvincing behaviour of the politician Paul Aremu towards the end, and inconsistencies such as the confusion about whether Chini works in the Cabinet Office or the Ministry of Consolation. If one adds to these the contrived plot, the weak characterization, the thematic confusion, the lack of psychological insight, the heavy-handed moralization and the tendency towards the sensational and sentimental, it will be seen why *Beautiful Feathers* represents Ekwensi at his weakest.

One would have liked to say that Ekwensi's latest novel *Survive the Peace* (Heinemann, 1976) shows signs that at last its author has learned from the mistakes of the past and mastered the novel form. Unfortunately, this novel is not likely to enhance Ekwensi's reputation much. In some ways there are improvements: though one would have expected that a novel about the Biafran War would naturally invite a concentration on the sensational, there is, paradoxically, less dependence in this novel on melodramatics to get the plot moving. The rather unexpected death of the hero, James Odugo, which might seem melodramatic to some, has in fact been rather carefully prepared for by the beautiful impression of peace, contentment and hope which precedes it and which must appear to the perceptive reader to be too good to be true. Ekwensi's control of language is also much surer here and he still retains his power of evoking remarkably vivid scenes, particularly at the start. In *Survive the Peace* he deserts his usual preoccupation with the problems of the city and modernism to give some attention to the Nigerian Civil War, but he is concerned here, not so much with the horrors of the actual war as some other Nigerian writers have been, as with the disintegration of family life that it causes, with the fragility of relationships during this catastrophe and the frenzied attempts, on the cessation of hostilities, to put the pieces together and 'survive the peace'. The treatment of the theme is generally satisfactory. However, it must be said on the debit side that Ekwensi shows no sense of plot and structure, the novel consisting of isolated episodes only tenuously held together by the overriding theme. As far as characterization goes, Ekwensi shows little psychological insight, little real understanding of how human beings will behave at particular moments: Vic's dash from the car which is taking her to safety on hearing that Odugo intends to make for his wife's village is unrealistic in the circumstances, and her sudden change into the callous unfeeling girl out to ensure her prosperity after the war should have been more thoroughly documented. The change in the Captain is not convincing either. Odugo, the hero, also fails to emerge as a credible character; he is too spineless, too passive, and says little that is memorable or that will help fix his character in the reader's mind. This last novel reinforces the impression that Ekwensi is incapable of creating lively, forceful and convincing male characters. The women are much more spirited here, as they are in the other novels. On the whole *Survive the Peace* is not a bad performance, but it is not by any means compelling. It is better than Ekwensi at his worst, but not as good as his best.

This survey has tried to show that Ekwensi has a very powerful and serious social and political concern, and his work is relevant to Africans for this reason. He is also capable of writing good passages, but he cannot sustain this power over the whole to produce an accomplished work of art. The good passages may show, as John Povey suggests, that he has potential; [15] but so far the potential has not been realized, even though his output has been prolific. It is not satisfactory to say that Ekwenski chooses to write shoddily because of his awareness of the limitations of his audience. An unsophisticated audience does not necessarily need shoddy work, and even if this were true Ekwensi should have realized, after the critics' strictures, that it was wrong strategy. We must seriously face the possibility that it is the combination of a distorted notion of what constitutes a good novel and an inability to sustain his good effects which has vitiated his otherwise thorough presentation of some of the evils of modern African urban society.

NOTES

1 See, in particular, three largely favourable articles: G. D. Killam, 'Cyprian Ekwensi', in *Introduction to Nigerian Literature*, ed. Bruce King (University of Lagos and Evans, Lagos and London, 1971), pp. 77–95; Ernest Emenyonu, 'African Literature: what does it take to be its critic?', *African Literature Today*, no. 5, *The Novel in Africa* (1971), pp. 1–11; John Povey, 'Cyprian Ekwensi: the novelist and the pressures of the city', in *The Critical Evaluation of African Literature*, ed. Edgar Wright (Heinemann, London, 1973), pp. 73–94.

2 Bernth Lindfors, 'Cyprian Ekwensi: an African popular novelist', *ALT*, no. 3 (1969), pp. 2–14.

3 Emenyonu, op. cit.

4 Povey, op. cit.

5 ibid, p. 74.

6 ibid., p. 75.

7 ibid., p. 77.

8 Killam, op. cit.

9 Lindfors, op. cit., p. 3.

10 Emenyonu, op. cit., p. 7.

11 All references are to the Heinemann African Writers Series edition, unless otherwise stated.

12 Cyprian Ekwensi, *Jagua Nana* (Hutchinson, London, 1961). All references are to this edition, now available in Heinemann African Writers Series (AWS 146).

13 I simply cannot bring myself to agree with Povey's view that Uncle Taiwo is a triumph of characterization. See Povey, op. cit., p. 83.

14 Killam, op. cit., p. 95.

15 Povey, op. cit., p. 93.

3. Chinua Achebe

▼▼▼▼▼▼▼▼▼▼▼▼▼▼▼▼▼▼▼▼▼▼▼▼▼▼▼▼▼▼▼▼▼▼▼▼▼▼▼

Chinua Achebe's *Things Fall Apart* (1957) demonstrates a mastery of plot and structure, strength of characterization, competence in the manipulation of language and consistency and depth of thematic exploration which is rarely found in a first novel. Although he has never quite been able to sustain this exceptionally high standard in subsequent novels, the general level of performance remains consistently impressive and he assuredly deserves his place as one of the most accomplished African writers. In the history of the anglophone novel Achebe comes next to Ekwensi in chronological importance, but his work is much more comprehensive in scope than that of the latter who confines himself almost entirely to contemporary situations. All the shaping forces which combined to stimulate the growth of modern African literature in the 1950s are discernible in Achebe's work. Broadly speaking, the African novel is a response to and a record of the traumatic consequences of the impact of western capitalist colonialism on the traditional values and institutions of the African peoples. This largely explains the African writers' initial preoccupation with the past. While recognizing the need for a redefinition and reordering of values in modern Africa in the wake of the disruptive effects of colonial administration, writers like Achebe and Soyinka also realize that before this reordering can take place there must be a confrontation with the past. In the article 'The novelist as teacher' Achebe talks interestingly of how he sees his role as a writer in society.[1] One of the consequences of the impact of western civilization on Africa, he says, is 'the disaster brought upon the African psyche in the period of subjection to alien races'. Africans were induced to prefer western culture and to regard their own with contempt. It is part of the African writer's business to teach his fellow-Africans that there is nothing shameful in African culture and tradition.

Here then is an adequate revolution for me to espouse – to help my

society regain belief in itself and put away the complexes of the years
of denigration and self-abasement. And it is essentially a question of
education, in the best sense of the word . . . I would be quite satisfied
if my novels (especially the ones I set in the past) did no more than
teach my readers that their past – with all its imperfections – was not
one long night of savagery from which the first Europeans acting on
God's behalf delivered them.[2]

In another article, 'The role of the writer in a new nation', Achebe
consequently suggests that the African writer must primarily concern
himself with the past in an effort to help his fellow-Africans regain that
lost dignity 'by showing them in human terms what happened to them,
what they lost'.[3] He goes on:

> There is a saying in Ibo that a man who can't tell where the rain
> began to beat him cannot know where he dried his body. The writer
> can tell the people where the rain began to beat them. After all the
> writer's duty is not to beat this morning's headlines in topicality, it is
> to explore in depth the human condition. In Africa he cannot
> perform this task unless he has a proper sense of history.[4]

The history of the colonialist impact on Africa proceeded in three
phases: first there was the stage of actual conquest when the white man
by sheer force of arms introduced an alien form of administration,
education and religion and taught the African to look down on his own
indigenous systems; the second was the period of resistance when the
now-awakened masses struggled to shake off the imperialist yoke;
finally there is the present post-independence stage with African
society seeking to reorder itself, having thrown off imperialist
oppression. The exploration of these three phases is the motive force
behind the African novel, and Achebe is central to this concern. He
deals with the first phase since in two of his novels he attempts to
demonstrate the destructive impact of westernization on indigenous
culture and to attest to the beauty of that culture; he touches on the
second phase although he is not as concerned as Ngugi with the
struggle to shake off the imperialist yoke, but he certainly shows the
beginnings of the rumblings of discontent; and he is very much
involved with the attempt at the re-ordering of values.

The theme of Achebe's four novels, then, all of which he had
planned as a tetralogy from the very first, is that of tradition versus
change: he gives a powerful presentation of the beauty, strength and
validity of traditional life and values and the disruptiveness of change.
It may be that Achebe's presentation of traditional life is not an

accurate reproduction of the historical truth. However, what we shall be concerned with here, in an attempt to see the picture of his Ibo society that emerges, is not a faithful anthropological documentation but the way in which Achebe sees it.

Things Fall Apart demonstrates the paramountcy of religious beliefs in nineteenth-century Iboland. Societies which the missionaries later branded as pagan were in fact more religious than anything that had been seen in the western world for a very long time. No major enterprise, whether national or personal, was undertaken without first attempting to divine the will of the gods. The religious system involved a complex hierarchy of gods and deities, major and minor, ranging from the personal god or chi, through the ancestral spirits and clan deities, to the major national gods. The chi, or personal god, which has been the subject of much literary debate, will be regarded here as a kind of guardian angel that ensured the individual's protection and was in a way responsible for his destiny. The spirits of the ancestors not only acted as mediators between men and gods but also occasionally took a hand in deciding human destiny; they could show their pleasure or displeasure with their descendants by making them prosper or sending them misfortune. An Ibo man's shrine contained wooden carvings which were the symbols of his chi and his ancestral spirits, and he had to pray to them and worship them daily with sacrifices. Then there were the village and clan deities like Idemili, Udo, Ogwugwu and Ulu, who were the immediate protectors of the village or clan, and the major gods – Amadioha, the god of thunder and of the sky; Ani, the earth goddess and the source of all fertility, the ultimate judge of morality and conduct; Ojukwu, the god who controlled the dreaded disease of smallpox; and Ifejioku, the god of yams. Above them all was the greatest: Chukwu.

In worshipping wooden representations of these gods the Ibo people, far from indulging in idolatory, were merely manifesting the belief, similar to the Christian theory of the omnipresence of God, that they were present in all aspects of creation through which they could speak to their people. The plurality of gods might also arouse the contempt of sceptical Christians, but the Ibo man, like the Christian, also believed in the supreme god, Chukwu, only he felt that Chukwu's might prevented him from being approached except through middlemen or lesser gods. Like all other religions, this elaborate religious system was designed to explain the mysteries of a seemingly irrational and frightening world and to provide sanctions for good behaviour. Adherence to its dictates therefore meant a stable society in which the norms were respected. In both *Arrow of God* and *Things Fall Apart* we see the powerful belief that the clan should not go to war unless its case was clear and just, for it could not otherwise count on the support of its deity. The fear of the gods, then, helped to sanction right conduct on both the personal and national levels. A man would never swear by his chi or his ikenga if he knew his cause was not just; no one would risk the wrath of Ojukwu or the thunder of Amadioha.

And yet, in spite of their faith in their gods and their conviction that their religious system is right and effective, the people of Umuofia and Umuaro in *Things Fall Apart* and *Arrow of God* display remarkable religious tolerance. They are generally kind and courteous towards the new religion, demonstrating a sophisticated liberalism and modernity which are completely absent from the new camp.

The elaborate religious order correlated with an equally elaborate social and administrative system ensuring decency, justice and stability. The notion held in some quarters that it was the white man who brought administration and order into African society, must by now be completely disproved. The administrative, social and judicial arrangements were interrelated and linked with the religious system. Through the social structure and the various initiation rituals, the individual came to learn the norms of behaviour. The belief in the ancestors who played a very important guiding role in the world of the living helped to strengthen personal moral awareness. The various social and administrative units – the family, the lineage groups, the age groups, the council of the elders and the chief priests – played their own roles, where appropriate, in resolving disputes and dispensing justice. The institution of chieftaincy was a subsequent imposition by an alien administration ignorant of the traditional system of government. This system as practised was perfectly democratic, since it did not allow one man or family to achieve absolute power. The various age groups, like the Okatagu age group of which Obika was a member, discussed matters immediately affecting the welfare of that group, while the council of the elders, a representative body consisting of the most responsible and oldest members of the clan, discussed weightier matters until a consensus was reached. The younger men did not have to stage coups, nor were they necessarily disgruntled, because they realized that their turn would come to sit on the council of the elders.

The sanctions imposed on those who fell foul of the norms were both punitive and deterrent. This partly accounts for their harshness. For instance, Okonkwo's seven-year exile from his fatherland and the destruction of all his property, though apparently a harsh penalty for the accidental slaying of a kinsman, was the only sanction the society possessed as a deterrent from murders within the clan. Respect for the gods also had to be enforced by heavy penalties against those who desecrated or destroyed their symbols or representatives on earth. The killing of Idemili's sacred python was therefore an abomination that could only be expiated if the offending party arranged very expensive funeral ceremonies for the dead snake. Such were the administrative, religious and social arrangements that ensured stability and coherence in Iboland. The society emerges indeed as one which observes great delicacy and decency in relationships, not only among the members themselves but also with neighbouring clans and foreigners. Okonkwo as an emissary offering peace or war is treated with great courtesy by the clan of Mbaino although his message is by no means pleasant. And even though Winterbottom's court messenger is insufferably rude to Ezeulu and the other elders, they treat him with great courtesy, as befits a stranger. Generally there is an acute sense of what correct protocol demands.

The society's culture embraces not just its customs and religious practices but also its art, of which Achebe gives several vivid glimpses. Particularly impressive is the care and devotion which individual artists bestow on their work, such as Edogo's attention to detail and his professional concern that his carving should be as good as the best. Then there is Obiozo Ezikolo, whose mastery of the ikolo, the king of all drums, is still unrivalled even in his old age. And even the lazy Unoka, Okonkwo's father, has at least one point in his favour – his artistry on his flute, his devotion to his singing.

This, then, is the picture of traditional society that Achebe presents in order to demonstrate the beauty and autonomy of African culture. Nevertheless, his attitude towards this society is quite different from the idealizing stance of the apostles of Negritude who are unwilling to accept that there was anything reprehensible in the African past. Generally Achebe demonstrates that practical realism which is one of the hallmarks of anglophone writing. He once said that the African writer should have sufficient integrity to resist the temptation to gloss over inconvenient facts.[5] Certainly, no one can accuse Achebe of doing this. He is far from flinching from the presentation of the harshness and cruelty of traditional African society, aware though he is of its strength and beauty. He makes us feel the full terror of a situation where, as a penalty for a woman's murder by another clan, an innocent young boy and girl are taken away from their homes and the boy is ruthlessly killed later on the orders of the oracle. The savage treatment meted out to twins and victims of the swelling sickness who are abandoned in the evil forest, osus who are ostracized from all normal human society, and individuals who infringe the sanctity of the week of peace, registers itself forcefully on the mind of the reader. Finally through Obierika's perceptive reflections we experience the harshness of a system that exiles a man for seven years for the accidental killing of a kinsman. All these apparently cruel customs were originally necessitated by the fear of the gods and of the unknown forces of evil; but Achebe wants to suggest that they erred on the side of thoroughness and probably caused more suffering than they were meant to alleviate. This is why in his novels he provides progressive thinking men like Obierika who, while accepting their society's customs, also seriously reflect on their fairness. In a sense, also, Achebe does not flinch from criticizing his society's resistance to change. While deploring the imperialists' brutality and conde-scension, he seems to suggest that change is inevitable and wise men like the early Ezeulu reconcile themselves to accommodating change. It is the diehards like Okonkwo who resist and are destroyed in the process.

The change is brought about, of course, by the white man with his new administration, education and religion. Though he accepts the inevitability of change and recognizes the benefits that it brings with it, Achebe still demonstrates that its total effect has been disruptive. The white man's arrival is first announced in *Things Fall Apart*. It is the missionaries who come first, bringing the word of God to supposedly benighted Africans, but as is the case with the whole history of the colonial exploitation of Africa, they are merely the advance guard paving the way for the administrator with his new form of government. The new administration leaves its stamp on the minds of the people with incidents of tremendous brutality and by its immediate disruption of the traditional order when, after a senseless massacre, men are forced to flee to lands where they have no kinsmen: a shocking reversal of the traditional system where even in times of difficulty men fled to their motherland. The new administration, having entrenched itself, behaves with astonishing arrogance and ignorance, imposing its own laws on a people who have ruled themselves with justice and stability for hundreds of years, without trying to find out the nature of indigenous law and custom or the points at which it clashed with white law. Achebe powerfully demonstrates, particularly in *Things Fall Apart*, the humiliation and degradation to which the tribe is subjected and the contempt that the white man shows for traditional ways and traditional dignity. Particularly disgusting is the way in which titled men, all of them leaders of their society, are treated as common criminals because they have unwittingly offended against the white man's law. One of the most moving scenes in *Things Fall Apart* is the confrontation between the elders of Umuofia and the District Commissioner as a result of which the elders are handcuffed and imprisoned until an enormous fine is paid. The incident demonstrates both the arrogance and the insincerity of the new administration which, unlike the elders, is guilty of treachery. Achebe's satire is scathing against the complacency and condescension of the District Commissioner.

> 'We have brought a peaceful administration to you and your people so that you may be happy. If any man ill-treats you we shall come to your rescue. But we will not allow you to ill-treat others. We have a court of law where we judge cases and administer justice just as it is done in my country under a great queen. I have brought you here because you joined together to molest others, to burn people's houses and their place of worship. That must not happen in the dominion of our queen, the most powerful ruler in the world.' (p. 175)[6]

The new administration induces Nigerians to laugh at their own culture, disregard their traditional system and insult their elders. This is ably demonstrated by the behaviour of the court messengers in both *Things Fall Apart* and *Arrow of God*. While grovelling with the utmost servility at the very mention of the white man's name, they are scornful in their comments on the traditional titles of their society: 'We see that every pauper wears an anklet of title in Umuofia. Does it cost as much as ten cowries?' Here we see the beginnings of that inferiority complex which contact with the white man has bred in some Africans, that feeling that Achebe complains of elsewhere, that everything associated with Africa must somehow be *infra dig*. while everything associated with the white man must be superior. Even when something of value is discovered in traditional culture its qualities are immediately transferred to the white man; without batting an eyelid, one of the court messengers can say: 'When a masked spirit visits you you have to

appease its footprints with presents. The white man is the masked
spirit of today.' This almost sacrilegious distortion of traditional
beliefs is all the more reprehensible since it is being used to serve the
purposes of corruption and extortion.

Indeed, the white man's administration breeds corruption in
African society. The view is held in some quarters that the present
widespread corruption in Africa will be difficult to eradicate because it
is almost endemic in Africa where 'dashes' are offered for services not
yet rendered. Nothing could be further from the truth. Achebe, here
and elsewhere, attributes the source of corruption where it belongs – to
the advent of the white man and his introduction of a money-based
economy. In the essay 'The role of the writer in a new nation' he
accepts that African society has always been materialistic, but he
asserts that in those days wealth meant the strength of a man's arm:
'No one became rich by swindling the community and stealing
government money.' This practice is a direct consequence of the
British administration's introduction of a cash-based economy and its
policy of placing in positions of responsibility men like the court
messengers and warrant chiefs who could operate outside the
sanctions of traditional society and use their positions to exploit the
people. This is the cause of the significant change from the traditional
situation where one voluntarily offered a present in gratitude to a
system where the gift was demanded even before the services were
rendered.

Achebe's disgust at the practice of the white administration in
Nigeria is summarized in the biting irony with which he treats the
posturing District Commissioner at the end of *Things Fall Apart*.

> The Commissioner went away, taking three or four of the soldiers
> with him. In the many years in which he had toiled to bring
> civilization to different parts of Africa he had learnt a number of
> things. One of them was that a District Commissioner must never
> attend to such undignified details as cutting down a hanged man
> from the tree. Such attention would give the natives a poor opinion
> of him. In the book which he planned to write he would stress that
> point. As he walked back to the court he thought about that book.
> Every day brought him some new material. The story of this man
> who had killed a messenger and hanged himself would make
> interesting reading. One could almost write a whole chapter on him.
> Perhaps not a whole chapter but a reasonable paragraph, at any rate.
> There was so much else to include, and one must be firm in cutting
> out details. He had already chosen the title of the book, after much

thought: *The Pacification of the Primitive Tribes of the Lower Niger.* (p. 187)

This is surely one of the most brilliant passages contrived by Achebe, the tone and language being perfectly controlled and the Commissioner's complacency and ignorance most effectively exposed.

The new religion, like the new administration, is a potent agent of disruption in Ibo society. In spite of the people's initial contempt and scepticism it continues to survive by sheer force of will and pertinacity. The people would have been prepared to allow it to continue to coexist peacefully with them, but the new religion is an aggressive one which breeds dissension in families, openly encouraging children to be disrespectful to their parents – a thing unheard of in traditional society. Like the new administration, the new religion shows scant regard for traditional beliefs and customs – Okoli, one of the new converts, commits the abomination of killing the sacred python and Enoch precipitates catastrophe by unmasking a masked spirit in the full gaze of the public. The simple-mindedness and tactlessness of the new religion are sometimes astonishing.

> He told them that the true God lived on high and that all men when they died went before Him for judgement. Evil men and all the heathen who in their blindness bowed to wood and stone were thrown into a fire that burned like palm-oil. But good men who worshipped the true God lived for ever in his happy kingdom. 'We have been sent by this great God to ask you to leave your wicked ways and false gods and turn to Him so that you may be saved when you die,' he said. 'Your buttocks understand our language,' said someone light-heartedly and the crowd laughed. (p. 132)

The missionary's underestimation of the people's intelligence is clear, but equally clear is the hard-headedness and tolerance of the people, indicated by the light-hearted rejoinder and the crowd's laughter.

Achebe does not play down the attractiveness of the new religion; he shows its appeal for all those who had been harshly treated by their society's more repellent customs – the osus, the mothers of abandoned twins and those like Nwoye who knew they would never measure up to the harsh demands of traditional life. Simple-minded and tactless though the new religion might be, it was, in practice, more humane than traditional religion and ministered to a vital need. Furthermore, Mr Brown, the first missionary is tactful and sensitive. Realizing that he cannot hope to make much headway in an open confrontation with the old religion, he decides to achieve his aims by means of education which proves a powerful attraction. He is also willing to learn more about the people's beliefs, spending long hours in the village talking about religion. Inevitably, however, the general aggressiveness of the new religion, particularly under the leadership of Mr Smith, results in confrontation which hastens the decline of traditional society. The closing section of *Things Fall Apart*, like that of *Arrow of God*, contains some very poignant passages lamenting the passing away of the old order.

Novels like *Things Fall Apart* and *Arrow of God* in which the author sets out to demonstrate the beauty and validity of traditional life and its destruction by an alien civilization must inevitably have a very high sociological content, since the nature of the society must be thoroughly documented before its collapse is shown. This need partly dictates the structure of *Things Fall Apart* and *Arrow of God*, the first parts of both novels being comparatively leisurely portrayals of Ibo society, whereas the second halves move much more rapidly, showing the forces which bring about the collapse. It also accounts for the high sociological content of the earliest African novels. However, a novel is not a sociological document; readers go to novels, not for sociological information, but for impressions of life powerfully realized. Sociological information will therefore appear tedious to most readers unless it is expertly handled in the novel, that is, unless it is made to appear part of the vibrant life of the people the author is describing and does not seem to be sociological lore *per se*. Novelists like Achebe and Amadi have proved themselves very adept at the incorporation of sociological material. Again and again we ask ourselves why it is that after reading hosts of novels which have been made tedious because of the preponderance of unassimilated sociological material, we can come back to Achebe's *Things Fall Apart*, half of which consists of sociological lore, and still be captivated by it. The answer is simply that in this novel the sociological does not call attention to itself as being purely sociological; it is presented as part of the life and activity of the people and is almost always related to some aspect of human character. At times the sociological is introduced as part of the detail which makes the book realistic and interesting. In Chapter 2 for instance, the traditional fear of the darkness and of dangerous animals, and the various superstitions concerning them, are incorporated into the general tension of the announcement of the meeting. When in Chapter 3 Nwakibie invites his wives to drink Okonkwo's palm-wine in their due order, the process is saved from looking like pure sociological information by the attention to detail and the concentration on the words and gestures of the participants, so that a sense of drama is generated and the whole seems to be part of life as it is lived among the Ibos. Even the songs have a relevance they do not have in the works of less accomplished novelists. For instance, the song the women sing after Okonkwo's success in the wrestling match is relevant to that contest and to Okonkwo's character, and the contest is itself presented as part of the lives and feelings of the people. Then the childhood song Ikemefuna remembers as he is on his way to his death heightens the poignancy of the events all the more.

In fact, in *Things Fall Apart* the presentation of the sociological goes hand in hand with the development of Okonkwo's character. In the very deepest sense of the words *Things Fall Apart* is a novel which shows the interrelationship of environment and character, one of Achebe's main aims being to demonstrate the way in which Okonkwo's character has been moulded by his environment. At every single point in the narrative Achebe tries to relate every belief, every activity of his society to some aspect of Okonkwo's character. If the novel is structured in such a way that at the end of the first part we have a powerful picture of the society that will collapse in the second part, it is also structured so that at the end of the first part the growth of Okonkwo's character has been perfectly traced and his personality established as one of the leading men in his clan; and it is that personality which will be largely in decline in the second. In this novel there is a masterly manipulation of plot and structure and a judicious deployment of the sociological which ensures that the development of Okonkwo's character and the presentation of his society are coextensive and contemporaneous.

This brilliant presentation of character by means of a skilful use of the sociological and deft manipulation of structure can be easily demonstrated. For instance, in Chapter 2 the sociological detail revolving around the meeting called to prepare the village for war is prevented from appearing purely sociological by the details and the sense of drama, and leads to Okonkwo whose importance in his community is emphasized since he is the emissary selected to carry Umuofia's message to Mbaino; in Chapter 3 the sociological – Unoka's consultation of the oracle of Agbala – is enlivened by the sense of drama and shown to be related to a man's personal activities and fortunes. In short, it is presented as part of the flux of life in this society, and it further illuminates Okonkwo's character, for it reveals why he is mortally afraid of failure and explains his resolute determination to become wealthy by the strength of his right arm. The sociological information about the week of peace in Chapter 4 is almost toned down by the drama of Okonkwo's senseless beating of his wife during the sacred week and is thus related to Okonkwo's restless energy, his latent capacity for violence and his fiery temper. The impact of the sociological in Chapter 5 – the New Yam Festival – is softened by anecdotes and jokes and serves as a preparation for the introduction of another sinister consequence of Okonkwo's violent nature: the attempted murder of another wife for no apparent reason.

Chapter 7 which describes the killing of Ikemefuna is an extremely important chapter. It starts with an incident which might seem on the surface to be merely another attempt to describe this society and its environment – the descent of the locusts and the people's joy as they collect them for food. But Achebe, by his superb artistry, connects even this to Okonkwo's character and fortunes, for it is while Okonkwo, Ikemefuna and Nwoye are happily crunching dried locusts that the blow falls – the news arrives that Ikemefuna is to be killed; and the actual killing itself displays Okonkwo's character in action, for it once more reveals his fear of being thought weak. The incident of the *ogbanje* in Chapter 9, like the blood-chilling Priestess of Agbala episode in Chapter 11, is again closely linked with the fortunes of Okonkwo's family and reveals the only spot of tenderness we are ever to see in this otherwise dehumanized man – tenderness towards his daughter and his second wife. The sociological in both is toned down partly by the insight the reader has into Ekwefi's feelings in her concern for her child, and partly by the remarkable serenity of Achebe's prose. In Chapter 10, the trial scene, where the prestigious masked spirits emerge to dispense justice, the portrayal of the society's customs is characteristically linked with the establishment of Okonkwo's character, for he is one of the nine masked *egwugwus*. Chapter 13 is infused with sociological material – the traditional announcement of Ezeudu's death and the description of the funeral ceremonies – but this is in fact one of the most dramatic chapters; it is actually here that the catastrophe occurs. In the midst of the ritual Okonkwo's gun accidentally goes off killing his kinsman – the dead man's 16-year-old son. It is the end of Part One – the end of the powerful presentation of traditional Umuofia society – but we have also seen the gradual establishment of Okonkwo's character and personality, both processes going hand in hand and reaching their climaxes at the same time. At every single point Achebe has been anxious to relate every episode, every sociological matter, to Okonkwo's character, which he has shown steadily growing in well-defined stages. Each act of violence is carefully prepared for, is shown to be more sinister than the former and closely related to Okonkwo's fear of weakness and his desire for action and success. The killing of Ezeudu's son is the climax of this double process; it is the climax to which everything – the presentation of the sociological and the portrayal of the hero's character and fortunes – has been leading in this remarkably well-constructed novel. It is to no less than this complex paralleling of sociological presentation, character portrayal and structural manipulation that *Things Fall Apart* owes that compactness, resonance and solidity which Achebe has not fully succeeded in capturing in his later novels.

One of Achebe's greatest claims to fame is the remarkable competence with which he handles the English language. Of all anglophone writers he has probably given most serious thought to the problems facing the African writer who is forced to write in English and he is probably the most successful in solving them. He may not attain the urbanity, verbal dexterity (which sometimes degenerates into linguistic gymnastics) and self-conscious mastery of Soyinka, but he displays much greater versatility and range. It was he who said:

> For an African, writing in English is not without its set-backs. He often finds himself describing situations or modes of thought which have no direct equivalent in the English way of life. Caught in that situation he can do one of two things. He can try and contain what he wants to say within the limits of conventional English or he can try to push back those limits to accommodate his ideas. The first method produced competent, uninspired and rather flat work. The second method can produce something new and valuable to the English language as well as to the material he is trying to put over ... I submit that those who can do the work of extending the frontiers of English so as to accommodate African thought-patterns must do it through their mastery of English and not out of innocence.[7]

Achebe's practice perfectly matches his theory. His own normal narrative style which is standard and idiomatic, radiates, to borrow his own phrase, a dazzling beauty. In *Things Fall Apart* in particular it possesses a grandeur and rhythmic beauty which distinguishes it from the prose of the other works. Achebe can also capture the nuances of speech of native Englishmen – the tone of voice of a Winterbottom, a Clarke, an Allen or a Mr Brown; flippant or naive, complacent or serious and earnest. He can make distinctions between the speech of the educated, sophisticated African and the not-so-educated. Edna's letter in *A Man of the People* reveals the linguistic uncertainties of a girl at her level of education, as do the speeches of Chief Nanga and Mr Nwege; nor must we forget the pomposity of the secretary of the Umuofia Progressive Union. And these are quite different from the speech of Obi and Christopher Okoli, the 'been-tos' in *No Longer at Ease*.

Achebe's rural characters who would normally use Ibo in actual situations are made to speak in English, but the English they use has been considerably modified in order to reflect an African rural community and the thought and speech patterns of native Ibo speakers. Without seriously distorting the nature of the English, Achebe deliberately introduces the rhythms, speech patterns, idioms and other verbal nuances of Ibo. The English is correct grammatically, indeed, the sentence patterns of English are largely retained, but the language is modified rhythmically and idiomatically. The effect of this is that while everyone who knows English will be able to understand the work and find few signs of awkwardness, the reader also has a sense, not just of black men using English, but of black Africans speaking and living in a genuinely black African rural situation. During the marriage ceremonies of Obierika's daughter this is how the conversation goes.

> 'Life to all of us . . . and let there be friendship between your family and ours.'
> The crowd answered: 'Ee-e-e!'
> 'We are giving you our daughter today. She will be a good wife to you. She will bear you nine sons like the mother of our town.'
> 'Ee-e-e!'
> The oldest man in the camp of the visitors replied: 'It will be good for you and it will be good for us.' (p.106)

The reader forms the impression that this is how the sentiments would be expressed in the native Ibo. Achebe often introduces direct translations from Ibo into English sentences, as when one of Ezeulu's wives, on seeing the new moon, says 'May your face meeting mine bring good fortune' or when Ezeulu, determined to see what is locked up in Oduche's box, says: 'Whether it be bad medicine or a good one, I shall see it today.' At times he tries to impart an African flavour even into his own narration.

He beat his *ogene* GOME GOME GOME . . . and immediately

children's voices took up the news on all sides. *Onwa atuo!* . . . *onwa atuo* . . . *onwa atuo!* . . . he put the stick back into the iron gong and leaned it on the wall. (*Arrow of God*, p. 2)[8]

Achebe is also aware of the use of pidgin in the urban environment, especially by Nigerians belonging to different tribes. This is reflected in the urban novels, *A Man of the People* and *No Longer at Ease*, where there is an extensive use of pidgin, whereas its use in *Things Fall Apart* and *Arrow of God* is more sparing.

One of the hallmarks of Achebe's language is the effective use of similes and images drawn from an exclusively African environment. Here is a striking example from *Things Fall Apart*.

Okonkwo did not taste any food for two days after the death of Ikemefuna. He drank palm-wine from morning till night, and his eyes were red and fierce like the eyes of a rat when it was caught by the tail and dashed against the floor. (p. 57)

This is Achebe's own narration which characteristically is in standard, grammatically correct, idiomatic English; but the powerful image of the rat caught and dashed against the floor, a common occurrence in most African rural environments, imparts an African flavour and appropriately conveys Okonkwo's internal torment. Almost all the similes in the novels set in traditional society are drawn from rural African experience.

The most significant aspect of Achebe's language, however, is his extensive use of proverbs in order to give a genuinely African flavour to the characters' speech. The proverbs are particularly noticeable in the speech of the older people, appropriately so, since the ability to use them expertly came with experience and was regarded as a sign of wisdom. Indeed, the proverbs represented the sum of traditional wisdom. Again and again in *Things Fall Apart* and *Arrow of God* we see their use by the older men to expose the inexperience and ignorance of the younger. The proverb is invaluable in debate, and the speaker's skill can be assessed by the facility with which he conjures up proverb after proverb in rapid succession to reinforce his points or to expose the hollowness of his opponents' arguments. In almost every case Achebe ensures that the proverb is appropriate. For instance, Okonkwo, talking to Obierika about his fears for his son, wishes to suggest that if Nwoye had been destined to become a brave young man the signs would already have been apparent. He says: 'A chick that will grow into a cock can be spotted the very day it hatches.' And in an attempt to absolve himself from responsibility for taking part in Ikemefuna's murder, he says: 'The earth cannot punish me for obeying her messenger. A child's fingers are not scalded by a piece of hot yam its mother puts into its palm.'

Arrow of God is, of course, a veritable storehouse of proverbs. Some continually recur like motifs and are essential to the novel's meaning: 'When an adult is in the house the she-goat is not left to suffer the pains of parturition on its tether' (p. 21). 'The man who brings ant-infested faggots into his hut should not grumble when lizards begin to pay him a visit' (p. 163). The first suggests that men in important positions should act sanely and responsibly when others around them are losing their heads. The second implies that a man should be prepared to take the consequences of his actions. Both proverbs have a relevance to the behaviour of both Nwaka and Ezeulu. *Arrow of God* is a novel of conflict in which the great issues which are at stake are significantly voiced out in great set debates, particularly those between Ezeulu and Nwaka. During the first debate both men speak with great skill, their speeches being riddled with proverbs as they attempt to demolish each other's arguments. After the disastrous affair at Okperi in which Akukalia is killed, Ezeulu, now speaking with the conviction of a man who has been proved right by events, makes a brilliant speech. The first part has no less than three telling proverbs, the most effective being 'he put a piece of live coal into a child's palm and asked him to carry it with care'. He then follows this up with the story of the wrestler who became so conceited that he challenged the spirits to a wrestling contest with disastrous consequences to himself, and he ends with two more appropriate proverbs. These are some of the devices Achebe employs to give a distinctively African flavour to his language. Since most of the proverbs incorporate vivid images as well, they also contribute to the colour of his style.

Achebe's style varies considerably from novel to novel. After the grandeur and solemnity of *Things Fall Apart* the prose style of *No Longer at Ease* is likely to strike the reader as terse and urbane: its wit possesses a sharp cutting edge. This is accounted for, not just by the move from a rural to an urban environment, but by the change of emphasis from the presentation of traditional society to social comment and social satire. *Arrow of God* returns to the presentation of the traditional, but since the society is now racked by dissension and conflict, the style, while remaining impressively elevated, appropriately lacks the rhythmic beauty of the best parts of *Things Fall Apart*.

In *A Man of the People* Achebe returns to the urbanity of *No Longer at Ease*, but this time the style is deliberately vulgarized in order to give the impression of the speaking voice and to expose Odili's inadequacies. It will be useful to consider *No Longer at Ease* and *A Man of the People* in this section on language, for it is largely by a skilful manipulation of language that Achebe makes his most telling points in these two novels.

No Longer at Ease deals with the plight of the new generation of Nigerians who, having been exposed to education in the western world and therefore largely cut off from their roots in traditional society, discover, on their return, that the demands of tradition are still strong, and are hopelessly caught in the clash between the old and the new. With corruption, bribery and immorality rampant in a modern urban Nigeria which has lost the values and sanctions of the old traditional order, the young 'been-tos' are severely tempted to abandon their idealism and conform to the new ethos. This situation holds good not just for Nigeria, but for all modern African states.

Obi Okonkwo, the grandson of the hero of *Things Fall Apart*, finds himself in precisely such a situation. On his return to Nigeria he discovers that the present corrupt reality is markedly at variance with the idealistic picture he had harboured during his student days; disillusionment quickly sets in. Although he initially scorns the mores of the new elite into whose ranks his new job automatically propels him, he soon discovers that it is not so easy to be different. He also has to acquire the artefacts which are the symbols of success of modern Nigeria, but at the same time traditional society continues to make demands and exert pressures on him which he is not able to resist. In the end, battered by financial and emotional problems, the once cocksure, idealistic Obi is forced to compromise his principles. He abandons his girlfriend, descends into bribery and is imprisoned. It is now a commonplace of African literary criticism that Obi Okonkwo is a pale reflection of his grandfather, lacking the former's courage, resilience and determination. Where Okonkwo is an impressive tragic character, his grandson falls far short of tragic stature. He lacks independence of spirit and the solid core which would have enabled him to resist temptation when his financial troubles began; he lacks initiative, merely allowing events to overtake him; and he is destroyed because he betrays his principles with astonishing ease, not, as in the case of his grandfather, because he champions them to the last.

Social comment and social satire therefore form the meat of the novel and Achebe's language rises to the occasion. *No Longer at Ease* is characterized by scintillating comedy, sophisticated wit and subtlety of irony. When Obi rather self-importantly denounces Mr Mark, who has come to bribe him, and turns him out of his office, this is how Achebe presents his elation.

> After his encounter with Mr Mark he did feel like a tiger. He had won his first battle hands-down. Everyone said it was impossible to win. They said a man expects you to accept 'kola' from him for services rendered, and until you do, his mind is never at rest ... A man to whom you do a favour will not understand if you say nothing, make no noise, just walk away. You may cause more trouble by refusing a bribe than by accepting it. Had not a Minister of State said, albeit in an unguarded, alcoholic moment, that the trouble was not in receiving bribes, but in failing to do the thing for which the bribe was given? And if you refuse, how do you know that a 'brother' or a 'friend' is not receiving on your behalf, having told everyone that he is your agent. Stuff and nonsense! It was easy to keep one's hands clean. It required no more than the ability to say: 'I'm sorry, Mr So-and-So, but I cannot continue this discussion. Good morning.' (pp. 87–8)[9]

The tone is marvellously controlled and the irony at Obi's expense unmistakable. That detail about 'stuff and nonsense' and the ease with which one could keep one's hands clean is superb. Achebe is implying that Obi is being too self-righteous and naive here. There is even a suggestion that he is merely acting the part of the upright man. We are prepared to believe that this kind of attitude will not really stand the shock of severe temptation. Earlier in the novel Achebe's irony at Obi's expense as the latter propounds his theory on the causes of bribery and corruption is equally masterly.

> 'The Civil Service is corrupt because of these so-called experienced men at the top', said Obi.
> 'You don't believe in experience? You think that a chap straight from university should be made a permanent secretary?'
> 'I didn't say *straight* from the university, but even that would be better than filling our top posts with old men who have no intellectual foundations to support their experience.'
> 'What about the Land Officer jailed last year? *He* is straight from the university.'
> 'He is an exception,' said Obi. 'But take one of these old men. He probably left school thirty years ago in Standard Six. He has worked steadily to the top through bribery – an ordeal by bribery. To him the bribe is natural. He gave it and he expects it. Our people say that

if you pay homage to the man on top, others will pay homage to you
when it is your turn to be on top. Well, that is what the old men say.'
(pp. 20–1)

The supreme irony is that Obi is going to be like the Land Officer and
he will take bribes like the old men he is denouncing. It is this ironic
exposure of Obi's arrogance, naivety and ignorance of the real
situation that prepares us for his capitulation to corruption later.

The satire at the expense of Mr Green, Obi's colonial boss, who feels
that Africans, particularly the educated ones, are useless and
irresponsible, and who views the present trend towards Africanization
and independence with dismay, is no less devastating, and it is done
largely by means of irony.

'You will do well to remember,' said Mr Green, 'that at this time
every year you will be called upon to cough up forty pounds for your
insurance.' It was like the voice of Joel the son of Pethuel. 'It is, of
course, none of my business really. But in a country where even the
educated have not reached the level of thinking about tomorrow, one
has a clear duty.' He made the word 'educated' taste like vomit. Obi
thanked him for his advice. (p. 95)

So too is this one at the expense of a minister of state, the Honourable
Sam Okoli.

'Do you have just one Assistant Secretary in your Ministry?' asked
Obi. 'Yes, at present. I hope to get another one in April. I used to
have a Nigerian as my A.S., but he was an idiot. His head was
swollen like a soldier ant because he went to Ibadan University.
Now I have a white man who went to Oxford and he says 'Sir' to me.
Our people have a long way to go.' (p. 69)

Many passages could be cited to show the range and effectiveness of
Achebe's scintillating comedy and sophisticated wit in this novel, but a
few will suffice here.

Mr Ikedi had come to Umuofia from a township, and was able to tell
the gathering how wedding feasts had been steadily declining in the
towns since the invention of invitation cards. Many of his hearers
whistled in unbelief when he told them that a man could not go to his
neighbour's wedding unless he was given one of these papers on
which they wrote R.S.V.P. – Rice and Stew Very Plenty – which was
invariably an over-statement. (p.10)

Mr Stephen Udom is quite often a target for satire.

A tiny boat came alongside with a young man at the oars and two boys in it . . . They wanted to dive for money. Immediately the coins were flying into the sea from the high deck. The boys picked up every one of them. Stephen Udom threw a penny. They did not move; they did not dive for pennies, they said. Everyone laughed. (p. 28)

The catastrophe that Achebe so brilliantly highlights in *No Longer at Ease* is part of the painful process of adjustment that society as a whole must make as it looks for new values to replace those so regrettably destroyed with the old society. Achebe's last novel *A Man of the People* is preoccupied with the same issue. In it Achebe raises the curtain on his society to reveal the full horrors of the *status quo* in most African countries – ministerial incompetence and corruption, social inequalities, rigged elections, thuggery, poverty, mass indifference and cynicism and intellectual bankruptcy. The hero is Odili, a young idealistic graduate teacher through whose eyes the corruption of the governing classes is largely viewed. It is through his eyes also that we see the most powerfully realized character – Chief Nanga, the man of the people. The latter is a man of tremendous charm and attractiveness and an expert at public relations; and he uses these with consummate skill as political weapons. But he also uses his political position to enrich himself at his country's expense and to indulge in immorality.

At the start of the novel Odili the hero is outraged by this glaring corruption, and contemptuous of the people's indifference which, in fact, helps to perpetuate the unhealthy *status quo*. But Achebe soon reveals the ease with which Odili, in spite of his high-minded idealism, becomes corrupt himself. As in *No Longer at Ease*, Achebe is emphasizing the inability of the new generation of educated Africans to resist temptation and abide by their principles. It is only when the clever minister outwits Odili and makes love to his girlfriend that Odili remembers his initial idealism and enters politics determined to wreak revenge by contesting Chief Nanga's seat. The outcome of the political fray is that a coup is staged and the minister rounded up. But Odili now shows what he would have done himself had he become a minister, when he uses his party's money as the bride-price for his proposed wife.

Achebe's artistic problem in this novel is the simultaneous exposure of both Odili and Nanga, for Odili is not much better than the minister. The problem is complicated by the fact that Odili tells the story in the first person. At times he is aware of his own shortcomings and teases himself good-humouredly about them, but he is also often unaware of them. Achebe must thus make the reader aware of the gap in point of view between himself and Odili; he must at the same time expose Nanga's corruption by using Odili as a mouthpiece. In order to achieve all this he makes brilliant use of irony directed at times against Nanga, at times against Odili and at times against both, and he manipulates the language so that he not only gives the impression of the talking voice, but contrives also to expose the essential hollowness of Odili's mind.

Apart from this ironic manipulation, the range of styles achieved by Achebe in *A Man of the People* is most impressive. There is normal, standard idiomatic English such as that used by John or Agnes the 'been-to'; there is the modified garbled variety used by Odili, not so much to impart an African flavour as to 'place' him ironically; there is pidgin which reflects the realistic linguistic situation among urban Nigerians; there is the modified version of English used by Odili's father and Edna's father which is Achebe's way of rendering the Ibo they would have actually used; there is the formal variety used in Chief Nanga's speeches; and there is the part-educated variety used in Edna's letter. It is in this, his last novel that Achebe unquestionably demonstrates his control over the language, his ability to bend it to accommodate his insights.

Since he is one of the earliest of modern African novelists, Achebe's relationship to the oral tradition ought to be examined. This is important if we are to establish that the African novel is an outgrowth of the oral tradition. We saw in the last chapter that Ekwensi, Achebe's immediate predecessor, owes little to that tradition. Though in a sense Achebe builds on what Ekwensi has started, in another sense he diverges from Ekwensi in concerning himself with the African past in two of his novels. It is therefore possible that Achebe's work could have derived independently from the oral tradition. Careful consideration of Achebe's first novel *Things Fall Apart* can only lead to the conclusion that there is little in its structure which recalls the oral tale. Certain aspects of its form suggest the influence of the oral tale, but this does not in itself prove conclusively that there is a direct line of development from the oral tale to the novel, or that *Things Fall Apart* derives from the oral tale. The point surely is that Achebe incorporates elements of the oral tradition into his work. This is the nature of the relationship between his work and the oral tradition. *Things Fall Apart* and *Arrow of God* contain several folk tales, like the stories of the quarrel between Earth and Sky (which is also found in Tutuola), of Mother Kite who sent her daughter to bring food, of the conceited wrestler who challenged the spirits to a wrestling contest, and of the jealous mother who sent her son back to the land of the spirits for his flute. Achebe has to tell these stories since in these two novels he is presenting a picture of traditional Ibo society and these tales were part of that society. Of course, Achebe also ensures that some of the tales have a thematic relevance. It is significant that in the two novels with an urban setting the influence of the oral tradition is not so obvious, whereas *Arrow of God* shows this influence most markedly. The history of Umuaro is told as it would be told by an old man (p. 17). Achebe also makes extensive use of proverbs which belong basically to the oral tradition, but he does so because proverbs are essential if he is to solve the language problem he is faced with, and because no picture of traditional society would be complete without them – it is part of the way in which the people converse. These elements from the oral tradition are used by Achebe, then, to achieve certain effects. They do not by any means suggest that the work has grown out of the oral tale. Perhaps the point needs to be restated that, much as we would like to, it would be difficult to trace a direct line of development from the oral tradition to the African novel. The techniques of oral lore are quite different from the techniques of the novel as practised by men like Ekwensi and Achebe. The novel form was initially western, the only literary genre that Africa has borrowed from the West. The earliest practitioners were men who had been exposed in their youth to the western novel. Achebe was himself stimulated into writing *Things Fall Apart* by the picture of Nigerian life presented in Joyce Cary's *Mister Johnson*, and it will be much easier to see the influence of Dickens, Rider Haggard, Conrad and Hardy on the novels of Ekwensi and Achebe than that of the oral tale.

Arrow of God

Arrow of God is Achebe's bulkiest and most ambitious novel so far, his main intention being no less than the presentation of as comprehensive a picture of traditional society as is possible in a novel; and the resultant work is accordingly of grand epic proportions. In addition to the breadth in which the work was conceived, Achebe also intended to give as powerful a portrait of the leading character as that he had given of Okonkwo in *Things Fall Apart*. The aims are grandiose indeed, possibly too grandiose, and in the present writer's opinion the effect has certainly not been as successful as in the first novel. The picture of traditional life is remarkably full, the characterization of Ezeulu is splendid, certain individual things are done well, but the novel as a whole is much less satisfying than the first one. To say that this novel is better than *Things Fall Apart* is to fail to see the brilliant interrelationship in the latter between characterization, structure, skilful presentation of the sociological and thematic exploration that I have attempted to demonstrate above. I shall later try to show why the achievement of *Arrow of God*, impressive though it is, does not rise to the excellence of the former.

Arrow of God is essentially a novel of conflict. There is the conflict between traditional authority and the white administration; there is the conflict between traditional religion and Christianity; there is the conflict between Umuaro and Okperi; there are minor jealousies and rivalries among Ezeulu's wives and sons; there is even a conflict within Ezeulu himself between his own inclinations and the will of his god, essentially a debate about the limitations of his power; but above all there is the conflict within traditional society in the struggle for power between Ezeulu the Chief Priest of Ulu and his opponents, and the rivalry between his deity and theirs. This, the major conflict, is either reflected in the other conflicts or is intensified by them. Ezeulu himself is at the centre of all the various conflicts.

The conflict with the administration is caused by the tactlessness of the latter in its attempt to impose a system of indirect rule on the people of Iboland. After the catastrophic confrontation of *Things Fall Apart* the power of the white man has become generally recognized if not universally accepted, and he, for his part, is trying to consolidate his influence by Lugard's policy of indirect rule. At the start of the novel we see that the broadminded, progressive Ezeulu has been able to establish such a cordial relationship with the reasonable, courageous and dedicated Winterbottom that the latter has been able to persuade the former to send his son Oduche to the Christian school. Both men have a mutual respect, but Winterbottom is only a cog in the British administrative machine which includes some extremely tactless, brutal and discourteous officials. When Winterbottom decides to appoint Ezeulu warrant chief of Okperi he sincerely thinks he is doing the right thing, since Ezeulu is the only man in the clan who has impressed him with his honesty, integrity and courage, and since he thinks that Ezeulu (whose name he mistakenly interprets to mean 'King of Ulu') already has the authority of a priest-king over his

people. But the incompetence of Winterbottom's subordinates and the
vulgarity and sycophancy of the native court messengers ensure not
only that Winterbottom's efforts are frustrated, but that conflict is
precipitated and intensified. Moreover, Winterbottom demonstrates
that in spite of his virtues he is still one of the breed of British
administrators and will not have his authority affronted by a mere
black man. He orders Ezeulu to be arrested and imprisoned, thus
initiating the chain of events which lead eventually to disaster. Most
Africans will applaud Ezeulu's behaviour in the confrontation with the
white man and his instruments. When he tells them that he does not
normally leave his hut and that the white man must come to him if he
wants to see him, or when he says 'Tell the white man that Ezeulu will
not be anybody's chief, except Ulu', he is affirming the dignity,
authenticity and autonomy of traditional life, and asserting, not only
that he will not be appointed to do the dirty work of a man who has
humiliated him, but that the only superior authority he recognizes is
that of his god Ulu. His great dignity and pride are drawn partly from
consciousness of his own worth and of the strength of his institutions,
and he makes what amounts to a stirring declaration of independence.
Predictably, the white administration does not emerge with credit
from the novel. Its administrative bungling, inconsistency and
ignorance are patent, and its effect, though not as direct as in *Things
Fall Apart*, is profound. It indirectly undermines Ezeulu's position,
intensifies the divisions within the clan and thus helps to hasten the
decline of the old order.

The religious conflict cuts deeper than that with the white
administration. Unlike the situation in *Things Fall Apart*, the new
religion has been in existence long enough to be fairly firmly
entrenched; its schools are prospering and it now numbers black men
among its catechists and other officials. But it is no less aggressive and
disruptive than it was in the earlier novel. This aggressiveness
contrasts markedly with the tolerance of the traditionalists, particularly
Ezeulu. However, the most aggressive and 'zealous' among the
Christians are not the white missionaries themselves, but the black
converts, men like the rigid fundamentalist Goodcountry who
encourages new adherents, not only to reject their own traditions, but
actively to destroy the shrines and other religious symbols of their
people. The similarity between Goodcountry and Joshua in Ngugi's
The River Between is striking. Utterly contemptuous of other Africans,
even the converted, he could also not be more contemptuous of the

beliefs and customs of the African people had he been a European. Basically, Goodcountry's failure, like Joshua's, is a failure of intelligence and sensitivity, an inability to respond to and interpret the genuine word of God; it is also a failure caused by lack of confidence in his own ability and authority, especially when faced with an astute layman like Moses Unachukwu. Like Joshua, he fails to see that the best way of ensuring the success of the church is to blend the best in traditional life with the best in Christianity, that a people with a thousand years of history cannot be made to forget their customs overnight. (This, in effect, is what happens in the end when the people are persuaded to offer their new yams to Christ.) Indeed, it is clear that even the leading converts find it difficult to reject their customs completely. This is a very common phenomenon in Christian Africa even today. Usually, it is regarded by orthodox theologians as the result of confusion or ignorance in the African mind, a mind that adheres both to Christ and to sacrifices. The more realistic, however, would surely see it as representing a people's determination not to be entirely alienated from their traditions and their roots.

The religious conflict in the novel comes to a head over the matter of the sacred python, the symbol of the god Idemili, which Goodcountry urges the people to kill. However, most of the Christians adhere firmly to their tradition, refusing to kill the python. Moses Unachukwu, in particular, is most vocal in his opposition. Achebe does not idealize Unachukwu, for he exposes his conceit and jealousy and suggests that his opposition to Goodcountry in this struggle for authority within the church is partly caused by the latter's contempt for him. In a sense he uses the debate over the question of the python as an opportunity to challenge Goodcountry openly. Nevertheless, Achebe recognizes his deep knowledge of the Bible and of the myths and legends of his people, and his determination to adhere to the basics of his tradition.

Ezeulu's son Oduche is caught up in this struggle for authority between Unachukwu and Goodcountry and is led unwittingly to humiliate Unachukwu in public. In reply, Unachukwu challenges him to live up to his reputation as a champion of Christianity and kill the sacred python. But though Oduche decides to kill the python, he is still sufficiently steeped in his people's lore to be terrified of the consequences. He therefore decides to imprison the python in the box Moses has made for him: 'The python would die for lack of air, and he would be responsible for its death without being guilty of killing it.' For the people of Umuaro such an abomination is heightened by its having been committed by the son of their religious leader who is supposed to be their champion against the encroachments of the new religion. The symbolism of the scene is pointed and the people's reaction suggests that it is not lost on them. The python, representing their religion, is locked in a box associated with the Christian religion since that kind of box is usually built by Moses only for Christians. It is gasping and struggling for air, struggling for life itself. The new religion has attempted to stifle the life, not only out of the old religion, but out of traditional society itself, to annihilate both completely.

Inevitably the religious conflict intensifies the conflict within traditional society itself. This conflict is the meat of the book, the others being merely reflections of it. The conflict is really a struggle for authority within the clan, starting as a struggle for supremacy between the chief priests of two deities, Ezidemili the chief priest of Idemili, and Ezeulu the chief priest of Ulu, the main clan deity. Since Ezidemili dares not challenge Ezeulu openly, he hides behind Nwaka the most powerful and wealthiest layman, one of the three surviving members who have taken all the titles of the clan. Nwaka comes from the largest village, Umunneora, and therefore naturally thinks that the leadership of the clan ought to be his. Hence a struggle for spiritual authority becomes a political battle, with Nwaka and Ezeulu as the protagonists.

Nwaka shrewdly uses the debate on the Okperi land case to present himself as the champion of the people's cause and to make a bid for the leadership. For him the matter is purely political. For Ezeulu, however, the political cannot be dissociated from the spiritual since a wrong decision would mean that the people of Umuaro would be disregarding a god who had once saved them from annihilation. Nwaka sees Ezeulu as attempting to impose his will on the people of Umuaro. He would draw a very rigid borderline between the functions of priest and those of a political leader, but he suspects that Ezeulu wants to combine both. Nwaka's manoeuvres result in a declaration of war which rages until Winterbottom intervenes and stops it, confiscating all the people's weapons. During the ensuing investigations Ezeulu gives his famous testimony which leads to his friendship with Winterbottom, and on the basis of which the disputed land is given to Okperi.

The dissension within traditional society thus leads to entrenchment in power for the white man. Ezeulu is seen in this situation as an ally of the conqueror, while he sees the people themselves as being responsible for the white man's intervention and the extension of his power by their obstinacy. 'The man who brings ant-infested faggots into his hut,' he insists, 'should not grumble when lizards begin to pay him a visit.' The conflict simmers underneath the surface until it breaks into full-blown fury once more when Winterbottom summons Ezeulu to appear before him at Okperi and the latter convenes a meeting of the elders to discuss the matter. Nwaka, who has all but disappeared during the interval, comes back to the attack with a brilliant speech in which he makes full use of all his powers as a skilled debater.

'But there is one thing which is not clear to me in this summons. Perhaps it is clear to others; if so someone should explain it to me. Ezeulu has told us that the white ruler has asked him to go to Okperi. Now it is not clear to me whether it is wrong for a man to ask his friend to visit him. When we have a feast do we not send for our friends in other clans to come and share it with us? And do they not also ask us to their own celebrations? The white man is Ezeulu's friend and has sent for him. What is so strange about that? He did not send for the priest of Idemili; he did not send for the priest of Eru; he did not send for the priest of Udo nor did he ask the priest of Ogwugwu to come and see him. He asked Ezeulu. Why? Because they are friends. Or does Ezeulu think that their friendship should stop short of entering each other's houses? Does he want the white man to be his friend only by word of mouth? Did not our elders tell us that as soon as we shake hands with a leper he will want an embrace? It seems to me that Ezeulu has shaken hands with a man of white body.' (p. 177)

The speech is done with remarkable skill. We notice the rhetorical questions, the use of repetition, balance and parallelism and the final telling ambiguity of Ezeulu having shaken hands with a man of 'white body'. As the speech as a whole draws to an end Nwaka uses Ezeulu's own favourite proverb suggesting that the latter ought to take the consequences of his own actions and not ask the clan to help him. And he uses three more proverbs in rapid succession to reinforce the point: 'You tied the knot, you should also know how to undo it. You passed the shit that is smelling; you should carry it away. Fortunately the evil charm brought in at the end of a pole is not too difficult to take outside again.' (p. 178)

Nwaka is holding Ezeulu responsible for the consequences of his friendship with the white man whose aim, however pleasant he himself might seem personally, is conquest and overlordship. Nwaka might be motivated by personal and political jealousy, but he is nevertheless

voicing the disquiet of a number of well-intentioned members of the
clan who have been resentful of Ezeulu's friendship with the white
man because they see the latter as an alien force posing a threat to their
independence and the purity of their traditions. They see Ezeulu as
thus undermining the basis of traditional society. The more unfriendly
among them even feel that by taking the stand he did on the land case
Ezeulu was betraying the cause of the people. Most of them, however,
are reasonably well disposed towards him. Recognizing the fool-
hardiness of resisting the white man at this stage, they suggest that
Ezeulu should go to Okperi accompanied by six elders of the clan. Our
recognition of this fact, that the majority of the people are more
reasonable than Nwaka and do not share his bitterness, will throw
Ezeulu's later decision to punish the whole clan into perspective. For
the moment he is more enraged by the more reasonable men than by
the hostile Nwaka, and his angry rejection of their commendable
proposal does not auger well for relations within the clan.

  The point is that Ezeulu fails to put himself into the position of the
people and to see that, from their point of view, some of his actions
might well look like betrayal. Even if Ezeulu does not think of himself
as king, he is certainly behaving like one, like a man who does not care
for the opinions of the people and who thinks that it is beneath his
dignity to explain all the motives of his actions to them. Akuebue, one
of his closest friends, talks to him seriously about the political and
religious implications of his flirtation with the white man. He is just as
astute an intellectual as Ezeulu and can see quite clearly the logic
behind the latter's actions. But he is also aware of the feelings of the
clan and the need to be responsive to those feelings. He significantly
warns Ezeulu that no man, however great, can win judgement against a
clan. He shrewdly tries to persuade Ezeulu to make a distinction
between the repulsive jealousy of Nwaka and Idemili, which is obvious
to all, and the genuine disquiet of the clan who feel that Ezeulu
betrayed them in the land case and is betraying them again by sending
his son to join in the desecration of the land. Akuebue accepts that the
clan as a whole is partly responsible for the intervention of the white
man, but he does not accept that they should therefore allow him to go
on befouling the land. He further asserts that whereas Ezeulu could
count on the support of some of his people even when he spoke out
against war with Okperi, he would have to stand absolutely alone in the
matter of his flirtation with the white man.

  Whether Ezeulu must be held responsible for the disaster which overtakes him and his society later, or whether the blame must be laid at the door of the white man, or of an instransigent society, or of Ezeulu's god, is one of the most fascinating issues raised in the novel. To discuss it fully we must take a close look at Ezeulu's character. In his own analysis Achebe describes Ezeulu thus.

> He is an intellectual. He thinks about why things happen – of course as a priest; you see, his office requires this – so he goes into things, to the roots of things, and he's ready to accept change, intellectually. He sees the value of change and therefore his reaction to Europe is different, completely different, from Okonkwo's. He is ready to come to terms with the new – up to a point – except where his dignity is involved. This he could not accept; he is very proud. So you see it's really the other side of the coin, and the tragedy is that they come to the same end, the same sort of sticky end. So there's really no escape whether you accept change or whether you don't...[10]

Achebe suggests that our sympathy ought to be with Ezeulu who is destroyed in spite of his willingness to accept change. It remains to be seen whether the portrait we have in the book bears out this analysis.

That Ezeulu is an intellectual is incontestable. The clarity of mind with which he analyses the issues facing his society, particularly the forces making for change, is impressive. This determines his attitude. If it is true that the white man has come to rule the country it will be wise to have a member of one's own family with him. Ezeulu's decision to send his son to join the white man is therefore partly dictated by prudence. He is being broad-minded, but also realistic, since he realizes that such a course of action is the only means of ensuring security for the future and guaranteeing the continued existence of his people. The proverbs he uses illustrate the point.

> 'The world is changing,' he had told him. 'I do not like it. But I am like the bird Eneke-nti-oba. When his friends asked him why he was always on the wing he replied: "Men of today have learnt to shoot without missing and so I have learnt to fly without perching." I want one of my sons to join these people and be my eye there. If there is nothing in it you will come back. But if there is something there you will bring home my share. The world is like a Mask dancing. If you want to see it well you do not stand in one place. My spirit tells me that those who do not befriend the white man today will be saying *had we known* tomorrow.' (p. 55)

Ezeulu also asserts that it is necessary to make tremendous sacrifices to meet the challenges of modern times.

'A disease that has never been seen before cannot be cured with everyday herbs. When we want to make a charm we look for the animal whose blood can match its power; if a chicken cannot do it we look for a goat or a ram; if that is not sufficient we send for a bull. But sometimes even a bull does not suffice, then we must look for a human. Do you think it is the sound of the death-cry gurgling through blood that we want to hear? No, my friend, we do it because we have reached the very end of things and we know that neither a cock not a goat nor even a bull will do. And our fathers have told us that it may even happen to an unfortunate generation that they are pushed beyond the end of things, and their back is broken and hung over a fire. When this happens they may sacrifice their own blood.'
(p. 165)

As the perceptive Akuebue recognizes, it is Ezeulu's son Oduche who is to be the sacrificial victim in order to ensure the survival of the clan. This pushing of things to their logical conclusion is, in a sense, impressive. The cerebral quality comes out even in Ezeulu's speeches. Where Nwaka's warm rhetorical flourishes appeal to the heart, Ezeulu's dry logical disquisitions are obviously meant for people who think. Impressive also are his honesty and integrity, his concern for truth and justice, his consistency in adhering to the will of the gods, his tremendous dignity and consciousness of his own traditional values, his almost regal presence, his power and his influence.

In spite of these admirable qualities, however, there is something rather chilling and unattractive about Ezeulu's personality, whatever Achebe's intentions may have been. The doubts about his personality begin to appear in the very first chapter of the book which significantly presents the ambivalence surrounding him. Ezeulu is assiduously pursuing his task of looking for the new moon, but he is also considering the limits of his power.

Whenever Ezeulu considered the immensity of his power over the year and the crops and, therefore, over the people he wondered if it was real. It was true he named the day for the feast of the Pumpkin Leaves and for the New Yam Feast; but he did not choose the day. He was merely a watchman. His power was no more than the power of a child over a goat that was said to be his. As long as the goat was alive it was his; he would find it food and take care of it. But the day it was slaughtered he would know who the real owner was. No! the Chief Priest of Ulu was more than that. If he should refuse to name the day there would be no festival – no planting and no reaping. But could he refuse? No Chief Priest had ever refused. So it could not be done. He would not dare.

Ezeulu was stung to anger by this as though his enemy had spoken it.

'Take away that word *dare*,' he replied to his enemy. 'Yes I say take it away. No man in all Umuaro can stand up and say that I dare not. The woman who will bear the man who will say it has not yet been born.' (pp. 3–4)

This is an extremely important passage, not just because it looks forward to the end when Ezeulu *does* refuse to name the day, but also because it shows him revelling in the power he possesses over the people and, if possible, wishing to extend that power. It shows also that long before the disastrous events towards the end Ezeulu has given serious thought to doing what none of his ancestors had dared – refusing to name the date of the New Yam Feast. In a very real sense he is here arrogating to himself powers that only his god could possess, arrogantly refusing to accept that he is merely an agent of the god – 'an arrow in the bow of the gods'. The realization that his opponents also know the limitations of his power maddens Ezeulu so much that he challenges them to state these limitations in public. But 'dare' also suggests that if need be Ezeulu *will* forget about the limitations and begin to exercise powers that only a god could. 'What kind of power was it if everybody knew that it would never be used?' Does this not suggest that Ezeulu is being strongly tempted to use this power in order to demonstrate to his enemies in particular that he has it? Does not the problem of the novel arise because Ezeulu begins to behave, not just like a king, but like a god? The point is raised again in the novel by no less a person than Ezeulu's son, Edogo, who accuses him of arranging things in such a way that the choice of a chief priest to succeed him would fall on his favourite son, Nwafo, whereas the choice had previously always rested with the god. Everyone knows that as Priest of Ulu Ezeulu is half man and half spirit, but he is strictly speaking only half spirit. Is he not trying to behave as though he were a spirit? Does not the trouble arise partly because Ezeulu cannot keep Ezeulu the spirit separate from Ezeulu the man?

Ezeulu's great pride and haughtiness make him extremely contemptuous of his opponents. He cannot brook a contrary opinion even when it comes from such a well-meaning and intelligent friend as Akuebue. Surely, only someone with a supreme contempt for the intelligence of others would expect them to think and behave like himself, as Ezeulu does. He never speaks to anyone as an equal. So conscious is he of his superiority that he scorns to unburden himself to anyone, even his closest friends, and the subsequent inscrutability is one of the causes of the misunderstanding between him and his clan. For an intellectual, Ezeulu is amazingly subject to wild outbursts of anger, directed not just at his enemies, but quite often against his sympathizers and members of his family.

Indeed, Ezeulu's relations with his sons reveal even more unpleasant aspects of his character. He is utterly contemptuous of the eldest, Edogo, whom he treats with great tactlessness, haughtiness and a complete absence of love. He is fond of Obika, but when the latter is whipped by Wright Ezeulu concludes, even before he hears Obika's account, that the young man must be guilty, and he allows himself to be blinded by anger from doing him justice. It is obvious that although he sends Oduche to be his eye among the white men he is scornful of his intelligence. His discrimination among his children leads to constant jealousies and rivalries. Edogo, during his detailed analysis of the relations between his father and his children, sees the main source of the problem as being Ezeulu's refusal to admit that his children are grown up: 'He must go on treating his grown children like little boys, and if they ever said no there was a big quarrel. This was why the older his children grew the more he seemed to dislike them' (p. 113). And the perceptive Akuebue, realizing that Ezeulu is too hard on his sons, has to talk to him quite seriously on the need for tact and patience. One must also mention that Ezeulu is not even on good terms with his brother; he refers to the relationship between the latter and Edogo as one between 'a derelict mortar and rotten palm-nuts'.

In sum, then, Ezeulu appears to be spiteful, ill-tempered, contemptuous, overbearing, tactless, proud, haughty, uncompromising and even vindictive. His apparent flexibility on the question of change contrasts oddly with his rigidity on other matters. All these qualities seem to be reflected in his somewhat dry, cynical speech. But we must also seriously consider the possibility of psychological instability in Ezeulu. The theme of madness recurs in the novel like a motif, thus reinforcing the impression that the madness which is immediately precipitated at the end by Obika's death is merely the culmination of a process which has been going on all through in progressive stages. If this is true, then Achebe has indeed given us a very interesting psychological study. We first encounter the madness theme during that important discussion between Akuebue and Ezeulu when the latter's reply to one of the former's questions is certainly not what he expected: 'It made him afraid and uneasy like one who encounters a madman laughing on a solitary path' (p. 162). Akuebue surely suspects that Ezeulu's increasingly irrational line of conduct on this and on other occasions is caused by incipient madness. Ezeulu's mother, we remember, was mad; Obika is quite often referred to, albeit jokingly, as mad; Moses Unachukwu refers to the madness in their family. Is there a suggestion of hereditary madness in the family? When Nwaka hears that Ezeulu has refused the offer of the chieftaincy, this is what he says: 'The man is as proud as a lunatic ... This proves what I have always told people, that he inherited his mother's madness' (p. 217). And another elder, Ogbuefi Ofoka, makes much the same comment later (p. 266). Achebe must have strewn so many references to madness in the text because he wanted us to believe that this is at least partly the cause of Ezeulu's otherwise inexplicable course of conduct.

The various strands that have so far gone into the novel's making are all firmly interwoven together in the climactic incident of Ezeulu's arrest and his subsequent refusal to name the New Yam Feast. It is obvious that Ezeulu has become obsessed with the opposition he feels he is receiving from his own people, failing to realize that in the bigger drama of change brought about by the new civilization, it is the white man who is the real antagonist, and that the intensification of the internal struggle on which he is bent would merely do the white man's job for him. During his imprisonment his hatred of his clan intensifies.

> His quarrel with the white man was insignificant beside the matter he must settle with his own people. For years he had been warning Umuaro not to allow a few jealous men to lead them into the bush. But they had stopped both ears with fingers. They had gone on taking one dangerous step after another and now they had gone too far. They had taken away too much for the owner not to notice. Now the fight must take place, for until a man wrestles with one of those who make a path across his homestead the others will not stop. Ezeulu's muscles tingled for the fight. Let the white man detain him not for one day but one year so that his deity not seeing him in his place would ask Umuaro questions. (p. 198)

Ezeulu is surely wrong in thinking that it is his clansmen who have led him into his present predicament. In what sense can it be said that Umuaro has gone too far? It was Ezeulu's own honesty and former friendship with the white man, and not the people, which caused the white man to send for him; and it was his own initial justifiable refusal to heed the summons, not the people's hostility, that caused the white

man to order his arrest. Nor did the people, like Nwaka, ask Ezeulu to
go alone and face the consequences; he himself had voluntarily decided
on that even before the great meeting. In what sense then could his
clansmen be said to be culpable? Ezeulu is spoiling for a quite
unnecessary fight with his people and relishing the thought of it, and it
is quite obvious that this view that the real struggle lies between him
and his people and not with the white man is wrong-headed and
irrational. It is the psychological instability which is beginning to
come to the surface. For a man who used to demonstrate so much
clarity of thought, Ezeulu's present inability to make important
discriminations is amazing. On his release from prison he sees the fact
that he is drenched by pouring rain as part of the suffering his people
are forcing him to endure and he is at once bitter and elated. He
deliberately begins to invent grievances where they do not exist; on his
arrival at Umuaro he refuses to speak to anyone and goes on planning
deadly revenge – exactly how deadly is indicated by the metaphor that
suggests itself to him.

> He must first suffer to the limit because the man to fear in action is
> the one who first submits to suffer to the limit. That was the terror of
> the puff-adder; it would suffer every provocation, it would even let
> its enemy step on its trunk; it must wait and unlock its seven fangs
> one after the other. Then it would be death to its tormentor. (p. 227)

Yet all the indications are that during his imprisonment the people
of Umuaro were well disposed towards him. His reputation has grown
with his resistance of the white man and on his return it is obvious that
Umuaro is not one hostile entity. The plain-speaking Ofoka confirms
what the reader knows, that the elders of Umuaro had not taken sides
with Nwaka against him and had agreed with his own suggestion that
he should go and confront Winterbottom because they genuinely
thought he was the best man to wrestle with the former. Ofoka's speech
is so persuasive that Ezeulu momentarily thinks of reconciliation, but
it soon becomes obvious that deep down he is still spoiling for a fight
because he wants to demonstrate the extent of his power.

> Behind his thinking was of course the knowledge that the fight
> would not begin until the time of harvest, after three moons more.
> So there was plenty of time. Perhaps it was this knowledge that there
> was no hurry which gave him confidence to play with alternatives –
> to dissolve his resolution and at the right time form it again. (p. 240)

The passage is important because it demonstrates both that the desire for reconciliation is not genuine and that even before hearing the voice of Ulu Ezeulu had already decided that he would use harvest time, the New Yam Feast, to hit Umuaro. And this is what he does after a long period 'of silent preparation' (p. 253).

The decision not to announce the date of the New Yam Feast on the flimsy pretext that two of the yams have remained uneaten while Ezeulu has been in prison is irresponsible in the extreme. It seems even more cruel in a man who has been so aware of his responsibilities. For Ezeulu's decision means that the crops on which the people's livelihood depends will remain rotting in the ground. It also means death, famine, disgrace, bankruptcy and general disaster for the whole clan; and Ezeulu is fully aware of the consequences. He is also intelligent enough to realize that the eating of the yams, though now a ritualistic procedure, is primarily a device to help the chief priest determine the right time for the New Yam Feast. The important thing surely, is the right date of the feast and of harvest, not the ritualistic eating of the yams. A distinguished collection of elders calls on Ezeulu to urge him to eat the yams and name the date of the feast in order to save his people from disaster. They even volunteer to take the consequences, if there are any, on themselves, and they use arguments about the necessity of changing with the times because they hope that these will appeal to Ezeulu who has always spoken in the past about the advisability of welcoming change. But on this occasion he is uncompromising. At the end of the meeting the elders continue talking about change and about customs which have been dropped in the past because they have begun to work hardship on the people; but Ezeulu, who once used so many proverbs to illustrate the necessity for change, is significantly silent.

When Ezeulu decides as a compromise to consult his god again, he announces that his consultation had produced 'no result'. Achebe deliberately chooses his words with care. He has said, not that the god advised Ezeulu to reject the pleas of his people, but that there has been no result. He is being deliberately ambiguous to leave open the possibility that Ezeulu's action does not have the endorsement of his god. During the consultation an incident occurs which ought to have warned Ezeulu that his action will lead to the collapse of traditional life and the destruction of his god; he hears the Christians' bell ringing as he starts his divination, and it sounds nearer here than it did in his compound. The significance is that the new religion is extending its influence even up to the shrine of Ulu and is about to usurp its privileges, but Ezeulu does not grasp the full meaning of the symbolism. The consequence of Ezeulu's conduct is that: 'In his extremity many an Umuaro man had sent his son with a yam or two to offer to the new religion and bring back the promised immunity'; immunity, that is, from the wrath of Ulu. 'Thereafter any yam that was harvested in the man's fields was harvested in the name of the son' (p. 287). Paradoxically, Ezeulu, who should have been the champion of his people's faith, becomes the agent of its destruction. But he is spared the knowledge of the final outcome, for when his pampered son Obika dies, he goes mad and lives his last days 'in the haughty splendour of a demented high priest'.

What, then, is the nature of the tragedy in *Arrow of God*? Ezeulu suggests several times that he is merely carrying out the will of his god. His friend Akuebue seems convinced that, proud and stubborn though he is, Ezeulu would not falsify the decision of Ulu, and to his in-law's remark that a priest like Ezeulu leads a god to ruin, Akuebue retorts that a god like Ulu leads a priest to ruin. Ezeulu's reaction on the death of Obika suggests that he feels Ulu has deserted him, indeed, struck him down, when he has merely divined his will and carried it out. To come to the conclusion, however, that the tragedy has been caused by a harsh irrational deity striking down a man who, far from offending him, has served him loyally, is to fail to respond to the full complexity of the text. Long before the will of Ulu could have been divined on the matter, Ezeulu had decided that as long as he was in Okperi he would never look for the new moon. By the time he hears Ulu's voice his plan of revenge, a purely personal one caused largely by private pique, is already formed. How then do we explain Ulu's message to him?

> 'Ta! Nwanu!' barked Ulu in his ear, as a spirit would in the ear of an impertinent human child. 'Who told you that this was your own fight?'
> Ezeulu trembled and said nothing.
> 'I say who told you that this was your own fight which you could arrange to suit you? You want to save your friends who brought you palm wine he-he-he-he-he!' laughed the deity the way spirits do – a dry, skeletal laugh.
> 'Beware you do not come between me and my victim or you may receive blows not meant for you! . . .' (pp. 240–1)

Ezeulu interprets this as a command from his god forbidding him from effecting a reconciliation and ordering him to step out of the fight so that the god himself can pursue the struggle with Idemili and bring him to the ground. I would like to submit, however, that it may not be Ulu's voice that Ezeulu hears; this is probably the figment of a fever-crazed imagination which has been subject to hallucinations, nightmares, dreams and visions during his long captivity. Even if it is the voice of Ulu, it is far from suggesting that Ezeulu's past conduct has been justifiable. Indeed, the voice takes him to task for daring to choose the lines of battle and arrange the basis of a fight which does not really concern him. If there is a struggle, it is between Ulu and his rival Idemili, not between Ezeulu and his people, and Ezeulu ought to leave it with Ulu to settle scores with Idemili, not decide to wreak personal revenge on his people. Ezeulu is behaving irresponsibly, like 'an impertinent human child'; he is trying to do what the god ought to do, behaving like the god when he is in fact no more than an arrow in the bow of the god. After Ulu's speech there is a passage which on careful consideration seems brilliantly ironical: we are told that the thought that he was merely an arrow in the bow of the god 'intoxicated Ezeulu like palm-wine'. The word 'intoxicated' is significant. Ezeulu is elated because he sees himself as being absolved from direct responsibility for the disasters he is about to plague his people with. Everything can now be laid at the door of the god: Oduche had imprisoned the python because he is also being used as an agent of the god; the white man's religion, the white man himself, are all agents of the god used to give Ezeulu appropriate weapons to fight the enemy. Indeed, Ulu had decided to use the white man as an ally from the beginning, and that explains Ezeulu's own decision to send his son to the white man's school. Since he is half spirit, those decisions have really been taken by the spirit side of him interpreting Ulu's will, while he in his ignorance thought that he was taking the decisions himself. It is the preposterousness of Ezeulu's line of reasoning that suggests the irony; this is the reasoning of a madman. Achebe's later suggestion that Ezeulu feels great compassion for the sufferings of Umuaro and that he is not deliberately punishing the clan is surely a major inconsistency. Achebe has already shown Ezeulu taking his fateful decision, and looking forward to the people's discomfiture with relish. The inconsistency is a major fault, suggesting not that Achebe is being deliberately ambiguous as that he has not thought out his themes clearly.

We are meant to understand that Obika's death is a punishment for Ezeulu. But far from being a merciless act from an ungrateful god, it is

Ezeulu's reward for stepping outside the bounds of his authority. The people's interpretation of the outcome of events is surely the right one:

> So in the end only Umuaro and its leaders saw the final outcome. To them the issue was simple. Their god had taken sides with them against his headstrong and ambitious priest and thus upheld the wisdom of their ancestors – that no man however great was greater than his people; that no man ever won judgement against his clan. (p. 287)

Achebe's tragic vision in this novel is thus no different from that in *Things Fall Apart*. He sees the hero embattled against tremendous forces, external as well as internal; these forces contribute to his downfall, but his own faults of character play a very important contributory role as well.

Arrow of God is a treasure-house of anthropological detail, but it lacks the compactness of *Things Fall Apart*. The sociological descriptions lack the excitement and even relevance of those in the earlier novel and are by no means as compelling. Where Achebe takes infinite pains in the earlier novel, as we have seen, to ensure that each sociological passage is relevant to some aspect of Okonkwo's character, few of those in *Arrow of God* do much to enhance characterization. They fill in the picture of traditional society, but the reader seldom gets the impression that they convey the pulse of life among the people. The first of these, Ezeulu's announcement of the new moon and his subsequent prayers to Ulu, seems almost laughable (p. 7). The Festival of the Pumpkin Leaves, one of the novel's centrepieces, merely has to be set beside the wrestling contest, the trial scene or the meeting scene in *Things Fall Apart* for the reader to see how much has been lost in dramatic impact and excitement. Its effect is marred right from the start by Ezeulu's lengthy and lustreless narrative about the history of his priesthood, and it calls attention to itself as purely sociological lore, as do the sacrifice of coverture and marriage ceremonies. The relevance of the songs, like Obiageli's lullaby, is questionable, and since the sociological lore lacks dramatic impact and relevance its frequent occurrence tends to hold up the movement of the story.

The novel starts well; an impressive first chapter introduces the major themes and characters. This process is continued through the next four or so chapters where the background to the various conflicts is filled in through a series of flashbacks, and the external forces who will help deepen the conflict are introduced. But then the pace becomes much too leisurely, and up to the entry of the court messenger the story seems rather rambling, largely because the events so far have not been as powerfully tied to Ezeulu's character as those in *Things Fall Apart* were to Okonkwo's. Furthermore, there seems to be a tendency towards repetitiveness in this novel. The similes and proverbs which Achebe uses as motifs, and therefore feels bound to repeat several times, jar on the ear after the second or third mention. Then the goodwill ritual of toe-painting, kola-nut splitting and chalk-drawing is repeated so often that it becomes tedious. Certain bits of information, like Oduche's having been sent to learn the secrets of the white man's magic, are given again and again as though Achebe has forgotten that he has already mentioned them. These details suggest that Achebe did not have as firm a grip over the materials of this novel as he had on *Things Fall Apart*, understandably so since the materials are bulkier and more intractable. But the novel is more than redeemed by the thoroughgoing analysis of conflict and change and the powerful presentation of Ezeulu's character.

NOTES

1 Chinua Achebe, 'The novelist as teacher', in *African Writers on African Writing*, ed. G. D. Killam (Heinemann, London, 1973), pp. 1–4.
2 ibid., pp. 3–4.
3 Chinua Achebe, 'The role of the writer in a new nation', in *African Writers on African Writing*, op. cit., p. 8.
4 ibid., p. 8.
5 ibid., p. 9.
6 Chinua Achebe, *Things Fall Apart* (Heinemann, London, 1970). All page references are to this edition.
7 'The role of the writer in a new nation', op. cit., p. 12.
8 Chinua Achebe, *Arrow of God* (Heinemann, London, 1971), All page references are to this edition.
9 Chinua Achebe, *No Longer at Ease* (Heinemann, London, 1962). All further page references are to this edition.
10 Chinua Achebe, in *African Writers Talking*, ed. Dennis Duerden and Cosmo Pieterse (Heinemann, London, 1972), pp. 16–17.

4. T. M. Aluko

▼▼

Although T. M. Aluko started writing before Cyprian Ekwensi, his first novel was not published until 1959, four years after Ekwensi's *People of the City*. He comes after Ekwensi, therefore, in the history of the African novel. It seems right to place him chronologically after Chinua Achebe as well, not only because Achebe's first novel was published earlier, but also because there are signs of a conscious, though largely unsuccessful, striving after Achebe's best effects.

Aluko has probably had as difficult a time with the critics as his countryman Cyprian Ekwensi. Most commentators deplore his insensitivity to the language problem facing African writers, his lack of thoroughness in the exploration of the issues he raises and his apparent inability to develop.[1] It is the purpose of this chapter to demonstrate that although the strictures are partly true, Aluko is not as insensitive to the language problem as has been commonly supposed, and he does show signs of development. At his best his work is possibly no more accomplished than Achebe's *No Longer at Ease*, but he seems to be a writer who is responsive to criticism and who has made a conscious attempt to improve. Consequently, there is a vast difference between his first novel, *One Man, One Matchet*, and his third, *Kinsman and Foreman*, which in the opinion of the present writer is undoubtedly his best.

It has been suggested that Aluko attempted to do for Yorubaland what Achebe so successfully did for Iboland, that is, to present an image of the past 'at that point where the civilization of the western world came into contact with it'.[2] This view must be substantially modified, for unlike Achebe's *Things Fall Apart* and *Arrow of God*, none of Aluko's five novels to date is set in the distant past, at that point in time when the western world first impinged on traditional Yoruba civilization. Aluko is therefore not concerned with the traumatic consequences of the impact of western imperialism on African life. Rather, he confines himself to the more modern period immediately preceding and succeeding independence, the period of adjustment and redefinition of values. Like Achebe, his main theme is the clash between the old and the new, but although the old is traditional society, the new is not the white man's civilization, but the efforts and ideologies of educated Africans who are striving to bring a measure of order into their society and take it into the modern world. The opponents of traditionalism here are not the white administrators, who are largely spectators in the drama, but the mainly western-educated African professionals – the doctors, engineers, lawyers and civil servants. Aluko's world is more the world of *No Longer at Ease* and *A Man of the People* than of *Things Fall Apart* and *Arrow of God*. He himself studied engineering in England in the late 1940s, eventually becoming one of the first professionally qualified Nigerians to hold a top post in the civil service. He therefore belongs to the same class and generation as most of his heroes – Titus Oti, Udo Akpan and Morrison. His work may be generally seen as an expression of disgust at all those forces which stand in the way of progress and modernization and impede the efforts of *the new, highly qualified, African professional* middle class. In order to plot Aluko's development this chapter will examine his use of language and his progressive treatment of the themes of traditionalism, the conflict between traditionalism and modernism, and the role of the alienated intellectual. *Chief, the Honourable Minister*, which is not really relevant to the purpose, does not feature in the discussion.

It is true that the early Aluko is largely insensitive to the language problem. His first novel, *One Man, One Matchet*, does not show much indication that he was aware of the linguistic modifications Achebe had made in *Things Fall Apart*. This is not to say Aluko's command of the English language is defective, his prose style being flawless and polished. The problem is that there is nothing distinctively African about it. Aluko does not seem to have realized that this style, which is perfectly acceptable for the educated author's own narration of events, will not be suitable to record the conversation of native Yoruba speakers or to penetrate their thoughts and present events from their point of view. If the following excerpt from *One Man, One Wife* has been often quoted by critics it is because it is the one which most tellingly illustrates the point.

'Nikun was the most beautiful damsel on earth. Her hair was of black silk; her teeth were as white as snow and looked like pearls. She was tall and graceful, and had ten baskets of clothes and trinkets.

'She was so beautiful that princes and wealthy men came from all countries to woo her. But she refused them all, and she always found fault with them.'[3]

There is little in the passage to indicate that the story is being told by a simple villager, still less by a little girl. Even more distressing is the intrusion of very English clichés, which though appropriate in the context of English story telling, are certainly not at home here. It does not seem to have occurred to Aluko that 'damsel', 'teeth . . . as white as snow' and looking 'like pearls' are not compatible with a traditional African environment. Furthermore, even if Aluko's normal reporting style has some of the virtues of English prose it also occasionally manifests some of its weaknesses. There is an over-fondness for clichés and stock phrases, and occasionally for the mannerisms of the English middle class as when Royanson's mother in *One Man, One Wife* says of one of the female characters: 'Joke is a darling . . . she descends from a long line of warriors. You could not hope for a better wife, dear.'

However, even in this shaky first novel, Aluko's linguistic strengths begin to appear. Obviously at his best when manipulating the language for satirical purposes, his gift for mimicry comes magnificently to his aid. One of the main butts of his satire is the half-educated man who, while pretending to be more learned than he really is, is yet one of the agents of corruption and thus one of the impediments to progress. In at least two of the novels he is brilliantly satirized by means of language. Here is part of a petition written by Royanson, a self-appointed letter-writer on behalf of an old farmer:

'I beg your honour most respectfully and respectively to carefully and patiently peruse these few lines of a tale of woe and persecution and prosecution perpetrated and perpetuated on your honour's most unworthy servant, to wit my humble self, Longe of Idoka village . . .

'The land that is the subject of this abominable act of man's inhumanity to man is the land of your honour's respectful, respective, unworthy servant, to wit my humble and unworthy servant. In the unwritten but verbal, verbose and oral history of Adasaland, the large piece of land was very generously and royally given by his Highness Oba Atakumasa, to his humble subject and loyal general for valiantly and courageously driving out the soldiers of the King of Ibadan away from Adasa Territory.' (p. 85)

Royanson is truly the cousin of Lakunle in Soyinka's *The Lion and the*

Jewel. However, although this technique is undoubtedly effective, Aluko does not seem to have realized that unless it is used with moderation it will bore the reader. By the time we come to Royanson's letter to the press reporting the riots at Isolo we surely feel that Aluko has overdone it. Most surprisingly, Aluko makes Royanson adopt this habit of duplication even in conversation with characters who, though literate in Yoruba, do not speak English. We are therefore incredibly meant to believe that Royanson uses this style not only for English conversation but even while speaking Yoruba with fellow native speakers of the language.

Linguistically, *One Man, One Matchet* is an advance on *One Man, One Wife*. It seems possible that Aluko has responded favourably to criticism and is now aware of the language problem and of Achebe's attempts at a solution. The speeches of some of the traditional elders suggest that he is making a conscious attempt to modify the English language in order to reflect the rhythms and speech patterns of Yoruba. Here is an excerpt from a speech by the Oba of Ipaja.

> 'Elders of Ipaja, I bid you welcome, and I bid you a pleasant evening,' the old chief said, waving the horse-tail. 'It was I who sent for you. I send for you all to come to my compound. There is cause for my asking you to meet me here, in my compound ...
>
> 'Many moons ago, we used to hold our meetings here, in my compound ... Here, the first Apaja, the founder of Ipaja, met his chiefs. And here my fathers met their chiefs and discussed state affairs. Now they all sleep there.' He indicated the furthermost end of the compound where his predecessors on the stool of Ipaja were buried.
>
> 'They all sleep there. But they hear everything we say. And they breathe peace.'[4]

No one would suggest that 'many moons ago', 'there is cause for my asking you', 'they all sleep there' and 'they breathe peace' are idiomatic English. Furthermore the deliberate simplicity is appropriate for the speech of a rural people. Later, there are even suggestions of direct translations from the Yoruba into English as when one of the elders says 'Fellow chiefs of Ipaja, this is word ...'.

Aluko's characteristic adroitness in exposing the linguistic incompetence of the half-educated man is also apparent here. The target in this novel is Benjamin, who sets himself up as the champion of the people's cause. But Aluko is aware that Benja-Benja (as he is called) is a much more formidable opponent than Royanson and therefore devises a less ludicrous style for him. Both Royanson and Benja-Benja

strive after bombast through a misconception that this is the best
English, but whereas Royanson resorts to duplication, thus using
hyperboles which are quite wrong in the context, Benja-Benja's
language is correct though pretentious. Here is an excerpt from an
article he writes for a local paper.

> We have been sounding the warning for some time now that the
> Imperialist Dragon now driven to the corner by the St George of
> Nationalism is seeking refuge in the Church. Trusting to the age-
> long tradition of the sanctity of the Church, the Monster is now
> seeking asylum in a place to which we would be the last to advocate
> forcible entry and attack – on one condition. That condition is this:
> the host must give a guarantee on behalf of his infamous guest that
> the latter would not hide behind the sacredness of the Church in
> order to continue to commit his atrocities against the people of this
> country. (pp. 91–2)

Particularly effective is Aluko's rendering of Benja-Benja's often-
quoted imitation of Lincoln's famous Gettysburg address which ends
thus:

> 'That we here resolve that this honoured dead shall not have
> died in vain, that this ancient city of Ipaja under God shall have a
> new birth of freedom, and that government of the people of Ipaja by
> the people of Ipaja for the people of Ipaja shall not perish from the
> earth.' (p. 114)

In this and subsequent novels Aluko demonstrates great skill in
composing speeches and sermons. He is also adept at conveying the
right tone of the white officials' conversation or communications. In
the following extract Gregory's characteristic flippancy and cynicism
certainly come through.

> 'Yes, Benjamin Benjamin; a most ingenious name, has rather a
> romantic flavour to it too. Well, I see he's already disputing credit
> for the discovery with Rodent. A weird exhibition – an English
> scientist and a half-baked African rabble-rouser disputing over a
> thing like that. One made his discovery through scientific methods,
> the other from African juju, alias Black science. I suppose they are
> both right. After all they have a common ancestor in Noah; he
> deserves the credit for the discovery.' (p. 155)

In spite of the generally favourable impression of Aluko's linguistic
ability in this novel, however, there are still a few lapses; the most
glaring of these is when Aluko, in a moment of flagging imagination,

makes one of his characters use almost exactly the same words in a similar situation as another character in *One Man, One Wife*; Chief Momo's son's letter in *One Man, One Matchet* begins and ends exactly as Joshua's son's letter in the former novel. Here is part of Chief Momo's son's.

> It is with much gladness in my heart that I write this letter to you. And I have the hope that it will get to you in happiness and in good health, as I am here. We all here are in good health, and there is nothing wrong at all. For this and other blessings, praise with me the Lord Jehovah.
> All my friends here greet you. All their wives greet you, as do all their children. They also send greetings to your wives, and all their children. My landlord greets you, together with his wives and his children. And they ask you to greet all at home, without exception. (p. 67)

Joshua's son's letter to his father begins like this.

> With much gladness of heart and love I write to you this letter. I hope that it will get to you in peace and in good health as I am here. I am very well, and there is nothing to complain about. For this and other blessings Jehovah's name be praised.

And it ends like this.

> My friends greet you. My master greets you. Together with his wives and children. My landlord greets you, and his wives. And his children. All in this village greet you. (*One Man, One Wife*, pp. 28–9)

It might be a plausible excuse that this was the conventional way in which the semi-educated greeted their relations in their letters and that Aluko is subjecting the whole process to ridicule. There can be no excuse, however, for the identity of the two old men's response to the letters, a similarity to which Lindfors has already called attention.[5] Aluko, then, seems to be making steady progress, but he yet has to match the sensitivity of Achebe.

Aluko's third novel, *Kinsman and Foreman*, shows an even further advance in the manipulation of language. Apart from the attempt to convey the feel of the native Yoruba even while using English words, there is a healthy infusion of proverbs to reinforce the African flavour.[6] Characteristically, a string of them occurs in old Pa Joel Tobatele's speech during Titus Oti's welcome ceremony: 'If a child boasts that he has as many clothes as his father, can he equally boast of having as many rags as his father? ... Does the thread not follow the path made by the needle? ... It is in spite of the snake that the bush rat nurtures its young to maturity.'[7] For the first time also we notice the use of pidgin in Aluko's work. Unlike the two earlier novels which were predominantly rural, *Kinsman and Foreman* moves quite frequently to the world of urban Ibadan, and the use of pidgin by some of the characters is therefore quite appropriate. Here is an example from a PWD worker: 'Layi, Layi ... Engineer want you. You go play with woman under mango tree you lef your work. Na today dem de sack you' (p. 15).

It is in this novel too that Aluko displays his remarkable flair for accurately capturing the affected style of the 'been-tos'. Titus's friend Chris says unashamedly on one occasion: 'Titus, the fellow's a great chap. You here at Ibala don't know his worth. Case of a prophet having no honour in his own town. He's a pillar of the Club – All Races, I mean' (p. 81). And in his letter to his fiancée Titus himself is not above saying: 'Won't that be heavenly, darling?' The occasional lapses are however still noticeable, particularly in the conversations between the educated Chris and Titus and the illiterate Auntie Bimpe who in spite of her handicap seems miraculously able to use English as impeccably as the other two – clichés and all. Nevertheless, one's general impression is that Aluko has learnt some lessons from Achebe and is making a determined attempt to modify the language to suit his purposes, and it seems to the present writer at least that this modification is sustained with occasional lapses even in *Chief, the Honourable Minister* and *His Worshipful Majesty*. He nowhere achieves the range and variety of Achebe and can therefore not boast of the latter's success; but it would be unfair to accuse him of insensitivity to the language problem.

Aluko's main theme is the clash between traditional attitudes and modern ideas – roughly the same field explored by Achebe. In the treatment of the subject, however, they seem to be poles apart. Achebe, while accepting the inevitability of change, still pays tribute to the dignity and majesty of traditional life. His vision of the process of change is thus always tragic, giving a powerful impression at the end of his novels of a great society destroyed. On the other hand, Aluko sees change as both inevitable and necessary precisely because there is little that is dignified or majestic about traditional life. He seems to endow his educated heroes with an unquestionable duty to drag African traditional society into the twentieth century even if they have to take it kicking and screaming. With the exception of Morrison in *His Worshipful Majesty* his 'been-to' heroes always emerge victorious in their struggle to modernize their societies. His vision therefore of the process is, in spite of the numerous deaths in his novels, essentially comic. Where Achebe's traditional elders like Akuebue, Ezeulu and Ezeudu are dignified, intelligent repositories of traditional wisdom, Aluko's obas and chiefs seem for the most part to be a bunch of doddering idiots in their second childhood.

This is a typical scene in which the council of elders in *One Man, One Wife* decide a case.

'This man claims to have spent thirty seven pounds. This woman admits only six pounds, five shillings. The gap between thirty seven pounds and six pounds is not narrow. What do you say to it, Chief Osi?' 'Thirty seven pounds, he says,' reflected Chief Osi, nodding his head. 'Six pounds, five shillings, she says. It is serious. What does Chief Ekerin think of it?' 'It is difficult, very difficult,' the Ekerin gave the final contribution. 'Very difficult indeed. But no case is ever too difficult for this court, Osi?' 'We will settle it, we must settle it. Thirty seven pounds! On one woman only. How can one believe it?' Chief Eketa looked round the court. (pp. 43–4)

This, in a way, is splendid comedy; but one cannot help wondering whether it is a fair picture of traditional society. On the other hand it is the educated elite to whom Aluko gives complete sympathy. It is to the Udo Akpans, Titus Otis and Morrisons that he is prepared to entrust the salvation of Africa, blinding himself to the fact that their language and life-style are almost completely western. (Udo Akpan is appropriately called by the people 'the black white man' while Morrison has a white wife.) Achebe faces the problem of the 'been-to' objectively, intelligently and thoroughly in *No Longer at Ease*; he is aware that the 'been-to' is caught in a dilemma since he is expected to be both modern and traditional but cannot really be either because he sees the defects of one society and has been completely alienated from the other. On the other hand, Aluko is hardly aware of the presence of any spiritual agony in his heroes, caused by alienation from traditional society and an inability to accept all the mores of the West. His heroes never try to operate within traditional society; Morrison's and Udo Akpan's families never appear and are hardly ever mentioned, while Titus Oti always treats his own relations with impatience. Unlike Obi these men are never exposed to temptation and they never fall; they remain upright, efficient and completely professional. Where Achebe intelligently refuses to offer any solutions to the problem of the 'been-to', Aluko offers one: the 'been-to' emerges triumphant, his enemies disposed of, and the process of modernization continues.

The white men, who are instrumental in Achebe's work, are only peripheral in Aluko's; as agents of change they are secondary to the educated elite. Where Achebe can hardly conceal a tone of contempt for his white administrators, Aluko's attitude to them is almost respectful. The ones he disapproves of are those like Gregory and Macbaine who secretly despise the highly educated African elite.

And yet it is the purpose of this chapter to demonstrate that even this view has to be substantially modified. Even in his treatment of traditional society Aluko's work shows signs of development; his latest novel, *His Worhsipful Majesty*, suggests that he has responded to the adverse criticisms of the earlier novels, for here there is a great measure of respect for traditional society. The awe-inspiring Alaiye of Aiye is a most majestic figure who is given real tragic stature, and the various religious rituals are described with sympathy and some reverence. Traditional society here is at least an equal match for the forces of modernism and the novel appropriately ends on a tragic note. There is also development in his treatment of the 'been-to'; at least the later novels show a much greater awareness of the problem and a more intelligent and mature treatment of the entire theme. It is these points that will now be demonstrated.

Aluko's first novel *One Man, One Wife* is easily his least satisfactory. One of the most muddled novels to have come out of Africa, it compounds all his obvious weaknesses – poor characterization, lack of psychological penetration and consistency, lack of thematic clarity, little sensitivity to language, little sense of plot and structure and an overabundance of melodrama. The theme of tradition versus modernism is particularized here in the clash between traditional religion and Christianity, but it is given very sketchy treatment and is certainly not sustained throughout the novel. Aluko soon moves over to other concerns. The title of the novel and the early scenes might suggest that the problem is caused by the conflict between the church's stipulation of monogamy and traditional society's encouragement of polygamy. But the 'one man, one wife' theme is slow to emerge and, even when it does, occupies a very small proportion of the book. In giving such a sketchy treatment to an important theme Aluko misses the opportunity so skilfully seized by a novelist like Mongo Beti of portraying the torment of individuals torn between their newly acquired Christian faith and their traditional inclination towards polygamy.

There is, however, a slightly more detailed presentation of the general theme of the conflict of Christianity and traditional attitudes. The hallmark of Aluko's treatment of the subject is his glib sarcasm at the expense of both sides. Christianity represents the new here, but since it is not the ideology of his educated 'been-tos' it can be laughed at with impunity. So, of course, can traditional religion. At times Aluko laughs at both of them on the same page. The champion of Christianity, and therefore of the new, is the Rev. David, but since he is less highly educated than the 'been-to' heroes and represents an ideology that Aluko does not apparently endorse, he is invested with very little of the glamour that attaches to the other modern champions.

His characterization is strangely inconsistent. At the start of the novel he appears almost as sympathetic and understanding as Pastor Olaiya in *One Man, One Matchet*, but he soon becomes a stern, unbending disciplinarian and his language degenerates into the language of fanaticism. Halfway through the novel, however, the theme of tradition versus change is lost sight of as the focus now turns on the activities of Royanson, the half-educated agitator who is clearly an early version of Benja-Benja and who is the object of Aluko's scorn.

In presenting Royanson like this Aluko seems unaware that he might lay himself open to the charge of inconsistency and psychological implausibility, and he seems, in any case, to be quite insensitive to some of the points in Royanson's favour. For the latter emerges as a champion of the oppressed, as an ambitious and resourceful young man in spite of the fact that he has laboured for years as a teacher on a meagre salary and has been judged very harshly by a hypocritical religion; indeed his semi-literacy is the effect of an unfair and inadequate educational system.

The novel's only claim to attention is its superb comedy. The satire, which is wide-ranging, can at times be biting, sneering or contemptuous, and there are occasions when, as in the portrait of Royanson, it is unfair and incomplete, though good fun. Characterization in this novel leaves much to be desired. None of the characters – not even Royanson and Joshua – is particularly well developed; and most of them, like Joshua, the Pastor and Jacob disappear from the scene for fairly lengthy periods, only to reappear mysteriously. Their actions are quite often inconsistent and we are given no inner view of their thoughts and feelings which might explain some of them. There is, characteristically, too heavy a reliance on melodrama, the scenes of Royanson's madness being perhaps the most incompetent and repulsive in the whole body of the African novel. No single theme is pursued for any length of time in this rather disjointed novel and at the end nothing is firmly pulled together. Aluko could hardly have made a worse start.

In this first novel, then, Aluko has barely got hold of the theme of traditionalism versus modernism and the problem of the 'been-to' has hardly emerged. In the second novel, *One Man, One Matchet*, the theme is much more clearly visualized and focused in the confrontation between two people – Udo Akpan, the young African District Officer, and Benja-Benja, the political rabble rouser. In this novel, which is a considerable improvement on the first, Aluko demonstrates greater control over the structure and the materials of the story in general; everything, with the possible exception of the disappearance of the Rev. Olaiya, is rigidly subordinated to the central conflict between tradition and progress. The characterization is also more successful; Benja-Benja and Udo Akpan are much more compelling studies than Royanson, and some of the minor characters are fascinating in their own right. Unlike *One Man, One Wife* the conflict is introduced quite early in the novel and sustained throughout. It is sparked off by the administration's decision to save the cocoa crop by cutting down the diseased trees during a severe outbreak of cocoa epidemic. Aluko has here chosen a better medium through which to expose the backwardness of traditional society. Unlike *One Man, One Wife* there is a rigid distinction here between good and evil with the forces of modernism being good and traditional society being evil and therefore the only object of satire. If we exclude *One Man, One Wife* where the theme hardly emerges, it is this novel which gives the most simplistic treatment of the tradition versus modernism theme; the Aluko who emerges here is a man who seems utterly contemptuous of tradition and absolutely endorses the modernism of his 'been-to' heroes. The administrative officers who come down to the village of Ipaja are presented as well-meaning, rational and scientific, while the villagers emerge as embodiments of mule-headed stupidity in their opposition to a measure which is designed to protect their livelihood. The satire extends beyond the mere question of resistance to the cutting down of cocoa trees to embrace the traditionalists' lack of a scientific attitude and their opposition to change of any kind. Their conservatism extends to a refusal to overhaul a corrupt and inefficient native administration and judiciary, and a hopelessly incompetent tax-collecting system. By this rigid dichotomy between black and white Aluko demonstrates that he has not yet fully grasped the complexities of the whole question of conservatism and change; he does not seem to realize that innovations have to be explained to traditionally conservative farmers through a massive programme of public education. It is this which is conspicuously absent in the efforts of Udo Akpan and the white officers to modernize Ipaja society.

Benja-Benja is the champion of traditional society in the novel although by education and experience he has been taken out of it; he espouses the cause both because he is fundamentally opposed to a white administration and also because he wishes to use his contact with the people to further his political ambitions. Aluko's hatred of the man can scarcely be concealed; he presents him as the half-educated embodiment of corruption and one of the impediments to progress. But in doing so Aluko, as in Royanson's case, blinds himself to the complexities in Benja-Benja's character which even the white administrator Stanfield is quick to recognize. Benja-Benja is obviously a highly intelligent man who in his schooldays has been the victim of a harsh colonial educational system. Although expelled from school prematurely, he is determined that this will not necessarily be a handicap to his progress and he sets about the task of educating himself with great energy. He eventually becomes a nationalist devoted to the cause of liberating the African peoples from the exploitation of the imperialist powers and, though imprisoned for his political activities, in the honourable tradition of all the redoubtable African nationalists – Kwame Nkrumah, Wallace Johnson and Jomo Kenyatta – he continues his education in prison with such success that he is able to write a thesis on 'The role of the chief in the Africa of tomorrow'. When we meet him he is assiduously collecting material for a projected history of the Ipaja people. To regard such a man as a rabble rouser is to demonstrate a lack of a sense of discrimination, to underestimate a formidable opponent, to undervalue his real appeal for the people and to judge him with the mores of the imperialists themselves.

Aluko shows himself to be completely detached from that powerful force of nationalism which was sweeping the African continent at that particular point in time. The issues that Benja-Benja champions in this novel – the struggle against excessive taxation, the resistance to the white administration, the protection of farmers and the people's way of life – were all major planks in the platform of all the major nationalist movements which led so many countries to independence in the 1950s and 1960s.

On the other hand, Aluko idolizes the highly educated African administrative officer Udo Akpan, who is African in name and colour only. He comes to Ipaja a completely westernized young man with impeccable Cambridge credentials; he operates completely and comfortably within the British civil service tradition and is hardly distinguishable from the white administrative officers. Deliberately or unwittingly, Aluko does not make him a native of the Ipaja district, so there is nothing to help root him down to the area. Towards the elders of Ipaja he is patronizing, rude and tactless, talking to them often with the tones of the white administrative officers. He makes no attempt at identification.

His mannerisms and manners, which are no doubt intended to convey the impression of the urbane, well-bred young man, are unmistakably English. He sees things from a European, not an African, point of view. As far as this novel is concerned the problem of the 'been-to' does not exist. Since Udo Akpan's family does not live in the district he is not called upon to play a part in traditional society; there is no question of an agonizing choice between traditional society and modern society. Udo Akpan behaves consistently as though he believes that traditional society is backward and must change; and he makes no attempt to understand it or to get near the people and be accepted by them. He never once, like Obi, questions the validity of the western civilization he is trying to impose on the people; there is no feeling of disenchantment with English life, which he has completely absorbed. The clash between traditionalism and modernism he sees as a personal confrontation between himself and Benja-Benja, and when the bungling administration decides to call a halt to the cutting of cocoa trees Akpan is piqued into resigning, not so much because of the administrative mismanagement as because the change of policy represents a victory for his arch-enemy Benja-Benja.

All this is not to say that there is nothing wrong with traditional society and its attitudes or that the administration is wrong-headed in its attempt to introduce modern ideas into Ipaja; for one thing we do see the widespread corruption that obtains, the exposure of which constitutes one of the main values of the work. The administration is obviously embattled against tremendous forces and some change is clearly desirable. But Aluko fails to see the bankruptcy of the administration's tactics and attitudes. Akpan's stay at Ipaja is not a success, as Stanfield calls it. Indeed, but for the riots at the end it would have been a complete disaster. It is melodrama which enables Akpan to triumph over Benja-Benja and the forces of traditionalism, not the discovery by a 'been-to' of a method of introducing peaceful change and modernization into traditional society. And at the end there is no suggestion that Akpan has learnt his lesson; he can still talk smugly with his characteristic English mannerisms about the shortcomings of lawyers. Aluko has obviously not solved the problem of modernizing a proud but conservative society, in spite of his optimistic conclusion.

In this novel Aluko has contrived some superb scenes though the humour is at times characteristically caustic. But though a major advance on the previous novel, *One Man, One Matchet* has its flaws, the most obvious of which is the blinkered treatment of important issues. Furthermore, the development of character could have been more masterly. We would have liked, for instance, to witness Owolokere's growing hatred for Benja-Benja, not merely to be informed after the murder that the latter had been having an affair with the former's wife. The plot and structure are more coherent than in *One Man, One Wife* but they are sadly marred by the irrelevance of the Rev. Olaiya's disappearance and reappearance at the end. The greatest weakness, however, is the continued heavy reliance on the melodramatic to round off the story. It seems as if Aluko is still unable to contrive conclusions deriving logically from what has been domonstrated in the body of the novel. He is making steady progress, but is still far from achieving an accomplished work of art.

Aluko's next novel, *Kinsman and Foreman,* which is undoubtedly his best, gives a much more intelligent and realistic treatment of the themes under discussion. The situation here is similar to that in *One Man, One Matchet,* with a newly arrived, highly educated and competent civil servant plunged into a corrupt and conservative society and entrusted with the task of modernizing its institutions and changing its attitudes. As in the earlier novel the conflict with traditional society narrows down to a confrontation between the 'been-to' and the partially educated, self-made man who is the visible embodiment of the society's corruption. There are, however, important differences between the two novels consonant with the more mature treatment of the theme. The hero of the novel, Titus Oti, the first qualified Nigerian engineer to be engaged on the senior staff of the Public Works Department, returns, not to a strange area as does

Udo Akpan, but to his own home base at Ibala; and the foreman,
Simeon Oke, with whom he comes into direct confrontation, is not a
stranger but his own kinsman. These changes suggest that Aluko has
really begun to understand the problem of the 'been-to' and the
complexities involved in the modernization of traditional societies,
and is prepared to give serious thought to them.

Two major problems confront the newly arrived young man who is
given a responsible position in his society; he has to adjust himself once
more to the traditional mores of his people and he has to battle against
unprogressive tendencies such as bribery and corruption. By sending
Titus Oti among his own people Aluko ensures that he cannot ignore
the claims of traditional society as Udo Akpan did; at least he cannot
behave as though they did not exist. He has to face the problem of
reconciliation and adjustment. By making the corrupt opponent
Titus's own cousin, Aluko shows his awareness that corruption is a
complex problem which is not susceptible to the kind of easy solutions
offered by Udo Akpan. Titus has to face the simultaneous problem of
learning to live with Simeon Oke while seeing the necessity of exposing
him. How is this going to be done? The novel is obviously more similar
to Achebe's *No Longer At Ease* than it is to *One Man, One Matchet,* for
both novels try realistically to face the problem of the 'been-to'. Titus,
like Obi, returns from England brimming with idealism and has to
adjust himself to the demands of traditional society from which he has
been somewhat alienated. At the same time he has to conform to
modern mores. Will he be more successful than Obi?

One of the earliest scenes in the novel shows the attempt of
traditional society to draw Titus back into its fold and to begin to exert
its constricting influence on him as though nothing has happened all
these years. Titus certainly feels the unwelcome pull.

> Titus began to have the feeling that he was gradually coming under
> some strange influence that he could not explain. Something deep
> down in him was telling him in a thin voice that he should break
> away from it all – he felt that he should run out of the airless room
> into the fresh atmosphere outside – an atmosphere that was free of
> ancestral spirits. But he found himself completely powerless to carry
> out his desire. He found himself unable to resist whatever he was
> ordered to do by his old great-uncle. He watched the old man, as in a
> dream pour out some water from a gourd into a calabash. (p. 8)

The dilemma is certainly there for Titus who inevitably becomes
locked in a sterile conflict with his relations, particularly old Pa Joel

who takes him to task for not giving him money and for not respecting him and his kinsman Simeon Oke. And yet this society which insists so much on its pride and dignity breeds corruption by the demands it makes on its members. The young Titus, who has hardly found his feet in his new job, is asked to be chairman at the local church bazaar, an exercise which would cost him £40, is expected to contribute generously to the church's building fund and is told to start saving money for the funeral expenses of his aged great-aunt. Society actually connives at Simeon Oke's corruption and expects Titus the engineer to make an even bigger fortune.

This is the strange situation that Titus has to cope with. At the start he is as much an idealist as Obi, being rigidly opposed to bribery and corruption and determined to do his little bit to modernize his society. The financial and other pressures on him are almost as great as those on Obi, but he succeeds where Obi fails partly because he is much stronger and more resolute than the latter; he never compromises his principles even if it means being rude and harsh to his mother. It is true that Titus seldom has to go through the agonizing dilemma Obi has to endure, but unlike Udo Akpan he is aware of the problems. If he does not go through Obi's dilemma it is because he knows precisely what he must do; he must turn down all those invitations and those pleas for contributions, and in the face of the combined opposition of his entire family he stands his ground. Because he does not yield to these financial pressures he is able to resist the temptation to take bribes when it occurs; he thus maintains his principles on corruption and fights his corrupt kinsman Simeon as far as he can.

Although Titus is a strong-minded character who refuses to allow his society to bully him, he is not as inflexible and unbending as Udo Akpan. He recognizes the need for some measure of adjustment; at a prayer meeting he attends at Auntie Bimpe's invitation he joins uninhibitedly in the clapping and singing. One would never imagine Udo Akpan doing this. There is no doubt also that Titus is a much more attractive character than Udo partly because he is much less stuffy, conceited and anglicized. The reason is also partly technical; we are with Titus from the beginning of the novel, seeing events mostly with his eyes and from his point of view. This ensures that we are with rather than against him.

But Titus is not ultimately able to solve the problem of corruption in his society. He is severely handicapped by the fact that Simeon Oke is his cousin. The problem is that Simeon has played his part well in traditional society. He has been the benefactor of Titus's father and indirectly of Titus himself. In order to do this he has plunged deeply into corruption, but traditional society is prepared to forgive him as long as he plays his traditional role. Should Titus with his modern idealism expose him or play his own role in traditional life and spare him? Although Titus knows about Simeon's corruption and criticizes it aloud whenever he has the opportunity, he is prevented by family pressures from doing anything active about it. The actions against Simeon are all taken by people other than Titus. When it is announced that Simeon is to be transferred to the Cameroons and rumour spreads that Titus is responsible for the transfer he spends time and energy strenuously denying all responsibility, although he knows that the transfer would be a very desirable thing. Simeon is eventually charged and taken to court, but although Titus has enough information to secure Simeon's conviction and the termination of his service, he is forced to withhold it diplomatically, during both the trial and the commission of inquiry, in the interest of family unity. Titus is therefore forced to make a limited concession to his traditional society and this prevents him from claiming total success.

Simeon is eventually exposed and sent to the Cameroons but this happens through the extraordinary Alasotele incident when, in the belief that the end of the world is imminent and that judgement is at hand, Simeon confesses his guilt. As in *One Man, One Matchet* the hero is enabled to claim success not through a logical culmination of the events demonstrated in the novel but through the intervention of melodrama. Although the treatment of the subject here is more thorough and intelligent than in the earlier novels, Aluko has still not really solved the problem of effecting drastic change in a corrupt traditional society. His thorough exploration of the subject ought to have shown him, as Achebe realized, that no easy solutions can be imposed. But Aluko is determined to make his been-to hero triumphant and he goes back on his own insights and offers solutions by means of melodrama.

Simeon Oke's corruption is well documented, but only by means of reportage, and his infrequent appearances lead to an inadequate realization of his character which is one of the weaknesses of the novel. As usual, Aluko partly exposes corruption by means of his brilliant comedy which is surely at its best in this book. There is good social satire also directed at a sycophantic civil service. When Titus turns up at headquarters a sullen-looking clerk who had spoken to him most disdainfully is suddenly transformed into the embodiment of courtesy and obsequiousness on learning that Titus is the new engineer. The comedy is quite often scintillating as during the thanksgiving service in honour of Titus's return from the UK. The plot of this novel is tightly knit, every incident contributing to the main design, although the effect is slightly marred by the usual resort to melodrama, as in the ghastly scene of Titus's encounter with the ghost. In spite also of a certain lack of solidity, density of texture and depth of presentation, there is some justification, all things considered, for regarding *Kinsman and Foreman* as artistically the most satisfying of Aluko's novels.

Aluko's latest novel, *His Worshipful Majesty*, though artistically not as accomplished as *Kinsman and Foreman*, gives the most realistic and intelligent treatment of the theme of tradition and modernism. Here Aluko at last resists the temptation to offer easy solutions. In this novel there are no obvious villains; traditional society is represented not by a corrupt, half-educated individual, but by the king himself, the Alaiye of Aiye. For the first time Aluko presents in his pages the majesty and dignity of traditional life. The conflict here is in many ways much more interesting than in the other novels for the protagonists are perfectly matched; each is the worthiest representative of his order that could be found. Instead of the shuffling doddering obas of the earlier novels we have in this novel an individual who is every inch a king. The splendour of his person and of his court is powerfully conveyed.

> Behind the drummers came the young ladies of the court, six of them selected for this occasion: they were the youngest of the King's wives. A number of them had been to school and were certainly good-looking. Each was dressed in an aso ebi that made her look truly lovely. They took their seats on the back row of the dais where two of the court eunuchs stood guard behind them. After more coming and going, the King himself came out, amidst shouts of 'Kabiyesi' from the crowd who had all risen to their feet. He wore a royal robe of alari with very ample sleeves. Both the agbada and the trousers were very heavily embroidered. He had on one of his many beaded crowns. His shoes were also beaded, with figures of birds in blue against a white background. He carried in his right hand a beaded horsetail. One hefty palace official supported the royal arm on one side and another on the other, as royalty himself descended the three steps to his seat. Others supported the ample folds of his garments.[8]

This is certainly a far cry from the Apaja of Ipaja or the Oba of Adasa. Highly conscious of his royal position, the King of Aiye regards himself as at least the equal of the King of England, with whose ancestor one of *his* ancestors had signed a treaty of friendship. Characteristically he speaks in the majestic plural and none of his subjects challenges his view that he is the owner of everyone and everything in his domain. A single sentence from him indicating the royal displeasure is enough to send the culprit rolling on the floor, licking the dirt, pleading for mercy and crying 'Kabiyesi'. When the situation begins to deteriorate and a commission of inquiry is set up to look into the organization of his royal household the king turns up, not to give evidence, which he thinks is beneath his dignity, but to address the court; and he treats the Secretary's attempt to administer the oath to him with the greatest disdain. Even at the very end, when all seems lost, the Alaiye does not lose his regal composure and dignity.

Aluko also deserves commendation for his description of other aspects of traditional life. The fascinating presentation of the Ancestor Festival is different from anything of a similar nature in the other novels. Here at last Aluko gives us a description of a traditional ritual which is worthy of Achebe himself. The language rises to the occasion and conveys, without the slightest hint of sarcasm, the dignity and solemnity of the scene and the significance of the events for the people. The king, appearing in his dual role as worshipper of invisible powers and as king, receives the worship and adoration of his subjects. Nevertheless, his awareness of the majesty of traditional life does not prevent Aluko from displaying its weaknesses. We are made to see the wicked treatment of Morrison at the end, the Alaiye's tyranny and despotism, the organizational confusion which distinguishes his household and the widespread corruption.

In order to rectify these shortcomings of traditional administration the government institutes new local government arrangements whereby the traditional rulers share power and the responsibility for the administration of the district with some of the more educated and progressive members of the society. These arrangements inevitably mean an erosion of the powers and authority of the traditional rulers, but since most of them indicate a willingness to co-operate, it is hoped that the new system will be off to a smooth start. In Aiyeland itself a brilliant barrister, Morrison, is invited to become chairman of the new council. The regulations, with traditional rulers and modern progressives sharing power, give the perfect opportunity for a clash between the old and the new.

Morrison is easily the most attractive of all Aluko's 'been-to' heroes. He is completely without the arrogance, conceit and condescension of Udo Akpan and the occasional uppishness, harshness and tactlessness of Titus Oti; and yet he is just as highly qualified and in many ways much more professional and competent than they are. Like them, he is not only an idealist but also a practical man of action dedicated to the eradication of corruption and dishonesty and the introduction of efficiency and progress into traditional life. He sets about his task of modernization with admirable energy and, above all, with tact, for he, unlike the other 'been-to' heroes, realizes that he has to deal with a traditional order that is proud, dignified and stubborn. Like Udo Akpan, Morrison is a stranger in the territory and is not called upon to operate within the extended family system; but he realizes that he has an immediate task of reconciling the modern with the traditional, and with great assiduity and professionalism he sets about informing himself about the history and customs of the people, soon becoming very knowledgeable on the subject. He is the only one of the 'been-to' heroes to show a genuine regard for traditional life. On one occasion during the Ancestor Festival he says, 'Whatever happens to the rest of our customs ... this communal labour system must be preserved ... Those who can see nothing good in the black man say that we have no governmental and organizational institutions worth talking about' (pp. 28-9). Later, on seeing other aspects of the festival, he is beside himself with excitement and enthusiasm; he inquires whether there are any books describing the customs and he cries out ecstatically, 'It is our custom. And ... we must preserve it.' Still later Morrison genuinely asserts and demonstrates that he is not against indigenous institutions. Although he realizes that the penalties sometimes imposed by customary courts are unfair and ought to be reviewed, he is against the abolition of such courts. Generally Morrison is sound, sensible, intelligent and tactful.

The conflict largely arises because the majestic Alaiye fails to understand the implications of the new regulations and his new role in the new system, and continues to behave as autocratically as he has always done. The fault partly lies, of course, with the departing British administration who have apparently given the Alaiye the impression that the new young men are being brought in merely to help the traditional rulers with their administration; it has not been made absolutely plain to the Alaiye that the changes will involve a diminution of his powers and authority and a different relationship with his subjects. At the start of the conflict, however, Morrison is extremely reasonable, tactful and accommodating. He does his best to meet the Alaiye and his chiefs halfway, agreeing to a proposed increase in salaries for traditional rulers, introducing an entertainment allowance for the Alaiye and a special vote, controlled by the Alaiye himself, for repairs to his court, and increasing the proportion of traditional rulers on the council. It is the Alaiye who still proves stubborn and unaccommodating.

Eventually the crisis comes to a head and Morrison decides that the time has come for the Alaiye to realize that he must move with the more progressive elements into the future. From now on the battle is joined with amazing ferocity, with the Alaiye refusing to budge an inch. It is a tribute to the growing maturity of Aluko's outlook that he recognizes the tragic possibilities inherent in such a conflict. He has come a long way from the simplistic *One Man, One Matchet* where a totally upright and unyielding modernist was pitted against a thoroughly corrupt traditionalist. Here an immensely dignified traditionalist locks horns with an eminently reasonable modernist. The tragedy is that they both have to be destroyed though each has so many good points in his favour. Aluko has at last realized that the struggle to modernize society is a difficult one fraught with peril for all concerned. Even the more junior officers are torn between loyalty to their traditional ruler and loyalty to the new regulations; in the course of the conflict some of them are destroyed or discredited. No one really wins in this struggle. Far from triumphing like Udo Akpan and Titus Oti, Morrison dies in the process. A solution has to be imposed from outside when on his death the government decides to depose the Alaiye, who is given real tragic stature at the end when he defiantly commits suicide.

Unfortunately, having come as near as he ever has to giving a convincing explication of the tradition versus modernism theme Aluko mars it all by characteristically resorting to melodramatics to round off the story. Riots break out, as so often in the novels of Aluko, spearheaded by the supporters of the Alaiye; Morrison, like Royanson goes mad, apparently because Jelenke and the palace boys have put a curse on him. Yet the novel still has its good artistic points. The satire and comedy, though not as compelling as in *Kinsman and Foreman*, are still impressive. Apart from the irrelevant melodramatics at the end the simple and straightforward plot and structure are tightly pulled together. The characterization of Morrison and the Alaiye is impressive though one is inclined to wonder whether Aluko need have made the Alaiye so obstinate.

Aluko may not yet have written his masterpiece but each successive novel has shown a clearer thinking out of his main theme and a greater awareness of linguistic problems. His educated men become progressively more acceptable because they are more flexible and more aware of the problems of change; his traditional villains become progressively less villainous and more representative of the dignity of traditional life. It seems therefore not entirely fair to talk of Aluko's insensitivity towards language or inability to develop.

NOTES

1 See especially: Bernth Lindfors, 'T. M. Aluko: Nigerian satirist', *ALT*, no. 5 (1971), pp. 41–52; Ayo Banjo, 'Language in Aluko: the use of colloquialisms, Nigerianisms', *Ba Shiru*, vol. 5, no. 1 (1973), pp. 59–69.

2 Arthur Drayton, 'The return to the past in the Nigerian novel', *Ibadan*, no. 10 (1960), p. 29.

3 T. M. Aluko, *One Man, One Wife* (Heinemann, London, 1972), p. 20. All further page references are to this edition.

4 T. M. Aluko, *One Man, One Matchet* (Heinemann, London, 1972), pp. 15–16. All further page references are to this edition.

5 See Lindfors, op. cit., pp. 46–7.

6 Even Ayo Banjo in his article points out that in this novel there are suggestions, minimal though they may be, that certain dialogues have been carried on in Yoruba. He also notices an attempt at linguistic differentiation.

7 T. M. Aluko, *Kinsman and Foreman* (Heinemann, London, 1970), p. 6. All further page references are to this edition.

8 T. M. Aluko, *His Worshipful Majesty* (Heinemann, London, 1973), p. 3. All further page references are to this edition.

5. Mongo Beti

▼▼

With the Cameroonian novelist Mongo Beti we begin an examination of the francophone novel and the francophone reaction to the consequences of the western infiltration of traditional African society which, as we have seen, was one of the motive forces behind the upsurge of African literary creative activity. All these writers – Beti, Kane, Laye, Oyono, Ousmane, Dadie and Ouologuem – must be seen against the background of the concept of 'Negritude', a movement which was the most forceful and articulate of all those attempts at reasserting the beauty and validity of African life and culture.

The imperialists who colonized Africa from the sixteenth century onwards were convinced of the barbarism of the areas that had thus come under their control; this was inevitably so, given their western yardstick for the measurement of culture and civilization. As far as they were concerned the foremost ingredients of civilization were technological advancement and literacy. Any people who were deficient in these were immediately classified as primitive. This conviction enabled them to give an altruistic halo to their colonizing mission; an expansionist venture into Africa which was basically materialistic or political could be almost disguised as missionary activity designed to bring light to a benighted people. The propaganda of the missionaries themselves actually reinforced this view; for they genuinely believed that Christian western civilization was best, and that they had a duty to spread it among members of their new empire, at times in the teeth of opposition from the political and administrative arm. The consequence of this missionary-imperialist activity was that African indigenous culture was devalued; traditional religion came to be equated with paganism and traditional education through the tribe's societies was regarded as the perpetration of the most barbarous, unhygienic and indecent practices. Very often the African people themselves, especially those along the west coast, were brainwashed into believing that their culture was primitive and that they could only hope for advancement by espousing western religion and a pseudo-western way of life. There were, however, significant differences between the English and French imperialist practices. The English administrators were generally content with exercising political, military and administrative control, leaving the civilization mission to the missionaries whom they generally regarded with a certain amused tolerance. They preferred the system of indirect rule, making use of the traditional rulers whom they were quite content to leave to exercise their functions within their traditional milieu. On the other hand, the French practised the policy of assimilation by means of which the cream of African traditional society were put through a thoroughly French system of education with the intention of making them *black Frenchmen* who were completely at home in French culture. Schoolchildren in francophone territories were taught to recite that their ancestors were Gauls, just like French children. However, during and after their studies in France, francophone intellectuals discovered that in spite of their impeccably French education and their genuine abilities, they were not totally accepted as Frenchmen. But on the other hand they had been alienated from their traditional roots. They were therefore caught in a cruel dilemma leading to a reaction against the system which had produced them, and a determined struggle to rediscover their lost identity. Hence their association with the concept of Negritude.

The Negritude movement was actually started, not by Africans, but by black Caribbean writers, notably Aimé Césaire whose *Cahier d'un retour au pays natal (Journal of a Return to my Native Country)* was published in 1939. It was he, in fact, who first used the term 'Negritude' in that poem. Aimé Césaire was a friend of Senghor, whom he had met in Paris, a third member of the group being Léon Damas from French Guiana who in 1937 had published a collection of poems, *Pigments*, which utterly denounced the French both for treating him as a white when he only wanted to be a negro and for their exploitation of Africa. The end of the Second World War in 1945 saw a consolidation of the Negritude movement with the publication in that year of Senghor's *Chants d'ombre* and in 1946 of Césaire's *Les Armes miraculeuses*. *Présence Africaine* was launched in 1947, and in 1948 Senghor published his *Nouvelle Anthologie de la poesie nègre et Malagache* to which the French writer and critic Jean Paul-Sartre contributed an introduction that has been generally considered the most penetrating analysis of the Negritude movement.

The central feature of the Negritude concept was its emphasis on the beauty, dignity and excellence of black African life and culture. Negritude writers generally glorified Africa to the extent, at times, of over idealizing her and blinding themselves to those aspects of African history and society which might not be entirely pleasant. Perhaps they felt that this was the only way in which they could counteract the imperialist tendency to devalue traditional African life. They extolled the beauty of the negro physique, the excellence of negro womanhood, the warmth of the negro's personal relationships, his attachment to his environment, particularly his reverence for the soil, his tremendous vitality and his zest for life. Correspondingly they decried the impersonality, decadence and materialism of western society which they saw as the consequence of unbridled technological advancement, and thus exposed the wrongheadedness of the attempt to impose western culture on Africa.

Largely because of their very different historical situation, the anglophone writers were little affected by the Negritude movement. Most of them were locally educated young men, and though conscious of the effect of imperialist practices on traditional life, they did not feel as alienated from their cultural roots as their francophone counterparts. Wole Soyinka's scathing remark that a tiger does not need to proclaim his tigritude neatly sums up their position. Generally the anglophones are pragmatic and more realistic. While demonstrating the beauty of traditional African life they also expose its shortcomings, as Achebe and Soyinka do in *Arrow of God* and *A Dance of the Forests*. The view is now generally held that Negritude is an outdated concept which may have excellently served its purpose as a rallying force for the restoration of a proper perspective on African life, but has outlived its usefulness. As far as the African intellectual is concerned, the emphasis today is on the need to examine critically all those tendencies which may be leading to a debasement of standards and values in contemporary Africa. The committed writer must now talk, not about the glory of the African past, but about ministerial incompetence, nepotism, social and political corruption, social inequalities, oppression and poverty. And for this exercise Negritude is quite irrelevant.

Mongo Beti's work falls within the context of this reaction against the imposition of western culture on African society. Taken as a whole it probably gives the most thoroughgoing exposure of the stupidity of the imperialist attempt to devalue traditional education and religion and replace them by an inadequate western educational system and a hypocritical Christian religion. One of the most elegant and sophisticated of African writers, Mongo Beti's urbanity of tone should not lull the reader into a feeling that he is complacent about the issues he raises. His intelligence and wide-ranging wit correlate with a determination to face the uglier realities and expose them.

Beti's first novel *The Poor Christ of Bomba* was so effective in its exposure of French imperialist attitudes that it provoked a storm on its publication in 1956. This largely underrated novel deserves more attention, if only because of the adroit manipulation of the rather naive narrator through whose eyes we see the events of the story. The focus is on the Rev. Father Drumont and his unavailing attempts to impose a rather austere and authoritarian version of Roman Catholicism on a proud people. The Father emerges as a harsh, obstinate, unfeeling, and conceited authoritarian in spite of, or perhaps partly because of, the unconcealed admiration he elicits from the naive narrator. The first few pages of the novel are brilliantly done.

> Surely it isn't blasphemy . . . oh, no! It even fills me with joy to think that perhaps it was Providence, the Holy Ghost himself, who whispered this advice in the Father's ear, 'Tell them that Jesus Christ and the Reverend Father are all one.' Especially when our village children, looking at the picture of Christ surrounded by boys, were astonished at his likeness to our Father. Same beard, same soutane, same cord around the waist. And they cried out, 'But, Jesus Christ is just like the Father!' And the Father assured them that Christ and himself were all one. And since then all the boys of my village call the father 'Jesus Christ'. Jesus Christ! Oh, I'm sure it's no blasphemy! He really deserves that name, that simple praise from innocent hearts. A man who has spread faith among us; made good Christians every day, often despite themselves. A man full of authority. A stern man. A father – Jesus Christ![1]

Our own experience, on the other hand, is of a Father who is utterly contemptuous of and brutal towards the African people whose shepherd he claims to be. Indeed it is his marked difference from Jesus Christ that strikes us in the church scene that follows; and the fact that it is he himself who draws attention to the similarity with Christ indicates his arrogance, conceit and contempt for the people's intelligence. Instead of a loving, forgiving Christ who is fond of children and asks that they be brought to him, we see a Father who shouts out angrily at mothers for allowing their babies to cry in church and who delights in punishing his charges for the slightest offence.

The impulses of this cruel, dehumanized Father are essentially anti-life. We also see his inhumanity, which is no different from that of the civil authorities, in extorting forced labour from the people in order to build his church. Particularly disgraceful is his exploitation of the Sixa girls whom he compulsorily houses within the mission, ostensibly to prepare them for the duties of a Christian wife, but in reality to provide cheap manual labour. Such cold inhumanity, such religious bankruptcy and dishonesty, are astonishing. So too is the Father's inflexibility on matters of church rules. It is an inflexibility which will not allow a penniless old woman to take the sacrament because her church dues have not been paid, even though everyone, including the uncritical narrator, is moved by the old woman's tale of woe and faith and expects the Father to relent. In spite of his zeal, however, the Father's brand of religion exposes him as being basically un-Christian. It consists in reminding his parishioners of their sins, even on those occasions when he finds an exemplary young man or woman. The concepts of love and mercy are completely absent from the Father's creed. In his view, being a good Christian consists in paying one's church dues and if one's relatives happen to be polygamous, then all connections with them should be severed. Prompted by the belief that only the miserable can have faith in God, the Father virtually encourages poverty and prays for the people's unhappiness. His religion is a life-denying force which fails to come to terms with indigenous law and custom. He fails to see that it is both unnecessary and undesirable to attempt to smother beneath the superficial trappings of Roman Catholicism the age-old culture of the people from which they derive their vitality and their sense of identity, and his most high-handed actions are concerned with his attempts to suppress some aspect or other of traditional life. He rages at the people for indulging in 'pagan' dances on a Friday evening and in an extremely entertaining sequence has a running duel with a traditional herbalist Sanga Boto who seems to have great influence over the minds and loyalties of the people. Though a charlatan in some respects, Sanga Boto owes the secret of his success, like most other African traditional herbalists, partly to his knowledge of the efficacy of herbs and partly to his excellence as an amateur psychologist. His practice illustrates a growing impression in Africa that the African discovered some truths about psychiatric medicine possibly earlier than western doctors. 'Sick people came to consult me and after going home they would suddenly imagine they had been cured ... It isn't my business to heal people, but to try to explain to them why they are unhappy ...' (p. 76). Behind Sanga Boto's accents one can hear the voice of Mongo Beti strenuously making a case for African psychiatry. The fact is that in spite of his alleged charlatanism Sanga Boto does more for these people than the Father. But when the latter catches up with him he hauls him out of his house, drags him shamefully through the streets of the village in his underwear, forces him on to his knees in front of the communion table and orders the drums to be beaten for High Mass. Absolutely lacking in compassion, absolutely inflexible, absolutely contemptuous of the people he pretends to serve, the Father must be one of the most repulsive white characters in the African novel.

And yet there is a very strong suggestion that the vice which the Father believes is rampant in the Tala country stems from his own person. He is the source of corruption, not only because of his encouragement of Zacharia and Raphael who spread vice throughout the countryside, but also because of his dubious relationship with the former which smacks of homosexuality. This is not explicitly stated by Beti, but it is carefully and deliberately suggested throughout the novel. Why is the Father so indulgent to this so-called cook Zacharia whose irresponsibility, corruption, lechery, dishonesty and laziness are patent even to the naive narrator? It is the assistant cook, Anatole, who does all the work, while Zacharia spends his time drinking palm-wine and wenching. During the tour we see for ourselves that Zacharia always abandons the cooking to the local boys, and yet it is always Zacharia whom the Father asks to accompany him as his cook on tour. Even the naive narrator senses that something is wrong: 'Lots of complaints have been made to the Father about Zacharia, but he refuses to believe them. Besides, he's so keen on his blessed cook that it would take the intervention of Christ himself to separate them' (p. 10). So attached is the Father to this useless cook that he builds a house in his village for him with brick walls and a tiled roof. Yet there is not the slightest sign that Zacharia likes or admires the Father, and in spite of his awareness of his own incompetence he continues to make more and more demands which the Father does not hesitate to meet.

The otherwise unyielding Father will brook insults from Zacharia that he will not tolerate from anyone else, and Zacharia knows that he can defy him to an extent that no one else dares. Where the slightest hint of immorality among the Sixa girls calls forth the most vicious sadism from the Father, he never thinks of punishing Zacharia. Even after the revelation of the cook's full villainy, the Father is still prepared to defend him and even fight for him. There seems to be little doubt that Zacharia has some secret knowledge about the Father which gives him a hold over him. What is even more alarming about the Father's relationship with his dependants is that he seems to be bringing up the narrator, the young boy Dennis, for the same purpose.

Ultimately the Father is shortsighted and deluded; he is a coward and a failure whose final strategy, faced with an apparently overwhelming situation, is always to give up and run away. Given the proud intransigence of the Tala people he decides to abandon them to their own devices for three years, in the hope that they will discover the need for God in the interval, but the plan backfires, and when he discovers its failure he decides to return home for good, leaving a mess behind him for others to clear up.

Mongo Beti's intention is to expose, not just the Father, but the Roman Catholic Church as a whole, emphasizing its lack of appeal for the people. He underlines the fact that, in spite of the Father's zeal, Christianity is a minority religion here, deeply distrusted by the majority of the people, even by those who espouse it. There are several reasons for their distrust, the first being that it cuts right across traditional customs. The church's attitude towards unmarried mothers is a case in point. In spite of the increasingly high rate of illegitimacy in the western world most western societies (and this is by no means confined to the church) have continued to regard unmarried mothers as being somehow immoral. In many African countries, on the other hand, having a child before marriage is neither unusual nor stigmatized, and many such countries are revising their concepts of legitimacy. In this novel the Talans' love for children leads them to rejoice whenever a girl has a baby before marriage. Even the naive narrator senses the folly of the Father's obsession with the subject of unmarried mothers whom he compels, nevertheless, to bring their babies for baptism on the payment of a special fee. Then there is the question of polygamy. The one-man-one-wife concept, which is a central Christian doctrine, is naturally repugnant to most traditional African societies where polygamy has been practised for countless generations. It is almost always the last stumbling block to the African's acceptance of Christianity and some of the more reasonable churches, while officially preaching the orthodox doctrine, have, with great understanding, been prepared to wink at irregularities. Not so the Roman Catholic Church that the Father represents. It attacks polygamy with crusading zeal and without a single thought about the economic and social implications of the problem. Few scenes could arouse our detestation of the Father's practice as much as this one.

> Then another woman came to the bar, crying pitifully and trembling all over. Matthew leant over and explained her case into the Father's ear. Her daughter had been married to a polygamist, but it wasn't this she was reproached with, since she was also in the power of a tyrannous husband. Her real sin was to make frequent visits to this daughter, even though she was now the wife of a polygamist.
> The woman wept still and covered her face with her hands. 'Listen,' said the Father, 'take care. Give up these visits to your daughter!'
> Through her tears the woman managed to stammer: 'Father, she's my child, my own child, and I love her ... Punish me in any way you like, Father, but don't forbid me to see my daughter. I would die! Have pity on me ...' The Father said he could change nothing. It was his rule that a Christian mother must make up her mind to cease such visits. (p. 62)

This lack of compassion, this total disregard of the people's traditions and this denial of their dignity, further explain the church's lack of appeal.

Moreover, Christianity turns out in Tala to be an extremely expensive and commercialized religion demanding much from its adherents and imposing several unreasonable tasks and obligations. It is also a religion that imposes its will by means of terror. We later see how the young Dennis's fear of eternal damnation as the consequence of sexual sin almost unhinges the poor boy's mind. Christianity here is an extremely naive religion that depends on a simple-minded and uncritical acceptance of its doctrines, thus suggesting its underestimation of the native intelligence of the African peoples. The identification of Christianity with a white civilization is another obstacle to its acceptance in these parts. Since the white priests are always in association with the white administrators, the people quite rightly regard the church as the ally of an oppressive imperialist administration, and the fact that Jesus Christ is always represented as white further intensifies the feeling that Christianity is a white man's religion which is completely unsuited to African conditions. The people are far from being deluded about the church's real nature. They are perfectly aware of its double standards; they know that the Father who rages against polygamy and immorality among Africans fraternizes with whites who live in concubinage with loose women and sees nothing wrong in supposed white Christians associating with 'pagan' women, although he preaches that after baptism the Africans should stop visiting their 'pagan' relations. Finally, they are aware that the church is a disruptive force that threatens to break up their once-stable way of life.

The central action of the novel is the Father's tour through the Tala country accompanied by Zacharia and the narrator, Dennis. Like Beti's second novel, *Mission to Kala*, *The Poor Christ of Bomba* takes the form of a picaresque tale whose significance lies, not so much in the events, as in the moral development of the participants. The journey is necessitated by one of the Father's most misguided policies. He discovers to his chagrin that, far from arousing in the people a stronger desire for the Christian faith, the three years' spiritual deprivation has caused them to forget Christianity and return to their traditional ways. Unlike the people on the road, the people of Tala have found a new independence and prosperity deriving largely from their success as cocoa farmers, and this prosperity is reflected in an obviously high standard of living. Against the Father's restrictive, life-denying morality the happy people of Tala posit their vigorous affirmation of life. The naive narrator's condemnation of them as living careless lives alerts us to Beti's real viewpoint at this stage. Since they live away from the towns and main roads, the Talans are not only rural people but also traditionalists who have not allowed their lives to be influenced by the values of western imperialism; and although the narrator dismisses them as backward, it is obvious that they are very alert and in their own way progressive.

The following exemplifies the condition in which the Father finds the church on his return.

I followed the Father and the catechist into the chapel, whose interior was in still worse condition. The mat roof, swinging from its nails, looked more like a fishing-net, and you could see the sky through it as if you stood in the open air. Naturally, the earth floor was pock-marked all over by the rain and the walls are streaked with laterite. Logs lie scattered about the floor, and these are the seats! The catechist says that the men all refuse to come and repair the place. If he goes to summon one individually, the news spreads like wild fire and everyone else vanishes. He even says they rendezvous in the forest on these occasions and hold dances, all mixed up with pagans. Finally, he discovered where they were meeting and surprised them there. He began by telling them how horribly they had sinned in joining pagan plays. Then he spoke to them of the chapel, which was all collapsing into lumps of earth and tatters of Raphia. No one replied to him on either point, except a bunch of pagans who began baiting him. Everyone just went on dancing without a care. (pp. 16–17)

Throughout the journey it is the same tale of dilapidated churches, polygamous husbands, unmarried mothers and non-payment of church dues. The message for the Father is clear; after nearly twenty years, Christianity has not really taken hold among these people. And it is significant that during the tour the once-feared Father attracts not only hostility but blatant disrespect.

Zacharia, whose irresponsibility should not blind us to his remarkable sanity and realism, plays a crucial role in the story. He is used by Mongo Beti as a kind of permanent check to the narrator's naivety and the Father's illusions about his mission. The author needs Zacharia on this journey to act as a useful corrective and to be the spokesman for the radical African point of view, and he is able to play this role effectively, not just because he is intelligent, but also because he is a perceptive man of the world who knows his people and is proud of them. He knows that these smart people have realized the importance of money in modern life and are going to chase it no less eagerly than the priests themselves. His corrective role is demonstrated again and again. Shortly before they set out on the tour he warns the Father that his three years' neglect will not have changed the Talans a bit, and he is proved correct. On their arrival at the village called Timbo where they meet with a splendid reception the Father makes a fulsome and patronizing speech, describing himself characteristically as the good shepherd who had deserted the people for their own good. It is a speech which would offend the sensibilities of any dedicated African, and Zacharia appropriately parodies it, calling it utterly ridiculous, and suggesting that its use of a different cultural reference makes it incomprehensible to the people. One cannot talk about 'a good shepherd' in a civilization where people do not know what a shepherd is. Zacharia's statement highlights not just the Father's arrogance, conceit and condescension, but also the blunders that can result from ignorance of a people's cultural patterns, and it certainly carries Beti's endorsement. It also exposes the Father's aloofness from the people whose customs and language he does not really know even after twenty years' sojourn. Because of his peculiar association with the Father, Zacharia can tell the former truths which no one else can, and, what is more he is about the only person to whom the Father listens. On one occasion he bluntly tells the Father that the

African did not first hear of God from the white man; if he agreed to embrace the religion of the latter it was because he hoped that such an association would give him the secret of the white man's power and knowledge. Zacharia can see right through the Father and the other whites; he knows their secrets, their illusions and their real desires and he is sensitive enough to be aware of the effect the Father is producing on the people. If the Father changes somewhat during the course of the journey, it is largely owing to Zacharia's influence.

The change that takes place in the Father is one of the most interesting features of the novel. The first signs of it appear shortly after that conversation with Zacharia and the catechist in which the former had tried to enlighten the Father about the real reasons why some of the people have turned to Christianity. In the ensuing conversation with the self-satisfied M. Vidal, the Father begins to express doubts for the first time about the purpose of his mission: and he mentions the point that Zacharia has made – that the people did not first hear about religion from the white man. The Father seems to be gradually groping his way towards a realization of the validity of traditional life and culture. When the bigoted Vidal asserts that the civilization they are trying to impart to the Bantu race involves much more than materialism and technological advancement, that it involves the Christian religion in fact, the Father suggests, following Zacharia, that any religion 'even if it hadn't inspired a policy of conquest, can be none the less real for its adherents'. This is a liberalism which we have never been led to expect from the Father. Vidal's callousness in proposing to build his road by forced labour also shocks the Father into a realization of his responsibility. Where he once expressed the wish that the people would be unhappy in order that they might return to him, he now sees it as his duty to protect them against the cruelty and depredations of Vidal. The Father cannot yet make a great point about this, however; for one thing, as Vidal sarcastically reminds him, there is the uncomfortable realization that he himself had once used forced labour in the construction of his religious buildings. Nevertheless, his conscience has been stirred and he has moved a very long way from both Vidal and the uncritical narrator who in his naivety rejoices at the people's forthcoming calamity.

At Evindi the Father has relented so far as to ask the catechist not to demand the receipts for cult dues, so that all the people can come into the church. However, the habits acquired over the years have become too ingrained to be entirely dispelled in a moment, Thus, he soon proceeds to break up the Christians' xylophones. The progress is therefore not unimpeded; but the change is no less real for that. Even the narrator realizes that in his new pensive mood the Father is for once prepared to discuss matters of doctrine and church rules with the people and listen to the views of even the non-Christians. Gradually he begins to see the black man's point of view and to support it in discussion with people like Vidal. Then comes the honest confession that he has blinded himself to the reality of things in his parish: 'There are so many things I should have seen long ago, if I'd only had the sense to notice them ... My God, what it is to be oblivious!' Later he appears to be seeing everyone for the first time in his or her real colours. This particularly applies to the cynical Zacharia whose potential for mischief the Father realizes only now.

Finally there is the realization in conversation with Vidal that he has been a failure and ought to return to Europe. This conversation is central to the novel's themes. It shows the Father's genuine concern now about the imposition of western culture on Bomba: 'These good people worshipped God without our help. What matter if they worshipped after their own fashion – by eating one another, or by dancing in the moonlight, or by wearing bark charms around their necks? Why do we insist on imposing our customs upon them?' (pp. 150–1). At the end of the conversation the Father arrives at a clear perception of what has been going on in Africa: the connivance between the missionaries and the administrators to keep the people in a perpetual state of subjection. The Father then launches on a touching analysis of the motives which had prompted him to come to Africa as a missionary: revolted by Europe's arrogance and technological preoccupation he had decided to extend the kingdom of Christ to people considered disinherited and simple. Arriving in Africa he felt flattered by the deference paid to him and failed to acknowledge the real worth of the people until jolted to reality by the Talans' spirit of independence and the failure of his stratagem. The real measure of the change that has come over the Father is indicated in his acceptance of the stupidity of his opposition to polygamy and his readiness now to be flexible about the question of unmarried mothers.

Everyone knows that the Father changes again towards the end of the novel. Before examining this final change, let us consider the narrator for a while. In the present writer's opinion the novel's greatest claim to fame is the brilliance with which the narrator Dennis is consistently manipulated. Mongo Beti's decision to make his

indictment of French colonial policy by looking at the events through
the eyes of naive boy was a stroke of genius. In a sense Beti's ironic
manipulation of the narrator here is a slightly simpler task than in
Mission to Kala where he has to deal with a more educated and much
less naive person. The easiest kind of irony to detect is that in which
the speaker makes judgements and assertions that always flagrantly
offend our normal values and standards. While Jean-Marie Medza in
Mission to Kala makes some correct responses, this narrator, who is so
single-minded in his admiration of the Father and is so consistent in
his endorsement of the Father's most outrageous actions and
statements, who is so uniform in his condemnation of Zacharia even
when the latter is at his most realistic and perceptive, seldom says
things that can be taken seriously. The irony, then, is patent; its
brilliance lies in the consistency with which the tone is maintained.

The ironic thrust of the work registers immediately in that masterly
first chapter, indeed on the very first page. The enthusiasm with which
the boy accepts the Father's new title of 'Jesus Christ' when we
can see the obvious blasphemy, arrogance and inappropriateness, the
effectiveness of phrases like 'made good Christians every day, often
despite themselves', 'that simple praise from innocent hearts' and 'A
father – Jesus Christ!', and the mocking tone of voice which suggests
the presence of Beti laughing at the narrator behind his back, all warn
us right at the start to be on our guard about Dennis's views. The
harsher the Father's behaviour, the greater is Dennis's admiration.
There is the simple-minded endorsement of the Father's decision to
abandon the Talans: 'He only abandoned them for their own good; so
they would become better and return to the true faith.' There are
occasions when the narrator denies his own humanitarian promptings
and endorses the Father out of the unshaken conviction that the latter
must be right. This uncritical endorsement would be extremely comic
at times if it did not also have some pathetic overtones.

> The man died as the Father was giving his absolution. What a lucky
> chance! This man who never dreamt of confession, who would have
> died without the sacraments, whose soul would have appeared
> before God in the worst possible state if the Father hadn't been
> present at the scene, behold him now already among the blessed! But
> how many people get a chance like that? And the tree had chosen to
> pierce him just below the belly, so he was punished exactly where he
> had sinned! In tomorrow's sermon the Father is sure to dwell on all
> these coincidences and draw them out before the faithful. (p. 27)

Even when the narrator seems to diverge a bit from the Father, his
responses are still the wrong ones. And he identifies himself with the
Father to the extent of yearning for the latter's country and
civilization.

> I do wish he would sometimes talk of his family and his country, but
> he talks so little! All he has told us is that the cold falls in large lumps
> from December to March and that everyone is a Christian and goes
> to Mass on Sundays. How grand it must be there! Provence! Yes,
> that's the name of his region – Provence. And there every man takes
> one wife only, and girls don't sleep with their boys until they are
> married in church. It's been like that for centuries and centuries!
> According to the Father, there are no forests in Provence. You can
> look out for more than five kilometres on every side and see the land
> all scattered with stone churches and tall belfries. How splendid!
> And it seems that in Summer-time, from June to September, the sun
> rises at four in the morning and doesn't set till ten at night. Cars,
> trains and aeroplanes without number. Ah, Provence what a place! I
> can see it now . . . (p. 47)

Such scintillating satire admirably demonstrates the effectiveness of
the use of the naive boy's mind as the reflector of events. The
excellence partly depends on the brilliance with which Mongo Beti can
penetrate this kind of mind. For instance, Zacharia's sexual antics in
the room next door leave Dennis completely puzzled at first.

> Hullo! there goes Zacharia's bed again. Will he never get rid of his
> diarrhoea? He's certainly got his due, anyway. Now he'll learn that
> one can't mock God or one of his ministers . . . My God! Who can
> Zacharia be talking to at this hour? There! A little stifled cry, like a
> child, or perhaps a woman. Yes, that's it perhaps, a woman's cry!
> Heavens, is it possible? Has Zacharia really got a woman with him?
> I'm going to listen carefully. At present, everything is still. There
> goes his bed, creaking again! Whatever can he be doing? Lord, there's
> no mistake now! A woman's cry. And the bed creaking ceaselessly.
> My, just think of Zacharia with a woman, here, in this house! Only a
> few metres from the Father, who's probably still talking to
> Matthew! What can they be doing together to make the bed creak
> like that? (p. 57)

And so Mongo Beti goes on, imitating with great adroitness the
language of simplicity: 'I've confessed! . . . At last, I've confessed and I
feel so good! I'm so happy. I feel just as I do after a good hot bath: all
the filth that covered me has slid away on to the ground, and freed of
that foul garment, how light and free my body feels in all its
movements! My God, how sweet it is' (p. 133). Since Beti wishes to

give the impression of the talking voice his narrator uses a colloquial style which helps reinforce the impression of naivety. The consequence of this accomplished artistry is that the author achieves the most vitriolic satire at the expense of the French while apparently remaining detached.

However, the narrator, like the Father, changes significantly during the course of the journey and in his own case the change is permanent. The change consists largely in a growth into sexual awareness, and the sexual scenes, though presented with a wealth of detail, are prevented from becoming prurient by the hilarious comedy caused by the narrator's naivety. At the start of the novel he is completely ignorant of sexual matters until Zacharia's and Catherine's activities next door alert him to the reality of things. Then Catherine takes matters into her own hands and seduces him. The next few scenes give a realistic impression of a boy being sexually aroused for the first time. The boy's ignorance of what is involved and what Catherine is trying to do to him, and his simple-minded calls on God later to witness that he was sorry and did not really want to do it, are incredibly funny. But Dennis soon becomes aware of Catherine's great attractiveness: 'How sweetly she smelt, Catherine! She smelt so sweet and her firm breast was pushing against my left arm. For a moment I thought of turning against the wall, but I didn't know what she was doing and so I stayed where I was . . . She tickled me! I laughed despite myself' (p. 85). In the end he allows Catherine to do as she wishes. With the narrator's growth into sexual awareness the style noticeably changes, becoming smoother, less jerky and less colloquial. Later his growth continues when he becomes drunk on palm-wine. Then follows a strong desire to have sex with Catherine again, not during the night, but by day so that he can have an opportunity of examining her naked body.

In spite of all his protestations Dennis is experiencing sexual passion for the very first time and he is not really repelled by it. At this stage we realize that the Father's effect on the boy has been to stultify his normal development. The constant need to go on tour has retarded Dennis's educational progress, but his emotional and psychological development have also been impeded. The Father's terror-inducing, life-denying religion has led the boy to believe that the affair with Catherine, though not initiated by himself, is mortal sin which has to be atoned for by confession and penance. But he dares not confess to the Father and therefore cannot take communion. We are made powerfully aware of the soul-racking torment the poor boy undergoes, the scenes demonstrating this being simultaneously among the most amusing and most pathetic in the novel. A struggle is raging between the choirboy brought up according to the Father's strictures and the adolescent powerfully aware of Catherine's attractiveness. Then, as Catherine's real identity and her association with Zacharia are revealed, and the ensuing scandal unfolds, Dennis's growth continues as his eyes are opened to villainy. He is the first to guess that Raphael, the director of the Sixa, must somehow be involved in the scandal and he justifiably wonders why it is only Anatole who does not seem to have been touched by it. Indeed, the chapter entitled 'Tebe' is almost entirely devoted to Dennis's thoughts as he gropes his way towards a full understanding of the reality of things at the Bomba mission. On their return to Bomba he has lost his innocence, but he has gained in knowledge. He even comes to some very perceptive conclusions about himself and the change that has taken place in him.

> At the time, the first days of that miserable tour seemed to me like a nightmare. But now it's no longer the tour that I look on as a nightmare, but rather all the preceding part of my life which seems dreamlike, cloudy and insubstantial, like something from which I have awoken ... yes, exactly as if I were waking from a long sleep, without quite knowing what use to make of my new day. My God! How bizarre it all is. My eyes open upon a colourless world; it neither rains nor shines and I can't even guess what time it is. (p. 147)

While Dennis's change remains permanent, the Father reverts to his original harshness. The fact is that although the Father had come to a clear realization during the tour of the futility of colonization and the attempt to impose alien customs on the people, he had retained his initial view of Africans as technologically, intellectually and morally backward. And it is what he now sees as the African's incorrigible immorality that administers the final blow and forces him to leave Bomba in a harsher frame of mind than seemed conceivable.

Zacharia's wife's revelation, after a dreadful fight with Catherine, that the latter is from the Sixa, prompts investigations which suggest to the reader, if not to the Father, that it is the latter's policies which are responsible for the descent of Catherine and the other Sixa girls into depravity. By putting a young man like Raphael in charge of a female institution like the Sixa with a lot of other young men around, the Father was merely presenting them with a ready-made brothel. The Sixa turns out to be a den of corruption, largely through the

Father's negligence, as Marguerite, one of the girls, tells him. The most startling revelation of all is that the Father's policy has created the perfect conditions for a venereal disease epidemic which now rages through the Sixa.

But the Father now irresponsibly blinds himself to the fact that he is largely the cause of the catastrophic turn of events at Bomba, unleashing his venom instead, not on the men, but on the girls who are the unfortunate victims of his own negligence and the men's incontinence. In a very real sense he has destroyed the lives of almost all these girls, not simply because they are infected with venereal disease, but because their fiancés, fed up with waiting and disgusted by the corrupt activities at the Sixa, have abandoned them. But this completely fails to register on the mind of the racialist Father who now sees the activities at the Sixa as the expression of the unbridled libido of the black race. 'They are all eaten up with lust; Ah, what a race!' (p. 177). We now see some nasty aspects of the Father's character that the relationship with Zacharia may only faintly have suggested. He now turns out to be a voyeur deriving a perverted pleasure from the girls' sordid revelations, vicariously enjoying the delights of sex at second hand. Under the pretence of conducting the investigations he calls up all the girls, one after the other, and forces them to give all the details of their sexual activities with the men, the more modest ones being encouraged with the aid of the cane. The Father also clearly becomes a sadist, for when each girl arrives for her confession she is first given several strokes of the cane on the Father's orders. This contempt for the dignity of the African race is repulsive in a man who is simultaneously demonstrating that he harbours the basest instincts himself.

Anatole, the assistant cook who administers the beatings, takes even greater pleasure than the Father in the girls' sufferings, revealing himself as a sexual invert of the worst kind.

> Anatole said to me with disgust: 'How pathetic these girls are! Even the hardest of them only need their arses tickled a little with my cane to make them begin farting out their nastiness... Talk about a brothel! And there was I, slashing away at their fat arses, flabby as mud. My cane really seemed to sink into their rotten flesh. Oh, how I detest the little mice! How I despise them! I'd like to spend my whole life thrashing them...' (p. 191)

Why is it, as Dennis pertinently observes, that of all the grown men, it is only Anatole who is not involved in the Sixa scandal! Is he impotent or homosexual or a woman-hater who channels his misogyny into these sadistic beatings? The obvious relish with which he sets about the business suggests evidence of strong sexual inversion. The Father's mission is completely corrupt.

The Doctor's report on the syphilis epidemic is a thorough condemnation of the Father's administration. It speaks of bad sanitation, bad housing, bad cooking arrangements, bad maintenance, low morale and exploitation. One would have expected that this would at last alert the Father to a full realization of his responsibility and moral obligation to the girls; but although he finally admits that he is 'the guilty party in the whole affair', it is an intellectual admission which is not deeply felt and is certainly not followed by repentant action. The height of his irresponsibility and impenitence are revealed when, instead of taking steps to cure the girls, as the Doctor has advised, he decides to pack them off to their homes, presumably to spread venereal disease throughout the country, asserting that they have brought dishonour to his mission. The Father shows at the end that he is even harsher than the opening pages have suggested. Worse still, he unnecessarily disbands the school without making provision for the furthering of Dennis's education; and when he leaves for France, he does not write to his young favourite as he has promised. He turns out to be a superficial and insincere man who in the end destroys the boy's career, for the latter can see no prospect before him other than employment as a small boy with a Greek merchant. The last scenes of the novel show the misery and desolation that the Father leaves behind him. By one of those ironic twists of fate Zacharia, the Father's erstwhile favourite, is going to marry Catherine and become a polygamist; and the Father who had once forbidden Christians to associate with polygamous members of their family advises the now destitute Clementine to stay with her husband. But Clementine the 'proper' Christian, refuses.

The thorough exploration of this novel's themes might lead one to overlook its artistry or to suppose that it is merely a string of episodes. It is, in fact, a very well constructed novel with a compact, unified plot. The fact that it is the same tale of woe that the Father meets at every station might seem repetitive, but it is necessary in order to demonstrate the Church's universal failure in the Bomba area. Most important, the reader is held spellbound by the gradual revelation of the various aspects of the Father's slow growth into awareness. It is quite obvious that in spite of the wealth of detail Mongo Beti had probably planned almost every aspect of this novel even before he started to write it. Particularly worthy of commendation is the brilliant exposure of the narrator's naivety and the consistency and effectiveness with which the author penetrates the depths of an adolescent mind in convincing language. This gives us splendid passages of introspection resulting in a very full picture, not only of the boy, but of the Father himself. Even more minor characters like Zacharia, Catherine and Vidal are realistically and convincingly presented.

No doubt there will be readers, particularly French ones, who will call the accuracy of Beti's presentation of the French colonial situation into question. It is quite possible that Beti has exaggerated, but exaggeration is a perfectly legitimate literary weapon. In order to assess the literary quality of the book, we must look within it, to the effectiveness of the methods used by the author, not outside to its historical truth. There is little doubt that, literarily speaking, Beti has produced a most effective denunciation of an unsuitable political and cultural system.

Mission to Kala

Mongo Beti's next novel, *Mission to Kala*, continues his denunciation of the French colonial exercise, turning the focus this time on the colonial educational system. His thesis, apparently, is that the formal classical education to which young francophones were exposed was ultimately valueless, since it alienated them from their roots in traditional society, taught them to consider the values of that society inferior to French ones and gave them little preparation for the life they were to lead. Beti's manipulation of his persona in this novel is a much more complex exercise. Unlike Dennis, the new hero, Jean-Marie Medza, though usually confused, wrong-headed and self-deluded, is not completely naive, and a simple reversal of his point of view would not necessarily tell us where Beti himself stands. Jean-Marie is often ironically treated in order to reveal his conceit, delusion and stupidity; at other times he himself looks back with disgust at his past follies, and on other occasions he is used straightforwardly as a mouthpiece to deliver Mongo Beti's satire against the French system. The exercise calls for a very deft manipulation of tone and language and suggests, not that Beti does not know what to do with his narrator, but that he is aware that he has a slightly more mature persona than Dennis to deal with this time.

Apart from the more complex manipulation of the persona the other major stylistic development in *Mission to Kala* lies in its richer comedy. One is immediately struck by the narrator's scintillating wit and flippant, ironic and sarcastic tone, even, at times, at his own expense. The comedy also resides in the great number of hilarious scenes, some of them bordering on farce and slapstick, such as the discovery of Jean-Marie in bed with Edima, his father's ravings on his return to Vimili, and the merry dance which he and Zambo lead their fathers in the skirmish at the end. The novel's picaresque nature is announced right at the start by the Fielding-like authorial chapter headings. As with most picaresques it takes the form of a quest during which the hero grows morally and spiritually and returns home a changed man. At the start of the novel Jean-Marie is chosen, in spite of his adolescence, for the task of bringing back his cousin Niam's erring wife, because his kinsmen assume quite wrongly that his classical education has transformed him into a white man possessing the latter's secrets and power. Jean-Marie is initially under no illusions himself about his suitability for the task. Aided by his perceptive aunt he does his best to resist this attempt to send him on what seems a stupid mission. His aunt, in particular, realizes that the solution of matrimonial problems is a traditional exercise, certainly an adult exercise which should not be undertaken by a boy who has just failed his school-leaving certificate examinations. But in his kinsmen's eyes Jean-Marie's western-style education has more than compensated for his lack of traditional experience. The people of Vimili are being severely criticized by Beti for endowing western education with an extraordinary mystique and assuming that it provides a grooming which will enable the educated man to play a significant role in traditional affairs. So it is, then, that a 16-year-old boy who has been partly moulded by the French educational system finds himself plunged into a totally traditional society which has been little influenced by that system.

Although Jean-Marie is rather diffident about his capabilities at the start, he becomes infected with a sense of his own importance from the moment he accepts his kinsmen's proposal, assuming that his education must give him distinct advantages over the people of Kala, his cousin's kinsmen, whom he now considers barbarous and primitive. From this point onwards he becomes the sustained object of satire. One of the hallmarks of Beti's style in this novel is the language he makes his hero use. It is language which simultaneously exposes Jean-Marie's pretentiousness and conceit and the inadequacy of the system of education to which he has been exposed. His speech is impregnated with western-type clichés and references, allusions to the classics and borrowings from cheap fiction and popular western magazines. These suggest both the kind of education he has received and the fact that he is prone to look at African phenomena through western eyes. Here are a few.

> They looked like a bunch of patriots who have just declared a holy war. (p. 4)[2]

> But here the individual was subordinated to that of the group in a way which would have made even Levy-Bruhl blink. (p. 78)

> It was just such an expression as is common among classics masters in the provinces, indicating that their pupils are incurably third-rate... (p. 80)

These western clichés and images, most of which are inappropriately used, suggest not only an addiction to western values and an alienation from traditional culture, but an incomplete assimilation of those values. A good many of the references are drawn from Jean-Marie's reading of the classics and are, in many cases, similarly inappropriately used.

> On the sports ground were about twenty big toughs, bare-legged and bare-chested, engaged in some game whose war-like nature even the Spartans would have recognized. (pp. 21–2)

> Every time he threw the ball the spectators shouted his name in chorus, as though he had been a friendly God to be supplicated at the siege of Troy. (p. 23)

> As we entered we received a roaring welcome that would have done justice to Caesar on his return home from the Gallic wars. (p. 30)

These examples suggest another dimension to Jean-Marie's images and references: they are not only non-African but also drawn from a grandiloquent frame of reference which reveals his conceit, his delusions of grandeur and his pretentiousness. With deft ironic touches Beti continues to expose Jean-Marie's condescension which becomes even more explicit as the novel progresses, so that although Jean-Marie gives himself grandiose airs, what we see is a silly, half-educated, pretentious young man who is completely ignorant of his country's traditional culture and unable, therefore, to operate within his society. On Jean-Marie's arrival at Kala he is full of contempt for the people whom he finds playing a traditional but apparently very skilful game. Jean-Marie proceeds, nevertheless, to denigrate it. Observing his cousin Zambo, who is giving a most magnificent display, he spitefully disparages his splendid physique. This paragon of masculine good looks appears to Jean-Marie's prejudiced eyes as 'a great hulking flat-footed devil, with a disproportionately lengthy torso and a slight pot-belly', and he goes on to call him a 'human baobab tree'. Having witnessed Zambo's performance, however, Jean-Marie begins for the first time to feel a sense of his inferiority *vis-à-vis* the people of Kala. This is the beginning of a process whereby Jean-Marie is gradually shocked out of his self-delusion and condescension.

However, the Kalans themselves, including Zambo, wrongly assume, as the Vimilians had done, that Jean-Marie must somehow be superior because of his learning and certificates. They therefore proceed to lionize him and expect to be educated by him. But Jean-Marie proves to be woefully inadequate for the task. Impromptu extra-mural sessions are held, during which the people, who are really much more intelligent than Jean-Marie has supposed, ask him very pertinent questions. Generally speaking, the nature of the questions asked at the first of these sessions suggests that Mongo Beti intended them to bring out the inadequacy of the kind of education to which boys like Jean-Marie had been exposed, for his basic ignorance is made patent again and again. The representative of the white man, the bearer of certificates, confronts the native people and he is worsted. The extremely intelligent and perceptive Kalans are able to prod his weaknesses and illogicalities with what he himself calls a 'needle-sharp clarity'. Fortunately Jean-Marie is himself able to see his inadequacy and to acknowledge the people's intellectual superiority. He is also honest enough to confess that he has never thought seriously about some of the points raised by the people.

If the first meeting is designed to test Jean-Marie's assimilation of what he has learnt at school, the second forces him to consider the role of educated men like himself in the community, a subject to which he has also never given serious thought. A woman in the audience makes the very relevant point that the education he is receiving will transform him into a Frenchman and cut him off from the lives of the people.

'You'll live in houses with a garden all round them, and a hedge to

fence them off from each other. You'll sit around in the evening
smoking cigarettes and reading newspapers. You'll drink your water
from a tap, not fetch it from a spring. You'll lose your taste for palm-
wine, and take to their red stuff instead. You'll travel around in a car,
and have a table-cloth at dinner, and boys to wait on you. You'll
speak nothing but *their* language. And perhaps, like them, you'll
come to detest the sound of tom-toms in the night. Very well. But
here's my real question – where do *we* come in to all this? (p. 82)

By asking about the relevance of Jean-Marie's education to the people
and the country as a whole, the woman helps to sharpen his ideas about
his future status and life-style and about the role of his generation in
the development of his country. In a very real sense it is Jean-Marie
who is being educated at Kala. It is clear that although the Kalans
revere him initially for his learning they are nevertheless aware of his
inadequacies, especially in so far as traditional life is concerned. He is
never called upon to use his superior knowledge in the negotiations for
the return of Niam's wife, for his cousin Zambo, realizing his total
ignorance of traditional custom, urges him to leave all the negotiations
in his hands; and Zambo conducts the affair brilliantly.

Jean-Marie's education continues as he becomes aware of aspects of
life in Kala to which he was never exposed in Vimili. He experiences
the warmth of personal relationships, not only among Zambo and his
friends, but also between Zambo and his father. The informality
which characterizes the latter case contrasts strongly with the strain-
ed relationship between Jean-Marie and *his* father. Whereas his development so far has been stultified, here in Kala he discovers the
joys of alcohol and experiences sexual fulfilment for the first time.

Inevitably, Mongo Beti idealizes the Kalans almost to the extent of
turning a blind eye to their faults. This is of course very much in line
with his Negritudist position. As far as Beti is concerned these
traditional rural people, living a life largely untouched by western
civilization, are vastly superior to their counterparts from the
westernized city. They must therefore by no means be regarded as
barbarous children of nature. This was Jean-Marie's first mistake.
Although largely isolated from western influence the Kalans, like the
Talans, are a proud, self-confident and even sophisticated people. On
arrival at the village the hero discovers that it gives a feeling of security.

...it was as though one was on a small island, pounded by heavy
seas, and yet safe from drowning. The neat huts and bungalows were
well spaced out down their long avenue; yet the whole place was

encircled and overshadowed by the immensity of the forest, like a
gully at the foot of a high cliff. As darkness fell, the street became as
noisy and animated as any town's native quarter. (p. 30)

The emphasis is on the Kalans' effortlessness and spontaneity. We are
meant to admire the excellence of their dancing and the expertise of the
young men's swimming. We also see their lack of inhibitions and of
complexes – the boys undress without any sense of shame and plunge
naked into the water, thus shaming the inhibited Jean-Marie into doing
the same, and they compare and joke freely about their sexual organs.
This naturalness results in a certain openness about sexual matters.
Zambo keeps a mistress at home with his father's consent and boys and
girls talk frankly about sex. Most of them have had sexual experience,
which is regarded as a matter of course here, and the fact that Jean-
Marie the 'city-slicker' has had none is regarded by them as a sign of
immaturity and suggests the stultification of his normal development.
We must not make the mistake of judging the people of Kala by an
alien moral standard and therefore accusing them of promiscuity and
lack of discrimination. They control sex here by keeping it in its proper
place, but they do not ban it. And it is significant that the Kalans are
entirely free from venereal disease since there are sanctions operating
against it. The very spontaneity of the people's life militates against it,
for since bathing here is communal among the young, any diseased
person would immediately be found out. Again and again in his novels
Mongo Beti stresses the sexual sophistication among the rural people.

The Kalans' informality and naturalness should not suggest,
however, that they are carefree, for they do have a proper sense of what
is the done thing. This is shown especially in their great hospitality to
strangers, particularly to Jean-Marie. Nothing is omitted which will
make him happy and comfortable. The Kalans are presented also as
industrious, perceptive and intelligent, and although their occupations
are diversified, they still retain their love for the soil and for
agriculture. The chief, for his part, is expeditious and fair in his
dispatch of administrative and judicial matters. On the whole Jean-
Marie's stay among them is a most pleasant interlude.

The consequence of his growth in Kala is that Jean-Marie becomes
a rebel against all those influences which have so far moulded him – his
education and his parental background. The reaction against the
educational system is particularly violent. Now, it is clear that Mongo
Beti largely supports his hero in his rejection of the French educational
system, but it is equally clear that some of the latter's comments are

extreme, and show a certain lack of discrimination. The point is quite
rightly made that the content of French education is largely foreign
and irrelevant to the needs of the African student. Some account must
be taken in the educational process of the African's own culture and
ancestral wisdom.

> 'It's perfectly reasonable to suppose that White children should
> learn faster than Black. What are they being taught? *Their* ancestral
> wisdom, not ours, isn't that so? Who invented aeroplanes and trains
> and cars and steamships? The Whites. Very well, then. Now if it was
> *our* ancestral wisdom that was being taught in this school, it would
> be normal to expect Coloured children to learn faster than Whites,
> wouldn't it?' (p. 61)

Even where the educational system has some relevance, its deficiency
in not giving the pupils proper instruction on important concepts has
been made patent. It has also been copiously demonstrated that the
largely classical education is unrelated to employment opportunities
and bears little relation to the day-to-day lives of the people. All this is
granted, and to a certain extent Jean-Marie's eventual hostility is
justified. The problem is that Jean-Marie proceeds to blame the
educational system for all his reverses at Kala when it is clear that other
forces are at least partly responsible. Faced, for instance, with the
essential superiority of his four friends, Jean-Marie attributes his own
backwardness to the educational system and longs for liberation from
its constricting demands.

> If only they wouldn't treat me just like a 'scholar' and nothing else!
> I'd have given all the diplomas in the world to swim like Duckfoot
> Johnny, or dance like the Boneless Wonder, or have the sexual
> experience of Petrus Son-of-God, or throw an assegai like Zambo. I
> wanted desperately to eat, drink and be happy without having to
> bother my head about next term, or such depressing things as
> revision-work and orals. The very least I could do was to conquer
> my fear of women – even divorcees. (pp. 58–9)

This is one of those passages which induce the feeling in some readers
that Mongo Beti is not quite certain about what he wants to do with his
persona – his first-person narrator. Judging from the general tenor of
the attack on education it would appear that on this occasion Beti
endorses his hero, since the latter is registering his distaste for the
educational system. But then the obvious lack of proportion in his
statement makes one want to hope that the author is treating him
ironically. Surely the acquisition of a formal education should not

necessarily prevent one from dancing or having sexual experience or participating in sports? Is it the educational system which is at fault here or Jean-Marie's parental background? Similarly, when he finds himself incapable of answering the questions put to him at Kala, he blames, not just this particular educational system, but education itself.

> The illusory nature of college learning could hardly have been better illustrated, as I learnt for myself that night. I was not without a certain pride in all I had learnt during the past academic year; yet at the first real test of my knowledge – a test imposed by genuine circumstances, not under the artificial conditions of an examination room – I had already discovered vast gaps in the frontiers of my tiny kingdom . . .
>
> Is there, as I am inclined to suspect, a kind of complicity, an unspoken agreement between the severest examiner and any candidate? And if so, does this complicity not rest on the implied assumption (which the Professor, at least, is consciously aware of) that all they both know is, in differing degrees, illusory and insubstantial? . . .
>
> My resentment against schools and educational systems mounted steadily as the days passed by. I saw a school as a kind of giant ogre, swallowing young boys, digesting them slowly, vomiting them up again sucked dry of all their youthful essence, mere skeletons. (pp. (pp. 67–8)

There is certainly wit here, and the powerful heady rhetoric suggests Beti's endorsement. But if the author endorses his hero here he would not merely be exaggerating (which is perfectly legitimate and was, in a sense, practised by some of the adherents of the more debased forms of Negritude), but ignoring vital areas of his own work. What must never be forgotten is that Jean-Marie failed his examinations. If he has hitherto taken pride in all he learnt during the past year, then he has no right to have done so since he obviously did not assimilate much; and if his pride takes a severe knock, the fault is purely his, not the system's (which quite justifiably failed him). How can he talk about an implied complicity between the severest examiners and the candidate when his own examiners have just failed him? And is he therefore justified in seeing schools as a kind of giant ogre devouring young boys? Has he any right to condemn education itself as he seems to be doing? One would like to think that Beti is treating him ironically, but one is not quite sure. Towards the end of the book the attack on education is resumed.

Do you remember that period? Fathers used to take their children to school as they might lead sheep into a slaughter-house. Tiny tots would turn up from backwood villages thirty or forty miles up country, shepherded by their parents, to be put on the books of some school, it didn't matter which. They formed a miserable floating population, these kids: lodged with distant relations who happened to live near the school, underfed, scrawny, bullied all day by ignorant monitors. The books in front of them presented a universe which had nothing in common with the one they knew: they battled endlessly with the unknown, astonished and desperate and terrified...

We were catechized, confirmed, herded to communion like a gaggle of holy-minded ducklings, made to confess at Easter and on Trinity Sunday, to march in procession with banners on the Fourteenth of July; we were militarized, shown off proudly to every national and international commission. (p. 165)

This passage certainly shows some signs of confusion of thought, largely due to the wide-ranging nature of its attack. There is material in it which would carry the endorsement of the author and most Africans – the denunciation of a system which forces the children to parade on the Fourteenth of July and to become Roman Catholics, which makes inadequate provision for the children's accommodation, permits them to be bullied by incompetent monitors and imposes a syllabus unrelated to their environment. But the eagerness for education demonstrated in the first few lines is a commendable thing which is still widespread in Africa (and would not be condemned even by the most fervent adherents of Negritude) even in these post-independence days, and which should by no means be denigrated. In post-independence Africa it has led to a desperate shortage of school accommodation in a number of countries. To see this as a peculiar phenomenon of French educational policy is to see the system through blinkers.

If we look at the novel carefully, it will be found, in fact, that it is not so much the French educational system, whatever its defects, which has caused the stultification of Jean-Marie's development, as his father's tyranny and determination that he should become a child prodigy. If Jean-Marie now reacts so violently against education and yearns for the liberty of his contemporaries, it is because he is actually conscious that his father, by pushing him so hastily through the educational system in his determination to make him a success, has denied him the pleasure of growing up gradually, which was his right as a child.

Looking back, I suspect Eliza had become my symbol of absolute
liberty, the freedom enjoyed by country boys like Duckfoot Johnny,
the Boneless Wonder, Son of God, and the rest. I saw this freedom
as the most precious possession I could acquire, and realized at the
same time that in all likelihood I should never have it. Without being
aware of it, I was no more than a sacrifice on the altar of civilization.
My youth was slipping away, and I was paying a terrible price for –
well, for *what*? Having gone to school at the decree of my all-
powerful father? Having been chained to my books when most
children of my age were out playing games? I did not exactly feel 'in
love' with Eliza, but I certainly desired her. (p. 63)

The truth is that at the back of all Jean-Marie's problems lurks the
nightmarish figure of his father. It becomes increasingly clear that we
should not (as has been the case hitherto) see *Mission to Kala* solely in
the context of Negritude and the French educational system. It may
have started as an attack on the latter, but it soon becomes a very
interesting psychological study of a boy's conscious and unconscious
reaction against his father and the influences to which the latter has
subjected him. Not enough credit has been given to Beti for his
expertise at adolescent psychology as demonstrated not only in the
penetrating study of Jean-Marie in this novel, but in the equally
brilliant portrait of Dennis in *The Poor Christ of Bomba*. Jean-Marie's
revolt against his father certainly comes out in the following passage.

My father: the word evoked twenty years of almost continual terror.
At any moment he was liable to materialize where I least expected
him. He was inescapable. And, at once, he would begin an
inquisition on my behaviour: what I had been doing, where had I
been, had I worked hard at school, were they pleased with me, would
I pass my exam? He was like a bloody policeman – no, worse: a
private dictator, a domestic tyrant. There was never any peace or
sense of security; nothing but rows, reproaches and fear. He had
packed me off to school as young as he could. My mother had been
unwise enough to protest, and this had earned her a formidable
dressing-down, poor dear. She said no more; simply formed a silent
opposition.
My father had been obsessionally determined that I should get
immediate promotion from one class to the next every term, without
ever staying put longer. There were endless private confabulations
with the masters. 'Please,' he would say 'punish him as often as he
deserves it. Do not be swayed by any regard for my feelings.' (p. 164)

If in the denunciation of the educational system there seems to be an
absence of a sense of proportion, it is due to Jean-Marie's hatred of the
father who has put him through such a rigorous system.

Indeed, the plot and structure of the novel seem neater and more meaningful if we look on it as a demonstration of a young boy's re-action against a tyrannical father. It starts with Jean-Marie return-ing home after failing his examinations, terrified of the father who is sure to react violently to his failure. However, the journey to Kala enables him to postpone the confrontation with his father, and it also presents him with a splendid opportunity to get a close view of a kind of life which his father's tyranny and obsession with success have prevented him from experiencing. And the tyranny is mentioned throughout the novel, not just at the end. It is mentioned, for instance, soon after Jean-Marie's arrival in Kala when he is informed that Zambo keeps a mistress under his father's roof: 'I reflected, gloomily, that if I imported a mistress at home my father would be anything but delighted' (p. 29). Then Jean-Marie observes the cordiality of the relationship between Zambo and his father which contrasts markedly with that between him and his own father, and gives him a glimpse of what the ideal father–son relationship ought to be. At Kala Jean-Marie loses the sexual innocence and immaturity he has hitherto retained largely owing to the influence, not so much of his education, as of his father. Hence the importance of the attempts to get him to go to bed with a girl. They mark a further stage in his development, a further step in his movement away from the rigid morality of his father. This is why his longing for Eliza becomes, as he says, his symbol of absolute liberty. In going to bed with her he would be registering his defiance of his father's scheme of values and he would be making a break for freedom. Comparing the freedom which his contemporaries at Kala enjoy with his own lack of it, he blames it all on an education into which he had been forced by his father. When he is worsted in argument during the extra-mural sessions he begins to see education as a giant ogre swallowing up little boys, but this is largely because of his revulsion at the way in which his father has bulldozed him through the system; the ogre could in fact have been suggested to his subconscious by the figure of his father. He begins to drink in Kala, which he would never have done at home; and when his uncle treats him like a grown man, he compares this to his father's treatment of him as 'a kind of small dog'. When he is duped at the end into marrying Edima his old fear of his father returns: 'He'll tan the hide off me for this . . . He'll do worse than beat me; he'll make my whole future life absolute hell. It's all my bloody elder brother's fault . . . If my elder brother hadn't been such a bonehead, my father would have worked out all his frustrated

ambitions on *him*. As things are, the old boy has to torment me instead'
(p. 154). Jean-Marie makes a very pertinent point here; disappointed
with the elder brother's stupidity and irresponsibility the father was
determined that this second son should be a success, and he therefore
put him through the rigours of the system.

It is clear that when it is proposed that Jean-Marie should marry
Edima, he could simply tell the chief that a mistake had been made and
that he has no intention of marrying; but he chooses quite deliberately
to recognize and treat the girl as his wife and take her home, because he
wants once more to demonstrate his new found independence. He now
knows he has grown up and is far beyond the reach of his parents. Jean-
Marie consents to the marriage, therefore, not so much because of his
stupidity, as because of his new found rebelliousness. He is quite
unconcerned about what his father will say about the marriage and he
decides to return and face him.

The novel has now come back almost to the point where it started. It
started with a boy returning home from school mortally terrified of his
father's reaction to his failure in his examinations; it ends with the
same boy returning home once more after an adventure of which the
father will almost certainly disapprove, but which has taught him
invaluable lessons about life, particularly about traditional life. The
boy has lost his fear as a result of his experiences and returns to
challenge the father: 'At the thought of our impending encounter, my
initial feeling of cold terror was soon replaced by a kind of anticipatory
excitement. I can't really explain this phenomenon. It was rather like a
young toreador going into the ring to meet his first bull . . .' (p. 163).
Then follows the most vitriolic denunciation of his father's influence
and a scathing exposure of the latter's capitalist tricks. The father
emerges as a thoroughly unscrupulous character who has no hesitation
in exploiting relations and enemies alike where his financial interests
are concerned. On the way home Jean-Marie regales himself with
palm-wine, his fear of his father completely gone: 'I was in a great
mood, ready to be as rude as hell at the drop of a hat, and whistling
nonchalantly to establish my reputation as a devil-may-care' (p. 169).
On his father's arrival Jean-Marie behaves like a grown man; the father
ignores him, but he continues to behave 'like a monarch surveying his
kingdom', shouting authoritatively to his younger sister and
determined that if his father attempts to beat him there will be a fight.
And that is precisely what happens.

Jean-Marie returns to Kala a rebel, not so much against an educational system, as against his father's tyranny. Indeed, he goes back to school and passes his exams, but the revolt against his father is complete. Leaving his home he becomes something of a delinquent and a wanderer. This is true to form, as a number of psychologists and social workers will testify. A home like Jean-Marie's is bound to produce juvenile delinquents in the end, and it is not surprising that this is what eventually happens to both Medza boys. But Jean-Marie would probably have gone on living in fear if his eyes had not been opened by other vistas of experience during the Kala adventure.

What then should we make of *Mission to Kala*? Is it that the work started as a denunciation of the French educational system and then changed direction to become an exposure of a tyrannical father? The two concerns are, in fact, interrelated. In order to demonstrate the father's tyranny the educational system must be denounced, first in order to show the rigours to which this father subjects the poor boy in his bid to make him successful, and secondly, and perhaps more important, because this rather westernized father uncritically accepts a defective and alien educational system for his child. The denunciation of an unsuitable system of education is therefore quite in place. If it is taken to extremes it is not because Mongo Beti is against education *per se*, but because the father's tyranny has bred in the young boy a temporary pathological hatred for all educational systems.

King Lazarus

Mongo Beti's third novel, *King Lazarus*, is a sad disappointment after the brilliance of the first two. Thematically, however, it is similar to the earlier novels since it is also concerned with the exposure of the pretentiousness of an alien cultural and imperialist system which shows little respect for the traditional life and dignity of the people. The attack this time is on the follies of both the Roman Catholic Church and the civil administration. *King Lazarus* differs in narrative technique from the other novels in being written in the third-person omniscient form. The change is for the worse. Gone is the brilliant manipulation of the naive narrator in *The Poor Christ of Bomba*; gone too is the brilliant wit and the captivating tone of voice of Jean-Marie Medza in *Mission to Kala*. Instead we have the rather garrulous omniscient narrator.

The novel is about the turbulent consequences of the conversion of the Chief of the Essazam to Christianity. The chief's new way of life clashes strongly with traditional beliefs and practices and disrupts the life of the community. Le Guen, the faceless assistant to Father Drumont in *The Poor Christ of Bomba*, is the representative of Roman Catholicism here. While lacking Father Drumont's intellect and capacity for rigorous self-analysis, he is more obstinate and insensitive than the latter, and is ultimately more disruptive of traditional ways. His simple, naive teaching illustrates the intellectual bankruptcy of the church and its contempt for the intelligence of the people it seeks to win to its fold. In the process of beseeching the chief to adopt a new way of life in keeping with his baptism, he 'threatened Divine Wrath, fanning the flames of eternal hell-fire under his nose, fore-warning him against the countless ways in which the Devil was liable to tempt into sin a soul aspiring towards God' (p. 101).[3] Le Guen completely fails to consider the effects of his advice and decisions on the lives of the people. When he advises the chief to put away all his wives but one, he is apparently unmoved by the fact that such a step cuts right across a tradition which the chief as traditional ruler is supposed to safeguard. Nor is he particularly concerned about the human aspects of the problem – about the fact, for instance, that some of the wives have been married to the chief for years and know no other home, that they are forced to leave without their children who are now deprived of parental love and care, since they are unceremoniously bundled on to 'respectable housewives' around the village with instructions to feed and bring them up. The fact is that Le Guen's ruse to enforce monogamy on the chief completely disrupts the kingdom, setting husband against wife, wife against wife, clan against clan, uncle against nephew, and plunging the tribe into civil war. The misery that his policy precipitates is very touchingly evoked, but he remains insensitive to all this. His zeal might have been partly excused if the conversion to Christianity had made the chief a better man. On the contrary, it seems to liberate the most repulsive impulses in him.

Inevitably, Le Guen comes into confrontation with the civil administration who do not welcome the prospect of an inter-clan warfare. This conflict between the religious and political arm recalls that between Father Drumont and M. Vidal in *The Poor Christ of Bomba*, but in this case it is the man of God who is obstinate while the administrator seems to be the embodiment of sound sense. He reminds the Father that the whole clan is against him and pleads with him to abandon his crazy policy of converting the chief.

You see, Father, we live in troubled times – times in which it is vital
that Africa should remain free of disturbances. Who can tell where
the slightest agitation might lead us? The most important thing for
all of us at the moment, Father – more important than the
conversion of souls to God, more important than anything else – is
surely the continuation of our presence here? Perhaps I should say
the continuation of that peace which we both, in our own way, have
succeeded in establishing among these disinherited people.
Consider their brutish ignorance of good and evil. I'm certain you
realize this, Father. Believe me – and I speak from a very long
experience of colonial administration – one outbreak gives rise to
another. This triggers off a third and so on to the next. What you get
in the end is real subversion, Father. (pp. 180–1)

And yet, as is evident from the passage, Beti is far from endorsing the
patronizing administrator. If he counsels moderation it is not because
of any regard for traditional culture. He merely counsels political
expediency to ensure the continuation of the French presence in
Africa. Beti's irony throughout this scene is a doubled-edged weapon
which simultaneously exposes the insensitivity and obstinacy of Le
Guen as well as the chauvinism of Lequeux. Towards the end
Lequeux is forced to bare his teeth and reveal in the crudest and most
violent kind of language that his entire career has been shaped by his
almost pathological hatred of communists, and Le Guen lets his own
weakness show in the flippant but naive letter he writes his beloved
mother: 'Imagine, Mama, I told him to his face that all his clap-trap
bored me stiff! He would persist in going on about Vietnam – tears and
melodrama turn and turn about. It seems he was born there. He also
tried to make me swear that I would give up my efforts to convert your
Bantu Monarch – your King Lazarus himself!' (p. 184). In the end the
administrator has the last word in contriving Le Guen's transfer to
another post. And the chief, though retaining the name 'Lazarus', soon
rediscovers the joys of polygamy and strict obedience to tribal ethics.

Inevitably the French administration is denounced in the most
scathing terms. The officials demonstrate a certain measure of
efficiency, but it is in the interest of perpetuating a corrupt and unjust
system. For supposedly insulting behaviour to one of his masters the
young schoolboy Chris is deprived of his boarding-rights without
being allowed to defend himself. And we are told that Maurice's
sentence of three months' imprisonment would have been at least ten
years' forced labour if the burglary had been committed on the
premises of a French businessman. Lequeux is a racist, and the other

whites are either egoistic and conceited like him, or silly and affected like Palnier who takes his new bride around wherever he goes and continually kisses her in public.

It must not be supposed, however, that Beti idealizes traditional society in this novel. This is a significant departure from his usual practice of showing tremendous responsiveness to the dignity and beauty of traditional life. *King Lazarus* presents a very unflattering picture of indigenous African society. The historical background with which the novel starts shows that owing to the impact of world forces on the Essazam they have become increasingly decadent. In this they are quite different from the magnificent people of Kala. They have been racked in internal feuds and vendettas; VD, alcoholism and other 'scourges' of modern civilization have made progressive inroads into their society. The chief is callous and pleasure loving; the young men and women are tireless fornicators; the elders are seen as 'pathetic orang-outangs who have reduced public debate to futility'; the diviners and priests are filthy, greedy old men more concerned with their own importance than with the efficient discharge of their duties; the warriors are even stupid in their fighting. Beti spares no pains to make the tribe as a whole look as ridiculous as possible. There is hardly a single character that Beti strives to make attractive; even the beautiful Medzo is an aggressive vixen and coquette, and the pathetic Makrita is an embodiment of ugliness: 'An old crone she was indeed, with scarcely more flesh on her bones than poor Yosifa. She was built like a man, flat-chested with a raddled face in which the eyes smouldered like those of a wounded tigress' (p. 165).

Beti's mood in this novel seems to be one of profound cynicism; it exactly matches that of the young Chris who of all the characters seems most to approximate to the author's viewpoint here. Flippant and irreverent, he arrives at the village ostensibly to protect his aunt who is one of the chief's abandoned wives and proceeds to observe the scene calmly and dispassionately. He can barely conceal his contempt for all the other characters and the people as a whole; and yet Beti seems to accord him almost complete sympathy. This would have been excusable if Chris had been exemplary in all respects, but he seems, in fact, to be a disreputable character who terrifies his mother, threatens to stab his elder brother and spends his time brewing illicit gin to be sold to the villagers whom he despises. It is not exactly clear what the roles of Chris and the other boys Bitama and Gustave are supposed to be, since they do very little to further the story. To identify Beti's point of view in the novel it is not really essential to know Chris's, so it could not be said that this is his role. On arrival at Essazam Chris does very little to achieve his ostensible purpose – the protection of his aunt. The Chris, Bitama, Gustave story has no relevance whatever to the main plot or the theme of the novel, and the inclusion of these boys constitutes a grave structural flaw. Beti probably intended to make more of them, but as the novel progresses seems to have forgotten what he wanted to do with them.

Beti's *forte* in *King Lazarus* is his power of description and ability to bring a scene to life which has by no means deserted him. The account of the onset of the chief's fever is brilliant and the later deathbed scenes are very effectively done. Brilliant too are the series of scenes which, with a maximum of economy, portray the relations between Mama and her children. So are the various battle scenes. Although the rich comedy of *The Poor Christ of Bomba* and *Mission to Kala* is absent here, Beti has still been able to contrive some very funny scenes like that between the hunter, Le Guen and Schloegel in the bush. Quite often, however, the comedy is of a grotesque sort. Indeed, it is evident that Beti demonstrates a predilection in this work for the grotesque; this comes out in both his comic scenes and his descriptions, and is generally in line with his cynical mood. Be that as it may, the description of people's personal appearance shows superb artistry. Particularly memorable is that of Yosifa, the chief's aged aunt.

> Incredibly ancient, with a long scrawny neck in which the veins and arteries stood out like rope, she had skin not so much wrinkled as *threadbare*... she had clearly suffered also from the attentions of men, who had used her till she was an ugly, worn-out crone.
> Her thin, shrivelled lips revealed a fine set of long, narrow teeth... Yellow-stained from chewing tobacco, they chattered continuously – the result of a senile tick in the lower jaw... Her pointed toes, curving inwards like those of a chimpanzee, were equipped with long, sharp nails reminiscent of vulture's claws. (pp. 40–1)

Characterization in *King Lazarus* is by no means as compelling as in the earlier two novels. The main reason for this seems to be that none of the characters' thoughts and actions are presented in such detail that he or she becomes memorable. There are hardly any passages of introspection. Both Le Guen and the chief, the two major characters, have a habit of disappearing from the scene for considerable periods, and in the case of the latter Beti fails to show the process whereby he changes once more from Christianity and monogamy to traditional ways and polygamy. The author's garrulousness is also partly responsible, for instead of allowing us to see and hear the characters wrestling with their dilemmas, he always stands between us and them.

This, then, is a novel marred by a number of flaws. Its prevailing cynicism suggests the bitterness of a man who is probably fed up with most things. It remains to be seen whether it really marks the decline of Mongo Beti.

1 Mongo Beti, *The Poor Christ of Bomba* (Heinemann, London, 1971), p. 3. All further page references are to this edition.

2 Mongo Beti, *Mission to Kala* (Heinemann, London, 1964). All further page references are to this edition. I have used Peter Green's translation, although I realize it is not very good, because it is the only one available in English. For a thorough discussion of Peter Green's translation, see Charles N. Davies, 'Whose mission to Kala? A study of the problems of translation', *Ba Shiru*, vol. 4, no. 2 (Spring 1973), pp. 25–33.

3 Mongo Beti, *King Lazarus* (Heinemann, London, 1970). All further page references are to this edition.

6. Ferdinand Oyono

▼▼▼▼▼▼▼▼▼▼▼▼▼▼▼▼▼▼▼▼▼▼▼▼▼▼▼▼▼▼▼▼▼▼▼▼▼

The Cameroonian novelist Ferdinand Oyono is surely among the most brilliant of Africa's comic writers. His wit is of a special quality; where Beti's humour is boisterous, Oyono's is elegant, but also has a sharp cutting edge. The nature of his art is quite deceptive. The slimness of the volumes published so far and his apparent light-heartedness might blind us to the real depth and earnestness of his work. Underneath the placid, urbane, comic exterior there is real anger and moral concern. He is, in fact, one of Africa's most effective satirists.

The deceptiveness of Oyono's art has given rise to an interesting controversy. In a review of Oyono's first novel, *The Old Man and the Medal*, Jeanette Kamara suggested that Oyono's chief aim in his works is to entertain, and that the details so familiar to the African novel are etched in to provide sufficient background to an essentially funny story.[1] This provoked a rejoinder from Mukotani Rugyendo, who asserted that, on the contrary, Oyono's chief aim has always been to expose the evils of the colonial situation in pre-independence Africa. The social and political preoccupation, rather than the humour, is the main interest.[2] Both views in a sense constitute overstatements of the respective cases. Mrs Kamara certainly overplays the humour, failing to relate it to the novel's moral and social purpose. In the light of Oyono's passionate denunciation of French imperialism it is surely too simple to say that his chief aim is to enterian. On the other hand, Rugyendo, while being powerfully aware of the work's moral and social significance, pays little attention to its technique. To say that the humour, which in *The Old Man and the Medal* is even richer than in *Houseboy*, is merely a sop to lure the reader to read the more unpalatable elements, is surely not quite accurate. Oyono's humour and other aspects of his technique are inseparable from his moral, political and social concern. They are the devices the author uses to make his moral and social points all the more effectively. The comedy fortifies the satire.

Where Beti and Kane are largely concerned with the cultural implications of French imperialism, Oyono is preoccupied with the social and political. His work is almost entirely devoted to a presentation of the ruthlessness of the French administration in those territories over which they had sway. In this sense his preoccupation is similar to Ngugi's, although there are differences in tone, broadly corresponding to the differences in attitude between anglophone and francophone writers. The francophones show a vehemence and stridency of tone which, with the possible exception of Armah, is almost absent from anglophone works. Ngugi's scenes of brutality in *A Grain of Wheat* are possibly more harrowing than Oyono's, and yet he does not reveal the same bitterness that the latter does in *Houseboy*; the vehemence of Beti in *The Poor Christ of Bomba* is to be found neither in Ngugi nor in Achebe. It is almost as though the spirit of defiance which in anglophone countries found expression in strong nationalist movements was channelled, in the francophone countries, to creative writing.

The Old Man and the Medal

Although *The Old Man and the Medal* aims some savage blows at the Roman Catholic Church, the political administration is the main butt of attack. The satire is effected through the presentation of the experiences of the old man Meka, a venerable patriarch of his community. The novel shows the process whereby Meka's eyes are gradually opened to the realities of French oppression in Africa. At the start we are impressed by his great strength and manliness, his pride in himself, his dignity, humility and religious devotion. Yet Oyono also stresses the naivety of his attitude to both church and state in order to highlight his complete disillusionment at the end. When Meka gives his piece of land to the church we are meant to see this not just as a manifestation of religious zeal but also as an index of his simple-mindedness in religious matters. Certainly Oyono's presentation of the scene leaves room for both interpretations.

> He had the special grace to be the owner of a piece of land, which, one fine morning, had proved pleasing to the eye of the Lord. A white priest had revealed his divine destiny to him. How could he go against the will of the Lord-who-giveth? Meka, who in the meanwhile had been reborn in baptism, humbled himself before

the messenger of the almighty. Full of enthusiasm he followed the raising of the house of the Lord on the land of his forefathers. On the eve before the church was inaugurated by the Bishop he was asked to choose his place in the church. Meka chose a bare dusty stretch of cement, covered with flies, reserved for the beggars at the far end of the nave beyond the last row of worshippers . . . For the Christians of Doum, Meka was the great favourite in the Paradise stakes, one of those rare mortals who would have no more than a mere appearance to put in at purgatory.[3]

The cutting sarcasm of the first and last sentences reveals Oyono's characteristic wit and suggests his laughter at Meka's expense. The irony is indeed double-edged, for it is both Meka's naivety and the church's deceit that are being exposed. Meka is surely simple-minded in his acceptance of the white man's values – the white man's religion, the white man's government and the inferior role to which the white man has relegated him. Even his own countrymen see his gift of his ancestral land to the church as an act of folly. When, on the decision to present him with a medal in recognition of his 'services' to church and state, the commandant says to Meka, 'You have done much to forward the work of France in this country . . . You are a friend,' many African nationalists would interpret this as an indictment rather than a commendation. The reader easily recognizes the hypocrisy and condescension in the commandant's words and the back-handed compliment in the loaded phrase – 'the work of France in this country', but these are lost on Meka who glories in the fact that he is to be regarded as the friend of the white man from now on. The point is also lost on Meka's neighbours and relations who completely misunderstand the political and cultural implications of the presentation of the medal. They feel that Meka is to become not only a friend of the white man, but a white man himself; his wife will be a white woman and they will all be privileged people.

'. . . Now that her husband is going to have a medal, she will become a white woman.'
    'Labour levies and all other nuisances, they are all over for him,' said Engamba thoughtfully. 'He has certainly been lucky.' 'And you here,' put in Mbogsi, 'if anything happens to you, all you'll have to do is to tell the commandant that you are the brother-in-law of the man the white Chief came to give a medal to.'
    'Yes, that's true,' said the stranger. 'Your family, your friends, and your friends' friends from now on will be privileged people. All they will have to say is "I am the friend of a friend of Meka's

brother-in-law", and all doors will be open to them. Even I myself feel a little touch of the medal's been given to me...' (pp. 34-5)

The splendid comedy does not obscure the very serious points being made. A passage like this takes on grimly ironic significance in the light of the novel's conclusion when Meka himself is brutally treated by the administration even while protesting that he is the man to whom a medal has just been given.

The cultural aspect of the situation emerges when Meka decides to have a western-style jacket made for the presentation. He looks quite ridiculous in the ill-fitting jacket, as the realistic Kelara points out: 'You're swimming in it like a little fish in the sea ... the jacket and you, it's like a dog listening to a gramophone' (p. 74). Moreover, Meka, whose feet have not been made to go into the white man's shoes, decides to have a pair for the first time in his life. The reader watches with mingled delight and pity the gruelling attempt to squeeze Meka's feet into the shoes and to get him to try to walk. Meka is really like a little child taking his first uneasy steps in a strange cultural milieu. Both the jacket and the shoes acquire a symbolic significance, suggesting the unnatural and fruitless attempts by Meka's friends and relations to force him into the white man's mould.

It is this sense of cultural disorientation that possesses Meka as he stands in the circle outside the headquarters at Doum waiting for the arrival of the chief of the whites who is to pin the medal on him. This is the beginning of Meka's realization of the absurdity of his and his countrymen's situation. He is isolated in the circle, appropriately placed between his own people who have now convinced themselves that Meka is as good as a white man, and the whites who are far from accepting him as such: literally a man caught between two worlds. But Meka is also powerfully aware of the realities of the political and racial situation. While the young administrators wear pith-helmets and wait for the chief of the whites in comfortable shelters, he, the black subject, is left standing bare-headed in the sun, his head baking like a lizard. Meka, who had earlier been extremely proud as the recipient of the white man's medal, now feels like a man constricted, a man who cannot be his real self and who even has to repress his urges. It is his adherence to the old old-fashioned concept of manliness that sustains him through this increasingly ridiculous ceremony. He must go through with it in spite of his disillusionment and discomfort because he is a real man who will not disgrace his race and his ancestry: 'A man, a real

man, never cries.' Soon, however, Meka feels an urge to urinate and a
brilliantly comic scene ensues.

> 'Almighty God,' he prayed to himself. 'Thou seest all that passeth in
> the hearts of men, thou seest that my dearest wish at this moment as
> I wait for the medal and for the White Chief, alone in this circle,
> between two worlds, O God, which thou has made utterly different
> from each other, that my dear wish and great longing is to take off
> these shoes and to have a piss...Yes, a piss...I am only a poor
> sinner and not worthy that thou shouldest hear me...but I beseech
> thee to aid me in this position which I have never been in before in all
> my life. In the name of Jesus Christ our Lord. So be it. I make the
> sign of the cross inwardly.' (pp. 88–9)

The prayer is a comment on both Meka's religious naivety and the
brand of religion that has been instilled into him. He has not yet seen
through the church's hypocrisy even though he has begun to realize the
insincerity of the elaborate political and civil ritual that is about to be
played around him. Meka's simple desire for a piss deflates the
pompousness of the ritual and exposes its pretentiousness and
insincerity.

As the heat intensifies and those alarming symptoms in his belly
become more pronounced, while the insensitive white officials delay
the moment of presentation, Meka's awareness of white duplicity,
hypocrisy and lack of consideration is heightened. Patent also is the
careful discrimination made between the treatment of Meka the black
man and Pipiniakis the Greek capitalist, who is also to receive a medal.
While Meka is left to cut a ridiculous figure outside, Pipiniakis waits
for the chief with the other whites in the cosy comfort of the
commandant's office. Pipiniakis's medal is different from Meka's, and
he gets it with the additional bonus of a kiss from the chief, while Meka
receives only a polite handshake. But in one of those significant little
touches which quite often go unnoticed in Oyono, Meka's hand
'swallowed up the hand of the Chief like a damp cotton rag'. Thus the
manliness and power of underestimated traditional society is
emphasized.

The shifting of the focus from Meka to his wife Kelara who is
watching the proceedings from among the African crowd brings out
the unfairness and insincerity of this elaborate charade all the more
powerfully. Kelara initially shared her husband's enthusiasm and
pride at the prospect of the presentation, but she is now plunged into a
disillusionment and despondency even greater than her husband's by a

young man's most perceptive comments: 'I think they ought to have
covered him in medals ... To think he has lost his land and his sons just
for that ...' (p. 94). The young man's comments indicate, not just that
the whites have failed to acknowledge the full extent of Meka's and
Kelara's sacrifice (a medal is after all a symbolic thing, even though
Meka's is in all probability inferior to Pipiniakis's), but also the
injustice of the white administration in taking away Meka's land and
sending off his sons, who should have been the mainstay of his old age,
to fight and die in a war not of their own making. Kelara's present
reaction now underlines this. She is revolted by her husband who
seems to be fraternizing with the very white men who have caused the
death of his two sons, and grinning with pride as the medal is pinned
on him. She cannot recognize her husband in the man over there and
she withdraws, weeping all the way home.

Meka's own utter disillusionment is soon to come. The whites'
behaviour soon indicates to him beyond the shadow of any doubt that
the award of a medal should not be taken as signifying an intention to
include him in their ranks. They make a circle round their chief and
exclude Meka. They are generally snobbish and condescending, and in
Father Vandermayer's case rude and contemptuous. They ignore
Meka on the way to the reception, making no provision for his
transportation; and although Father Vandermayer, in an attempt to
atone for his rudeness, offers him a lift in his van, he puts him in the
back, though he has no one with him in the cabin. The reception scene
itself is one of the most brilliantly executed in the novel. Once more the
scintillating comedy does not obscure the moral points. The entire
scene brings out Meka's spirit of manly independence and
determination to be himself. Utterly contemptuous of the formal
western habit of sipping meaningless toasts out of slim champagne
glasses, which he attributes to a weak western fear of alcohol, he drinks
his in one go without waiting for the formal toasts, and asks for another
helping. The scene thus emphasizes the cultural clash. The blacks,
inspired by Meka's courageous leadership, begin to behave spontaneously, thus deflating the formal pompousness of the reception.
Then Meka, ignoring M. Fouconi's threatening gestures, moves to
the dais and delivers an address in which he invites the chief of
the whites to a feast at his home. It is a very sincere invitation which,
among other things, is intended to test the genuineness of the
friendship between Africans and Frenchmen that the high commissioner had spoken about in such glowing terms. But it is politely

declined. However, Meka rises even further in the estimation of his fellow-Africans because he has been courageous enough to express sentiments that they all feel.

The liberating effect of the alcohol enables the Africans to give expression to their hitherto bottled-up impressions and thoughts about their imperialist oppressors. Released from their inhibitions and with their eyes now fully opened to the reality of things, they lash out at the white men, denouncing their basic unfriendliness, insincerity and oppression. They also lash out at the wretched interpreter who, having been brainwashed into accepting the white man's superiority, takes it upon himself to unbraid his countrymen for what he thinks is the unseemliness of their behaviour. The interpreter has not learned the lesson of the last few moments, which is, that these men, far from degrading themselves, are rediscovering their dignity and independence. He is justifiably pounced upon by the Africans, and forced to apologize and take to his heels for safety.

The whites soon show their own claws, demonstrating the truth of the Africans' allegations, when Gullet the police chief intervenes, brutally breaking up the party. Meka, who has fallen asleep in the meantime, is inadvertently left behind. He wakes up later in the midst of a terrible storm, blunders eventually into the location and is confronted by an African policeman who has been brainwashed by the white administration into behaving to his countrymen with the utmost brutality. He arrests Meka on a charge of loitering with the intent of stealing from the whites in the area. Meka's weak protestations of innocence and his claims to being an elder and a friend of the governor merely elicit the most shocking display of ruthlessness and obscenity, and a complete disregard for the traditional respect usually accorded to age. The facade of friendship between white and black involving receptions and presentation of medals is now completely shattered to reveal the horrifying realities of life under French colonial oppressors. Meka's appeal to his Christianity is powerless to save him.

> 'I am a Christian, officer! The mouth that receives the saviour is forbidden to lie ... officer.'
> 'Your mouth will receive some cat shit if you're not careful, you old tortoise ... Come on, on your way.' (p. 123)

So too is his pathetic appeal to his grey hairs:

> 'My son,' said Meka, gasping for breath, 'you are young enough to be my son, officer,' he entreated. 'Why do you want to shed blood

as old as your own Father's? O officer, why do you want to bring
down a curse on you and yours ... O officer! Do my words run off
you like water off a duck's back?'
    'Shut up,' roared the constable, shaking him like a mango tree.
(p. 124)

Meka is unceremoniously thrust into a cell where he has leisure to
contemplate the degradation and helplessness of the African situation:
'My God! ... The shame of it, the shame ... Poor us.' The sense of
shame reminds him that he hails from illustrious ancestry – that he is
the descendant of the great Mekas, 'The-stock-unshakable-beneath-
the-storm', 'the River-without-fear-of-the-forest', the 'Pythons',
'Rocks', 'Cotton-trees', 'Elephants', 'Lions', the son of 'Men who had
never bowed to another man's strength'. This sense of his manly
ancestry first produces contempt for the constables and a resolution to
be generous to them in the morning when they would have discovered
their grave error. But the realization that humility and innocence are of
no avail in a world with scant regard for virtue and honesty helps him
to summon his enormous reserves of courage and strength, and to hurl
magnificent defiance and invective at the officers. When he is ordered
in the morning to see Gullet, he demonstrates his great strength, to the
consternation of the constables.

> Meka felt himself shaking from head to foot. As in a dream he seized
> the constable's arm, yes, in the same way he would grasp the head of
> a porcupine he found half dead in one of his traps ... He felt his
> fingers sinking into the man's soft flesh like the flesh of a ripe
> avocado pear. The constable leapt back with the pain and
> shook himself free. Meka made the very most of his victory. He put on a
> terrible look though in his heart he would have been happy enough
> to leave things where they stood – and anyway this great lout could
> easily have the best of it. Nevertheless, he placed one knee on the
> ground and challenged the huge constable to wrestle with him.
> (p. 133)

The remarkable prose and the effective images powerfully evoke
Meka's great strength and determination. Here, as elsewhere in this
novel, traditional strength and virility are contrasted with the effete
softness associated with the white administration which has to enforce
its will, not by inherent strength, but by torture and the gun.
Inevitably Meka is overpowered by the officers and taken into the
presence of Gullet who brutally lashes at him with his riding crop and
spits into his face. It is at this point more than at any other that we

realize that this novel is intended to do much more than merely
entertain. The writer who exposes Gullet's brutality and inhumanity
with such passion is most definitely committed to the African struggle
although he displays his commitment by demonstration rather than by
polemics or assertion.

Throughout these scenes, however, Meka never loses his dignity.
On his release his thoughts return to the past and to the values of
traditional society, as he walks home. He thinks of the good old days
before the white man conquered the country, of the skull of the first
white man – a German – which his grandfather, the great Chief of the
Mvemas, gave him on the day he killed his first panther. But he threw
the skull into the river the day he was baptized. Now with a flash of
insight Meka realizes that the day he was baptized was the day he
became a slave. His eyes are thus fully opened not just to the
oppression of the political and civil authorities but to the hypocrisy of
the Christian Church. This is why, as he walks home, the traditional
beliefs which he has hitherto been taught to regard as superstition
replace Christian belief. For instance, when a bird's droppings fall on
his head he rubs in the 'heavenly manure' which is supposed to be a
sign of good luck. As Oyono comments: 'All these superstitions had
sprung up again in his mind like a great tide sweeping away the years of
Christian teaching and practice.'

Back in his village amongst his traditional trappings Meka feels
refreshed and invigorated. His new antagonism to Christianity gets
powerful expression in a vehement outburst against Mvondo.

> 'You shut your mouth, shut your rotten mouth,' roared Meka,
> raising himself onto his elbow. 'Look at me,' he went on, 'all of you.
> You aren't men at all except that you've got a pair of balls ... The
> whites have just been taking it out of me and killing me, and what do
> you do?' Turning to Mvondo. 'You start talking about the Lord.
> Since you started sprinkling yourself with holy water your wrinkles
> haven't disappeared! And he comes talking to me about the Lord . . .'
> (p. 147)

And at the end the entire chorus of relations and neighbours join in the
denunciation of the white man and his values: their mood is one of
resignation to the hopelessness of their cause.

To say that *The Old Man and the Medal* is a light-hearted panorama
would be like saying that *Gulliver's Travels* is light-hearted. Both are
gloriously comic works, but it is not so much that the tragedy does not
obscure the charm and gaiety as that the gaiety does not obscure their

essential seriousness. Underneath the superficial light-heartedness there is real anger and the most determined commitment to the exposure of man's inhumanity to man. The gaiety is, in fact, partly created by the people's tremendous sense of fun and zest for life. In the midst of their sufferings they can find time to laugh. Towards the end of the novel, for instance, as everyone discusses Meka's terrible experiences, Essomba comes out with a side-splitting joke.

> 'Well, Meka should have shown them what they could do with the medal they were going to give him – by turning up – with nothing on ... except a *bila*! ... I-I-say, he should wear a *bila* ... because if he did ... the Chief of the whites ... have to bend down and pin the medal on— on— his *bila*!' (pp. 165–6)

The tension is relieved; the sense of fun makes the people's position tolerable, but their antagonism to the whites is not lost sight of. In fact, the joke amounts to an assertion of cultural autonomy and a refusal to be reconciled to the white man's values.

Generally, the picture Oyono presents of traditional society and the indigenous people is even more attractive than Beti's in *Mission to Kala*. There is an unmistakable sense of fellow-feeling among the people. When it is announced that Meka is to receive a medal, neighbours and relations, distant as well as near, share spontaneously in the joy. There is not the slightest suggestion of envy. Oyono also uses dialogue effectively to create the sense of a chorus of neighbours who sympathize with Meka in time of trouble, rejoice with him in time of joy, and offer advice. We do get the impression of a solid, cohesive and neighbourly society which is, in so many ways, superior to the imperialist tormentors.

Although the church is not the main butt of attack in this novel, Oyono's elegant irony and sarcasm expose its hypocrisy and naivety. It is seen as a mere tool of the administration, supporting and operating the latter's policies in the most simple-minded ways. In a bid to force the people to buy expensive French drinks Father Vandermayer has no scruples in denouncing the native drink *arki* with the most repulsive lies. The church's falsehood here is on a par with the deception practised on Meka in order to persuade him to donate his land to the church. Oyono also stresses the disruption that the church causes in the traditional order. Its blatant disregard for and ignorance of local custom and tradition leads to misery, as in *The Poor Christ of Bomba*. The dangers of a simple-minded adherence to Christian teaching are exemplified in the fanatical Ignatius who is a figure of fun. But the church's moral bankruptcy is most glaringly exposed in Father Vandermayer. The scene in which he reveals himself in his true colours to Meka during the reception is one of the most meaningful in the novel.

The richness of Oyono's comedy should be apparent. But we must be aware of the distinctive quality of his humour. Where the more boisterous Beti, for instance, achieves the bellyful of laughter, Oyono is more urbane, more restrained and yet more cutting. He depends for his effects, not on farce or slapstick, but on irony, sarcasm and the particularly witty turn of phrase. The special quality can be seen in that excellent statement: 'He had the special grace to be the owner of a piece of land, which, one fine morning, had proved pleasing to the eye of the Lord.' He can create scintillating comedy of character while apparently keeping a straight face.

> Mbogsi put the old overcoat on every morning to go to chapel. He had only worn the pith-helmet once. That was when he went to propose to the Lady who was President of the Association of Saint Anne in the village, an old tape-worm with a head like a bat's. After twenty years squatting on his heels in front of Engamba to share his meals Mbogsi decided to get married so he wouldn't have to keep on confessing to the priest before all the major feasts his everlasting sin of 'impure thoughts'. The ancient President of the Association of Saint Anne who already had swellings from old age behind her ears and on the back of her neck and had lost all her inscisors refused him and Mbogsi found comfort in the sterile commentaries of the Simplified Bible which he carried everywhere he went. (p. 28)

Very occasionally the comedy descends to the level of the grotesque: 'He was taken to be a young administrator until the day when his first boy ran off with his false teeth. His nose stuck out sturdily from the middle of his bloated face which the sun had turned as red as the bottom of a chimpanzee' (p. 46). Quite often, of course, the comedy becomes vicious as when a sow reminds Meka of the profile of the chief of the whites: 'I see now ... Why didn't I think of it before? It's the profile of the Chief of the whites ... No one can deny the same workman made the Chief of the whites and this pig' (pp. 143–4).

The sense of realism and solidity created in Oyono's novels is partly due to his impressive use of detail: most things – gestures, actions, characters or scenes – are described minutely, demonstrating that Oyono can really keep his eye on the object under observation. Here is an example of the technique applied to people.

Evina had been cook to the priests and had retired to Doum after he had lost his last tooth in the service of the white man. His mouth had sunk in, dropping his chin down on to his neck and making his nose stand out. His nostrils were so wide that you could see the whitish stagnating snot. His wife had left him. He was no good to her – with his bent back and hands that shook like a leaf in the wind. (p. 18)

As can be seen from the above passage, it is also partly the detailed description which helps fortify the comedy. Here is an example of the technique applied to actions.

The stranger stroked his lower lip and nodded his approval to Mbogsi. He pulled out an old camphor bottle. He uncorked it and took a pinch of chestnut-coloured powder and pushed it as far as he could up his nostrils which were as black and hairy as a gorilla hide. His eyes filled with tears but with a sharp toss of his head he forced them back and offered the open bottle to Mbogsi. He rubbed the end of his nose with the back of his free hand. When Mbogsi had helped himself he passed the bottle on to his neighbour who passed it on to the next man. (pp. 30–1)

The processes of people's thought, particularly Meka's, are also documented in detail. There are several occasions too when Oyono seems to be reporting events in his own person, but is, in actual fact, merely recounting minutely what goes on in Meka's mind, looking at the events very closely with Meka's eyes. Oyono's ear for the detailed statements of his characters also accounts for the novel's impressive dialogue, and the detailed observation of almost every aspect of a scene is largely responsible for the many powerfully realized scenes.

The attention to detail is also undoubtedly responsible for the brilliant characterization. The peculiarities of each character, whether they relate to action or appearance, are given in detail. Their personal histories are also sketched in, and they are shown in action making use of detailed dialogue. The result is that even the more minor characters are fully presented: there is the conceited, incompetent, vulgar and pretentious tailor, the generous, neighbourly, faithful and efficient Amalia, her greedy husband Engamba, and the determined, tough-minded, bossy and blunt Kelara. Even Agatha, who makes only a brief appearance, emerges as quiet, submissive, helpful and friendly.

The excellent translation by John Reed effectively captures the lucidity and urbanity of the author's elegant prose. Oyono is outstanding among francophone writers for manipulating the foreign language in which he is obliged to write to suit his own purpose.

Proverbs and images, taken largely from traditional life, abound, as in: 'If the ghosts mutter it will rain in the night', and 'It is a long time before the pot where the goat is cooked loses the smell'. The novel is richly infused with expressions reflecting indigenous speech, such as: 'Give up your place to a man of years' and 'O man that passes . . . May your morning be good . . . O man who is a friend, may yours also be good.'

In *The Old Man and the Medal* Oyono has not tried to be as ambitious as other African writers. The very simple plot and structure, with the novel merely moving from village to city and back to village again, underlines this. He concentrates instead on a few selected scenes. But within the modest limits he has set himself he has been eminently successful. The area of focus may be limited, but the gaze is penetrating and sharp, giving rise to powerful insights and a most competent artistry.

Houseboy

Houseboy is even more impressive than *The Old Man and the Medal*, though it exudes less of the characteristic Oyono humour. The remarkable dexterity with which the author has used the mind of a growing boy as the reflector of the evils of the French administration compels admiration. The novel is told in the first person in the form of a diary by Toundi the hero, thus enabling Oyono to achieve a measure of detachment. But the triumph of the method is the brilliant penetration into the growing boy's mind and the fascination with which we watch his development as his eyes are gradually opened, like Meka's, to the realities of French imperialism. The boy's eventual suffering at the hands of his superiors exposes the brutalities practised by the French imperialists, and as in *The Old Man and the Medal* the deceptively placid surface and the matter-of-fact tone of the diaries mask real anger and bitterness. *Houseboy* emerges as possibly the most passionate denunciation of French colonial rule in African creative writing.

The young Toundi's naivety is patent in the opening pages of the book as, in a penetrating display of a young boy's mentality, Oyono makes him say: 'My ancestors were cannibals.' The tone suggests that, whether the statement is true or not, Toundi is applying the standards of the imperialists to an evaluation of his people. The style is deliberately simplified to reflect the outpourings of a very naive young boy's mind.

> My name is Toundi Ondoua. I am the son of Toundi and of Zama. When the Father baptised me he gave me the name of Joseph. I am Maka by my mother and Ndjem by my father. My ancestors were cannibals. Since the white men came we have learnt other men must not be looked upon as animals.[4]

The irony at this stage reveals a simple-mindness in the boy which is as startling as Dennis's in *The Poor Christ of Bomba*. The irony is double-edged since Toundi will eventually be treated like an animal (kicked about like a little dog *inter alia*) by the very whites who pretend to preach about universal brotherhood. We are made aware of the boy's naive attraction to the white man and his values, an attraction which is closely linked to his greed: 'In fact I just wanted to get close to the white man with hair like the beard on a maize cob who dressed in women's clothes and gave little black boys lumps of sugar' (p. 12). There is satire here, directed not just at the boy's naivety, but also at the white man's effeteness and the spiritual bankruptcy of the Roman Catholic Church whose priest attracts boys to Christianity by throwing them lumps of sugar. The scramble for the sugar leads to Toundi's estrangement from his father, but not before the latter has made what turns out to be a prophetic statement about the possible consequences of his greed.

Thus, in a highly significant scene, Toundi is induced to turn his back on traditional life and on all of his ancestors, and to run away to the mission on the eve of his initiation, 'when I should have met the famous serpent who watches over all the men of my race'. In this he is abetted by Father Gilbert who not only encourages the boy to be disrespectful to his father, but humiliates the latter in the boy's presence, an incident which, we are informed, causes the father's death. Once in the shelter of the mission Toundi wrong-headly assumes that he is now going to be like a white man; but in spite of his naive admiration of Father Gilbert the latter merely treats him like a pet animal, showing him off to his friends, the other whites, as 'his masterpiece'. In fact, the Father exploits him, for in addition to serving mass he does all the housework for no reward except that 'now and then he gives me an old shirt or an old pair of trousers'.

Gradually, however, the growing boy's eyes begin to be opened to the reality of things. He is quick to observe that the behaviour of

Father Vandermayer, who makes another appearance in this novel and is generally much worse than his superior Father Gilbert, is at least odd; and he unwittingly brings out his arrogance and cupidity. At this stage, however, the boy merely remarks oddities of behaviour without grasping their full significance. For instance, he notes that Father Vandermayer, delirious with malaria, shouts obscenities all night, without bringing out the implications of this for a priest. On Father Gilbert's death, however, Toundi has progressed so far as to see the significance of people's conduct. He sees through the pretence of those who come to mourn the Father.

> Everybody who wanted to show how attached he had been to the dead Father was there. Workers forcing out their tears. You could see from their contorted faces the difficulty they were having to make their eyes wet. Stupid-looking catechists uncertainly stroking their rosaries, starry-eyed catechumens hoping that perhaps they would be lucky enough to be present at a miracle. (pp. 21–2)

The reader also observes the obvious change in the prose style as the boy grows older and gains in perception. In fact, the death of Father Gilbert marks a turning point in Toundi's fortunes, for the unsympathetic Father Vandermayer promptly hands him over to the commandant as a houseboy. It is another sign of the boy's growing perception that he realizes that his life from now on will not be as comfortable as it has been in the past. But he accepts the new situation with resignation. 'I shall be the Chief European's boy. The dog of the king is the king of dogs.'

Toundi is initiated into his new master's household by an act of wanton brutality on the part of the burly commandant whom he ironically describes as 'the kind of man we call "mahogany-trunk" because the trunk of the mahogany tree is so strong that it never bends in a storm'. We shall soon see this 'mahogany trunk' bending in a storm, but for the time being he is master and Toundi is 'the thing that obeys'. We now begin to see the full implications of Toundi's description of himself as the dog of the king; for the commandant literally kicks him like a dog, and continues to exploit him.

Toundi's discovery that the commandant is uncircumcised marks a very important milestone in his development. His attitude towards his master now changes completely. Though partially exposed to a Christian education, Toundi has not so completely lost touch with his traditional culture as to have scant regard for the traditional concept of manliness which is supposed to be one of the consequences of circumcision. He completely loses his fear of the commandant who now appears to him both literally and figuratively in all his nakedness. The discovery emboldens the nearly mature Toundi, making him both more stoical and more impertinent. When he discovers the commandant swallowing two raw eggs he asks him sarcastically whether he would like raw eggs at lunchtime. 'My coolness surprised him. I took my time over whatever he told me to do. He shouted at me as he always did but I did not move. His eyes had once struck panic into me. Now I stood unconcerned under their gaze' (p. 33).

Though developing rapidly, Toundi has not yet completely lost his naivety or fear of the consequences of annoying the white man in general. For instance, while on tour, the engineer's threat effectively prevents him from touching the latter's lovely mistress, Sophie, who has to spend the night alone with Toundi in a hut. On the arrival of the commandant's wife he goes into raptures over the latter's beauty and bursts into lyrical song when she shakes his hand.

> My happiness has neither day or night. I didn't know about it, it just burst upon my whole being. I will sing to my flute, I will sing on the banks of rivers, but no words can express my happiness. I have held the hand of my queen. I felt that I was really alive. From now on my hand is sacred and must not know the lower regions of my body. My hand belongs to my queen whose hair is the colour of ebony, with eyes that are like the antelope's, whose skin is pink and white as ivory. (pp. 55–6)

The skill with which Oyono manipulates the language in order to make his points about Toundi is truly admirable. The passage's irony becomes starkly obvious in the light of the idolized mistress's eventual brutal treatment of Toundi; furthermore, the purity he associates with Madame here sharply contrasts with her filthy conduct in the affair with M. Moreau.

Though much more perceptive now than he was earlier, Toundi is so bedazzled by Madame's glitter that he fails to see the affectation and insincerity of all her actions. His admiration for his mistress blinds him once more to the reality of things, just as his admiration for Father Gilbert and the other whites did earlier. Some of the most significant gestures and statements of the whites fail to register now; once more, he merely reports them. But his eyes gradually begin to be opened to his mistress's real nature. His discovery of her lustful glances at the engineer marks as decisive a turning-point in the boy's development and his relations with Madame as the earlier discovery that the

commandant was uncircumcised. Toundi now really begins to
understand the meaning of Madame's gestures and expressions. He
sees that she is secretly attracted to black sexuality; in later
conversations he realizes that she is actually trying to make advances;
but the now-mature Toundi carefully steers her to more harmless
topics.

When Madame's flirtation with M. Moreau starts, Toundi is an
innocent no longer: 'I wonder why he didn't come with the others to
welcome Madame. Has the lion waited till the shepherd has gone before
coming to devour his ewe?' (p. 71). Her use of Toundi as a go-between
in the scandalous affair with M. Moreau is the beginning of the boy's
corruption, a corruption which will take horrifyingly physical form
later when he lies on his deathbed, a bundle of rotten flesh. But there is
now no doubt of his maturity and worldly wisdom, or of his profound
sympathy for his master who he feels is being abused. With his keen
eye for detail he now correctly interprets the various signs dropped by
Madame and her lover, and the language now assumes a new elegance
to match the mature Toundi's sophisticated comments on this affair.

> These Europeans certainly take chances when their emotions are
> involved. I hardly expected M. Moreau to come to the residence
> now the whole of Dangan knows about him. But the Commandant is
> too convinced of his own importance to suspect his wife. (p. 82)

Another incident now occurs which marks a further turning-point
in the relations between Toundi and his mistress. When, on his return
from tour, the commandant attempts to kiss his unfaithful wife, the
latter's and Toundi's eyes meet once more, this time over the
commandant's shoulder. Madame is now sure that Toundi fully
understands the implications of this and several other scenes, that he
has seen through to her infidelity, deception and insincerity and, what
is more, that his eyes are judging her. From this moment her attitude
towards the houseboy becomes conspicuously hostile.

Toundi's moral sense remains strong. He disapproves of what he is
being used for although he cannot help it. He is powerfully aware of
the injustice and cruelty of the whites and the hypocrisy of the church.
On one of his errands to the prison director he finds M. Moreau
mercilessly beating two Africans suspected of stealing from the Greek
M. Janopoulos.

> M. Moreau is right, we must have hard heads. When Ndjangoula
> brought down his rifle butt the first time, I thought their skulls

would shatter. I could not hold myself from shaking as I watched. It was terrible. I thought of all the priests, all the pastors, all the men, who come to save our souls and preach love of our neighbours. Is the white man's neighbour only other white men? Who can go on believing the stuff we are served up in churches when things happen like I saw today...

It will be the usual thing. M. Moreau's suspects will be sent to the 'Blackman's Grave' where they will spend a few days painfully dying. Then they will be buried naked in the prisoners' cemetery. On Sunday, the priest will say, 'Dearly beloved brethren, pray for all those prisoners who die without making their peace with God'. M. Moreau will present his upturned topee to the faithful. Everyone will put in a little more than he had intended. All the money goes to the whites. (p. 87)

Who would have dreamed that the Toundi who was such a fervent admirer of Father Gilbert would have said this? Indeed, the scene represents a brilliant piece of structuring for it obviously looks forward to the end and prefigures the fate that awaits Toundi himself. Toundi's fate is assuredly sealed, not just because he knows about the affair, but because he is imprudent enough to let Madame realize that he feels morally superior. From now on he begins to behave rather superciliously towards his mistress. He is overreaching himself, making it too obvious that she is, in a sense, in his power. His crime is not so much that he has seen the whites in all their nakedness, as that he is openly scornful of what he sees; he has to be destroyed because he is setting himself up as a judge of that nakedness. The cook is quick to warn him of his danger: 'You're going to be in trouble, talking to Madame all the time with a smile at the corner of your mouth ... didn't you hear how she said, "Thank you, Monsieur Toundi"? It's a bad sign when a white starts being polite to a native' (p. 90). Now that Madame realizes that Toundi is deliberately adopting a tone of moral superiority, her attitude is not just one of hostility but of icy politeness: 'He's Mon-sieur Tound-i (stressing every syllable) ... he rather fancies himself. He has ideas about his own importance. Just lately he has been taking liberties. But he knows now how far he can go.' The brilliant contraceptive episode exposes the viciousness of which Madame is capable.

Although he has developed quite significantly, Toundi does not seem to be sufficiently experienced to realize that having discovered the secrets of the whites he must behave with greater circumspection than ever, and that the whites will never allow someone who has discovered their nakedness to give the impression that he will publish it to the world, still less allow him to adopt a tone of moral superiority. One of the novel's puzzles is why Toundi chooses to stay, even though he must be aware of the storm clouds gathering around him. Kalisia, the new chambermaid, warns him of his danger in even clearer terms than the cook and urges him to leave: 'If I were in your place . . . I'd go now before the river has swallowed me up altogether . . . As far as they are concerned you are the one who has told everybody and they can't help feeling you are sitting in judgement on them. But that they can never accept' (pp. 115–16). But Toundi stays on, even after the commandant openly accuses him of having been the go-between. Far from thinking of leaving he begins to display a certain cocksureness, indicating that the feeling of moral superiority is still there. Even when the commandant and his wife make up their differences and both turn against him, he still continues to display the same superciliousness instead of thinking of departure. Is Toundi's general behaviour meant to indicate a resolute mood of defiance, a refusal to cringe to this morally inferior white man? Or does it suggest a mistaken conviction that his master and mistress, knowing that they are in his power, would not dare move against him? Oyono does not really make it very clear.

Toundi is eventually arrested on the pretext that he is the accomplice of Sophie, who has absconded with the agricultural engineer's money. One would have expected him to try to prove his innocence, as he could quite easily have done, but he makes no real attempt at this. Is this a flaw in the novel, or is it due to a realization by both Toundi and his creator that defence would be useless? Or must we trace it again to that resolute spirit of defiance? However, we admire Toundi's courage as he heroically tries not to give in under torture. But the cruelty proves too much for him; his body lets him down and he breaks down and cries. Toundi's pathetic story is that of an innocent boy seduced from a traditional environment which would have given meaning to his life, corrupted and then destroyed by the brutal imperialist oppressor.

The church is even more savagely denounced in this novel than in *The Old Man and the Medal*. It is seen here, as in that novel, as a hypocritical agent aiding and abetting the imperialist oppressors. It helps to promote Toundi's corruption by first seducing him from his traditional environment and then handing him over to the mercies of the political administration. Father Gilbert's condescension and evangelizing activities cause friction in the neighbourhood, and his

latent violence is seen writ large in the repulsive person of Father
Vandermayer, who appears in an even worse light here than he does in
The Old Man and the Medal; for here we see his arrogance, high-
handedness and capacity for violence. He loves to beat the Christians
who have committed adultery, making them undress in his office and
asking them in his bad Ndjem: 'When you were kissing, weren't you
ashamed before God?' Where black men are concerned Father
Vandermayer is prepared to debase the sacred ritual of confession
because of his predisposition to degrade the African. In the process he
degrades himself and becomes a voyeur and sexual invert.

The absurdities of the religious scene are revealed through the
penetrating eyes of the growing boy. This is how he sees the ceremony
of Holy Communion.

> All the faithful come up to the altar with their eyes shut, and their
> mouths open and their tongues stuck out as if they were pulling a
> face. The Europeans receive Communion separately. They haven't
> got nice teeth. (p. 17)

The passage also highlights the discrimination that is practised in this
church, where the Africans sit on trunks in the nave while the
Europeans are comfortably seated in the transept on cane armchairs
covered with velvet cushions. Yet in spite of the church's discrimination and degradation of the African, we notice the statue of
St Peter, 'who had been so blackened by the weather that he could pass
for an African'. In his description of the church scenes Toundi's irony
is cutting and his observation sharp. The unusually calm tone in which
his statements are made conceals real bitterness and the most
penetrating insight into the foibles of these people. There is the
brilliant satire created by the presentation of the activities of the whites
during Communion while the catechists are busy pouncing on the
blacks for the least sign of inattention.

> Mme Salvain was sitting next to the Commandant. In the row
> behind, Gullet and the agricultural engineer leant over as in a single
> movement toward the two fat girls. Behind them the Doctor now
> and then pushed up the gold braid that hung down from his
> overlarge epaulettes. His wife, pretending to be lost to the world in
> the perusal of her missal, followed out of the corner of her eye what
> was going on between Gullet, the agricultural engineer, and the two
> fat Mesdemoiselles Dubois. From time to time she raised her head
> to see how far the Commandant and Mme Salvain had got. (p. 40)

The scintillating comedy which is created as we look at these people through the narrator's eyes brings out their hypocrisy, immorality and artificiality. The matter-of-fact tone also underlines this artificiality and suggests the pointlessness of these people's lives and the aimlessness of their conversation.

> The Doctor's wife returned to the attack. She mentioned a newspaper that had praised the Japanese ballet. When she had run out of things to say, one of the Mesdemoiselles Dubois took over. She mentioned the names of several white men who I suppose might have been musicians or had something to do with music. She was very sorry she had not had Madame's opportunity of being in Paris at the beginning of the week. She lamented that the tennis courts had already turned to mud in the first rains and that she had not found anyone who could really play well at Dangan. Mme Salvain spoke of horses, complaining that the tsetse fly of the forest zone had made it impossible for the Africans to rear them. The engineer said something could perhaps be done ... M. Janopoulos discussed the price of cocoa with the Commandant. The Doctor expressed the desire to have a European midwife. (p. 61)

The aimless drift of the conversation and the painful process of finding an acceptable subject to sustain it is underlined by the rather staccato style of the passage.

Among the whites themselves there is envy, malice and intrigue; they are only united in their hatred of the Africans, most of whom, they assume, are prone to gonorrhoea. Father Vandermayer, who so obviously terrorizes the Africans, they see as a saintly man devoting his life to the service of ungrateful savages. And yet the whites are quite prepared to exploit the African for sexual purposes, though they hypocritically try to keep this concealed. The Africans, on the other hand, emerge as a people of great dignity and cleverness, morally and intellectually superior to the whites. Thus the wily Ondowa insults the agricultural engineer even as he does his bidding and on Toundi's arrest the constable who acts as Gullet's interpreter cleverly omits those details which might incriminate Toundi and Sophie, and ensures that the neighbours do not inform against them. Here, as in *The Old Man and the Medal*, the Africans demonstrate tremendous fellow-feeling, solidarity and humanity. Even Kalisia, the woman of the world, warns Toundi of his danger, and when he is arrested they all rally round him. The giant Mendim me Tit, specially brought up from almost foreign parts to torture his fellow-Africans, thinks up a clever scheme to save Toundi some suffering. Of course, not all the Africans are presented in an attractive light. Some, like the blustering Akoma, are shown to be mere tools of the French. This man, who is the only Dangan chief to have been to France, obviously relishes what he thinks is the importance conferred on him thereby, and makes himself a figure of fun. On the other hand, Mengueme speaks French fluently but wisely pretends that he does not. Oyono's generally sympathetic treatment of the Africans may be partial, but it is difficult to accuse him of bias, since he demonstrates their good qualities within the context of the novel.

Next to Toundi himself, the most interesting and most fully presented character is his mistress. Her initial portrait through Toundi's admiring eyes suggests beauty, innocence and purity – 'like a newly-opened flower'. But this dazzling beauty soon reveals her true nature as an immoral nymphomaniac. Her initial tolerance towards Africans is soon transformed into immense hostility; she becomes the Africans' greatest enemy – the indirect cause of the worst atrocities perpetrated in the novel. The facade of innocence also soon disappears revealing a most deadly nature and the deadliness is suggested by the image of the snake with which she is clearly associated. Even her impassivity is the impassivity of the snake waiting to pounce. In particular, the similarity between her eyes and those of a snake is stressed again and again. They often go quite hard and contract to two white dots. On one famous occasion Toundi actually feels he has trodden on a snake after seeing the snake-like look in Madame's eyes.

> I lowered my eyes. For a fraction of a second I raised them and they met Madame's eyes. I saw them grow small, then large as if she could see something that astonished her. Instinctively I looked down at my feet to make sure I wasn't standing beside a poisonous snake...
>
> I stood for a few moments at the foot of the steps rooted to the spot by the look in Madame's eyes. I ferreted about the stems of the citronellas, a favourite place for the little deadly poisonous green snakes, I felt something soft and sticky under my feet. With a shriek I leapt into the air. My master rushed to the window. I was ashamed at myself, ashamed because I had shrieked when I felt a banana skin with the sole of my foot. (pp. 77–8)

We are shocked by Madame's immorality, infidelity and filth. This 'newly-opened flower' is not above throwing her used contraceptives under the bed and asking her houseboy to sweep up the mess; nor does she hesitate to ask the laundryman to wash her sanitary towels.

Oyono lays great stress in *Houseboy* on the importance of eyes, particularly the narrator's and Madame's eyes. It is, of course, through Toundi's eyes that we see the Dangan world but, more significantly, it is his eyes which strip the Europeans naked, revealing their brutality, immorality and filth. Toundi's moments of greatest perception are usually when his eyes meet someone else's, particularly over someone else's shoulders. The Africans in general use their eyes. There is even a suggestion that the eyes of the Africans are much more penetrating than those of the whites: 'The eyes that live in the native location strip the whites naked.' The whites, on the other hand, go about blind. The Africans' eyes not only perceive but judge. This is why Toundi's eyes are so important. He is himself an eye. 'For him . . . you'll be something like the eye of the witch that sees and knows . . .' M. Moreau recognizes that Toundi is a threat by the look in his eyes.

> 'You see, he can't look us in the eye. His eyes are shifty like a pigmy's. He's dangerous. Natives are like that. When they can't look you in the eye it's a sure sign they've got some idea fixed in their wooden heads . . .' (p. 91)

For the African, on the other hand, refusal to look someone in the eye is a sign of guilt. Thus, when Madame realizes that Toundi knows her secret she is unable to look him in the eye.

The brutality of the whites is copiously demonstrated from the very first picture of the dying Toundi. It is reflected also in the commandant's violence, in Gullet's mindless destructiveness, in M. Janopoulos's wanton cruelty and in the engineer's degradation of Sophie. But it is the scenes at the prison and the hospital that bring out the brutality and indifference of the whites most powerfully.

> I lay down on my stomach in front of the constable, Gullet handed him the hippopotamus-hide whip he always carried. The constable made it hiss down on my buttocks twenty-five times. When it started I determined not to cry out. I must not cry out . . . Behind my back Mendim was beginning to pant.
>
> 'Scream, for God's sake,' he yelled in the vernacular, 'cry out. They'll never let me stop while you don't cry . . .' He counted twenty-five, then he turned round to the whites. 'Give me the whip,' said Gullet. He brought down the hippopotamus-hide lash across the constable's back. The constable gave a roar of pain. 'See, that's how I want him whipped. Start over again!' Mendim rolled up the sleeves of his khaki jacket, his lips twisted in pain.
>
> 'Scream, scream,' he begged as he went to work on me again. 'Are your ears blocked with shit?'

The lover of Sophie shouted at him to shut up. He gave me a kick under the chin. Then he called 'stop, stop'. (pp. 130–1)

The degrading conditions in which the Africans are forced to live, even at the hospital, are also forcefully demonstrated. The reassurance which the sympathetic doctor temporarily inspires is dissipated by his own sense of hopeless despair about the conditions he has to work in. Toundi, who has been hit on the chest by a rifle butt, cannot be X-rayed because the white doctor in charge has walked off with the keys of the X-ray room. And when he turns up and is told about the broken rib, all he can say is: 'Meanwhile what about his temperature? . . . only 103 – that's not serious for them. He won't slip through your fingers' (p. 130). The most urgent need apparently is not to save the man's life, but to assure the police chief that he will live to be tortured further.

That the novel's effect is the consequence of the most accomplished artistry cannot be doubted. Here, as in *The Old Man and the Medal*, Oyono proves himself an expert in the comic art. The comedy is occasionally the result of masterly understatement and the calm tone of the most devastating comments makes the satire all the more effective. The powerful observation and attention to detail also heightens the comedy.

The Chief himself wore a khaki jacket on to the sleeves of which his red badges and their silver braid had been sewn, apparently in some haste. From each sleeve trailed a length of white cotton. A middle-aged man wearing a pyjama top over his loin-cloth shouted 'Eyes front!' Some thirty urchins, unnoticed until now, sprang to attention. 'Forward marsss' ordered the man. (p. 47)

Almost every word counts . . . the khaki jacket clashing with the red badges and the silver braid, the improvisation for show reflected in 'in some haste', the absurdity of the pyjama top over the loin-cloth and the ridiculous guard of honour. The tone of the passage is rather condescending at the villagers' expense perhaps, but it is very effective satire none the less. This is the kind of reception the Frenchman likes when he goes on tour. The satire therefore is ultimately at the expense, not of the villagers, but of the Frenchman, as it ought to be.

1 Jeanette Kamara, review *'The Old Man and the Medal'*, *ALT*, no. 3 (1969), pp. 50–2.

2 Mukotani Rugyendo, 'Ferdinando Oyono: a dissenting view', *ALT*, no. 6 (1973), pp. 152–6.
3 Ferdinand Oyono, *The Old Man and the Medal* (Heinemann, London, 1969), p. 10. All further page references are to this edition.
4 Ferdinand Oyono, *Houseboy* (Heinemann, London, 1966), p. 11. All further page references are to this edition.

7. Sembène Ousmane

▼▼▼

Sembène Ousmane's educational background is quite different from that of most other writers from francophone Africa. Starting life as a fisherman, he progressed through the local *école* to careers as plumber, bricklayer and mechanic in Dakar, and docker and trade union leader in France. Not for him the hours of the *lycée* followed by the heights of academe at the Sorbonne. Ousmane has reached the top of the intellectual pinnacle as writer and film director, not through exposure to the classical French education designed for prospective middle-class *assimilés*, but through his own determined exertions.

The outlook of such a man is likely to be slightly different from that of his more conventionally educated counterparts. Indeed Ousmane seems to have more in common with anglophone writers than with his francophone compatriots. In the first place, he has little time for Negritude, preferring to deal with the anti-colonial problem on the level of political rather than cultural polemics.[1] It is now fairly established that francophone intellectuals were much more concerned with the superimposition of an alien culture and the consequent erosion of the indigenous personality than with political domination. With the possible exception of Guinea, the anti-imperialist struggle was much more strident in anglophone than in francophone Africa. National leaders with seats in the French Chamber of Deputies or even in the French Cabinet were not likely to press vehemently for independence. Sembène Ousmane did not share this complacency. Indeed one detects in his works the suggestion that the masses, though inarticulate and largely illiterate, were much more politically aware than their leaders, and there is a certain amount of scorn for the indifference of leaders whose education and position cut them off from the aspirations of the people. The passion with which Ousmane portrays the evils of political domination puts him in line with novelists like Achebe and Ngugi.

Secondly, Ousmane has an almost unrivalled ability, among

francophone writers, for portraying the lives of ordinary men and women. By background, temperament and inclination he is a man of the people, and he can penetrate their thoughts with great insight, and present their predicament with sympathy and humanist regard. In his pages will be found a more convincing portrait of traditional life than in most other francophone novels; his presentation of life in the little village of Santhiu-Niaye in *White Genesis* is as compelling as Achebe's portrayal of Umuofia.

Thirdly, Sembène Ousmane is one of the few francophone writers to turn his attention to the corruption and decadence threatening modern African society. Where the Negritude writers extol the virtues of traditional society, Ousmane, like Soyinka, forces his countrymen to take a realistic look at the uglier aspects of African life in *White Genesis*, undeterred by arguments that, writing such a story would bring dishonour to the black race.

> I also know, and so do you, that in the past, as well as in the present, there have been many anonymous heroic actions among us. But not everything we have done has been heroic … The debility of AFRICAN MAN – which we call our AFRICANITY, our NEGRITUDE, and which, instead of fostering the subjection of nature by science, upholds oppression and engenders venality, nepotism, intrigue and all those weaknesses with which we try to conceal the base instincts of man (may at least one of us shout it out before he dies) – is the great defect of our time.[2]

Such a declaration puts Ousmane in line with the mainstream of contemporary anglophone writing, and his own exposure of the corruption and incompetence engendered by a clogged bureaucratic system in *The Money Order* is as revealing as Achebe's *A Man of the People* or Soyinka's *The Interpreters*. In this chapter I intend to look at three of Ousmane's works: briefly at *White Genesis* and *The Money Order* and in greater detail at *God's Bits of Wood*, showing how they reveal the man and the artist.

The two novelettes, *White Genesis* and *The Money Order*, published in translation recently,[2] demonstrate all the distinctive characteristics of Ousmane's art: the feel for the lives of ordinary people; the tough, precise, evocative language; the powerful characterization, especially of the womenfolk; and the deep moral and social concern. In *White Genesis*, Guibril Guedj Diob, chief of the little village of Santhiu-Niaye commits incest with his daughter, is discovered, ostracized and put to death. To these bones of a story, Ousmane grafts the way of life of a whole village, a village doomed to economic and moral decay. The powerfully written story shows that Ousmane possesses what Lawrence would call the power of sensuous understanding, the capacity to portray the feelings and aspirations of the people and relate them to the environment. Not only is the village in decline, the whole basis of the order on which it has operated is being challenged. Ngone War Thiandum, Guibril's wife, is plunged into a situation in which she is forced to question a traditional order which condemns her to a secondary role – that of a wife who must always be obedient and never express an opinion. She questions the order, particularly since it is its most prestigious representative, her own husband, who has polluted it and exposed its corruption and hypocrisy through his infamous conduct. The historical, economic and sociological analysis of the village in the opening pages is most significant. It presents the village as decaying, life denying and constricting. Santhiu-Niaye is a village to get out of, and its deathliness and decay are only the outward manifestation of an inner moral corruption and decadence. One of the novelette's claims to excellence is the powerful portrayal of Ngone War Thiandum, a truly tragic heroine, torn between her moral sense, her love for her daughter, her devotion to her husband and her family pride – all culminating in her courageous suicide. There is also a convincing portrayal of the workings of the lunatic's mind in Ngone's son, Tanor Ngone Diob, a victim of the war in Indo-China. The chorus of villagers, created through very skilful dialogue, forms a very fitting background, which eventually becomes the foreground hounding Guibril to death.

The Money Order is equally powerfully written. In this tale Ousmane uses the slender framework of the penurious Ibrahim Dieng's attempts to cash a money order to expose certain evils in his society. Dieng discovers that before the order can be cashed a lot of red tape has to be got through and various officials bribed; and when at last he thinks he is on the point of getting the money he discovers that an influential relative, who is supposed to be helping him, has outwitted him and used the money for his own purposes.

Here at last is a work of fiction from francophone Africa which faces up to the disintegration threatening modern African society. But unlike some other writers who have handled this theme there is little didacticism or overt moralizing. Ousmane achieves his effects through superbly realized scenes. There is excellent dialogue, tremendous economy of language, and although there is pathos, there is no sentimentality. The brilliant comedy is directed partly at Dieng's naivety but mostly at society's corruption. Indeed, the work is infused with a sense of the decadence of modern Senegalese life, with the dishonesty, corruption, bribery and the evil effects of bureaucracy. The hero, Dieng, represents the ordinary man, trampled by friends, neighbours and officialdom. As in *White Genesis*, we feel the pressure of society here. We experience its solidarity, but also its malevolence and greed, caused, in fact, by the general suffering. Although the hero grows in knowledge of his society, the final note is one of despair.

On the basis of these two first-rate novelettes, Sembène Ousmane must surely rank as one of Africa's first writers. But *God's Bits of Wood*, written much earlier, is his masterpiece. To say that *God's Bits of Wood* is merely about a moment in history – the strike of 1947 – is to radically misunderstand it and to underestimate its importance and that of its author. For the novel encompasses the same span as Ngugi's *A Grain of Wheat*; like that novel, it is about the mobilization of a whole people into political consciousness. The strike is symbolic of something much bigger – the struggle of a people for equality and for the right to be treated as decent human beings. All the main participants in the drama recognize that they are involved in much more than a strike. Bakayoko, the leader, is aware that he has started a movement whose ultimate consequence will be equality and the disappearance of the old feudal network; the workers themselves are astonished at the forces they have set in motion and are uncertain how to control them; even Dejean, the racialist, is aware that the issue is much more than a confrontation between employer and employees.

> A discussion between employer and employees presupposes the fact that there are employees and there is an employer. But he, Dejean was not an employer; he was simply exercising a function which rested on the most natural of all bases – the right to an absolute authority over beings whose colour made of them not subordinates with whom one could discuss anything, but men of another, inferior condition, fit only for unqualified obedience.[3]

The conflict is seen by all as a racial confrontation in terms of the people against the *toubabs* – the white authorities. The railway, spanning as it does almost the whole of former French West Africa from Bamako to Dakar, serves as a unifying force and reinforces the novel's epic span, suggesting a groundswell of resistance to the French imperialists, not just in Senegal, but throughout the region. The powerful presentation and analysis of the important railway junction of Thies suggest that it is a product, not just of bad railway administration, but of colonialist and capitalist exploitation and neglect.

> Hovels. A few rickety shacks, some upturned tombs, walls of bamboo or millet stalks, iron barbs, and rotting fences. Thies: a vast, uncertain plain where all the rot of the city has gathered – stakes and crossties, locomotive wheels, rusty shafts, knocked-in jerricans, old mattress springs, bruised and lacerated sheets of steel. And then, a little farther on, on the goat path that leads to the Bambara quarter, piles of old tin cans, heaps of excrement, little mountains of broken pottery and cooking tools, dismantled railway cars, skeletons of motors buried in the dust, and the tiny remains of cats, of rats, of chickens, disrupted by the birds. Thies: in the midst of this corruption, a few meagre bushes – wild tomato, dwarf peppers, and okra – whose pitiful fruits were harvested by the women. Bald-sided goats and sheep, clotted with filth, came here to graze – to graze on what? – the air? Constantly hungry, naked children, with sunken chests and swollen bellies, argued with the vultures. Thies: a place where everyone – man, woman and child – had a face the colour of the earth. (p. 27)

It is against such degradation that the people are fighting. Ousmane's theme, then, like Ngugi's, is political; and like Ngugi he makes his political points, not through bald political statements, but through a demonstration of the impact of political activities and decisions on the life and feelings of people. Seldom has a writer been able to generate such passion, anger and sympathy for the people's sufferings while appearing detached and uninvolved. Ousmane never intrudes. We seldom hear him speaking in his own voice. Everything is presented through the interaction of character, scene and setting. There are several scenes revealing the brutality of the authorities as they pounce on a people determined not to be cowed into submission. Their first expedient is to turn off the water and cut off all necessary supplies. The privation and suffering of men, women and children thus doomed to thirst and hunger is very tellingly rendered. They are forced to buy water when it is available, eat vultures and pawn almost all their belongings. Without the slightest provocation the security forces open fire on massed strikers at Thies, killing several people including the blind Maimouna's helpless baby. When the women at Dakar march on the police station to support the heroic Ramatoulaye, they turn fire hoses on them, breaking the neck of Houdia M'Baye, widowed mother of nine. Isnard senselessly kills two apprentices and fatally wounds a third. At the gates of Dakar the soldiers open fire on the marching column of harmless women, killing the legendary Penda and Samba N'Doulougou. At Bamako, as elsewhere, the authorities resort to arbitrary arrest and detention without trial: the innocent aged Fa Keita is seized in the midst of his meditation, his wife old Niakoro battered to death, his grand-daughter Adjibidji knocked senseless on the floor, while he himself is led to prison. The scenes at the prison are among the most degrading in the entire novel, and they are as powerfully done as anything of the same nature in Ngugi or Oyono. Without degenerating into sentimentality or false pathos, Ousmane manages to arouse tremendous anger and pity at the contemplation of such suffering. He shows how ill-treatment in prison has brutalized and corrupted men who are forced to live in the dark and wallow in each other's excrement. The racialist Bernadini, who is the officer in charge of the camp, seems to specialize in inventing new refinements in torture with which to plague his victims.

> 'Silence!' Bernadini repeated. 'Now who was talking? No one, of course! I am accustomed to that. But let me tell you that I was in the camp at Fodor, in Mauretania, and I swear to you that no one who was with me there is likely to forget it!'
> He went over to the stammerer, who seemed to be muttering something to himself, and lashed at his face with the riding crop. 'That's just in case it was you who was talking! If you open your mouth again, I'll plant my foot here.' He flicked at the man's groin with the butt of the whip. 'That should make you come, *Macaco*! All right, chief, on with the promenade!' (pp. 314–15)

Obviously Bernadini's intention is to debase human beings to the level of animals.

It is a tribute to Ousmane's powers of characterization that, momentous and absorbing though the events are, the characters are not dwarfed by them. A story of such epic proportions will inevitably feature scores of characters. Many of them are of little significance and are soon forgotten; but a good many also stand out starkly individualized. In a sense, the novel is a study of individual suffering and fortitude in the face of adversity, and Ousmane interweaves with the events the personal tragedies of a number of characters. The work also presents the little jealousies, rivalries and animosities, and the complexity of motives dictating human actions. It is these which give the novel its resonance and substantiality.

First there is Maimouna, the blind mother of twins. Far from being an object of pity, she is an object of admiration, a reservoir of quiet strength and dignity, a source of inspiration and a symbol of endurance and the will to survive. When we first meet her she is characteristically singing the legend of Goumba N'Diaye – the woman who measured her strength against that of men before she went blind. The song suits her and a number of other women in the story, for in spite of her blindness, her courage and resilience make her more than a match for the men. It is one of the novel's grim ironies that while she sings in praise of living, one of her twins crawls away and is trampled to death beneath the boots of the soldiers, in a scene whose terror is vividly conveyed by Ousmane's superb descriptive power. Demonstrating tremendous fortitude in the face of this tragedy, she recovers and plays a leading role in the resistance. She becomes not only a source of strength, but an agent of rescue and of healing, and a repository of knowledge and wisdom.

Then there is Houdia M'Baye, mother of nine children, whose husband had been one of the victims of the first fighting in the strike. After his death she is unable to return home to her family because of the strike, and because she is again about to have a baby. When the baby is born they christen him 'Strike', and there are some telling scenes as the baby suffers because its mother's breasts have run dry through starvation. In the end Houdia M'Baye is brutally killed by the authorities' fire hoses. Ousmane lingers over her death-scene, focusing attention on each of her movements in order to arouse maximum horror and pity.

There is also Sounkare, the old watchman whose portrayal demonstrates Ousmane's power of psychological penetration. He embodies not only deprivation, but also the loneliness which is an inevitable by-product of these troubled times. In a brilliant flashback, Ousmane fills in details from Sounkare's early life, thereby generating profound sympathy for him. After a comfortable childhood, an advantageous marriage had been arranged for him, and he had saved enough money for the bride-price; but then came the accident in which he jumped from the locomotive and broke a hip. All the money went in doctors' fees and, worse, the accident left him impotent – unable to leave someone to bear his name. His precarious position makes him originally ignore the strike call, but after the 'trial' of another collaborator, he is forced to stay at home and face poverty unrelieved by neighbours who have now ostracized him. Ousmane gives us several convincing passages of introspection as Sounkare is led by calamity to question the very existence of God. There are some bizarre details as the starving watchman looks at Aziz the Syrian stuffing himself with food and as he tries ineffectively to kill a fat rat for his dinner. His end is macabre: completely overcome by hunger he falls into a pit and becomes food for rats. Once more the remarkably controlled language enables Ousmane to generate pathos without degenerating into sentimentality.

Although Ousmane presents his black characters sympathetically, he does not over-idealize them. Like Ngugi in *A Grain of Wheat*, he is alive to the weaknesses of both blacks and whites. This is another index of his intelligent objectivity. We can take his presentation of Bakayoko as an example. If anyone could be said to be the hero of a work in which so many characters jostle for importance, then it is probably Bakayoko, the organizer of the strike. Ousmane delays Bakayoko's appearance for a considerable period of time, building up in the meantime an impressive atmosphere of expectancy from rumours and reports. We already know, before his appearance, of his restlessness, of his oratorical gifts and his hypnotic influence over the workers. Beaugosse wonders: 'Who was this man whose shadow reached into every house, touching every object? His words and his ideas were everywhere, and even his name filled the air like an echo.' But we also hear of some of his more unpleasant qualities: his heavy-handedness and his ability to instil a certain awe into even his admirers.

On his appearance we recognize his sheer intellectual force, his tremendous self-confidence and self-possession and his ability to master a situation completely. He is the visible embodiment of the drive towards liberation. His ability to disregard destiny or bend it to his will makes him the soul of the strike, the source of the people's strength in their great struggle. But there is something rather chilling about Bakayoko. Ousmane does not fail to stress that his confidence and self-possession could easily degenerate into arrogance and conceit. We are aware of his harshness, lack of tact and scorn directed even towards blacks like Beaugosse. Character after character, including Lahbib and Alioune, his greatest friends, mention his callousness, his lack of feeling shown in his refusal to go home after his mother's death or to attend Doudou's funeral. The perceptive Maimouna warns Penda that if she falls in love with him he will occupy her heart, and then pass through it leaving nothing but bitterness, for 'In Bakayoko's heart there is no room for anybody. He is blinder to his neighbour than

I am.' And this is precisely what he does to N'Deye Touti, whom he abandons quite unceremoniously after the latter has given up her principles and a most eligible suitor, and offered to be his wife. Several images are used to suggest Bakayoko's callousness and lack of consideration for the feelings of others. For instance, he smiles as a child crushes a crab with a blow of his heel; he watches as a bird hops towards a trap and he is pleased when some boys subsequently gather round the trapped bird; and in one of our final views of him he is laughing delightedly at a sparrowhawk who has just startled him by pouncing on a rat. Perhaps the rather special situation demands men who will not allow feelings or sentiment to interfere with their singleness of purpose; but there is no doubting the stress laid on Bakayoko's harsher qualities.

Nor does Ousmane flinch from exposing the inadequacies of the other characters and the complex motives of their actions. Thus Beaugosse, tortured by sexual jealousy of Bakayoko, is driven to resign from the union and ally himself with the imperialists; Tiemoke devotes all his energies towards bringing Diara to 'trial', not just out of devotion to the cause, but because he wants an idea of his to play a part in the lives of thousands of people – he wishes to prove himself, to discover his worth as a human being; and Doudou devotes himself to the strike out of a yearning for popularity. Of course Ousmane is most scathing when he turns his attention to the collaborators. Both Mabigue and the *imam* are ridiculous figures. Ousmane's description is so apt: Mabigue's pink, delicately lined palm, 'which was as soft and plump as a woman's', reveals not only his effeminacy but his complacency and indifference. His castrated ram, with which he is closely identified, is combed and brushed and sleek, while men, women and children go around naked, hungry and thirsty. The *imam* in his wisdom finds theological reasons to justify the perpetuation of colonialist exploitation; French imperialism becomes equated with 'the will of God'.

The society Ousmane presents in *God's Bits of Wood* is a society in the process of change, going through political social and economic evolution. The railway itself, with its tremendous speed and power, is both symbol and agent of change, like the road in Cary's *Mister Johnson*. Ousmane's remarkable prose enacts the power of the diesels: 'The massive diesels, their copper still gleaming, were formed in solid ranks, standing clean and powerful, and remote as gods. This building was their temple, and the acrid odour of hot oil their incense. Here they

were ministered to and worshipped by the best mechanics in the land
...' (p. 186). Men who work with such machines are likely to feel a
sense of power themselves. It is not surprising, therefore, that the
drive towards emancipation is spearheaded by the railwaymen, the
most mobile of all workers and therefore the most likely to have the
most comprehensive view of their country's suffering. When they
force every machine within a thousand miles to halt, they become
conscious of their strength.

The railway has transformed the area from a predominantly
agricultural and feudal order into an industrial one where everyone
claims equality. As Fa Keita puts it: 'I think it is the machine which has
ground everything together this way and brought everything to a
single level. Ibrahim Bakayoko said to me, not long ago: "When we
have succeeded in stirring up the people of this country and making
them one, we will go on and do the same thing between ourselves and
the people on the other side of the ocean"' (pp.132–3). The rise of the
railway is thus clearly linked with the drive towards political
liberation. It has produced a whole new breed of men, scornful of the
feudal order, impatient with the wisdom of their ancestors, pinning
their faith on education and the written word. In a culture where
everyone is illiterate the memory of the elders is the repository of
history, hence their importance; but with the spread of education and
the availability of written records, the importance of oral history
declines and the elders are no longer consulted.

And so the novel starts with old Niakoro's consciousness of change –
young men planning a strike without consulting their elders – and Fa
Keita subsequently laments the passing of an old order when
everything happened within a framework that no longer exists. The
precocious Adjibidji, unconvincing though she is as a character, is
perhaps the clearest symbol of future trends. Most significantly there
is a dramatic change in the role of women, for the momentous events
have produced not only a new breed of men, but a new breed of women
as well. From the secondary position which a Muslim feudal culture
traditionally accorded them, the women move into the foreground not
only to support their men, but quite often to take the initiative, and this
happens all along the line from Bamako to Dakar. To the chagrin of
some of the men they begin, quite unbidden, to address public
meetings; they play a leading role in the various battles with the
security forces, unsupported by the men in some cases, and in others
standing firm while the men take to their heels. They begin to feel

closer to the lives of their men and force them to acknowledge the narrowing of the gap. Several of them like Penda, Mame Sofi and Ramatoulaye demonstrate great inventiveness and resourcefulness, and at the end they demand a share in the running of things, and the men are forced to acquiesce.

Indeed, one of the hallmarks of Ousmane's writing is the great importance of women. One can say, in fact, that his world is one in which women seem to be supreme. They are always much more powerfully portrayed and demonstrate much greater moral courage than the men. One thinks of Ngone War Thiandum and her daugher Khar Madiagua Diob in *White Genesis*, Dieng's wife Metty in *The Money Order* and Ramatoulaye, Penda and Maimouna in *God's Bits of Wood*.

Ramatoulaye in particular, a woman who is head of an enormous household, arouses our admiration by her courage, determination and presence of mind. In the scenes with the police officers and the *imam* she is given real moral stature as she delivers the most biting rebuke to the former; and the victory is completely hers. In the eyes of the other women she looks like a being transformed, someone whom they would never have thought capable of such heroic acts of defiance.

Then there is Penda, the tough and originally despised prostitute who identifies herself completely with her people's struggle, eventually becoming a sympathetic and extremely competent leader of women, and dying heroically at the Gates of Dakar. But perhaps the most interesting of all is the young girl N'Deye Touti. In her portrayal, Ousmane probably comes as near as he ever will be to the Negritude writers, for he obviously exposes the inadequacy of her largely 'French' education which has left her unprepared for life. Ousmane suggests, however, that the fault lies partly with N'Deye Touti's own attitude, her acquaintance with the wrong books and the wrong films, leading to a superficial idea of French values. She becomes a dreamer attached to European ideals and completely cut off from the life and ideals of her people. 'N'Deye herself knew far more about Europe than she did of Africa ... she had never read a book by an African author – she was quite sure they could teach her nothing' (pp. 84–5). N'Deye Touti does not identify herself with her people's struggle until she is humiliated by the very Europeans to whom she is drawn. Later, after the disastrous affair with Bakayoko, she is ennobled through suffering. She becomes a model of self-denial and an object of admiration by everyone.

The events of the novel culminate in the women's historic march to Dakar which proves the final test of their courage and their ability to support their husbands and to sustain their new role. The march is not without its problems; jealousies and rivalries break out among the women and superstition almost defeats their efforts. But they carry on to the end, sustained largely by Penda's determined leadership and the blind Maimouna's courage and inspiration. Even when the supporting men flag and complain, Maimouna, her baby strapped across her back, walks steadily forward humming her endless refrains: 'All the women seemed to want to walk behind Maimouna, as if she trailed a protective wake in which they would be safe.' Soon fellow-feeling and goodwill are re-established, the quarrelling parties are reconciled, and the success of the march is the turning-point, the decisive blow which leads to victory in the struggle.

The weakest point of Ousmane's art in this novel is probably his portrayal of the white characters. One has the feeling that they lack the depth of the blacks. Nevertheless, Ousmane still achieves variety in their portrayal. Isnard, who has devoted his life to working for the country, and ends by being forced to leave for the tragic killing of the apprentices, is more broad-minded than the stupid, obstinate careerist Dejean. The latter is an embodiment of the most irrational anger, and a creature of the wildest passions, while the former is at least prepared to use gentler methods. And these two are distinguishable from the smooth Edouard and the disillusioned drunkard Leblanc. The uncomfortable feeling persists, however, that Ousmane makes his white characters just a bit too stupid and beastly; they are, in fact, rather one-dimensional.

To be fair to Ousmane it must be pointed out that he never condemns the whites in his own person, preferring to present their absurdities and brutalities through action and dialogue. It is from Bernadini's own mouth that we are apprised of his worst excesses.

Ousmane's achievement in *God's Bits of Wood* is largely due to his wonderfully controlled artistry. First there is the quality of his prose. One has to be cautious in discussing the stylistic aspects of a translated work, but a few tentative points can still be made. Ousmane's language is so precise and economical; the choice of words is so exact. One has the impression of confident mastery of language, not of an uncertain beginner fumbling with words. This is writing which is the product, not just of erudition, but of observation and experience, as when he says 'Mabigue's face was an astonished mask of soft black wax' or 'The loose sleeves of his tunic flapped like the wings of a long-legged bird preparing for flight'. The impression conveyed is that almost every phrase, simile or metaphor is backed by the weight of lived experience and carries an intellectual force. Without resorting to floridity, Ousmane contrives majestic prose with an attractive rhythm.

In order to refute Charles Larson's view of the African writer's frequent difficulties in writing convincing dialogue, one only has to turn to the pages of Sembène Ousmane.[4] Here is the most meaningful and convincing dialogue – in the scenes between the workers, or between the white characters or between the women. And it is dialogue which functions not only towards the fixing of character, but also towards creating a sense of community, as in *White Genesis*. It is partly owing to the skilful dialogue that we get the views of the various members of this community and feel their force.

Ousmane's strongest point is probably his descriptive power. He usually starts his novels with scenic description in beautiful, majestic, rhythmic prose, moving gradually from the general to the particular. *White Genesis* starts with a powerful general description of the *Niaye*, narrowing down to the particular village of Santhiu-Niaye and eventually to Ngone War Thiandum's hut and Ngone herself. *God's Bits of Wood* begins with what looks almost like an aerial view of Bamako before our attention is focused on the Bakayoko household and finally on old Niakoro. The cinematic technique gives glimpses of the artistry of the man who was subsequently to become a successful film director. Ousmane also gives the most detailed description of people's physical features – again with the sureness of the film maker's eye, as the realistic portrayal of old Niakoro suggests.

> On either side of her little, high-arched nose the drooping lids half covered her eyes. Her lips were tattooed – a souvenir of youthful vanity. The line of her mouth was drawn back to a perpetual sucking motion, and her cheeks moved in and out to the rhythm of her breathing, so that she seemed always to be swallowing. Her head appeared linked to her body only by threads of flesh, and by the flabby dewlaps that drooped beneath her chin. (pp. 11–12)

Ousmane can give the most powerful description of place – witness his evocation of Thies or Bamako – of events, such as Houdia M'Baye's death, and of landscape. No matter what he is describing, he keeps his eye on every detail, every movement, every gesture. His use of detail is as impressive as anything to be found anywhere else in African literature. It is techniques such as these which are responsible for the large number of superbly realized scenes in the novel, such as the meeting between the workers and the employers at Thíes, the confrontation between the women and the security forces culminating in Houdia M'Baye's death and Mama Sofi's skirmish with the water seller. His passages of introspection are equally detailed and convincing, as can be seen from his penetration into old Niakoro's ruminations or Sounkare's thoughts.

Unlike some works by francophone writers, Ousmane's novels have a truly indigenous flavour. This is partly due to his unique ability to enter into the lives and feelings of ordinary people, but also partly to his clever use of certain devices. For instance, like Achebe, he often introduces literal translations from the people's speech, as in expressions like 'a blessing for your care' and 'has everyone passed the night in peace?'. His similes and metaphors are taken largely from rural traditional life, as in 'this strike is like a band of monkeys deserting a fertile plain' and 'she fell on her side, her shrivelled breasts drooping out from her body like gourds left too long in the sun'.

God's Bits of Wood has its flaws; apart from the inadequate portrayal of the white characters there is an occasional drift towards melodramatics as in Betrice Isnard's death. And although Ousmane usually checks any tendency towards sentimentality, Adjibidji's ecstatic declaration about the spirit washing the water is a trifle trite and sentimental. But these are small faults in the face of Ousmane's towering achievement. He remains one of Africa's most exciting writers, speaking with conviction to both francophones and anglophones.

NOTES

1 See G. D. Killam (ed.), *African Writers on African Writing* (Heinemann, London, 1973), pp. 148–52.
2 Sembène Ousmane, *The Money Order* with *White Genesis*, trans. Clive Wake (Heinemann, London, 1972), pp. 5–6.
3 Sembène Ousmane, *God's Bits of Wood*, trans. Francis Price (Heinemann, London, 1970), p. 244. All further page references are to this edition.
4 Charles Larson, *The Emergence of African Fiction* (Indiana University Press, Bloomington, Ind., and London, 1971), p. 18.

8. Yambo Ouologuem

▼▼▼

Bound to Violence

Yambo Ouologuem's *Bound to Violence* is one of the most remarkable novels. It can genuinely claim to have derived from purely African sources since, to a much greater extent than most other African novels, its narrative technique owes much to the oral tradition, which is reflected not only in the style of narration but in the extensive use of African myths and legends. Indeed, one of the most striking features of this novel is the skilful blending of the mythological, the legendary and the factual. The novel is remarkable also in its concentration on violence and sex in their rawest forms. And yet it is obvious to the most casual reader that *Bound to Violence* does not set out to be a sensational thriller and is, in effect, neither cheap nor fourth-rate. Within the context of the novel the violence and sexual details are seen to be absolutely necessary to the author's purposes. Ouologuem's complete lack of self-consciousness in his portrayal is due to the need to expose the violence that has characterized Africa throughout the ages.

The originality of Ouologuem's inspiration has been seriously challenged. Charges of plagiarism have been bandied back and forth, and the matter has not been satisfactorily settled. Ouologuem himself has not put up the spirited defence his supporters would have liked. In the heat of the argument the publishers suspended circulation of the work. That they have now decided to reissue it can be taken as indicating their conviction that the novel can stand on its own as an authentic work.[1] This is not the place to raise the whole thorny and complex question of plagiarism as it relates either to Ouologuem's novel in particular or to modern critical attitudes in general. The allegedly plagiarized sections of *Bound to Violence*, even if the charges were true, certainly cannot account for the strength, solidity, power and density of texture of this astonishing novel which is so African in its inspiration. Critical discussion of it can therefore proceed uninhibited.

Most of the novels discussed so far are concerned with one of the three phases associated with the impact of imperialist expansion on Africa. *Bound to Violence* is unique in being concerned with all of them. Through a powerful presentation of oral lore it explores the nature of African society before the advent of the white imperialists and then goes on to show the process of imperialist conquest and the conflict between the new alien values and traditional ones; then it portrays the reaction against imperialism and finally the contemporary process of readjustment and rediscovery of new values during the post-independence phase. There is one factor that all these phases have in common – violence. The continent has indeed been 'bound to violence'. Unlike other francophone writers, like Beti and Oyono, Ouologuem aims to show, in one comprehensive presentation of Africa's plight, that oppression on the continent has not merely been the consequence of imperialist occupation, but has been going on throughout the ages. It is, so to speak, Africa's legacy, the consequence of exploitation not just by whites, but by Arabs, whites and black notables. Ouologuem seeks to dispel all the myths about Africa and to reveal the candid truth. He goes against the conventional wisdom which normally blames the imperialists for the disasters of the African past, presenting a picture of a well-organized, stable and respectable Africa before the advent of the conquerors. He shows instead that the African past has been astonishingly murky and that Africans themselves must shoulder a large proportion of the blame for the disasters that have always overwhelmed the continent. Obviously, then, Ouologuem, though a francophone writer, does not belong to the Negritude school. His realistic and clear-sighted attitude to the African past and present puts him in the company of the anglophone writers.

Bound to Violence starts appropriately with a presentation of the history of the Nakem Empire, going back to the year 1202. The picture is far from being flattering. What strikes the chronicler as he recounts the story is 'the desperate flight, before God's "implacable blessing", of its population, baptized in torture, hunted as far as the Rande ... torn by internecine rivalries and warring with one another for the imperial power with a violence equalled only by the dread it called forth' (p. 4).[2] The Nakem history turns out to be a record of the worst imaginable chaos, degradation, wanton carnage and maddening cruelty. The legendary Saifs themselves, with a combination of Jewish, negro and Arab blood running in their veins, seem to demonstrate the worst qualities of all three peoples. It is an age of feudalism and slavery with the Saifs turning out to be the worst slave owners and traders in history, their chief victims being the blacks, the paupers and the 'niggertrash'. One of them, Saif al-Haram, in order to provide for his extravagances, extends and blesses the slave trade.

> Amidst the diabolical jubilation of priest and merchant, of family circles and public organs, niggers, who unlike God have arms but no soul, were clubbed, sold, stockpiled, haggled over, adjudicated, flogged, bound and delivered – with attentive, studied, sorrowful contempt – to the Portuguese, the Spaniards, the Arabs (on the East and North coasts), and to the French, Dutch, and English (west coasts), and so scattered to the winds.
>
> A hundred million of the damned – so moan the troubadours of Nakem when the evening vomits forth its starry diamonds – were carried away. Bound in bundles of six, shorn of all human dignity, they were flung into the Christian incognito of ships' holds, where no light could reach them. And there was not a single trader of souls who dared, on pain of losing his own, to show his head at the hatches. A single hour in that pestilential hole, in that orgy of fever, starvation, vermin, beriberi, scurvy, suffocation, and misery, would have left no man unscathed. Thirty per cent died on route. And, since charity is a fine thing and hardly human, those amiable slavers were obliged when their cargo was unloaded to pay a fine for every dead slave; slaves who were as sick as a goat in labour were thrown to the sharks. Newborn babes incurred the same fate: they were thrown overboard as surplus . . . Half naked and utterly bewildered, the niggertrash, young as the new moon, were crowded into open pens and auctioned off. There they lay beneath the eyes of the all-powerful (and just) God, a human tide, a black mass of putrid flesh, a spectacle of ebbing life and nameless suffering. (pp. 11–12)

It is the complete disregard for human life, the treatment of a lower class of people as though they were animals and not men made in the image of God, that makes this passage so scarifying, and the cruelty is largely perpetrated by black Africans on other Africans. The narrator's bitterly ironic tone reinforces the horror all the more.

On the other hand, the life-style of the Saifs is one of luxury, dissipation and the utmost decadence. Every form of depravity, corruption, bestiality and perversion abounds in their courts. The most depraved of all was probably Saif Tsevi, who seduced his sister and became her lover, while she, having married, became an adulterer, 'choosing her concubines with impunity among boys of ten...'. On one page alone (p. 20) the reader is treated to orgies, bestiality, public copulation, incest, buggery, homosexuality and human sacrifice. Those were years without glory, the fulfilment of Saif Isaac's curse on al-Haram. The history of the Saifs is also a fearful story of a bloodthirsty struggle for power, of family feuds, intrigues and eventual disintegration; it is a history in which, on the death of a Saif, one claimant to the throne marries all his father's four wives, including his own mother, in order to strengthen his claim, and throws his brother, the legitimate heir, into a dungeon where he dies. After the death of Saif al-Heit a period of disintegration and fragmentation of authority sets in, with regimes succeeding each other with astonishing rapidity. Indeed the colonial conquest was facilitated by this disintegration. Making use of oral lore Ouologuem makes his point that the history of Nakem under African rulers does not bear looking into.

In this novel the author uses violence in much the same way as Armah and Swift use images of filth and obscenity – to shock us into a realization of the repulsiveness of violence and its presence in African society. Ouologuem pulls no punches; he shows not the slightest signs of self-consciousness and he refuses to flinch from the presentation of the most mind-boggling details. The Saifs seem to be pastmasters at the art of discovering the most ingenious methods of torture and brutality, unleashing a reign of terror and suffering on their innocent people. We hear of multitudes of men being immured alive, having been smeared with the blood of butchered children and disembowelled mothers (p. 4); of seventeen foetuses expelled from the gaping entrails of mothers in death agony – mothers whose husbands, having been forced to rape them, killed themselves through shame; of a Herod-type Saif who kills all newborn babies and lines the walls of his antechamber with their countless heads. As in the Christ story, one mother is fortunately able to flee with her husband and child under cover of darkness; the baby thus survives to become a kind of saviour – the most illustrious and the most just of the Saifs. We hear of eighteen notables being roasted alive and simultaneously poisoned by asps, of conquered chiefs being sacrificed and devoured.

> The capture of rebel tribes, of free men, of defeated warriors, the sacrifice of their chief and the feasting on his flesh, became ritual acts, which entered into the customs of those jittery jigs, whose barbarity fell in with the plans of the emperor and his notables ...

Through intermediaries, Saif al-Haram encouraged the raiders to bless the wounded captives with a stroke of the sabre, to carry their skulls pitted on lances and assegais to the door of the victor who – God wills it! – was feasted as a hero. And as though a Black really had the soul of a man, the chief of the prisoners and his family were first given over to the mercies of the village women and children who whirled around them, leaping, dancing, singing, shouting insults, and spitting on them in order, so they swore, to cleanse their souls of Satan's blackness ... Then each villager in turn danced around the prisoners with a crudely carved wooden knife and 'stabbed' the chief once for every year of his own age and once for every relative he himself had lost in the last slave raid ... On the night of the third day, his ankles weighed down with tinkling bells, the chief of the prisoners – bound hand and foot as the women whirled around him, lewdly uncovering their nakedness for a flashing moment, arching their backs and tapping their pubic hair with the palms of their hands – was castrated ... And paralysed with pain, the castrated husband, his thighs sticky with blood, looked on helpless as his wives – first standing, but in that same instant rolled in the dust – became the harlots of the victorious village, stripped, and then to the mad rhythm of the tom-tom taken each in turn by every man and woman in the village ... On the seventh day of their captivity, they were rubbed with peanut oil and tied to a pole, half dead with pent-up rage under the taunting words and gestures of the villagers. Made feverish by the thought of their impending death, with burning eyes and foaming mouths, the captives butted the air with their heads and, frantic to kill their enemies, clawed and bit and snarled at them as they passed.

On the evening of this seventh day all the prisoners, glutted with palm wine, drunk on millet beer, were howling like dogs. At midnight they died on the wood fire, in the crackling hiss of their fat, presenting to the expert fingers of the cannibals human flesh as white as that of a suckling pig. The brains and the women's sexual parts were set aside for the 'eminent' men, with clearly aphrodisiac intent, the chief's testicles were sprinkled with pepper and strong spice, to be relished by the women in their communal soup. (pp. 14–15)

The violence continues right up to more modern times under the regime of Saif ben Isaac al-Heit himself.

Apart from the scenes of violence, there are several illustrating the macabre and weird. Incidents involving sorcery and black magic, cannibalism, rape, castration, incest and all kinds of sexual orgies are presented with the same calmness of tone characteristic of this narrator. The horrifying details of the operation to prove Tambira's non-virginity are typical. It is significant that although this novel abounds in sexual incidents, only in one case – the encounter between Tambira and Kassoumi – are abnormal ingredients completely absent. Apart from those involving incest, homosexuality and bisexuality, there are scenes portraying voyeurism, masturbation and sadism, at times in the most unusual and unnecessary circumstances as in the encounter between Raymond Kassoumi and his wife. The scene between the administrator Chevalier and the Saif's instrument Awa is probably hard to beat for sadism and abnormal sex. A number of readers might feel that these episodes of abnormal sexuality are overdone. It is clear, however, that they do not read like similar scenes from the pages of cheap fiction. Far from intending to titillate, Ouologuem is in deadly earnest, his powerful prose style alone being an index of his seriousness of purpose. Indeed, the role of this magnificent, resilient and lyrical prose in toning down the obscenity can hardly be underestimated. Similarly, although the actions of his characters may seem abnormal and horrifying, their psychological motivations are usually given, so that the acts, though terrible, are plausible. This is true of the scene between Chevalier and Awa and no less true of that in which Sankolo, unable to control his feelings while watching Madoubo's and Sonia's love making, begins to masturbate frenziedly, and brutally kills his fiancée whom he discovers watching him. If the scenes of violence and the macabre almost turn the reader's stomach it is because this is precisely Ouologuem's intention.

There can be little doubt about Ouologuem's success in the demonstration of his main theme – the exploitation of Africans by African notables and Arab and European conquerors. His thesis is that the colonial conquest, which was in fact facilitated by the dissolution and turmoil of the Arab-ruled Nakem Empire, was not the root cause of Africa's evils. The notables' practice of slavery, and forced labour gave the white imperialists a plausible pretext for intervention and allowed them to hide their expansionist policies under the cloak of humanity and philanthropy. Without slavery and the oppression practised by indigenous rulers, colonization might have lost some of its glamour as a 'duty of international charity ... to suppress the slave trade that was devouring all Africa'. Forced labour, a form of slavery, had become the mainstay of economic life; consequently the niggertrash, who saw the prospect of liberation from slavery, welcomed the white man with joy. But the whites turn out in practice to be no less cruel than the black imperialists. They treat their captives with the same wanton disregard for human life.

A woman is found squatting. Big with child. They push her, prod her with their knees. She gives birth standing up, marching. The umbilical cord is cut, the child kicked off the road, and the column marches on, heedless of the delirious whimpering mother, who, limping and staggering, finally falls a hundred yards further on and is crushed by the crowd. (p. 27)

Once more the horror is all the more effectively generated because the information is conveyed in the same flat matter-of-fact tone while the narrator calmly passes on to other matters. Violence has become a way of life and this incident is a minor matter, all in the day's work, as it were.

Having established their power, the French imperialists begin their policy of assimilation. The policy is given a perspective going back to the reign of Louis XIV when Aniaba, the son of the King of Assinia, had visited that monarch's court. The young prince had been baptized with Louis himself as godfather, and then commissioned as an officer in the French army. When the prince became king on the death of the King of Assinia a kind of coronation ceremony was performed in Notre Dame Cathedral and on the day of Aniaba's departure Louis said to him: 'Now there is no other difference between you and me than the difference between black and white.' Ouologuem's sarcastic tone brings out the hypocrisy and condescension, the blatant disregard for the young prince's own religious beliefs – the same qualities which are later to characterize the practice of assimilation. Now the hypocrisy and condescension are even more blatant when Saif's son, Madoubo, visits France and, in his gloss to Louis's words, Governor-General Delavignette says: 'He meant that both were kings, brothers in kingship, and that, though differing in colour, they were united by the identity of their royal nature. And now, by extension, there is an extension of royal nature between Africa and ourselves' (p. 33).

The hero of the novel is Saif ben Isaac al-Heit, descended in the maternal line from the illustrious Saif Isaac el-Heit, the glory of whose reign he tries to recapture. He even encourages the popular belief that he is a messianic figure, like his distinguished ancestor whom he is said to resemble in every feature. In an empire noted for the brevity of its regimes, the Saif's long reign of more than half a century, from pre-colonial times to the more modern days of independence, is astonishing; it is a measure of the remarkable grip he has on his country and his unrivalled ability for turning even what looks like disaster to his own advantage. Ouologuem uses the Saif partly to make one of his most important points: that the imperialists, while fondly imagining that they were the colonial overlords, were merely pawns in the hands of the African potentates. The Saif, whom Ouologuem presents as the greatest colonial overlord of all, is diplomatically more than a match for the French conquerors whom he uses for his own purposes. He is therefore absolutely central to Ouologuem's thesis that the disasters that have overtaken modern Africa are due not just to the exploitation of European imperialists, but largely to the tyranny of Africans themselves. Thus the Saif needs to be put at the centre of events. He is clearly the central character in this prolonged drama; all the various incidents – the encounter between Chevalier and Awa, the love affair between Tambira and Kassoumi, the fate of Raymond Kassoumi – are there to display some aspect of the Saif's remarkable character or some feature of his reign.

Descended like most of his ancestors from a combination of Jewish, Arab and negro lineage, the Saif is a man of tremendous magnificence, dignity and refinement whose intelligence and charisma enable him to retain his hold over his empire and twist the imperialists around his lifttle finger. Nevertheless there is a certain ambivalence about him which is reflected in Ouologuem's attitude: he is possibly the most oppressive in the long history of the Saifs, though his shrewdness ensures that he never really loses the loyalty of the people. This skill is demonstrated when early in his reign he converts the traditionalist populace to Islam, since he shrewdly realizes that it will thus be easier to hold them down and exploit them. However, whatever his faults (which are many), the Saif might appear to many African nationalists as a champion of his country resisting the imperialist advance. He is given real moral stature in the heat of the battle when he shouts, like Richard III: 'Give me an army, I ask no more. An army!... The subjects of my empire have risen against me, seeking refuge with those apes in helmets. An army and I'll send those white apes packing.' Defeated, he signs a peace treaty with the French which turns out to be not worth the paper on which it is written since the Saif is able to use it as a cover for his devious manipulations, which include the systematic murder and harassment of French administrators and missionaries. In consequence, he is able to transform defeat into genius 'and the dictatorship of a tyrannical dynasty into eternal glory'. The Saif is fighting a rearguard guerilla action against the imperialists, and although Ouologuem presents him rather unflatteringly in these scenes, there is little doubt that his action would be applauded by many contemporary Africans.

The splendour of the Saif's court, even in the moment of defeat, is powerfully captured by Ouologuem.

> Surrounded by a court as magnificent as in the days of his glory, clothed in the imperial insignia, he sat on his throne; his feet rested on satin carpets embroidered with golden flowers. Over his short tunic he wore a large, richly embossed dashiki, open at the throat; from his neck hung two fetishes; on his head a fez surrounded by a jet-black turban; on his legs dark trousers and on his feet Moorish boots with hippopotamus hide soles.
>
> Raising his arms, he set upon his head a golden diadem whose points were studded with pearls. Soberly but richly clad, his loyal retinue were more dejected than usual, their eyes submerged in the darkness of dreams.
>
> Forgetting the salaam, Saif did not rise to greet the French delegation, but merely motioned them to be seated. Behind the emperor, two masters-at-arms, dressed all in red, thrust their assegais into the ground and stood motionless in an attitude of barbaric nobility, their arms extended as though to swear an oath. In their left hands they held a sharpened axe and a silver mace fastened with lion hide, the emblem of royalty. Two gleaming muskets were slung over their shoulders. On their faces they wore masks made from the skin of the king of beasts. (p. 31)

Ouologuem may disapprove of the Saif's tyranny, but there is no doubt of his responsiveness to the majesty and dignity of his person and the splendour of his court.

The Saif is a consumate schemer who lays his plots with the calculation of the brilliant chess player that he is. The reader watches spellbound, for instance, at the complicated but masterly plot he engineers to bring about the administrator Chevalier's death; a kind of awe surrounds his figure even as he sets about this mission of slaughter, and he is so successful that on the death of the administrator he is rewarded by the unsuspecting French who create him a Chevalier of the Legion of Honour.

Saif's skill in manipulating the whites is further shown in the elaborate deception he practises on the German anthropologist Shrobenius. The latter is one of those western scholars whose uncritical adulation of African history and culture can be even more condescending and offensive than the sarcasm of detractors. The essential emptiness of Shrobenius's criticism can be seen in the glowing tribute he pays to the excellence of Negro culture and the Negro personality.

> 'But these people are disciplined and civilized to the marrow! On all sides wide, tranquil avenues where we breathe the grandeur, the human genius of a people ... It was only when white imperialism infiltrated the country with its colonial violence and materialism that this highly civilized people fell abruptly into a state of savagery, that accusations of cannibalism, of primitivism, were raised, when on the contrary – witness the splendour of its art – the true face of Africa is the grandiose empires of the Middle Ages, a society marked by wisdom, beauty, prosperity, order, nonviolence, and humanism, and it is here that we must seek the true cradle of Egyptian civilization.' (p. 94)

Ouologuem's powerful demonstration of African pre-colonial violence and degradation effectively exposes Shrobenius's ignorance of the facts of African history, and it is a mark of the ignorance of the West about African affairs that such wordy nonsense earns him a chair at the Sorbonne. Shrobenius himself personifies 'mercantile intellectualism', the creed of those who make reputations out of their stupid fulminations on Negro art: 'Thus the Nakem artist has no universe. Or rather, his universe is a vast solitude; no; a series of solitudes ...' And all this is based on fake masks. Ouologuem has brilliantly captured the meaningless academic jargon that can so easily pass for scholarship.

It is a measure of the Saif's great skill that in spite of the oppressiveness of his rule he contrives to retain the favour of notables and serfs alike. The niggertrash revere him even when he is being most cruel to them. For instance, on the outbreak of the First World War he is able to whip up the niggertrash into a frenzy of enthusiasm for the alien conflict with the voice of 'celestial inspiration'; and they run joyfully to their deaths confident of resurrection, while the Saif negotiates with the French authorities that not a single hair of the heads of the notables' sons should be touched.

Although Ouologuem is responsive to the Saif's effectiveness and magnificence, it is central to his purpose to emphasize the cruelty and degradation of his regime. He does not flinch from the portrayal of the squalor and degradation of the serfs. The case of Sankolo, who is reconditioned as a zombi or walking corpse in order to be used as unpaid labour, is typical. He and lots of others like him continue to inhabit the twilight zone between life and death, consciousness and unconsciousness. Appropriately, Ouologuem uses surrealistic techniques to describe the march of Sankolo and the other zombies, to communicate the impression of beings who have been robbed of their human personality, moving about in a permanent trance-like state, perpetually under the influence of powerful drugs and living almost entirely in a world of fantasy. In this state of semi-awareness they can only shout for more women and drugs. The helplessness of people like these and of the niggertrash in general under the Saif's rule surely comes out in Sankolo's cry of anguish: 'Don't you see, a nigger is nothing; a nigger woman is good enough to fuck. We're helpless; we haven't got the law on our side ... Oh, horrible' (p. 107).

The plight of the niggertrash is focused on in the story of Tambira and Kassoumi who are generally meant to be representative of the serfs. Tambira is a serving woman in the Saif's household and Kassoumi is a slave cook. Their personal tragedy is skilfully interwoven with the story of the corruption and tyranny that obtain in the Saif's empire. Kassoumi is presented right from the start as an ungainly, grotesque figure who is eventually to become a symbol of suffering, a worthy object of compassion. His ill-fitting clothes are themselves a symbol of the degraded unpaid worker. Kassoumi finds relief from his dreary oppressive existence in a spot in the shade of a banana tree where he goes whenever he is off duty. It is a spot which reminds him of his home, the only place where he could feel happy. Ouologuem's prose rises to heights of lyricism as he traces the development of the love affair between Tambira and Kassoumi. He demonstrates the exquisite beauty of this relationship in the midst of the carnage, squalor and corruption. He also effectively communicates Tambira's sheer vitality and sexual appeal: 'Her wide, firm lips open over dazzling white teeth, and her questioning eyes brought out the velvet softness of her skin – the colour of old mahogany, firm and desirable, burnished by the blood-kindling air of the Yame ... she pranced with malicious merriment and clucked for joy' (p. 40). Ouologuem also skilfully demonstrates the power of love as it takes full possession of a man's mind: 'He was obsessed and on edge; the thought of Tambira filled him, he felt driven toward her by his whole heart and body. He wanted to hold her, to crush her, to take her into himself. In his rage he shook with a sense of importance, with impatience and irritation, because she did not belong to him' (p. 41). Ouologuem presents the declaration of Kassoumi's passion and the consummation of their love against the background of a beautiful and approving nature; there is the lovely detail of the bird bursting into ecstatic song as Kassoumi confesses his love, and on hearing the song of the bird Tambira's heart melts with tenderness and she presses the man's hand. When they make love in the tall grass the leaves murmur as a light breeze brushes softly over them. In the midst of all the intrigue, pretence and self-seeking that obtain in this realm, this love is presented as perfectly natural and innocent. Ouologuem's account of the love making is realistic without being obscene. The whole affair is managed with great skill – without prurience or sentimentality, and yet with detailed demonstration. Characteristically, the Saif seeks to pervert this honest, natural love. His consent to the marriage is only a trick, an affectation of paternalism which he finds highly profitable. And of course, he claims the privilege of 'the first night'.

As his children grow up, Kassoumi looks on education as the means of saving them from slavery, and Tambira shows justifiable pride and happiness in her sons and a keen interest in their education. However, it is not ordained that she and her husband will escape the doom of the niggertrash, for in the end she is exploited and destroyed by the inhumanity of the system. While consulting a sorcerer about the success of her children in their final elementary school examinations she is raped by him, and then blackmailed and raped and killed by the Saif's evil agents Kratonga and Wampoulo. Tambira's terrible death is another of those episodes which might possibly suggest to some readers that Ouologuem overdoes the violence. Some stomachs might well not be able to take the discovery of Tambira's body in the latrine and Kassoumi sucking out the worms from her nostrils. Nevertheless, we admire Kassoumi's touching devotion as he pulls out his wife's body, washes it and buries it. It is one of the few instances of genuine devotion to be found in the whole novel. Kassiumi's own fate is scarcely less terrible. He is treated in the same way as Sankolo and sold into slavery; and his family is all but destroyed. Ouologuem could hardly have used a better method to demonstrate the suffering of the niggertrash.

The novel partly deals with the impact of French colonialism on indigenous African society and therefore includes the theme of tradition versus modernism, which is handled particularly on the educational level. The people are forced to decide whether to accept the white man's education and send their children to school, or continue in the old ways. For the serfs like Kassoumi and Tambira, education is the ultimate source of deliverance from the scourge of slavery; but the crafty Saif sees it as an undesirable and alien imposition on the traditions of the people and decides that only the sons of the servant class should be constrained to undergo it. Following the Saif's example the notables encourage marriages among the servants with the object of producing as many children of the serf class as possible who would go to the French mission schools instead of their own children. Thus the Saif and his aristocracy shrewdly arrange a compromise which ensures that they both conform with the demands of the French imperialists and prevent the future nobility from being contaminated by a foreign culture.

One such serf child is Raymond Spartacus Kassoumi, eldest son of Tambira and Kassoumi. A brilliant success at school, Raymond initially earns the malevolence of his fellow serfs. Even in those early days it is clear that French education has a perplexing effect on him for he is torn between French and traditional ways. Characteristically the wily Saif encourages his educational ambitions, but only with a view to using the educated Raymond as his instrument to further his intrigues with the French. He even encourages the love affair between Raymond and Tata, which duplicates that between Raymond's parents, with the intention of using it for his own sinister ends. The general point is that the aristocracy are going to use the educated sons of the serfs as their instruments: 'The life that Raymond lived from that day on was the life of his whole generation – the first generation of native administrators maintained by the notables in a state of gilded prostitution' (p. 136).

On being sent to continue his studies in Paris, Raymond goes through the spiritual agony experienced by other intelligent young men like him from francophone countries. A child of violence from traditional Africa, he finds he has to come to terms with white European society. Gradually white culture takes possession of him and he begins to despise his native Africa. Raymond is trying deliberately to disguise his African personality and adopt a white one, but the consequences are disastrous because instead of understanding French culture he merely blindly accepts it. Yet, though France continues to fascinate him, he discovers it is as difficult to get rid of Africa 'as a plant of its roots'. The result, inevitably, is confusion and aimlessness. He forgets his family and plunges into the sexual decadence of the West. What we are witnessing is the destruction of Raymond's, the educated serf's, soul. However, he is brutally shocked into a realization of the aimlessness of his life when he discovers that his own love partner in a brothel orgy is no other than his sister Kadidia whom he has not seen for several years. His young sister is a prostitute and he has committed incest with her in the worst possible circumstances. Raymond is cruelly confronted with the fate of his generation, his class and his race. He learns in addition that his father has been sold as a slave and that his brothers, having been drugged, have gone mad. The symbol of prostitution is very significant. Raymond's class has been prostituted to the needs of blacks and whites alike. While his sister has been used to satisfy the lusts of white and black men, he himself has been prostituted not just to French civilization but also to serve the political needs of the African aristocracy in his country.

There is no doubt that Ouologuem juggles with the plot a bit in order to bring about this series of horrifying incidents. It seems too much of a coincidence that Raymond's sister should be a prostitute in the very brothel he and his friends choose to enter and that the girl allocated to him as his sexual partner should be his sister. It also seems incredible that Raymond, who has not been away from home all that long, should be unable to recognize his sister. Nevertheless, the point Ouologuem wishes to make is clear; the niggertrash have been exploited and destroyed by both blacks and whites in both Africa and Europe.

When Kadidia is killed by a sadistic customer, the shock and the information she has revealed about their family throw Raymond into a state of depression. His studies suffer, he loses his scholarship in consequence and his financial situation deteriorates sharply. Although he makes one determined attempt to revert to his old Nakem habits, he continues to drift aimlessly. In this condition he meets a homosexual who confidently makes advances to him. Though Raymond is aware that the man's confidence is a reflection of his own degradation and of the fact that he is a 'nigger', he is not revolted. Financial need is pressing. Raymond realizes that this is the destiny of the serf class, whose life is one of unending prostitution. He prostitutes himself, just like his sister: 'The student stood up: he had consented to sell himself.' But over and above the question of prostitution these two men are bound together by the similarity of their condition. Like Raymond, Lambert the homosexual is an exhausted shell who has known suffering and solitude and they both seek through this love to escape their anguish. Raymond, indeed, has the look 'of a beaten dog'. There is little doubt that Ouologuem presents this homosexual affair with great sympathy. The quality of his prose rises once more to heights of lyricism and dazzling beauty equalled only by the description of the affair between Tambira and Kassoumi. Certainly, the accounts of the other heterosexual scenes do not match the excellence of these homosexual ones. The touch of beauty and the note of responsive sympathy is surely evident in this passage.

> They were no longer man and man, lover and partner, but a creature apart, issued from some strange power of life, apogee of the natural order of love, a great sea that stretched out in a hammock and never spoke, but shuddered. Pressed together to the full length and breadth of their good, warm bodies, they breathed everlastingly the air stirred up by the sound of their pairing ... At these moments a different tenderness aroused a surge of gratitude in both of them. Saying nothing, they took each other's hands and kissed each other at length. In slow sips Kassoumi, with the wretched look of a beaten dog, drank their fitfully whispered confessions of love, drank them with a gentle pressure of his tongue against his palate as he might have eaten flowers, airy-fingered roses. He loved this taste of rose petals when he kissed the man, relishing even the insipid taste of the air in his nostrils. And each breath seemed to carry an imperceptible train; the winnowing of harvests forever repeated: and what was born and what died, the sap that flowed, wrapped in the guilt of their two bodies, was he, Kassoumi, the son of a slave, the cornered, alienated nigger engaged in being reborn well-born. At the height of his effervescence he rose to inhabit the long silence of his birth. He germed like the earth ... (p. 155)

The passage contains hints of ritual and there are suggestions of generation and even, paradoxically, of fecundity. Mention is made of 'the sap that flowed', of Raymond germing 'like the earth' and of 'his effervescence'. It seems as if, through this amorous encounter, Raymond is going through a process of rebirth; he is 'engaged in being reborn, well-born'. In what sense, however, can Raymond be said to have been 'reborn, well-born'? Is there not something offensive to the African sensibility in the implication that as a result of mating with a white man the Negro Raymond is 'reborn, well-born'? It soon becomes clear, however, that this is a ritual not so much of rebirth as of rediscovery. Ouologuem's comment is that Raymond's search was not so much for ecstasy as of the profound meaning of his own destruction. For after the lyrical bout of love making, images and events from his past life in Nakem come out of 'the depth of forgetfulness to confront him'. It was his history and destiny, that of a slave whose name is Spartacus, that had inevitably led him to prostitute himself to this white man. The next day the glamour of the pairing disappears, and although Raymond is led back compulsively to the white man, it is in

fact 'to his own identity: fear, the problem of his body and his skin' (p.
157). The point is that hitherto Raymond has been trying to live like a
Frenchman, trying to forget his African identity and slave origins. It
takes Kadidia's revelations and his own degradation by the homosexual to make him realize the full implications of his ancestry –
that he is, after all, a black man, a slave oppressed and used by blacks
and whites alike. The affair with the homosexual is therefore a ritual of
rediscovery and only in this sense of rebirth.

Lambert turns out to be a very callous man who merely uses
Raymond to satisfy his own needs, even though he saves him from
want and gives him enough financial support to make it possible for
him to resume his studies successfully and regain his scholarship.
When Lambert's mother, with whom he has been secretly in love,
orders him to get married, he abandons Raymond as nonchalantly as a
paid daily charwoman. But Raymond continues to do brilliantly,
winning all the academic honours, becoming the ideal student, 'the
pearl of French culture'. Having become assimilated, he even marries
a Frenchwoman. His marriage to this unattractive daughter of a vulgar
ex-laundress is a sign of Raymond's recognition of his real position in
this French society, even though he is now a highly successful
academic and architect. This is the position that French society is
prepared to accord him. He realizes that 'the society in which his
mother-in-law moved was no better than an "advanced" nigger, living
among whites, was entitled to' (p. 160). But Raymond's prostitution
has gone so far that he is prepared to accept this position. He even
builds a house for his mother-in-law and flings himself body and soul
into the defence of invaded France during the Second World War, just
as a quarter of a century earlier the niggertrash, at Saif's persuasion,
had enthusiastically gone to their deaths in support of France. History
has repeated itself; the niggertrash, educated as well as uneducated, are
still being exploited by blacks and whites alike. Raymond is left for
dead on the field of battle. But through sheer determination and
courage he escapes and deserves to be treated as a hero, but he is
ignored. He discovers that in spite of all his sacrifice and achievements
he is still a *French subject*, not a Frenchman.

Raymond's return to a Nakem-Ziuko which is now thirsting for
reform marks the end of his alienation, but not the end of his
prostitution. Realizing the deplorable condition of his country, he
wishes to be revolutionary; in a sense it is his duty to be revolutionary,
but he is forestalled by the wiliness of the Saif and his notables who are

determined to use the educated sons of the serf class to defend their interests in the French National Assembly in Paris. Consequently, although Raymond returns home amidst general rejoicing as the people's man, he merely becomes a pawn in the hands of the French and the Saif who continues to retain his customary hold over the people. Raymond has once more sold his soul; this is the fate of the poor niggertrash.

Although the Saif shrewdly continues to manipulate events in Nakem, he is eventually prevailed upon to temper his cruelty to the governed through the efforts of the Abbé Henri, a patently good and self-sacrificing man, who is also the voice of morality in the novel and obviously a foil to the Saif. The Abbé reclaims the Saif for the world of morality, not just through his humility and Christian charity, but by sheer force of intellect and subtlety. He is the only one, in fact, who proves to be a match for the Saif. It is he who discovers, through patient research, the Saif's method of killing men with asps. Both the argument and the game of the chess between the two men at the end of the book are of immense significance. The Abbé starts the discussion by telling the Saif of a film he has seen (*Zamba*) which was inspired by the history of Nakem-Ziuko. The film which is about violence, is an analogue of what has been happening in Nakem, and the villain who stands at the centre and pulls all the strings is obviously the Saif himself. The Saif is quick to realize from this account of the film that the bishop is aware of all his schemes, but he goes on to make excuses. He blames humanity's chaos on the world's oddity: 'We are wanderers in disaster, that's a fact.' In this way the Saif tries to disclaim personal responsibility for the disasters into which Nakem has been plunged. If Nakem suffers, he goes on, it is because the human machine has broken down, but Destiny is always there, ready to forgive. Suffering and antagonism are inevitable in human history and politics. 'Man is in history, and history is in politics. Politics is cleavage. No solidarity is possible. Nor purity' (p. 175).

The game of chess is symbolic on more than one level; it is symbolic of the game of life and politics in which the Saif and countless others are engaged in their own way, but is it also a battle for the bishop's life, for the Saif intends to kill the former with an asp in his usual way and the bishop can only escape death by demonstrating superior intelligence and beating the Saif at his own game. The bishop is the only match for the Saif because he, like the Saif, is realistic; he also has faced up to the 'ultimate lie or the ultimate truth of existence'. In the game the bishop explains all the Saif's moves to him, thus showing that he is aware of his methods: 'And all that, the whole panoply, is only to save the king's head – your conscience – the immobilized piece' (p. 179). He also lets the Saif know that he is aware that the cylinder contains an asp trained to kill him. This immobilizes the Saif and simultaneously puts the bishop in a winning position in the game. The Saif thus realizes that he does not have the moral right to kill him. Where the Saif had hitherto believed that the triumph of right is the triumph of its might, the bishop now teaches him that though right without might may be a caricature, might without right is an abomination. When the Saif throws the cylinder containing the asp into the fire it symbolizes not just his inability to vanquish the Abbé, who has now proved at least his intellectual equal, but his rejection of violent methods to achieve his ends. The rest of the match demonstrates that the bishop and the Saif have come to an amicable understanding. As the Saif himself says: 'Nakem was born generations ago, and only in the last fifteen minutes have men learned to discuss the state of its health' (pp. 180–1). The Saif has the assurance that although he has rejected violence, 'the king will not die'. He has come to accept the religion of love and tolerance: 'There is always one who loves and the other who turns his cheek.' He and the Abbé envisage a future Nakem where both the peacemakers and the politicians will be able to coexist. While the Abbé says 'Blessed are the peacemakers, for they shall see God,' the Saif replies: 'Blessed are the politicians, for they shall understand life.' And Ouologuem ends the novel with a most beautiful coda.

> That night, as they sought one another until the terrace was soiled with the black summits of dawn, a dust fell on the chessboard; but in that hour when the eyes of Nakem take flight in search of memories, forest and coast were fertile and hot with compassion. And such was the earth of men that the balance between air, water, and fire was no more than a game. (p. 182)

The most cursory glance at *Bound to Violence* ought to suggest that Ouologuem is heavily indebted to the oral tradition. The novel is obviously the product not only of remarkable intelligence, but of first-rate research ability. The first chapter, 'The Legend of the Saifs', consists almost entirely of a reworking of myths and legends derived from the tales of griots and troubadours and the epics intoned by the elders. At times Ouologuem tries to tell the story in the same way as the

griots and troubadours would have told it. The accents of the story
teller are surely evident in the following.

> Our eyes drink the brightness of the sun and, overcome, marvel at
> their tears. *Mashallah! wa bismallah!* ... (p. 3)

> The Most-High did this in His infinite mercy – prayer and peace
> upon it! (p. 6)

> His countenance was like the lightning and his gown was white; his
> reign was just and glorious. (God keep his soul.) (p. 8)

> A perfect crime. And as such often repeated. *Mashallah! wa
> bismillah!* The name of Allah upon us and around us! And forgive
> us, O Lord. (p. 47)

The prayer tag at the end of such passages, couched at times in Arabic,
and occasionally in the local language, is one of the indicators of the
influence of the oral tradition; this, surely, is the way in which the
griots, who had a quasi-religious function, would have related it. At
times Ouologuem conveys the nuances of the oral tradition even in his
own obvious commentary as in: 'When the Immortal One makes the
sun – diamond of the house of His Power – set, then, along with the
tales of the oral tradition, the elders intone the famous epic...' (p. 6).
Clearly Ouologuem is not here quoting directly from the oral tradition
nor is he retelling the story in the style of the griots, since he makes
reference to the oral tradition itself and to a particular epic.
Occasionally he quotes directly from the oral tradition, making
reference to the particular tale the account comes from.

> The consequences of his audacity are related by Mahmud Meknud
> Trare, descended in an unbroken line from griot ancestors and
> himself a griot in the present-day African republic of Nakem-Ziuko:
> 'After that the Saif decided that only the sons of the servant class
> would be constrained to undergo French education...' (p. 46)

Apart from leaving the impression that the work is an extended oral
tale, the oral tradition has other significant effects on the style. It can
impart dignity to the prose as in 'A hundred million of the damned – so
moan the troubadours of Nakem when the evening vomits forth its
starry diamonds – were carried away' (p. 12). Then the prayer tag at
the end of passages can be used to devastating sarcastic and ironic
effect, as in 'In reality the nobility, warriors in the days of the first
Saifs (Glory to the Almighty God), had become intriguers for power:
Amen. At the death of the accursed Saif (Blessed be the Eternal One!),

conscious of their own need of stability (So be it!), they had flung the people into a bath of pseudo-spirituality, while enslaving them materially. (And praised)' (p. 23). Indeed, one of the hallmarks of this novel's style is the peculiar quality of the narrator's tone of voice. Usually ironic and sarcastic, it is also characterized by wry sardonic humour as in 'The Saif dynasty went from bad to worse with the grandsons of Saif Rabban Johanan, the eldest of whom, Jacob, so the griots relate, "spent his nights expounding all manner of abstruse theological problems to his cat"' (pp. 18–19). At times Ouologuem eschews even irony and sarcasm, commenting adversely on his characters in his own person.

> Shrobenius, that human crayfish afflicted with a groping mania for resuscitating an African universe – cultural autonomy, he called it – which had lost all living reality ... displayed his love of Africa and his tempestuous knowledge with the assurance of a high school student who had slipped through his final examinations by the skin of his teeth ... Then, obliged to acknowledge the spiritual aridity of certain manifestations of social life, he fell into a somnolent stupor, no longer capable even of sadness. (p. 87)

The similarly mordant satire at the expense of Raymond's mother-in-law descends almost to the level of downright abuse.

> As wrinkled as the rear end of a she-ass, loud-mouthed, hard-working, maniacally stingy, she yacked incessantly ... Madame Teyssedou, Suzanne's mother, had the spacious udders of a buffalo cow. She was stubborn and narrow-minded, the kind of woman who goes through life without ever suspecting any of its undercurrents, subtleties, or shadings, who perceives nothing and deforms everything, blind to the possibility that anyone might think, believe, or act differently from herself. (p. 160)

One of the distinctive marks of Ouologuem's art, like Ousmane's, is his brilliant use of language. There can be no doubt of his mastery of his French medium which one suspects is even reflected in the excellent English translation. At times his prose exudes the tough intellectual quality obvious in:

> The crux of the matter is that violence, vibrant in its unconditional submission to the will to power, becomes a prophetic illumination, a manner of questioning and answering, a dialogue, a tension, an oscillation, which from murder to murder makes the possibilities respond to each other, complete or contradict each other. (p. 173)

This is taut cerebral language, and the reader is far from forming the impression that it is meaningless jargon. At other times it can be simple, though still remaining powerful, as in this account of the sexual encounter between Raymond and his wife.

> Her lips are edged with honey-coloured flesh. Her tongue, soft and light in her open mouth. He nibbles it, bites it, draws it to him, devours it, savouring his revenge ... Immobile, passive, holding down the white woman's neck with both hands, he pours out his hatred. Her hair falls over her eyes as frantically, with trembling hands, she busies herself with his body and slips off his shorts. (p. 168)

The prose can rise to heights of loveliness as in:

> She walked with a slight swaying motion, as though carried by a skiff, seeming to curtsy nimbly at every step. He could not take his eyes off her and was seized with an overwhelming desire for this woman. His back broke out in a cold sweat, and he was filled with a dull rage, a helpless anger. But then, brusquely assuming an air of detachment, he tried with gentle gestures to bring himself to reason, to forget his madness. (p. 39)

It can be lyrical, as in the description of the Tambira–Kassoumi love affair, and it can exude a poetic grandeur as in Sankolo's account of his experiences. Ouologuem also makes occasional attempts to modify the language and give it an African flavour, as in 'May your path be straight' or 'May God hear you and reward you'. His superb descriptive power is partly due to his use of images. They are drawn largely from the world of traditional life as in 'the members of that society who had no more courage than a wet hen' and 'his face in anger turned as yellow as pepper'. Appropriately, in a novel concerned with violence, most of the images are taken from the more repellent aspects of the animal kingdom as in 'The crown forced men to swallow life as a boa swallows a stinking antelope', 'That same night, at the hour when the jackals fill the bush with their howling, the emperor gathered together his whole court...' and 'the Arab conquest ... settled over the land like a she-dog baring her white fangs in raucous laughter'.

Ouologuem's realization of his characters is also faultless. So many of them stand out in this motley throng because the author presents then in detail through thought and action. Apart from the superb portraits of the Saif, Raymond, Tambira and Kassoumi, the reader is not likely to forget Sankolo, Bouremi, Chevalier, Awa, Wampoulo, Kratonga, Shrobenius and even Kadidia. Ouologuem relies not so much on a complex plot and structure as on a full and detailed presentation of the experiences of his characters, thus achieving a novel of remarkable solidity and significance. His achievement is rare in the whole history of the African novel.

NOTES

1 Some editions expunge the allegedly plagiarized portions.
2 Yambo Ouologuem, *Bound to Violence* (Heinemann, London, 1971). All further page references are to this edition.

9. Ayi Kwei Armah

▼▼

Two Thousand Seasons

Ayi Kwei Armah's first three novels, *The Beautyful Ones Are Not Yet Born*, *Fragments* and *Why Are We So Blest?*, sought to expose political and social corruption not only in contemporary Ghana but in Africa as a whole. On the other hand, his fourth novel, *Two Thousand Seasons*, delves into the past and in one majestic sweep of Africa's history seeks to demonstrate how those pure African values and traditions which used to exist in an almost prehistoric past were destroyed through the exploits of Arab predators and European destroyers. The similarity with Ouologuem is obvious; but where the anti-Negritudist Malian author seeks to dispel all the myths about African history, declaring that black notables, no less than Arab and European conquerors and imperialists, were responsible for the historical degradation of the continent, Armah adopts an essentially Negritudist position, the net effect of his presentation being the total condemnation of the Arabs and Europeans as the destroyers of the pristine values of a pure Africa. It is true that even in Armah's work there are indications that the black people had started losing 'the way' before the advent of the predators and destroyers; indeed there is a suggestion, as in Ouologuem's novel, that their subjugation by the imperialists was itself the consequence of the black people's loss of the way. But the venom Armah directs at the imperialists, a venom unequalled in African literature, and the constant reference to the imperialists as the destroyers, indicates that he lays the blame squarely at their door. It would be a remarkable twist of fate if the anglophone writers begin their flirtation with Negritude at precisely the moment when the francophones seem to be abandoning it; for this exercise in racial retrieval, this attempt to rediscover a glorious African past unadulterated by all those forces associated with the imperialists, is now to be detected, not just in

Armah, but to a certain extent in Ngugi and in some of Soyinka's recent pronouncements.[1]

As might be expected in a work dedicated to the celebration of pure African values unadulterated by the mores of the West, the language of *Two Thousand Seasons* is deliberately given an African flavour. With the possible exception of Okara in *The Voice*, Armah makes a much more conscious attempt than any other African novelist to impart an African flavour to the language he employs. The rich traditions of African oral and lyric poetry are invoked here. The powerful prologue itself is written in the style of African vatic utterance or that of the African dirge, as in:

> Woe the headwater needing to give, giving only to floodwater flowing desertward. Woe the link from stream to stream. Woe the link receiving springwater only to pass it on in a stream flowing to waste, seeking extinction.
>   You hearers, seers, imaginers, thinkers, rememberers, you prophets called to communicate truths of the living way to a people fascinated unto death...[2]

Predictably, Anoa's seminal prophesy is also cast in vatic form.

> 'But our voice is not harsh enough for your hearing. You are hastening into destruction so fast its flavour, its very name, will be sweetness to you, to your children, to so many generations of our people hurtling down the whiteness of destruction's slope. Two thousand seasons: a thousand you will spend descending into abysses that would stop your heart and break your mind merely to contemplate... Two thousand seasons: a thousand dry, a thousand moist.' (p. 25)

At times the language is patently that of the praise song.

> Water hanging clear, water too open to hide the veined rock underneath, water washing pebbles blue and smooth black, yellow like some everlasting offspring of the moon, water washing sand, water flowing to quiet meetings with the swift Esuba, to the broad, quiet Su Tsen, river washing you, Anoa, water washing you.
>   Land of the Duiker, best of animals, attacking none, knowing ways to keep attackers distant, land that should have been perfect for the way, land that will yet be: your praisesong should be woven from the beauty of sounds found only in the future, a beauty springing in its wholeness when the way is found again, Anoa. (p. 89)

It is to devices such as these that the novel owes its intensely poetic quality.

Indeed, the style of the novel demonstrates that Armah has made use of certain aspects of the African oral narrative tradition. *Two Thousand Seasons*, like *Bound to Violence*, reads for the most part like an African oral chronicle. We are aware of the talking voice – the African talking voice – with Armah deliberately manipulating structure and idiom so that the prose has a genuine African ring, as in: 'Concerning reasons why this fearful holocaust was to come upon us, whether truly it was a vision directed unto us and not something that merely chanced unluckily to glance across the mind of one, two, three among us; concerning all this the first three were as mute as the mighty odum tree' (p. 19), or 'Hau! Many, so many of the predators from the desert died that beautiful night of blackness' (p. 34), or 'Hear this for the sound of it' (p. 54) and 'There was no ease to that conclusion's coming' (p. 63). Inevitably, however, Armah finds it impossible to sustain this illusion through language of an African oral narrative. When he gets really immersed in absorbing episodes, especially those describing the exploits of the idealistic group of initiates or the schemes of the white destroyers, the style tends to lose its African oral quality and approximates to something like normal standard English: 'What we do know is that after the success of our escape the white predators executed another terrible slaughter among those who chose to stay. The relatives of all who had spurned oppression were burned to ashes' (p. 71), or 'In his worst nightmares the king imagined himself caught in a whole society of unimpressed eyes, sceptical ears, staring, listening, undeceivable. If ever the society became that way it would be impossible for him to remain king' (p. 114). There are even occasions when, having lapsed into standard English idiom, Armah seems to pull up short and remind himself that he must retain the quality of the African oral narrative. On such occasions the style has a self-conscious ring about it.

The air was heavy with its motionless humidity. Among us the sound of coughing, at first staggered and subdued, grew to be a strong, constant noise. Even the white destroyers in their greed grew alarmed for our health. They changed the method of our feeding. Now, except for the irons on our legs, we were freed in little groups, seven, ten at a time, and driven upward by an armed askari to take our corn. Water also we drank up there, after being made to jump and run for air and for the loosening of stiffened bodies.
Ask the destroyed. They alone can tell you, they who have been taken into whiteness ... (p. 197)

There is a noticeable change in the style at 'Water also we drank up there', which becomes even more pronounced with 'Ask the destroyed ... they who have been taken into whiteness'. And quite often, when Armah launches into a condemnation of oppression and cruelty, the sentiment comes nakedly from the author's own voice and the oral narrative quality disappears, as in 'The time's tale is of jealous, cowardly men determined to cling to power, and the result of that determination: the slaughter of honest people, the banishment of honest words, the raising of flattery and lies into the authorized currency of the time, the reduction of public life to an unctuous interaction' (p. 14).

In *Two Thousands Seasons*, as in *The Beautyful Ones Are Not Yet Born*, Armah reinforces his points by a powerful deployment of images and symbols. Images of life, vitality, fecundity and meaningful movement associated with the pristine African 'way' play against images of death, aridity and inertia associated with the world of the predators and destroyers. The colours black and white themselves assume a symbolic significance. Whiteness becomes synonymous with alien values and with death and destruction, not just because in the African imagination it is the colour of death and disease, but because it is the colour of the destructive imperialists. It is significant that Armah regards both the Arab predators and the European destroyers as white. On the other hand black is the colour associated with racial triumph and eventual fulfilment. Then the setting sun associated with the path towards death is set against the rising sun which is associated with life. Correspondingly the West, where the sun sets, is regarded as the home of the destroyers, is often referred to as the 'falling' and associated with death; whilst the East, the 'rising', is the source of life and vitality. But by far the most important symbols are those of the desert and water. The desert is an agent of destruction associated with the whites. It is presented as a monstrous devouring force, sucking and converting everything into its own destructive and unproductive self, rather like 'caves' in E. M. Forster's *A Passage to India*. Everything that has posed a threat to the vitality and purity of Africa and the black race is subsumed under the compelling but frightful image of the desert. Everything that is heading for destruction, disintegration, decadence and death is heading desertwards. The desert is, of course, the home of the white Arab predators, the first imperialists, and by association it is linked also with the white European destroyers. Armah can therefore say with some conviction that the desert was itself created by a people 'whose spirit is itself the seed of death'. This suggests that the desert is not just a physical entity, but the total situation created by the imperialists. It represents a state of mind, a set of values and attitudes, and it is cultural, economic, political and religious.

On the other hand the symbol of water is set against that of the desert; it represents the pure, cleansing, regenerating, life-giving indigenous forces of Mother Africa. In particular, the waters of Anoa receive honourable mention: '. . . the waters of Anoa – water suspended bubbling at the lip of its forest fountain, water falling like long, translucent threads airing in the wind before the masters of the weaving art take them for their use, water flowing, rushing, water slowed down behind new obstacles, water patiently rising till it overflows what can never stop it. . .' (p. 117). The symbol of water is particularized in the symbol of the clear, pure spring. And it is the spring which is constantly contrasted with the desert. Where the spring lives by reciprocity – giving and receiving – the selfish, destructive desert knows no giving; it can only take. The threat to African values and the safety of African life is represented by the image of the desert sucking the spring into itself.

> Springwater flowing to the desert, where you flow there is no regeneration. The desert takes. The desert knows no giving. To the giving water of your flowing it is not in the nature of the desert to return anything but destruction. Springwater flowing to the desert, your future is extinction. . .
>
> Woe the headwater needing to give, giving only to floodwater flowing desertward. Woe the link from stream to stream. Woe the link receiving springwater only to pass it on in a stream flowing to waste, seeking extinction. . .
>
> It is for the spring to give. It is for springwater to flow. But if the spring could continue to give and the springwater continue flowing, the desert is no direction. Along the desert road springwater is the sap of young wood prematurely blazing, meant to carry life quietly, darkly from roots to farthest veins but abruptly betrayed into devouring light, converted to scalding pus hissing its own vessel's destruction. Along the desert road springwater is blood of a murdered woman when the sun leaves no shadow. (pp. ix–xi)

It is impossible to change the nature of the desert, just as it is impossible to change the nature of white men; it can only be overwhelmed by the concerted effort of all the waters of the universe. However, it must not be supposed that all forms of water are beneficent. The sea is different. Being the place where the white destroyers come from, it is almost as destructive as the desert. While *en route* to the coast the idealistic initiates are quick to notice the difference between the calm river they have been rowing on and the raging angry sea they now encounter. The river's easy flow gives way to a wild turbulence. The river is indigenous and reassuring, whilst the sea is alien and threatening, and the clashing meeting between river and sea symbolizes the coming conflict between the indigenes and the alien Europeans: 'The seawater came in long, curling waves to a meeting with the darker water from the land. In both waters there was a forward motion, so at the place of their meeting there was no quiet mixing but a violent upward surge from clashing waves' (p. 118).

The most significant fact about *Two Thousand Seasons* is Armah's positing of a far-distant past when all the black people belonged to one vast African nation with its own genuine, pure system of values or way of life that the author consistently refers to as 'the way' – 'our way'. And he posits this fact in spirited defiance of the Europeans who distort the essentials of African history: 'That we the black people are one people we know. Destroyers will travel long distances in their minds and out to deny you this truth. We do not argue with them, the fools. Let them presume to instruct us about ourselves. That too is in their nature' (p. 4). The main characteristic of this authentic African 'way' is what Armah refers to as reciprocity – the principle of mutual giving and receiving. Giving and receiving are intertwined and together constitute a principle of life; death ensues when the two are separated. 'Receiving, giving, giving, receiving, all that lives is twin. Who would cast the spell of death, let him separate the two. Whatever cannot give, whatever is ignorant even of receiving, knowing only taking, that thing is past its own mere death. It is a carrier of death' (p. xi). 'The way' is therefore a way of life as opposed to the destroyers' way of death. 'The way' had its own clearly defined political and religious systems. As far as political organization is concerned, it emerges as a communistic egalitarian system with 'each participant an equal working together with all others for the welfare of the whole'. Land was held in common, the principle of the individual ownership of land being a later innovation of the imperialists. The people of the way had and loved possessions, but they were not materialistic, since materialism implies the individual hoarding of possessions. The people of the way, on the other hand, used possessions for the enrichment of the whole: 'The disease is not in the abundance of things but in relationships growing between users. The people using all

things to create participation, using things to create community, that
people have no need of the healer's art, for that people is already whole'
(p. 315). There is a great sense of unity and tremendous emphasis on
communal activity: 'The body that is whole moves always together.'
Although this genuine African system was characterized by egali-
tarianism and communal activity, the way was not antipathetic to
leaders, or what Armah refers to as 'experts' and 'caretakers'.
However, these were not positions of selfish consumption at the
expense of the sweat of others as they subsequently became in colonial
and post-independence times, but 'productive agencies requiring care
and the patient use of skill exactly learnt'.

Armah also posits a religion of 'the way' quite distinct from Islam or
Christianity, which he sees as alien religions associated with the death-
dealing Arab predators and European destroyers. In this Armah goes
much further than avowedly Negritudist writers such as Laye and
Kane who present Islam as a traditional African religion accepted by
the people. He groups Islam with Christianity as 'shrieking theologies'
with which the Arab predators and white destroyers assail the black
people alike, and he refers to the myths of both religions as mere fables.
As far as Armah is concerned the people of 'the way' had no need to
invent 'fables' to explain their origins; they did not wish to know who
made the earth and sky for it was not necessary for the earth to have
been created by any imagined being. Such fables were for children and
soft minds. It becomes obvious that Armah's religion of 'the way' is
even different from most traditional African religions which at least
assume the existence of one or more supreme beings and include
'fables' explaining the origin of the world and man's relationship to the
divine. According to the religion of 'the way', a supreme being, if there
is one at all in the world, is equivalent to the will and determination of
the people, not an external supernatural force:

> ... there is indeed a great force in the world, a force spiritual and able
> to shape the physical universe, but that force is not something cut
> off, not something separate from ourselves. It is an energy in us,
> strongest in our working, breathing, thinking together as one
> people; weakest when we are scattered, confused, broken into
> individual, unconnected fragments. (p. 151)

Indeed, the system of 'the way' laid tremendous emphasis on
'connectedness', that is, meaningful communication or an awareness
of relationships. 'The way' involved 'connected sight', 'connected

hearing', 'connected thinking' – a vision, a system of thought and action that focuses on the entire pattern, sees the interrelationship between past, present and future, concerns itself not just with the expediencies of the present, but with the prophecies of the past and the lessons of history, and takes thought for the welfare of posterity. The reverse is 'unconnectedness' – fractured vision, fractured hearing and fractured thinking – which is associated with the white predators and destroyers and therefore with destruction and death. There is a sense in which Armah is almost impatient with the present, which he refers to on one occasion as 'the senseless present' whose sounds are merely a 'brazen cacophony'. Instead, he emphasizes the need for going back to origins and determining future purposes: 'A people losing sight of origins are dead. A people deaf to purposes are lost.'

There was, then, a glorious African past when the people had not yet strayed from 'the way', from 'the cycle of regeneration'. Disintegration set in when they started to deviate from the path of reciprocity to that of unbridled generosity. The disintegration actually began during the period of the rule of the Fathers – a harsh time, characterized by warring gangs and clans, and rulers determined to cling to power. This was succeeded by the rule of the Women, a time of peace and abundance, a fertile time. But the consequence of this prosperity is that generosity becomes a vice – a giving without worrying about receiving – and this leads to ease and fertile softness. Armah's thought here is not entirely clear. It is difficult to accept that the disintegration could have set in solely as the result of an unbridled generosity, especially as we ourselves can see that even before the rule of the Women and the ensuing 'fertile softness', there had been a rule of Fathers which was harsh and tyrannical, and from which the people had to be liberated by the Women. What caused this harshness and tyranny, this deviation from 'the way'? Surely not generosity! But on this Armah is silent. In fact, it would seem from Anoa's celebrated prophecy, that the onset of disintegration was caused as much by 'thoughtless ease' and a kind of materialism as by generosity: 'The present path creates not harshness but a soft abundance, your minds are crammed with kapok and you too now confuse the way with thoughtless ease ... The way is not barrenness. Nor is the way this heedless fecundity. The way is not blind productivity. The way is creation knowing its purpose...' (p. 27).

So Anoa prophesies the doom of centuries of slavery and subjugation that will inevitably overtake them for deviating from 'the way'.

'Slavery – do you know what that is? Ah, you will know it. Two thousand seasons, a thousand going into it, a second thousand crawling maimed from it, will teach you everything about enslavement, the destruction of souls, the killing of bodies, the infusion of violence into every breath, every drop, every morsel of your sustaining air, your water, your food. Till you come again upon the way.' (pp. 26–7)

The first imperialists – the Arabs whom Armah also regards as white men coming from the white desert – were able to obtain a foothold precisely by exploiting the people's generosity. They first appeared as beggars, and since 'the way' also prescribed that strangers should be given sustenance, they were treated charitably. But 'the way' also suggested that a guest who turns contemptuous is a guest no longer but a parasite. Unfortunately the people were heedless of this and therefore fell victims to their own generosity. Armah could scarcely conceal his scorn for the Arab conquerors and their religion Islam. He describes Ramadan as the predators' season of 'hypocritical self-denial' and sees Allah as a slave-owner benefactor God. The Muslim rulers are presented as bestial beings indulging in the most repulsive orgies involving drugs, food and sex, and they have no qualms in calling on their slave-owner God at the height of their indulgence in unspeakable rites. The passages describing their activities are reminiscent of Ouologuem's own account of similar practices.

Great was the pleasure of these lucky Arab predators as with extended tongue they vied to see who could with the greatest ease scoop out buttered dates stuck cunningly into the genitals of our women lined up for just this their pleasant competition. From the same fragrant vessels they preferred the eating of other delicious food: meatballs still warm off the fire, their heat making our women squirm with a sensuousness all the more inflammatory to the predators' desire. The dawa drug itself the predators licked lovingly from the youngest virgin genitals – licked with a furious appetite. (p. 33)

And there can be no mistaking the relish with which Armah describes the women's slaughter of these Arab predators.

Mohammed, the Sheikh Mohammed, brother of Shaq'buht: Each woman, so commanded, stroked the licking tongue, the neck, the back of Mohammed's head. Sekela, she stroked the expectant tongue with a thin, sharp knife. The tongue, curled around its latest morsel of spiced meat, dropped just in front of Mohammed's mouth. Too amazed to feel the still imminent pain, the Arab was

staring dumbfounded at his severed tongue when a sharper knife
held in Nywele's hands slid deep into his neck and was jerked
sideways to the left, sideways to the right. Mohammed died with his
forehead stuck to the floor, like every good man of his enslavers'
faith. (p. 37)

However, the Arab predators are enabled to return and make a
second conquest due largely to the rivalry between chiefly houses and
factions in an unseemly scramble for power, and the activities of
zombies and parasites who prefer the rule of alien whites. At their
second coming the Arab predators make full use not only of these
parasites who are ready tools to their purpose, but also of their religion
which they use to smash the feeblest minds. 'The predators had
discovered that the capture of the mind and the body is a slavery far
more lasting than the capture of bodies alone.' They thus skilfully
exploit the divisions among the people, merging the struggling for
power into a holy war.

In *Two Thousand Seasons* Armah directs almost as much venom
against the beings he refers to as zombies or parasites as against the
white imperialists themselves. The worst kind of zombies are the
askaris, the immediate servants of the imperialists who have been
conditioned to do their master's bidding. Armah's picture of the askari
is a mindless robot, who has been totally brainwashed, his soul
completely voided out of his body, and he himself conditioned to doing
automatically whatever his master wishes, even if it means killing his
own grandmother.

> The mind can also suffer attack, the mind can also fall to conquest. A
> mind attacked and conquered is guided easily away from the paths of
> its own soul. The body is then cut off from its spirit as in sleep, yet
> still instinct with the conqueror's imposed commands, a soulless
> thing, but active. In this state of souldeath the body blindly, sleepily
> obeys the conqueror. Such a body is set to persist in such obedience
> even if its conqueror be a distance of days and days away, a time of
> seasons separate. Such are zombies. And among us such were the
> askaris. (p. 44–5)

But in a sense the askari commands our sympathy since he is not really
responsible for his own actions, and we feel that a terrible crime has
been committed against him by the imperialists who have robbed him
of his original human personality, just as Sankolo is deprived of his in
similar circumstances in *Bound to Violence*. The other classes of
zombies – the 'parasitic elders' and 'ostentatious cripples' – deserve

much less sympathy since they seem to be willing collaborators in their own degradation. These include the schizophrenics who have been alienated from their own culture and traditions and yet are stupidly proud of their transformation, the fifth columnists who, having lost confidence in the ability of their people to govern themselves, yearn for the return of the imperialists, and the puppet rulers whom the imperialists place over the people to do their dirty work. Now bloated, fat and contented, voided of their souls and reluctant to lose their position and influence, 'they do their zombi work, holding up the edifice of death from falling in vengeance on the killers' heads'. Armah includes under the umbrella term of 'zombi' all those who, either by force or through their own volition, have become collaborators with the imperialists, have lost their own original indigenous personalities and now help to consolidate imperialist power and culture in preference to indigenous traditions and institutions. In this sense Bradford George, the son of King Koranche, is also a zombi, for he has been alienated and detribalized through his education, raised as a servant of the white destroyers and sent to Europe where his African soul has been voided out of him and his name 'Bentum' changed to 'Bradford George'.

In the wake of the Arab predators' second conquest some idealists among the people decide that rather than submit to slavery and the Muslim religion they will leave in search of new lands where they would re-establish 'the way'. They thus embark on an epic journey. The journey motif, including images of movement and travelling, is a prominent one in the novel. It soon becomes clear that the journey is not just physical but spiritual and psychological; it is partly a journey into the racial psyché – to rediscover authentic values and standards – the way. That the journey and movement are partly psychological and spiritual has been indicated when earlier in the work we are told that the African people were not afraid of motion. 'We are not a people of dead, stagnant waters.' There were those among them who had travelled 'but not over land and not over water. Movers in the mind, their news was of communities we would have forgotten without them...' Armah is suggesting that the African people were neither insular nor introspective before the advent of the imperialists, nor did they lack a spirit of intellectual curiosity; they were perceptive to ideas from outside, and were capable of analytic thought.

The epic journey, like the march in Ousmane's *God's Bits of Wood*, is not without its drawbacks. The people are plagued not only by hostile communities and the uncertainties of the physical landscape but by dissension, doubts and outbreaks of violence among themselves. And even on arrival at the promised land – Anoa – disintegration continues. The way is lost almost as soon as it is found again. Men begin to cast blame on the spirit of reciprocity itself, yearning once more for the methods and systems of the white predators; and it is this movement that wins the day: 'The way was lost in the fascination with the white heat of easy roads to power.' Hence new 'ostentatious cripples' arise, new rulers, caretakers and kings, whose cruelty is no less detestable than that of the white predators themselves. Once more Armah does not flinch from the details as he presents the mind-boggling tyranny of this race of black kings of whom Jonto is typical.

> It was his never-finished craving for newer abominations that ended him. He loved particularly the tender arseholes of boys not yet in their thirtieth season. Some he had oiled for ingress but in his happiest moods he dispensed with oil, preferring as lubricant the natural blood of each child's bleeding anus as he forced his entry. (p. 101)

Perhaps Armah overdoes the details but he probably feels he needs to be as realistic as this in order to bring out his utter detestation of the cruelties of kingship. As he says: 'The quietest king, the gentlest leader of the mystified, is criminal beyond the exercise of any comparison.'

These traumatic events in the new land occur several centuries after Anoa's famous prophecy of two thousand seasons of suffering. The fulfilment of the prophecy now continues with the arrival of the white European imperialists (destroyers), this time from the white sea. Once more it is the people's generosity which proves their undoing, for the white men make several apparently unreasonable requests: they ask for permission to extract the country's mineral wealth, to hunt and destroy or carry away the country's wild life, they want land specially set aside for themselves to grow their crops and wish to make use of forced labour in doing so, and they propose to give gifts to the king and his courtiers. Characteristically, Armah's presentation of these gifts reveals his contempt not only of the European imperialists but also for the greedy and simple-minded king and courtiers who allow themselves to be captivated by such trifles. The gifts suggest the Europeans' complete contempt for the African mind, but unfortunately the behaviour of the king and his courtiers confirms the

European imperialists in their view. Armah always insists on the gaudiness of these trifles – they are red as daytime blood, or deep blue, and they *shine* fiercely in the sun.

The first white destroyers include a soldier, a hunter, a trader and a priest. Armah thus suggests in a parabolic way the categories of imperialists who have helped further the subjugation and exploitation of the black peoples. The priest is particularly significant. Armah goes to great lengths to expose the moral bankruptcy of Christianity, as he does with Islam. The white missionaries not only help to further the aims of their white imperialist brothers, but also find theological arguments to sanction oppression and dictatorship by the black puppet kings themselves: 'it was an incontrovertible teaching of the white religion that a king had a right, a duty in fact, to impose his will strongly on his people, for to the white man the king was always the head, the people merely the body' (p. 155). Thus the missionaries show their complete misunderstanding of and contempt for indigenous customs and their willingness to impose alien systems upon a proud people. The satire against Christianity can be biting. The simple-mindedness of the new religion and the complete incomprehensibility of its doctrines to the ordinary African mind are gloriously ridiculed, even as the priest boasts of its virtues.

> 'Our coming here is a high favour unto you, o heathen people. We bring you whiteness, which is godliness itself. We bring you the miracle of belief to save you from the damnation that is doubt. How could you have known before our coming unto you that a god invisible, unheard, but still known to us the whites, created this universe? How could you have known before our coming unto you that this god sent his only offspring to be a teacher unto you, an expert in how to suffer without resistance against those who make you suffer, without bitterness even, a teacher to teach you to aim for excruciating deaths after lives of pain? How, abandoned to yourselves, could you have known? Come and be saved. Come to the church, come into whiteness, come into purity. Throw your names to oblivion. Take white names, and denounce those who would fight against the whiteness of our new road. Rebels against whiteness they are, rebels against god.' (pp. 311–12)

Armah powerfully demonstrates the cruelty, hypocrisy and ingratitude of the white destroyers. But what is even more disturbing is the way in which they are able to seduce some of the kings and courtiers like Koranche and his flatterer Otumfor to support their wicked purposes. As Armah puts it, 'the naturally decaying class of kings and courtiers were being deliberately supported and helped to multiply by the white destroyers from the sea for their own ends'.

The king, Koranche, is the most memorable single character in a novel which seems to be sadly deficient in characterization. This and other weaknesses are probably due to the work's narrative form, a combination of oral chronicle and parable – a parable of the history and sufferings of the entire African peoples. We hear the voice of a narrator in our ears rather than see the activities of powerfully realized characters in vividly presented scenes. The work is also deficient in dialogue and in vivid evocation of setting. As might be expected from a parabolic kind of work, the landscape, as in *The Beautyful Ones Are Not Yet Born*, is vague. Only on a few occasions is the setting used meaningfully. On one occasion the initiates who are being taken into slavery suddenly become aware of the large number of crocodiles in the river. Then on the rather luxuriant river bank they see a crocodile surfacing briefly to pounce on an unsuspecting duiker and drag it into the killing water. The relationship between the crocodile and the duiker is of course the same as that between the enslaved initiates and their new captors. Slightly later they see a seabird flying towards them. The bird significantly comes from the sea, and even more significantly flies in a *white* streak directly above them. It then suddenly plunges into the water, catches its prey and flies backward to the sea. Once more the symbolism of the white seabird and its prey is obvious. Immediately after this they land in an area whose gloomy forbidding nature seems to match the purposes of their white captors.

> Simply, the place held no great promise of anything a seeker might want. But now in its diseased secrecy the white destroyers had found a fitting place for their purposes. Here was stagnant water choked with dead matter, animals floating bloated with here, there a remnant limb sticking in the air out of the water, dead palm trunks breeding grubs, too light to sink in this heavy water, too sodden with decay to float. All things here passed us by in a dragged-out dance of rotten things. (p. 176)

The emphasis is on stagnation, rottenness, decay and death. The setting matches not only the imperialists' intentions, but the mood of the captives.

Apart from these few examples, all of which significantly occur within two pages in one chapter, Armah makes little attempt at the evocation of setting or creation of local colour. However, in the second half of the novel, with the intensification of the activities of the group of initiates, the work tends to lose its air of parable and oral chronicle and comes to look increasingly like a thriller or adventure story. It is at this stage that a few realistic, properly delineated characters like Isanusi, Abena, Kamuzu and Koranche emerge.

Koranche the king plays as central a role in the events of the story as the Saif does in *Bound to Violence*. To a more limited extent he also has a capacity for intrigue and deception; but there the similarity really ends. Where Ouologuem is alive both to the Saif's devilry and to his magnificence, there is no mistaking Armah's superb contempt for Koranche. Ouologuem's Saif is given stature as a freedom fighter against the white imperialists, whereas Koranche is a traitor who collaborates with the imperialists to bring about the subjugation of his country and the destruction of his people. Where the wily Saif manipulates the imperialists for his own purposes, the moronic Koranche could only be their tool. It is the quality of mindless imbecility that Armah stresses in the adolescent Koranche, his only other noticeable quality being his capacity for quiet malevolence. As king, Koranche knows that because of his mediocrity the more perceptive among his people hold him in contempt, and his power can only rest on the masses' gullibility and preference for the superficies of things. Few sights could be more degrading than that of the king dancing with glee at the sight of the white men's trifles. Armah so detests this monarch that he even takes the unusual step of penetrating into his mind to show how things appear to his warped mentality. Above all, Armah convicts him of the same sin as the white destroyers – the inability to reciprocate: 'they give more than they receive. I, the king, I only know how to take. They are full vessels overflowing. I am empty. In place of a bottom I have a hole' (p. 115).

Abena functions as a moral voice, courageous in her defiance of the king, determined in her loyalty to the group and consistent in her search for 'the way'. Isanusi plays about the same role here as the teacher in *The Beautyful Ones Are Not Yet Born*. He is a pillar of wisdom, a repository of history, a man of undoubted integrity and inevitably the rallying point for the opposition to Koranche's tyranny. He sees it as his function 'to keep the knowledge of our way, the way, from destruction; to bring it back from an oblivious people, all else failing, at least as remembrance' (p. 139).

It is in order to rid the country not only of the curse of the destroyers who have inflicted slavery upon the people, but also of the tyranny of men like Koranche, that the group of idealistic and determined initiates, under the guidance of Isanusi and the inspiration of Abena, set about their task of liberation. Their efforts must also be seen as a parable of the attempts of heroic and well-intentioned Africans throughout history to free Africa not only from the burden of slavery, but also from the scourge of contemporary African leaders who have brought about a new enslavement of their peoples. The two thousand years of misery prophesied by Anoa are not yet ended, and the struggle to free Africans from tyranny and re-establish 'the way' continues. The activities of the initiates are therefore both missionary and revolutionary; in fact, they provide a blueprint for the continuing African revolution.

The initiation procedures themselves comprise a system of traditional education, perfectly suitable for equipping the initiates to cope successfully with their environment. They consist of an exposure to all the various trades and arts, ending in specialization in the particular art for which the initiate shows most aptitude. The initiates are warned that it would be fatal to their arts to misuse the skills they have learned and that they must never turn these skills to 'the service of things separate from the way'. Having been thus schooled, the determined group of twenty initiates decide to resist the tyranny of Koranche who wishes to select the best among them – Abena – as the bride of his zombi son, Bradford George. They flee to the fifth grove where they are exposed to more moral lessons from Isanusi. But in their innocence they are soon led to believe that the king has relented and foolishly accept his invitation to a feast on board the white men's ship. This behaviour of the group seems to lack psychological plausibility. It is unlikely that having already experienced Koranche's treachery and received strong warnings from Isanusi they would fall so easily for such a simple ruse. As it is, they accept the invitation, and once on board the ship they, who had been distinguished by their idealism and antagonism to everything associated with the white man, are easily seduced by the latter's trifles. They thus put themselves on the same level as the ridiculous Koranche and his courtiers. Inevitably they are enslaved and sent down to the coast to be shipped abroad.

In this section of the novel there are some poignant passages demonstrating the horrors of the slave trade. We are aware of the bleak hopelessness of men who even on regaining their liberty cannot go back to their homes because they will be sold again by their own people. We notice the courage and patriotism of Tawia, who would rather be killed than leave her native shores for the dreaded unknown, and the cruel repugnant zeal of the half-white zombi John, who persecutes black people out of revulsion at the thought that some black blood runs in his veins. But it is in the midst of this persecution on board the slave ship that the enslaved people begin to rediscover 'the way'. As they forge a new harmony among themselves, a new unity of purpose, a common mind and a common soul, they move gradually towards connectedness, one of the cardinal principles of 'the way': 'Connected thought, connected action: that is the beginning of our journey back to our self, to living again the connected life, travelling again along our way, the way' (p. 209). They are thus able to conceive and execute a coherent masterplan against the white slavers. Once more, there is no mistaking the relish with which Armah describes the killing of the white men. This is, as it were, the moment of Africa's revenge.

> Thirty victim eyes searched for each destroyer and found him. Seven hands caught each ashen limb. One white destroyer was thrown into the water with not one of his limbs: these followed after. Another had his left thigh stretched away from the right till the bones between them cracked. He was hurled off the ship in the wake of the first. The third was strangled by so many pulling hands his neck turned longer than a chicken's, ungraceful in its slender death. The fourth and last white destroyer, they went down together, bound tight with rope from the flapping sailcloth overhead. (pp. 222–3)

Since they have been sold by Koranche, the liberated initiates cannot hope to return to their homes; in fact, they do not wish to 'return to homes blasted by triumphant whiteness'. On the other hand their idealism would not allow them to remain passively where they are in 'invalid security'. They thus dedicate themselves to a grand design whose aim is the utter destruction of all the destroyers and their collaborators, and the total liberation of their peoples. And they commit themselves to the re-establishment of the way: 'That is our destiny: to end destruction – utterly; to begin the highest, the profoundest work of creation, the work that is inseparable from our way, inseparable from the way' (p. 246). But they see this not as a temporary matter, but as the work of a lifetime, a continuing exercise in which generations of others yet to come will have to join: 'This lifework, its fruit should be the birth of new seers, other hearers, more numerous utterers. And the fruit of all our lifework together: that should be destruction's destruction.'

In their preparation for the struggle the initiates are helped, not only by Isanusi, but also by Kamuzu. But Kamuzu is motivated only by materialism and the drive for personal power: 'Kamuzu does not hate the enslavement of our people. What he hates is his exclusion from the profits of the trade' (p. 249). Indeed, once they capture the white men's castle at Poano, Kamuzu begins to behave like a white governor himself. Armah no doubt intends Kamuzu to represent all those contemporary African leaders who, having 'led' their countries to independence, now behave like the imperialists themselves and subject their people to a new form of slavery. He flies his own flag in place of the destroyers', erects a statue to himself, takes delight in the firing of cannonballs on the slightest pretext, becomes obsessed with wealth, self-glorification and women and begins to call the castle 'his' castle. He even concludes a pact with the white destroyers. The events of this section of the novel read distressingly like *Animal Farm.*

But the initiates free themselves from Kamuzu's influence and, having engineered the destruction of the castle, in consequence of which Kamuzu is hanged, move on to the liberation of their own land of Anoa and the destruction of Koranche. It may be seen as a weakness of this novel that after the execution of Koranche in what is virtually a coup, the group of initiates merely seem to withdraw into the background, putting nothing in place of the power vacuum thus created. Bradford George is allowed to assume the throne, to become the tool of the white destroyers and send to them for help, so that in effect the struggle between the liberators and the destroyers is perpetuated. On the other hand the initiates' complete success must have meant the end of the struggle, whereas according to Anoa's prophecy their misery should last for another two thousand seasons. The struggle therefore goes on, and there is now constant war between destroyers and liberators.

It is possible to argue that *Two Thousand Seasons* is a racist work. And yet in spite of the venom directed at the white predators and destroyers and the author's obvious relish at their destruction, one can argue, with Wole Soyinka, that the work is rescued from a destructive, negative racism by the positive nature of its message.[3] It is a rousing call to Africans to liberate themselves from all those alien forces – economic, political, spiritual – which initially led to the destruction of African traditional values and are the real cause of the present decadence on the continent. It also urges Africans to make a spiritual and psychological journey back to origins to rediscover and re-establish that pure African system unadulterated by alien values. Only in the possibility of such a rediscovery can there be any hope.

NOTES

1 See Wole Soyinka's *Myth, Literature and the African World* (Cambridge University Press, Cambridge, 1976).
2 Ayi Kwei Armah, *Two Thousand Seasons* (East African Publishing House, Nairobi, 1973), p. ix. All further page references are to this edition.
3 Soyinka, op. cit., pp. 111–12.

10. Wole Soyinka

▼▼

The Interpreters

With Wole Soyinka's novels we come to the theme of social comment. At the Scandinavian African Writers' Conference held in Stockholm in 1967, Soyinka delivered a lecture which has had important consequences for the development of African literature.[1] In it he urged his fellow African writers to cease their preoccupation with the past and focus their attention instead on those forces which threaten the disintegration of African society. In doing so Soyinka was not necessarily deploring commitment to the past; he certainly endorsed Achebe's aim of teaching his people about the grandeur of their heritage and showing them 'where the rain began to beat them'. He himself realized that before Africans could understand the present there must be a remorseless confrontation with the past and he has used the past meaningfully and effectively in his poems and plays. Soyinka was merely suggesting that an unduly prolonged pre-occupation with the sins of the imperialists and their allies might lead African writers to neglect the chaotic state of the continent in contemporary times and to ignore the responsibilities of Africans themselves for its present state. When Soyinka delivered his lecture most African countries had already become independent, some over a decade earlier, and the first military coups had taken place in Ghana, Nigeria, Sierra Leone and other places. The Congo (Zaïre) had had its disastrous civil war and the Nigerian Civil War was just beginning. African society was indeed going through a turbulent period of readjustment in the wake of the traumatic consequences of the imperialist occupation. Although the policies of the imperialists were no doubt partly responsible for the problems of readjustment, African countries had been independent long enough for Africans themselves to take responsibility for a large proportion of the mess. Wole Soyinka was pointing out that the African writer, being among the most sensitive minds in his community, has a duty to act as the conscience of his nation. In the task of discovering new values he has a very important role to play, but he can only play it effectively if he faces up to the truth and forces his countrymen to see themselves as others see them; he must alert them to the debasement of standards in their community, to the prevalence of corruption, incompetence, nepotism, brutality, injustice, poverty, social inequality, materialism, hypocrisy and snobbery. The African writer in contemporary times must be socially committed and involved, and he must be prepared to expose his society's shortcomings and suggest alternative scales of value.

The consequence of Soyinka's call is that in the later 1960s and early 1970s the focus in African writing shifted from historical, cultural and sociological analysis to penetrating social comment and social satire. Of course, Achebe had in a sense anticipated Soyinka with the publication of *A Man of the People* in 1966, but his novel was rather too political, whereas Soyinka was asking for attention to be paid to the presence of decadence in all areas of African society. His call has been heeded by several writers, but he himself had showed the way with the publication of his first novel, *The Interpreters*, in 1965. This novel is probably the most comprehensive exposé of the decadence of modern African society that has so far been published. It has, however, given rise to sharp controversy among critics and readers. On the one hand are those like Professor Jones who give it unqualified praise;[2] on the other hand there are those like Derek Elders and the present writer who do not believe that the novel is the accomplished masterpiece it has been claimed to be.[3] Soyinka has become such an established figure in the African literary cannon that it is almost sacrilegious to register an opinion of his work which falls short of total praise. Let it be said at the outset that the relevance of Soyinka's exposure of decadence is not in question; but in conformity with the general critical method of this study, all aspects of the novels discussed – both message and technique – must be examined for a balanced evaluation. Even where technique is concerned one is aware that Soyinka does certain things extremely well – much better than most other African novelists – but one is also uneasy about the language and structure of the novel. In raising questions about these two aspects of Soyinka's art one is, in fact, articulating the responses of hosts of intelligent readers who find them not just difficult but rather affected. One is not merely objecting to structural unorthodoxy. The practice of novelists like Sterne, Virginia Woolf, Conrad and Ngugi – to name only a few – has attuned the mind of the modern reader to novels which do not progress in linear time but which are perfectly acceptable because even in their apparent haphazardness they obey a formal logic of their own, and the reader is convinced that no other structural principle could have been devised to make the author's points effectively. Soyinka, like Ngugi in *A Grain of Wheat*, makes use of flashbacks, but where one can see a kind of logic and inevitability in their use in Ngugi's novel it is difficult to make the same case for Soyinka's. The density of the novel's verbal texture which has been so often hailed by critics can easily degenerate into a pointless wordiness. I shall try to demonstrate these points by a detailed consideration of the novel's structure.

The novel starts with all five or six interpreters at a nightclub in Lagos; a hundred and five pages and six chapters later, when Egbo is discovered in a drunken stupor in his girlfriend's flat, we realize that the story has hardly moved at all in present time. Instead, Soyinka has taken us back in a number of flashbacks whose purpose presumably is to throw some light on the characters of his interpreters. The novel delves into the past almost immediately after it begins – the sight of Egbo's beer dissolving in a puddle formed by the rain at the nightclub takes his mind back to a journey he made up the creek to his grandfather's domain. The puddle thus forms the link between the present and the past, but it is surely a very tenuous link, nor is the need for a flashback at this stage demonstrated. No theme has as yet been announced, no problem about Egbo has been presented which the flashback is needed to clarify, unless it is his very isolated statement during his reverie: 'Well, I made a choice. I can't complain.' On page 10 there is a flashback within this flashback, taking the reader even further back in time to the young Egbo's presentation to his grandfather.[4] On page 14 we return to the present and the nightclub, but on page 16 Egbo's reveries take us back once more to his childhood, and on page 17 we return to the present. The flashbacks so far have thrown considerable light on Egbo, but it is not made clear why it had to be Egbo at this stage, nor is the information thus received used to illuminate any act of Egbo's in the present, for when we return to the present the focus is turned mostly on Sagoe until about page 26 when it is switched to Sekoni with a flashback to Sekoni's past. This flashback, which is about Sekoni's dreams about how he will apply his engineering skills to the modernization of his country, is immediately collapsed into a scene demonstrating the dreary routine of Sekoni's tasks in his new job, the only indication that we have moved forward in time being the four dots at the end of the word 'desk'. Having given us a glimpse of Sekoni's fortunes the narrative returns at the start of Chapter 2 to the present, as the interpreters leave the nightclub. There is no real link between the flashback illustrating Sekoni's past and the scene immediately preceding it in the present, unless it is the few words Sekoni speaks at the end of that scene, and when we return to the present it is not to Sekoni but to Sagoe and Dehinwa. We remain with these two in the present for the whole of Chapter 2, but in Chapter 3 the focus swings over to the Faseyis whom we have not met before, and the time sequence of the whole chapter is not clarified. We assume that it is the present, but we cannot be sure whether it precedes the interpreters' exploits at the nightclub (and is therefore a flashback) or whether it follows them; nor are we sure whether the action has shifted to Ibadan or not. Since Faseyi is associated with the Ibadan Teaching Hospital we assume that it has, but nothing definite is said about this and our doubt is deepened even further by the fact that the reception at which we first meet the Faseyis is given by an ambassador whose sphere of operations would properly be Lagos. Chapter 4 delves back into the past with the story of Egbo's relations with Simi. This flashback presents Egbo as a highly sexed schoolboy, thus illuminating his affairs not only with Simi but also with the Ibadan university student. But there is no reason why it had to come at this particular point; it could be transposed elsewhere without materially damaging the story. Since we were with the Faseyis at the end of Chapter 3 there was no problem about Egbo which the flashback had immediately to illuminate, and even if there has been some illumination the connection is not made, since we return at the start of Chapter 5 to Sagoe and Dehinwa. There is really no logical connection between the flashbacks, no reason why a particular one is where it appears.

We remain with Sagoe in the present for a short while and then plunge into the past to his interview for the newspaper job. In the midst of the Chief Winsala episode, where the latter calls at Sagoe's hotel to collect his bribe, there is a flashback within the flashback to Sagoe's early childhood and the beginnings of his preoccupation with voidancy. Then on page 90 the scene shifts again almost imperceptibly to the present and Chief Winsala's discomfiture at the hotel. In Chapter 6 we are still with Sagoe; the scene has moved slightly forward but not yet to the present for we are given a glimpse of Sagoe's first experiences at his new job. Then on page 99 the focus swings over to Sekoni and his illness, but once more there is nothing to indicate whether this is contemporaneous with Sagoe's first experiences at his new job, or whether it precedes or follows it; and the only link between this flashback and the preceding section is the one word 'silence'. At the start of Chapter 7 we return to the present and to Sagoe in Dehinwa's bedroom and it is only now, as Sagoe, having woken up from his drunken stupor, makes his way to Sir Derinola's funeral, that the narrative really moves forward. From now on the story moves consistently forward with the solitary exception of the flashback to the scene of Egbo's first encounter with Simi. Soyinka does try to suggest something of a closely knit narrative with the stories of Sagoe, Lazarus and Noah, and the Uguazors and Faseyis; but in reality the narrative consists of independent episodes which are thematically and symbolically rather than causally and logically linked together. There is no doubt that the flashbacks in the first half of the book throw a considerable amount of light on Sagoe, Egbo and Sekoni; but there is little logic in their arrangement, and the linking devices, where they occur, are very tenuous. It would be a large claim to say that Soyinka uses flashbacks as adroitly as Ngugi does. The work begins to look increasingly like a clever pastiche consisting of a series of highly entertaining episodes which nevertheless add up to a picture of life.

If there are reservations about the novel's structure, there can be none about the thoroughness of the satire at society's expense. Soyinka's wide-ranging wit takes in all sections of a corrupt society – the brutal masses, the aimless intellectuals, the affected and hypocritical university dons, the vulgar and corrupt businessmen, the mediocre civil servants, the illiterate politicians and the incompetent journalists. The focus is largely on the five brilliant interpreters of this society – Sagoe the university educated journalist, Egbo the foreign service official, Sekoni the engineer and sculptor, Kola the artist and teacher of art and Bandele the university lecturer. All are talented intellectuals who have retained their African consciousness although they were largely educated in the western world. Yet their western education enables them to look at their changing society with a certain amount of detachment. They are therefore uniquely qualified to be interpreters of this society. The reader is impressed by their honesty, sincerity, moral idealism, concern for truth and justice and aversion to corruption, snobbery and hypocrisy; but anyone who assumes that Soyinka presents all the interpreters as models of behaviour will be completely misreading the novel. He is careful to expose their selfishness, egoism, cynicism and aimlessness. Indeed the conduct of the intellectuals both in and out of the university is a major preoccupation of Soyinka's in this novel. The aimlessness and superficiality of the lives of most of the interpreters is patent. With the exception of Sekoni and Bandele they all seem to be lacking in wholeness and solid core; this is seen in Egbo's inability to decide between a life of power in the creeks and the tedious routine of the foreign office, and in Sagoe's pointless chat about his drink lobes. When Sekoni dies the weaknesses are glaringly brought out as Egbo, unable to bear the grief and the funeral, flies to the refuge of his grove; Sagoe is characteristically awash in beer and vomit for a week and Kola is completely unable to work. Only the strong and resourceful Bandele retains his composure and takes upon himself the onerous task of consoling Sekoni's unfortunate father.

Egbo, who is possibly the sharpest intellect among them, is also the most selfish, egoistic and cynical. In a sense he is typical of all the interpreters in that he has to make a choice between the apparently aimless life he lives in modern Lagos and a return to traditional society. All modern young men and women who face the problem of hammering out new values for themselves in a rapidly changing and largely unsatisfactory situation have to make similar choices. When we first see Egbo he is undertaking the journey up the creek to the ancestral home in the hope of making a choice between the sterile unrewarding career in the foreign service and the much more challenging job of leadership of his traditional society. Egbo is in a real dilemma since neither prospect is attractive. On the one hand the leadership of the creeks represents immense power, wealth, sensual pleasure and the real possibility of becoming a powerful instrument of change, while life in the civil service is mere 'pith to hollow reeds'. But on the other hand Egbo doubts whether he has the necessary resources to make a success of this job which is, in spite of its privileges and other attractions, a demanding one. There is a sense therefore in which his soul-destroying but less demanding job at the foreign office is ulti- mately preferable to life as a traditional ruler. Thus when he makes the pilgrimage up the creeks Egbo hesitates to go ashore, and in the final analysis he baulks at a decision. It is here that we see his lack of fibre. He knows he must face the issues, but he is unable to make an unequivocal decision: 'Perhaps he had hoped they would simply move and take the burden of choice from him.' At the crucial moment he merely says: 'all right, let's go', without indicating any definite direction. When Bandele characteristically forces him to decide he can only say weakly: 'with the tide'. It is a choice of the grey file-cabinet faces at the foreign office rather than the warlord of the creeks. But it is not, in fact, a deliberate decision. The expression 'with the tide' suggests not only a return to the aimlessness of the city, but a choice wrung out of him when his will is almost paralysed to choose.

Other flashbacks give us an insight into Egbo as an adolescent. His turbulent and difficult childhood (he came near expulsion six times) and his early rebelliousness against tradition and authority prepare us for the callous, cynical and truculent Egbo who will turn his back on his people's traditions and bear down on his friends with unexpected violence. His lustful thoughts and his sexual initiation by the courtesan Simi prepare us for the callous indifference with which he treats both Simi herself and the innocent student whom he unscrupulously seduces and makes pregnant. It is clear that Egbo merely uses women for his pleasure without a thought for their convenience or their future. True, he has a stab of conscience when Bandele informs him towards the end of the girl's pregnancy and of the scandal it has given rise to; but even so his cowardice is revealed, for apart from a melodramatic assault on Dr Lumoye he can do nothing positive to help the girl who has heroically decided to have and take care of her baby. And even though he makes a show of abandoning Simi at the end, he is still uncertain whether to cast his lot with the student.

Egbo's habitual retreat to his grove is an attempt to come to terms with his inadequacy. He initially discovered the shrine after his original flight from Simi when he spent a night of terror beneath the bridge. The grove acted then, as it now continues to do, as a source of sustenance and consolation. Consequently he ritualistically retreats to it whenever he needs to be reassured. 'When I come here I discover, it is enough. I come, shall I say, to be vindicated again, and again and again.' Unlike Bandele and Sagoe, who can be flexible and tolerant to human foibles, Egbo can remain arrogantly unreasonable and unsympathetic. During the visit to Lazarus's church, an institution for which he harbours the greatest scepticism, he is the most difficult of all, sullenly refusing, unlike the others, to have his feet washed, offering no explanations, merely making negative gestures of the hands and head. His natural predisposition to violence comes out in a number of episodes, particularly during the scene of the sacrifice when he almost plunges a knife into Bandele's throat. His egoism is revealed in his obsession with the way in which he is portrayed on Kola's painting. On seeing the final version he is so disgusted that he leaves in a huff with his ram. But it is a stroke of genius which has induced Kola to portray Egbo as the violent, rapacious destroyer, Ogun, for Egbo is nothing if not violent. Like the god Ogun, he is associated with blood – the blood of the virgin he deflowers and the blood of the ram which he flicks on to Bandele's shirt. His representation as Ogun is thus an externalization of a basic quality. We also see his irresponsibility in abandoning Noah through annoyance with the way he is represented in the painting; and this is an act with disastrous consequences, for Noah, left on his own in a strange environment, falls into the clutches of the homosexual Joe Golder and jumps to his death when the latter tries to assault him indecently. Yet when Egbo is subsequently informed about Joe Golder's homosexuality, he recoils in utter disgust, quite oblivious of the fact that he is just as culpable for Noah's death as Joe Golder. Soyinka concentrates attention on the violence of Egbo's reaction to the revelation.

> As from vileness below human imagining Egbo snatched his hand away, his face distorted with revulsion and a sense of the degrading contamination. He threw himself forward, away even from the back seat, staring into the sagging figure at the back as at some noxious insect, and felt his entire body crawl in disgust. His hand which had touched Joe Golder suddenly felt foreign to his body and he got out of the car and wiped it on grass dew. Bandele and Kola stared at him, isolated from this hatred they had not known in Egbo, and the sudden angry spasms that seemed to overtake each motion of his body. (p. 237)

Sagoe is much more human than Egbo. He is also the most important of the interpreters since it is largely through his activities as a journalist that we are made to see the antics of contemporary Nigerian society. We applaud his consideration and sympathy when he joins the small band of eleven mourners and takes a wreath from Sir Derinola's cortege to bestow on the poor man's. We contrast his humanity with the brutality of the Lagos crowd during the pursuit of Noah. He is even considerate in his treatment of Chief Winsala and Sir Derinola. Nevertheless, the unattractive aspects of his character are apparent. His piercing gaze strips Nigerian society bare, but his own shortcomings are simultaneously exposed. He can be irreverent, cynical and, when steeped in beer as he often is, aimless and irresponsible. He can muse over which political party a taxi driver thugs for, but on discovering that he has no money on him to pay his

taxi fare is dishonest enough to bluff his way out of the jam by
pretending to be a police officer and threatening to arrest the driver.
His integrity and concern for truth and justice make him champion
Sekoni's cause when the latter is so brutally treated by his employers,
and he justifiably registers his disgust at the connivance of his own
newspaper bosses with the proprietors of another paper to suppress
the truth. But he lacks the courage to pursue matters to their logical
conclusion and resign his job as he once weakly threatened to do.
Instead he takes refuge in his pointless voidante philosophy.

The voidante philosophy serves the same purpose for Sagoe as
Egbo's grove does for the latter; it provides a refuge from the
frustrations of life in Nigeria. But the fact that he has to resort to such
wordy nonsense for consolation is an index of his personal inadequacy
and lack of wholeness. The voidante philosophy is jargon. Expressions
like: 'To shit is human, to voidate divine' are not likely to recommend
themselves to the discriminating reader. Here is a typical passage.

> Voidancy is not a movement of protest, but it protests: it is non-
> revolutionary, but it revolts. Voidancy – shall we say – is the
> unknown quantity. Voidancy is the last uncharted mine of creative
> energies, in its paradox lies the kernel of creative liturgy – in release
> is birth. I am no Messiah, and yet I cannot help but feel that I was
> born to fulfil this role, for in the congenital nature of my ailment lay
> the first intimations of my martyrdom and inevitable apotheosis. I
> was born with an emotional stomach. If I was angry, my stomach
> revolted; if I was hungry it rioted; if I was rebuked it reacted; and
> when I was frustrated, it was routed. (p. 72)

The unnecessary wordiness and the pointless aliteration of the 'r's are
an indication that Soyinka is also alive to the mindlessness of this kind
of exercise and is deliberately using the voidante philosophy to
comment adversely on Sagoe.

With regard to tolerance and flexibility, Sagoe stands midway
between Egbo and Bandele. While lacking Egbo's almost irrational
conservatism and rigidity, he does not rise to the heights of Bandele's
ability constantly to make allowances for people. Unlike Egbo, he can
tolerate Joe Golder even when he learns about his homosexuality, but
he cannot understand Bandele's toleration of the German, Peter. Nor
does he understand what Bandele abundantly realizes – that civilized
society is only possible if one is prepared to disguise one's feelings and
be accommodating even towards those one secretly despises. On the
contrary, Sagoe is brutal, brusque and blunt, particularly during

the Oguazors' party. Soyinka mercilessly strips the mask off these posturing people, but he is also careful to contrast Bandele's courtesy and tolerance with Sagoe's rudeness at a party to which he was not, in fact, invited.

At his job Sagoe is thoroughly professional, but rather selfishly so, since he sees all the participants in the events he observes primarily as actors in a sensational newspaper drama, thus blinding himself at times to real human suffering. Fortunately he is reclaimed at the end for the world of humanity by Dehinwa who consents to marry him and gets him to burn his books of enlightenment. Instead of a recourse to voidancy, therefore, he finds a much more respectable and effective refuge in the solid Dehinwa.

Kola, the artist of the group, has few of Sagoe's redeeming features while sharing his cynicism and selfish professionalism. He always sees people in terms of their suitability as sitters for his painting; and as long as he gets his sitters and is able to concentrate on his work he does not care how much misery he causes. He completely fails to appreciate Lazarus's religious sincerity and significance, and is indifferent to his story and his church. And he demonstrates his irresponsibility and selfishness in his determination to take Noah back with him at all costs – a decision which indirectly leads to the boy's death. Our first insight into one of his main qualities is given by his irreverent portrait of the portly woman dancing by herself on the floor of the nightclub. Where Egbo and Sekoni see nothing but beauty in the woman, Kola places a goitre on her neck and encases her feet in wellington boot canoes, thus revealing his characteristic cynicism, viciousness and spite. These qualities are also displayed during the scenes involving the Faseyis where he seems to take a sadistic pleasure in increasing the immature, ultra-sensitive and absurd Faseyi's internal torment at the contemplation of the consequences of his wife's unconventional conduct. Nor is the repulsiveness of Kola's conduct lessened by our awareness that his aversion for Faseyi is partly motivated by his growing love for the latter's wife. Kola also shares Egbo's predisposition for violence though on a slightly smaller scale. The one apparent point in his favour – his immediate sympathy for the child albino Usaye for whom he gets a pair of glasses – is nullified by the uncomfortable feeling that he might have been motivated by the desire to please Monica Faseyi, and is certainly tainted by Kola's obvious interest in the child as a sitter for one of the figures in his painting, the Pantheon. And yet, in spite of all this professionalism, Kola is not as accomplished an artist as Sekoni who is, if anything, an amateur. He has to admit the obvious superiority of Sekoni's work.

> And Kola found that he was indeed jealous. Unless 'The Wrestler' was one of those single once-in-a-life coordinations of experience and record, Sekoni was an artist who had waited long to find himself but had done so finally, and left no room for doubt. Certainly there was no self-doubt in Sekoni's hand, and none showed in this his first attempt. Joe Golder's verdict was the same. Kola struggled futilely with his canvas for a while, then gave up for the day, confessing, 'Sekoni's wrestler has put me off. Let's continue tomorrow.' (p. 101)

Of the entire group of interpreters, Sekoni the engineer elicits the greatest sympathy. If he is also the most vulnerable it is precisely because of his basic honesty and courage and his determination not to compromise his principles and sacrifice his insights in order to accommodate the reactionary elements in his society. Apart from an occasional display of temper provoked by his frustration in a soulless society and heightened perhaps by his stutter, Sekoni seems almost entirely free of any flaws. Nor does he show any signs of the inadequacy that plagues Sagoe, Egbo and Kola. Indeed, in spite of his eventual madness, there is a wholeness in Sekoni which is quite lacking in Egbo, Sagoe, Kola and Lasunwon. He always seems to move on a plane of mysticism, conveyed not just by his stutter but also by his unusually concentrated and poetic language.

> 'N-n-no. Oh no, KKola is right. After all, lllife, lllove, the-they are p-p-paths to the Universal D-d-dome. And d-d-domes of moisture . . . optimistic ap. . .proach, view of hhhumanity. Wh-what Kola hhhas d-ddone wwwith our friend's c-c-creative symbols. Re. . .member, a woman is the D-d-dome of love, sh-she is the D-d-dome of Religion . . .' (p.26)

The densely concentrated language suggests the operation of a powerful probing intellect and a wide-ranging imagination. The passage above leads into a flashback which sets the tone for the powerful treatment of the Sekoni story.

> Sekoni, qualified engineer, had looked over the railings every day of his voyage home. And the sea sprays built him bridges and hospitals, and the large trailing furrow became a deafening waterfall defying human will until he gathered it between his fingers, made the water run in the lower channels of his palm, directing it against the primeval giants on the forest banks. And he closed his palms again, cradling the surge of power. Once he sat on a tall water spout high

above the tallest trees and beyond low clouds. Across his sight in endless mammoth rolls, columns of rock, petrifications of divine droppings from eternity. If the mountain won't come, if the mountain won't come, then let us to the mountains now, in the name of Mohammed! So he opened his palm to the gurgle of power from the charging prisoner, shafts of power nudged the monolith along the fissures, little gasps of organic ecstasy and paths were opened, and the brooding matriarchs surrendered all their strength, lay in neat geometric patterns at his feet. Sekoni shuffled them like cards and they reshaped to magic formulae in sweeping harbours. (p. 26)

The density of texture and the tremendous power of the language match the power of Sekoni's imagination and genius and the breadth of his vision, which is really what the passage is out to communicate. There is an almost other-worldly quality about the prose; it is as though the author were trying to describe events beyond the processes of time and space. Expressions like 'mammoth', 'primeval', 'monolith', 'eternity', 'petrifications', 'giants' and 'divine' are significant. The sexual innuendoes in 'little gasps of organic ecstasy and paths were opened', and 'the brooding matriarchs surrendered all their strength' suggest the act of creation. Sekoni appears like an almighty creator feeling the surge and the pulse of power beneath his fingers and relishing his success as he compels the primeval forces of nature to bend to his will. Perhaps there is a slight suggestion that Sekoni's dreams are too grandiose for the reality of the situation. Nevertheless, the passage celebrates the triumph of human ingenuity and power. Of course the contrast between these magnificent dreams and the mundane tasks Sekoni is assigned is most marked, and it justifiably elicits Sekoni's wrath. When his ingenious power station is condemned through a combination of jealousy, stupidity, conservatism and corruption Sekoni batters it to pieces himself and goes mad. The Sekoni story poignantly demonstrates the destruction of brilliance and originality by a narrow-minded and corrupt society. There is also the suggestion that through this destruction the vast potential of the country, which someone of Sekoni's vision would have succeeded in harnessing, remains untapped. The ruined power station is therefore symbolic on more than one level; and Sekoni himself emerges as a genius of the first order, as a man of vision and imagination and above all as a man of integrity.

The wholeness which Sekoni demonstrates in spite of his madness is revealed when he takes to sculpture on his return from his convalescent trip to the Holy Land. He once more emerges as the artist *par excellence*, as the powerful creative agent taming the magic spirit of the wood. The object he creates, 'the wrestler', is a symbol of power, strength and indomitable energy, and it reflects not only Sekoni's inner intensity and wholeness but his power. The language communicates this power as well as the vigour that the piece of sculpture exudes: 'Taut sinews, nearly agonizing in excess tension, a bunched python caught at the instant of easing out, the balance of strangulation before release, it was all elasticity and strain' (p. 100). But in spite of this power that the piece exudes there is a spontaneity and effortlessness about Sekoni's work that makes Kola green with envy. It is his first piece of sculpture and he has asked no one to sit for him, but the finished product, which has obviously been inspired by the nightclub brawl, is unmistakably Bandele. Sekoni's wrestler is thus a symbol not just of energy and power but also of struggle and, above all, of a grim determination to conquer in the struggle. One feels sure that if death in the accident had not cut short Sekoni's life he had the power within him, in spite of his madness, to give the lie to his society and win through.

Bandele, who is perhaps the most perfect of the interpreters, is the embodiment of Soyinka's positive values in this novel. There is hardly a flashback to Bandele's past, with the result that his presentation is not as detailed as Egbo's or Sagoe's; by the same token he seems to be the least talkative of them all. Yet there is no doubting the effectiveness of his presence throughout the novel. Apart from being Soyinka's spokesman and therefore the norm of conduct, he is the conscience of the members of his class and generation. Like Soyinka his creator he is not only aware, as the others are, of the shortcomings of his society, he can also achieve a certain measure of detachment and see with great clarity the weaknesses of his fellow interpreters. He can always be relied on to criticize the foibles of his friends sharply, whether it is Egbo's indecision in facing the choice confronting him, or Sagoe's selfish brand of journalism or Kola's indiscretions with the Faseyis. And there is no doubt that on each occasion we and the author endorse his judgement. Bandele's habitual reticence is the correlative of much more heightened powers of observation than the others. On several occasions Soyinka stresses the difference between his reactions and those of the other interpreters to the same people and situations – to Peter, the Oguazors, Lazarus and his group, Joe Golder and the Faseyis. And he emerges as easily the most courteous, the most tolerant and the most compassionate. He is supremely capable of ensuring that people do not feel embarrassed even when, like Peter, they are the cause of their own embarrassment. He is even capable of pretending that he understands the point of view of people like the Oguazors and Faseyi, and sees no point, like Sagoe, in throwing Mrs Oguazor's vulgarity and affectation in her teeth, or, like Kola, in tormenting Ayo Faseyi for his stupidity, affectation and hypocrisy. He knows about Joe Golder's homosexuality, but tolerates it, and even after the disaster of Noah's accident tries to make things smooth for Joe Golder when he virtually tells a lie to Lazarus about the circumstances of Noah's death. He is thus both peacemaker and consoler.

The difference between Bandele and the other interpreters is most clearly revealed in the Lazarus scenes where we find him genuinely trying to unravel and understand the circumstances of the albino's 'death' while the others are being cynical. He is perceptive enough to realize that Lazarus must not simply be dismissed as an impostor and that he has not just brought them to his church to promote his fund-raising activities: 'This man did go through some critical experience. If he has chosen to interpret it in a way that would bring some kind of meaning into people's lives, who are you to scoff at it' (p. 179); and from this moment onwards Bandele's criticism of his friends becomes more scathing as he points out their selfishness and their indifference to human suffering.

With the events of the novel moving towards their disastrous climax Bandele becomes more and more aloof from the others, an almost superhuman creature presiding in judgement over not only the other interpreters, but this corrupt society as a whole: 'And Bandele held himself unyielding, like the staff of Ogboni, rigid in single casting.' And later: 'Bandele sat like a timeless image brooding over lesser beings' (p. 245). His moral superiority at the end is fully justified by his earlier flexibility. He has also earned the right to look down on the others because his conduct has been free from censure. It is this inflexibility and this inexorableness of his judgement which the images describing him towards the end are meant to suggest. On one occasion he is likened to 'a palace housepost carved out of ironwood'. When he turns majestically on the university group, including Lumoye and the Oguazors, for their callousness in the discussion of the pregnant girl's case we are told: 'Bandele looked at him then thoughtful, and he looked round the circle, calm, his body lax again. He was looking at them with pity, only his pity was more terrible than his hardness, inexorable. Bandele, old and immutable as the royal mothers of Benin throne, old and cruel as the *Ogboni* in conclave pronouncing the Word.' And the word he pronounces with such deceptive calmness is the terrible doom: 'I hope you all live to bury your daughters' (p. 251).

Dehinwa, Sagoe's girlfriend, is a fitting anchor and refuge for the latter. Although merely a girl struggling to make a life for herself in the Lagos jungle, she is personally more successful than most of the interpreters. Always sane and sensible, she is as solid and dependable as Bandele. Her struggle to keep Sagoe calm after Sekoni's death is as heroic as Bandele's consoling of Alhaji Sekoni, and towards the end she sensibly endorses everything that Bandele says and does.

In Joe Golder, the American homosexual, and Peter, the German, we see the interpreters' lack of wholeness and spiritual integration abstracted as it were and looked at in itself. In a sense they can be said to represent the problem of the interpreters magnified a thousand times. They do not know where they are or where they are going. Joe Golder's sexual and racial ambiguity is a reflection of his lack of wholeness and of roots. In the powerful scene between him and Sagoe, Soyinka skilfully penetrates the mind of the ultra-sensitive and largely unsuccessful homosexual. If what we know of his background did not make his story pathetic, his grotesque behaviour would be almost comic as in the desperation of his yearning he tries to probe the new 'pick-up' with the most personal questions, trying to find out whether he is a kindred spirit who is likely to succumb to his advances. He is so sensitive and his need is so great that he becomes unreasonably irritable when Sagoe does not seem to be co-operative. With very keen psychological penetration Soyinka reveals the internal torment of the homosexual in an unpermissive society. Joe Golder badly needs Sekoni's wrestler, not only because it represents masculine strength at its best and therefore ministers, in a sense, to his homosexual needs, but because the piece of sculpture represents a wholeness which is a contrast to his own inadequacy. The song he sings at his recital – 'Sometimes I feel like a motherless child' – fittingly mirrors his spiritual, sexual and racial dislocation. Peter the German's hallmark is national ambiguity; he is a German who is striving to be an American and the result is grotesque in the extreme. The scene between him and Sagoe in Bandele's home is one of the liveliest in the novel. It is perfectly visualized by Soyinka. It would have been scintillating comedy were the reader not put off by the German's incredible vulgarity. What is so striking about him is his insensitivity, his complete lack of comprehension of his crudity and the effect he has on other people.

Although the interpreters have their shortcomings, they are distinguishable by their honesty, courage, moral idealism and concern for equity from the generality of the Nigerian public whose frivolities Soyinka so brilliantly exposes through their eyes. The satire is most scathing when directed against that pillar of the establishment, Ibadan University. As the seat of higher learning, the source of the nation's higher level of manpower and the home of academics who are presumably engaged in the pursuit of truth, the university ought to be a powerful agent of change in this society. But the attitude of its members makes it hopelessly inadequate for the task. Soyinka strips off the veneer of respectability to reveal the malevolence, pettiness, vulgarity, affectation, hypocrisy and cruelty that go on underneath. The university group is largely seen through Sagoe's eyes during the Oguazors' party. The sentence which introduces the group is a perfect epitome of what goes on: 'A buzz of wit, genteel laughter and character slaughter welcomed them from the drive and they entered the house of death' (p. 141). It suggests the repulsiveness of what is going on underneath the genteel surface. The hallmark of the group is affectation and insincerity.

The avidity with which the university community tries to ape English mannerisms and the outdated English cultural patterns is grotesque. At a strategic moment, for instance, the women retire to the ladies' room while the men, 'house-trained and faultless', pretend not to see. It does not occur to the professor and his wife that this particular item in the books of etiquette is not only completely outmoded but utterly irrelevant in an African situation where more sensitive minds are busy hammering out new values. In the wake of Sagoe's savage onslaughts, however, the cracks begin to appear in the veneer of gentility revealing real malevolence and vulgarity. This most vicious society indulges in back-biting, intrigue and character assassination. After a slight 'indiscretion' of Sagoe's 'Each guest began to ask his neighbour, "I hope it wasn't you who brought him," and sighed, disappointed that the candidate had not lost his chance of nomination to some committee' (p. 148). There is pretentiousness, social climbing, deceit and malice. Dr Lumoye has no scruples in going against the code of professional ethics and revealing the confidential medical information that one of the girls is pregnant; and he sees nothing immoral in his own subsequent statement: 'If I tasted of it myself I would at least have something to show for it.' Soyinka comments: 'And the laughter rose genteel over the champagne bubbles' (p. 149). It is not only the narrow-mindedness that strikes us, but the callous indifference to the happiness of a young person, and the moral myopia in not realizing that Dr Lumoye, who is worse than the girl, has no right to sit in judgement on her. 'Genteel laughter' and 'champagne' suggest the bogus sophistication which masks real crudity and vulgarity.

Eventually the conversation itself becomes openly crude with the guests revealing their preoccupation with sexual scandals. Soyinka captures the gossip and the tone of the conversation with brilliant accuracy: 'Dr Ajilo denied that he took prostitutes home. Never further than his garage, he swore, but Oguazor was just behind him, and he was not amused ... "Who is Salubi going with these days? That boy is morally corrupt, I tell you. He doesn't even keep off the students"' (p. 150). At Kola's exhibition the professor's blindness to his own and his community's moral weaknesses and Lumoye's malevolence are more blatantly revealed. Captivated by the salacious details of the case, Lumoye reacts to the information that the pregnant student intends to have her baby and then return to college. But even as his laughter booms out his drunken vulgarity is exposed.

> 'You mean she wrote, she actually wrote and said she wanted to return?'
> 'In her condition?' said Caroline.
> 'Wit in full belly?' Lumoye, still open-mouthed.
> 'But why are you surprised? Morals mean nothing to these modern girls.'
> 'And she looked ever such a nice, quiet girl,' Caroline added.
> 'Ha ha,' warned Dr Lumoye, 'the quiet ones are generally the fastest. As soon as she came to the clinic I knew it. One of the quiet ones I said, I bet her trouble is old penalty kick into the net ha ha ha ... Oops, beg-pardon.' (p.249)

The satire on the university group is particularized in the attack on the ridiculous Professor Oguazor and his beloved consort, the formidable Caroline. Professor Oguazor is an enormous figure of fun who, having worked his way up the establishment ladder and achieved a professorship, feels he ought to deny the African in him and adopt a conspicuously English life-style; but his attempt to live the life of an Englishman has disastrous consequences, for his speech, mannerisms and home in general are a grotesque parody of the actual thing. In his pathetic striving after a western life-style which he clearly does not fully understand, he merely degenerates into ridiculousness of speech and vulgarity of taste. The plastic fruits and other artificial decorations in his home, which Sagoe so effectively ridicules, are an indication not just of a life-denying sterility or unnaturalness, as Professor Jones suggests,[5] but of vulgarity and a complete misunderstanding of western culture. Sagoe's ridicule of the plastic cornucopia is neatly dovetailed into the exposure of Mrs Oguazor's affectation, arrogance and condescension. She is disgusted that Sagoe has turned up at her party without putting on a tie and she has no scruples about showing her feelings on the subject. Her husband's affected speech is ridiculed simultaneously with his grotesque aping of the outmoded etiquette of the English upper classes.

'I thought Ceroline was here.'
'She was a moment ago.'
'O der, end the ledies are wetting for her.'
Just then Mrs Oguazor herself emerged from a group and came to the professor.
'Ceroline der, the ledies herv been wetting for you.'
'I know. I was just looking for you to tell you we must go upstairs. Will you handle things at this end?'
'Ef cerse, der.'
'Ah I see you've met the *new* lecturer' – Sagoe distinctly perceived the exchange of understanding – 'I have asked Bandele to bring him to tea; he is not yet used to things here.' From the marionette pages of Victoriana, the Professor bowed. The contempt in his manner was too pointed for any error, and it was with the greatest difficulty that Sagoe refrained from looking down to see if his fly was unbuttoned. 'Cem en der,' and the Professor took his good lady's hand, 'We mesn't keep the ledies wetting.' (pp. 144–5)

But in spite of this pretended sophistication the professor and his good lady turn out to be rude in the extreme. They have no conception of real hospitality, of courtesy, of the rules of real decency and good breeding, no idea of the consideration which is due to guests. When the arrogant Caroline fails to persuade the courageous and unconventional Monica Faseyi to go upstairs with the other ladies, she loses her temper and almost launches out into abuse.

It was a brilliant stroke of Soyinka's to juxtapose Professor Oguazor's denunciation of Salubi's 'meral terpitude' with the information about the professor's 5-year-old daughter, 'the plastic apple of his eye', whom he tucked away in a private school in Islington because he could not publicly acknowledge her since he got her by the maid. It is the moral obliquity and hypocrisy of this society, the blindness of its members to their own glaring moral faults in their readiness to point out the faults of the others, that is so striking. The satire at the expense of the university is perhaps the most effective thing in the book.

No other member of this community seems more pathetic than the ridiculous Dr Ayo Faseyi. A highly talented young man who is considered to be the best X-ray analyst on the entire continent, Dr Faseyi should not normally need any external trappings to boost his social acceptability. But so concerned is he with status that he behaves like a nonentity striving to get society to recognize him. His aping of English mannerisms and values is even more ridiculous than Professor Oguazor's. He is a pathetic social climber who is prepared to deny the African in him and to use whatever unscrupulous methods come his way in order to enhance his standing in the community and further his material prospects. But in the process he ironically humiliates himself.

We first meet the Faseyis as they prepare to enter an embassy reception and we are shocked to see that Faseyi 'inspects' his wife thoroughly, presumably to make sure that there is nothing about her that will 'disgrace' him at such a gathering of the establishment. He himself wears a bowtie and when he is satisfied with Monica he kisses her 'formally on the forehead'. The scene continues.

'You might as well put on your gloves now,'
　'What gloves? I didn't bring any.'
　Faseyi thought she was teasing, and, out of character though it was, Monica was certain that her husband was teasing.
　'Come on now, put on the gloves.'
　'You stop teasing, now. Who do you see wearing gloves in Nigeria?'
　Faseyi was no longer joking. He had snatched the handbag from her and found that there were no gloves inside. 'Do you mean you didn't bring them?'
　'Bring what, Ayo?'
　'The gloves, of course, what else?'
　'But I haven't any gloves. I gave the ones I had away soon after I came.'
　'I am not talking about two years ago. I mean the gloves you've bought for tonight.' ...
　'But you didn't say anything about gloves.'
　'Was it necessary to say anything? It was right there on the card.

In black and white.' He took the card from his pocket, dragged it from the envelope and thrust it under her eyes.

'Read it, there it is. Read it.'

Monica read the last line on the card. 'But Ayo, it only says those who are to be presented. We are not, are we?'

Ayo held his head. 'We *are* to be presented.'

'You didn't tell me. How was I to know?'

'How were you to know! It took me two weeks to wangle that presentation, and now you ask me how were you to know. What would be the whole point of coming if we were not to be presented?'

'I am sorry,' said Monica, 'It never occurred to me ...'

'Nothing ever occurs to you ... But at least you could have used some initiative. Even if there was no question of being presented, you knew their Excellencies would be here.'

'I am sorry.'

'Darling, if the Queen was attending a garden party, would you go dressed without your gloves? ... Darling I am surprised at you. These are simple requirements of society which any intelligent person would know.' (pp. 40–1)

The passage exposes Faseyi's uncritical absorption of non-African values, his willingness to descend to whatever depths are necessary in order to ensure social success and his complete unawareness that gloves, the Queen and garden parties are completely irrelevant and out of context in an African setting. But the criticism extends beyond Ayo Faseyi to include the upper stratum of Nigerian society which *does* condone this uncritical transplantation of English upper-class values to African soil. So scandalized is Ayo Faseyi by his wife's indiscretions during the reception and the Oguazors' party that he becomes almost hysterical and demonstrates an incredible immaturity degenerating into stupidity. He makes himself an easy prey to the malevolent Kola's taunts. Faseyi behaves in this slavish way because he thinks he can use the contact with the professor and his kind to make headway in Nigerian society.

'Do you know a Minister was present? Yes, and one or two other VIPs. Oguazor knows people, you know. I saw four corporation chairmen there, and some Permanent Secretaries. A thing like that, Kola, one is simply socially finished.'

'Yes, you, of course.'

'Look, let's face the facts. The university is just a stepping-stone. Politics, corporations – there is always something. Not to talk of these foreign firms, always looking for Nigerian Directors. I mean Kola, you are an artist, but I am sure it is all a means to an end, not so?' (p. 203)

The behaviour of the university group is symptomatic of what goes on in the nation as a whole. This in itself is a sad comment on the university which, as the seat of higher learning, might have been expected to possess better values and standards of conduct than the mass of the people. Yet the sad fact is that in most African countries universities can lay no greater claim to virtue than the nations they are meant to serve. They manifest the same prejudices and at times demonstrate the same capacity for corruption that is to be found outside the learned walls. The portrayal of Sir Derinola and Chief Winsala is central to this exposure of corruption in Nigeria as a whole. Sir Derin is one of the pillars of the establishment – a chairman of several companies and an eminent and respected judge whose conduct should normally be above suspicion. But the actual reality is quite different. Sagoe's hallucination in Dehinwa's room is instrumental in stripping the veneer of respectability off Sir Derin. His near-nakedness in this scene suggests that now that he is dead, he has been levelled with the rest of ordinary humanity and the pomp which was associated with wig and gown is no more. But the nakedness also suggests the stripping away of the sham respectability and the revelation of Sir Derin for the corrupt man he is. In Sagoe's hallucination Sir Derin keeps on the brassiere because he would like to pin on it the medals he received with his knighthood. The contrast between the medals and the brassiere is ridiculous in the extreme and shows the absurdity of Sir Derin's posthumous desire to retain his knighthood even though he has given up his other external trappings. He does not see that the knighthood and the clothes belong to the same veneer of respectability which has nothing to do with a man's innate worth. But when he reappears he has come to a full realization of the truth and is even prepared to take off the brassiere and to be buried completely naked: 'Now I am satisfied. Don't let them bury me except as I am now. Not even a shroud' (p. 69).

Sir Derin's corruption – his involvement in bribery in association with Chief Winsala – is copiously demonstrated in the novel. In the process he exposes himself to unspeakable embarrassment and humiliation. In a sense Chief Winsala, who does not pretend to Sir Derin's respectability and comes out openly with his corrupt demands, is a more honest figure. He is even a likable character, an enormous Falstaffian figure of fun, a noted lecher and a genial rogue who is always drunk, even for interviews. The scenes in which he features are always comic and he attracts some sympathy through our realization that he is being used by much bigger and more hypocritical fish. Sir Derin's fantastic funeral is used as a medium of social comment by Soyinka, particularly through the contrast with the funeral of one of the brothers of Lazarus's church. The hideous crudity of the latter serves to show up the pointless extravagance and insincerity of the former. Sir Derin's mile-long funeral procession consisting of forty cars piled high with gory carnations and a thousand mourners on foot routs the more humble one and pushes it to a corner. The inflated hyperboles of the public orator enumerating virtues that never existed further show up the absurdity of such a splendid funeral for a man who really ought to have ended in disgrace.

The social comment gets added point with the description of the activities at Sagoe's newspaper offices. The contrast between the slum surroundings and the opulence of the boardroom is insisted on, as is that between the filth of the general lavatory and the comfort of the 'neuter lavatory' used by the top officials: 'Matthias was in front, but Sagoe's nose arrived long before them both and the sight of soggy scraps of newspaper stuck in urine only confirmed its probing' (p. 77). With admirable economy Soyinka exposes the managing director's corruption and lack of a proper order of priorities. The newspaper's boardroom, which is, in a sense, an expression of the managing director's personality and tastes, suggests not only extravagance and corruption but also vulgarity and lack of real taste. There is a radiogram, but no records; only the radio is ever used and that just for news. The radio has nine winking lights, all differently coloured. The pride of the managing director, he picked it up on his eleventh round-the-world mission. In an effort to seduce the German salesgirl who showed it to him he said:

> 'By the way ... do come to my hotel and show me how it works.' 'Aren't we to ship it home for you, sir?' 'Of course – of course,' said the Director. 'I meant come with the leaflets, and explain it all to me; I don't read German, you see.' 'It is there in English also,' said the girl, 'and in French and Spanish and Arabic.' Dragging his long trail of traditional splendour after him the Director turned to his private secretary and said, 'Aren't these German girls stupid?' (p. 76)

Tea is served to the members of the board in a delicate china set which the managing director picked up during the tenth economic mission to American China. He donated it to the board, remarking: 'You know, Shanghai Chek has exactly this kind of cup and saucer.' The board itself is composed of incompetent, corrupt idiots, fittingly described

by Sagoe as 'a desk of illiterate, unctuous, aggravating toads', who
irritate the latter so much with their inane questions that he has to walk
out of the interview in disgust. The scenes enacted at the newspaper
offices constitute some of the most brilliant comedy in the book.

The conduct of Sekoni's employers gives us further insight into
corruption and incompetence, this time in the civil service. Soyinka's
accurate turn of phrase neatly captures the amateurishness of the
service and the officials' preoccupation with trivia when they ought to
be concerned with the problems of nation building: 'If you'd just look
up these applications for leave and put up a roster . . .'; 'Please join a
preliminary Committee of Five to sort out the applications for the post
of Third Class Clerk . . .'; 'Don't forget the meeting of the Board. You
are one of our ex-officio members . . .' (p. 27). There is good satire
directed at the fondness for expatriate experts, especially when a
brilliant idea by an indigenous person has to be condemned. The
expert arrived, 'And he winked, a truly expert expat. expert's wink.'
He goes to Ijioha, sees Sekoni's project and does what he is expected to
do – condemn it without allowing it to be tried out. Meanwhile the
chairman's subsidiary company registered in the name of his 2-month-
old niece, which has been sole contractor for the Ijioha project, clears
out a few thousand in immediate compensation and files claims for a
few thousand more. The expatriate expert puts in a claim for injuries
sustained in the course of duty and collects £8000 lump sum
compensation for the termination of his contract. The reader is
astonished by the cynicism of it all, by the corruption, inefficiency,
hypocrisy, envy, bureaucratic stifling of initiative, destruction of
indigenous genius and the thoughtless waste of the country's
resources.

Soyinka's satire broadens out to include the masses whom he shows
to be ruthless and bloody-minded particularly in their harassment of
the young thief who turns out to be Noah. The religious references in
this section to the thief Barabbas who was actually freed by the Jewish
masses highlights the Lagos crowd's malevolence. Soyinka's bitterness and scorn are apparent in spite of the calmness of tone. He
certainly brings out not only the hypocrisy of people who fawn on
leaders who are ten times more fraudulent than Noah, but their
brutality and bloodlust, which is particularized in the driver who with
grim concentration tries to crush the thief's legs as he goes past his
bonnet. Nor does Soyinka forget the politicians, even though most of
the novel is concerned with social rather than with political corruption.

The mindless stupidity of Chief Koyomi is ruthlessly exposed through Sagoe's journalistic antics. In reply to the chief's demand for a concrete proposal from him, Sagoe, in a moment of tremendous cynicism, has proposed a plan for the utilization of excrement. He does not know that the chief will take it very seriously and make the proposal in a speech in Parliament which is an almost verbatim report of his proposal.

> 'I told Chief Koyomi special night trains would be run, coupling sealed wagons of local contribution at every station, night collection rail-rolling to the North, fertilizing less productive land. In a year, I told him, the country's farm products would be doubled.'
>
> 'Wait a minute, wait a minute,' and Egbo grabbed the newspapers, looking for the report. 'Aha, I thought so, that's almost the man's speech word for word.'
>
> 'I must concede it to him, he has a fantastic memory, unless he knew shorthand of course and took it down behind his back. Mind you, I had had a few and that is when my air of conviction is truly irresistible. I think I pointed out the metaphysics of the plan to him too – bringing the wheel full circle.'
>
> 'I have it,' Egbo exclaimed, 'that must be what he called mental physics and chemistry.'
>
> 'You see. I told you the man went loose on imagination.'
>
> 'Listen to this – another piece of your reportage I bet ... The collection of sewage pails, declared the Honourable Koyomi, was inhumane, and as the honourable member spoke, his long repressed brain grew fertile and the scheme became grandiose and sprouted the most unexpected offshoots of various colours and odours ... (p. 240)

It is difficult to ascertain what attitude Soyinka expects us to adopt towards Lazarus and his brand of religion. Certainly Lazarus's account of his death and resurrection, the event which led him to establish his church, sounds incredible, especially as he himself seems convinced that he did die and was not merely buried alive. He also sounds sincere when he claims that he became an albino only after his 'resurrection'. If, like the other interpreters, we demonstrate a tendency towards scepticism, then Soyinka's mouthpiece, Bandele, acts as a useful corrective. He is convinced that Lazarus is not just another religious quack, but a man who genuinely thinks that his religious experience can help him to be of service to others. This seems to be the fairest opinion of Lazarus. His account of his experiences after death may be melodramatic, some of the details of the service may be gimmicky, and the ordeal by fire to which he subjects Noah may be repugnant to most people's sensibilities, but his religious sincerity is enacted. He also carries conviction when, in conversation with Kola, he demonstrates his genuine concern for saving the souls of the worst criminals. And there can be no doubt about his determination that the ex-thief Noah should not return to the gutter. He features generally as an agent of rescue and salvation even though he has to admit failure over Noah. Like Bandele, and unlike the other interpreters, he gives an impression of wholeness and sureness of purpose.

The final scenes of the novel bring to the surface the tensions and conflicts which have broken out among the interpreters and some of their associates. Bandele has moved farther and farther apart from his friends whose aimlessness, cynicism and selfishness he has now all too clearly seen; Egbo is moving away from Simi the courtesan who is portrayed as both attractive and destructive, yet he seems unable to decide conclusively to cast his fortunes with the young under-graduate who carries his child; Kola is on the point of coming to an understanding with Monica Faseyi who is now about to be separated from her husband. Instead of a resolution of conflicts, therefore, the final scenes move towards a falling apart. The night of the gathering at Kola's exhibition is one, not of harmony, but of 'severance' in which Kola admits that every man is going his way (p. 246). The events of the previous few days have taken a severe toll on them all, and the novel ends in disillusionment and pessimism.

Most critics have shown awareness of the fact that Soyinka's language and style suggest that this is very much a poet's novel. The poetic quality is imparted not only by the host of allusions, cryptic images and metaphors, but also by the liberties with syntax and vocabulary one normally associates with poetry. The net effect is of tremendous density of texture, compactness and economy of language. Soyinka, by means of fusion of images, suggestive allusions and metaphors reverberating far beyond themselves, can condense into a brief paragraph what other novelists might need a whole page to say. The density of texture is evident in 'Osa drowsed in hard shadows and sun vapours, in vivid white reflecting momentary blindness, motionless...' (p. 10) and in 'Rain ribbons in club greens and orange ringed her, falling off the edges of the open "state umbrella" and her reflections were distorted on the four sides of the mirror stem' (p. 22). However, the use of this kind of language can be overdone. Is it really necessary in this passage for instance? 'The rains of May become in July slit arteries of the sacrificial bull, a million bleeding

punctures of the sky-bull hidden in convulsive cloud humps, black,
overfed for this one event, nourished on horizon tops of endless
choice grazing, distant beyond giraffe reach' (p. 155). One may need
the image of the bleeding arteries of the sacrificial bull to suggest the
tremendous force of the rains of May, but need Soyinka pursue it to the
details of humps and overfeeding on grass tall beyond the reach of
giraffes? And is the following really necessary to describe the gods on
Kola's Pantheon?

> And of these floods of the beginning, of the fevered fogs of the
> beginning, of the first messenger, the thimble of earth, a fowl and an
> ear of corn, seeking the spot where a scratch would become a
> peopled island; of the first apostate rolling the boulder down the
> back of the unsuspecting deity – for they must learn the first stab in
> the back and keep inferiors harmless within sight – and shattering
> him in fragments, which were picked up and pieced together with
> devotion; shell of the tortoise around divine breath; of the endless
> chain for the summons of the god and the phallus of unorigin
> pointed at the sky-hole past divination ... (p. 225)

This is not justified even by the fact that Soyinka is making forays into
the world of legend; where there is little justification it must appear
that he is merely demonstrating his undoubted control over words.

It must surely be conceded that of all anglophone writers Soyinka
exhibits the most complete control over the language. One notes the
judicious use of pidgin for Matthias's speech and the effective
mimicking of the half-educated man's speech for satirical purposes.
Here is the managing director of Sagoe's newspaper: 'Just let him go,
Chairman. How can an interview be conductable with someone who is
not taking the matter serious? ... Don't talk when I am talking,
otherwise just get out. We want the kind of person who is going to
respect his superior, not conceited boys of your type. Suppose you are
not begging who is interested in that. Your betters are begging my
friend so go and sit down' (pp. 79–80); and this kind of register is
different from that used by the less educated elder of Lazarus's church:
'The rich man, he die. The poor man, he die. God does not take bribe.
He is a man of impartiality' (p. 170). If Lazarus's sermon is a *tour de
force* it is partly because of his rich use of language. In the description
of the contest between Christ and Death he uses images and allusions
drawn from a world familiar to his audience, images which make the
account intensely dramatic and vivid.

'He wrestled with Death and he knocked him down. Death said, let

us try *gidigbo* and Christ held him by the neck, he squeezed that neck
until Death bleated for mercy. But Death never learns his lesson, he
went and bought boxing gloves. When Christ gave him an uppercut
like Dick Tiger all his teeth were scattered from Kaduna to Aiyetoro
...' (p. 165)

Mention must also be made of the brilliant rendering of Sekoni's
stammer. When the reservations to Soyinka's occasional tendency to
drift into pointless verbosity have been made, tribute must finally be
paid to the control he exercises over language.

The discussion so far should have suggested that Soyinka's ability to
realize a scene is probably greater than that of most other African
novelists. So many of his scenes are memorable. We think of the
Oguazors' party, of the embassy reception, of Sagoe's interview, of
Egbo's initiation by Simi, of Dehinwa's interview with her mother and
aunt, of Lazarus's sermon, of the chase of the thief Noah, and hosts of
others. The effective realization is partly due to his use of language
which sweeps the reader vividly along, and partly to his concern for the
details of movements and gestures. In the wrestling scene in the nightclub, for instance, Soyinka describes almost every aspect of the thug's
and Bandele's movements. Similarly, he can keep his eye on the object
and describe it effectively, as in this picture of the albino Lazarus when
we first meet him: 'Across the floor, an albino sat slanted like a leprous
moonbeam without the softness. Freckles on his face like poisoned
motes, dark scabs, and they floated on sheer phosphorescence of the
skin' (p. 157). The use of detail can also be effective in the portrayal of
the inner thoughts of individuals giving us interesting passages
of introspection, as with Egbo's guilty ruminations after his loss
of innocence in Simi's bedroom. Above all, it is probably the quality of
Soyinka's dialogue which contributes most to the liveliness of his
scenes. Very few other African novelists equal him in this regard.

Soyinka's presentation of character is also sure. Even the minor
characters are established by the few words they utter or by a striking
image. No reader of the novel is likely to forget the German Peter, or
the student Egbo seduces, or Mrs Faseyi senior, or Dr Lumoye, brief
though their appearances are. The major characters, like the five
interpreters Bandele, Sagoe, Egbo, Kola and Sekoni are, of course,
presented in depth, as are the Oguazors and the Faseyis. In a novel in
which the characters are legion, it is a tribute to the novelist's powers
that so many of them are substantial. The only lapses seem to be the
portrayal of Noah and Lasunwon who remain shadowy figures,

Lasunwon to such an extent that the reader tends to forget that he is one of the interpreters; he only seems to be distinguished by his habitual stupidity. Soyinka achieves great variety in his characters: there are the aimless but brilliant interpreters, the pillars of rectitude and sound thinking like Bandele, the arrogant, affected but vulgar academics, the social climbers like Faseyi, the embodiments of corruption like Sir Derin and Chief Winsala, the stupid politicians like Chief Koyomi, and the courageous, blunt and genuine ones like Mrs Faseyi, Monica Faseyi, Dehinwa and the female student. He has managed to encompass a tremendous amount of life in this novel.

Finally there is the quality of his humour. *The Interpreters* remains one of the funniest novels from the pen of an African. At times the comedy takes the form of farce as in the closing stages of the Oguazor's party. It can also be created by the author's occasionally sarcastic tone of voice. But usually it is simply comedy of character. People like Sagoe's managing director, Professor Oguazor and Ayo Faseyi are bound to be comic whenever they appear. *The Interpreters* will remain a book about which a good many readers will have reservations. But even these will in the last resort pay tribute to the comprehensiveness of the scope of its satire and to the powerful view of life that it presents.

Season of Anomy

The difference in tone between *The Interpreters* and Soyinka's second novel, *Season of Anomy*, is revealing. Where he has contrived some hilarious scenes in the earlier work, the mood of *Season of Anomy* is unmitigatedly grim. It was published some eight years after *The Interpreters* and a lot had happened during that period to affect Soyinka's outlook profoundly. There had been two military coups in Nigeria involving great bloodshed and violence, a bitter civil war with ugly allegations of genocide, the death of a number of promising personalities like Okigbo in the strife, a military dictatorship with political parties abolished and the normal democratic processes suspended, and Soyinka's own imprisonment and eventual voluntary exile. The situation of the African continent had deteriorated to the point of bleak hopelessness. To many, it seemed that the continent was retrogressing to a state of barbarism where the ordinary human being was deprived of all rights and his life was of no account to the authorities. It seemed, in fact, to be going back to the historical state so powerfully described by Ouologuem in *Bound to Violence*. The immediate post-independence phase of social and political corruption and intellectual dishonesty was now giving way to a bleaker phase of dictatorship, victimization, thuggery and violence organized occasionally at the highest level, and a prevailing atmosphere of fear. If *The Interpreters* raised the curtain on a kind of comic opera, *Season of Anomy* takes us into a chamber of horrors to reveal the full extent of human degradation and inhumanity.

The novel is about the evil consequences of greed and lust for power and the apparent futility of any attempt to introduce proper values into a society where power-drunk rulers interpret any such action as a threat to their hold on power, and see it as their duty to eliminate the instigators. At a first glance, *Season of Anomy* might not seem to equal *The Interpreters* in structural complexity and although Soyinka still retains his mastery over the episode, the best scenes in *The Interpreters*, like the Oguazors' party, seem livelier than the best scenes of *Season of Anomy*. Yet, taken as a whole, this new novel gives the impression of greater compactness and power and is altogether a more satisfying work of art than *The Interpreters*. For in it Soyinka skilfully interweaves a number of elements – reality and fantasy, the literal and the allegorical, the modern and the classical, African nature myths and rituals and European archetypal allusions – into a compact whole. There is also a series of interesting and functional contrasts: the natural rhythms of life associated with the community of Aiyero are set against the unnatural activities of the dictators; the regenerating, life-affirming rituals play against the Cartel's appetite for slaughter; and Ofeyi's idealism as he sets out on his quest through the devastations of this contemporary waste land is set against the corruption of the authorities and their henchmen.

Images and symbols from the world of vegetation, fertility and the natural processes are central to the meaning of *Season of Anomy*. This is evident in the names of Aiyero's institutions and in the titles of the various sections of the novel. Significantly, the head of the ideal and self-sufficient society of Aiyero is called 'Custodian of the Grain'. The grain suggests not merely food, but germination, revitalization, fertility, healthy luxuriance and prosperity. It represents the germ of a promising idea which will grow into a powerful movement that will (it is hoped) eventually revitalize the entire country bringing material prosperity, spiritual health and a concern for the proper values. The images therefore suggest Aiyero's potential role in the propagation of a decent life for all.

The relevance of the headings of the various sections is readily apparent. The first, which is mainly about Aiyero, the home of the grain, is called 'Seminal'. It thus suggests the sowing of the idea which is to grow and spread its roots throughout the entire country. This is the beginning of the attempt to infiltrate the country with the Aiyero ideal of moral and spiritual purity, and since the authorities are corrupt, the dissemination of the Aiyero ideal means sowing the seeds of discontent. The second section is called 'Buds', because the grain having been planted and the seeds of discontent sown, they have now sprouted and put forth buds. Consequently this section concentrates on Ofeyi's evangelizing activities. However, the use of this metaphor from the world of vegetation does not necessarily suggest complete success in the infiltration of the Aiyero ideal, for the corruption of the all-powerful authorities completely inverts what should have been the logical fruition of nature's processes. Thus 'Buds' involves not just the spreading of the Aiyero ideal of moral and spiritual purity, but also the authorities' growing uneasiness and their first counter-attack in the hounding of Ofeyi who is forced on to the defensive. The title of the third section makes the point even clearer. 'Tentacles' suggests not only the people's growing discontent, and the spreading of the Aiyero roots into other parts, but also the Cartel's plans for a vicious counter-attack. In fact, the tentacles also belong to the Cartel. Ironically 'Harvest' is not about the successful fruition of Aiyero's ideals, but a harvest of blood and murder; and 'Spores' suggests not the preparation of the grain for another sowing season but the grim putting together of the mutilated pieces. The vegetation myths are thus inverted; the landscape is not healthy and flourishing but barren and death dealing, and the harvest is a harvest of blood and corpses.

Other images and metaphors from the natural processes, the seasonal rhythm and the world of vegetation recur throughout the book, serving like motifs binding the whole. But there is always a hint that the luxuriance and fertility they suggest is an illusion. When Ofeyi and the dentist, for instance, come upon a grove of rain-trees beguiling in its luxuriance, the prose itself suggests its illusory nature.

> They came to the grove of rain-trees, the famous stretch planted by a now forgotten missionary eccentric. It led from the small town of Omola and spread for miles in an arcade of interwoven branches high above the road. The sun filtered through in yellow shafts,

weightless insubstantial bamboos, organ pipes which yielded to contact on the car, ran lightly over the panels, ran through the windscreen and played on their faces. Bird song came down those gilded pipes, played among the restful shadows.

Sensations, mere sensations. He felt as always dissatisfied, cheated. Those golden wafers were so cruelly beguiling, he stretched his hand through the window and they danced all over his arm in elfin abandon. Within that glade they were cut off from the world, wrapped in a mist of sun-motes in a forest of song. Ofeyi sank deep into the enchantment, consoling himself by thinking, I store it up for later needs. (p. 148)[6]

This is surely one of Soyinka's most beautiful descriptive passages, possibly his most beautiful in this novel. But the keynotes of the grove are titillation, enchantment and an invitation to abandonment. The element of unreality is confirmed when the grove soon gives way to bleak desert terrain.

The pervasive images of natural healing processes in this novel are set over and against images of disease and attempts to subvert those healing processes. On the one hand we are told of the healing powers of the women of Gborolu: 'What Gborolu did not kill with liquor it cured with its waters. In the dark damp of fermentation sheds the old women of Gborolu also nursed strange fungoid growths to which many even from the far metropolis, turned for alleged miracles of pharmacy when all else had failed' (p. 131). But on the other hand whenever healing powers are attributed to the Cartel the note of irony is unmistakable: 'What they are doing now, uproot it where they can, destroy the men whom they hold responsible for the spread of the virus of thought' (p. 117). The images of healing associated with the dentist are usually of drastic surgical or dental processes to remove the decayed or carious portions before they infect the whole. Humanity in general is seen to be grievously sick of a cancer which is gradually spreading its tentacles to the whole and against which there is apparently no remedy: 'Those secretive fingers with the sensitivity of grass, cattle and egrets, of ultimate repose – what chance do they have truthfully, against the tumored belly of humanity with its periodic seepage of pus and bile into the living streams of earth?' (p. 195). The baobab tree, normally a symbol of life, plenty and nourishment, is here an abnormal embodiment of the disease that plagues the waste land; it looks like an undernourished, deformed, diseased human being.

Against the landscape rose a single baobab, dry and stunted. Its trunk was broad and even up to a few feet, then it was overtaken by an abnormality or retardation that seemed, from the lumps, swellings and contortions, a blight of human infections – rickets, beri-beri, kwashiokor, and a variety of goitres. A distended belly in the middle of the trunk thrust its wrinkled navel at the black horizon. From malformed shoulders balanced on a flat chest writhed an abortion of limbs. Where the head might have been thinner branches hissed skywards, daring forked tongues in a venomous protection of whatever mystery hoard lay within the so-called tree of life. For there was nothing that called for protection from this wasted emanation. (p. 212)

The snake-like images associated with it suggest that it is also linked with monstrously unnatural evil. The author is accusing the Cartel of perverting the whole of nature.

The Cartel is appropriately associated with images of the unnatural and the abnormal. It is the snake which must be scorched before it has time to strike or a monster-child that the rationalists have given birth to. Unlike Aiyero, which observes the natural rhythm, the Cartel is committed to unnatural and abnormal growth. In a novel which lays so much stress on germination and vegetation rituals, the Cartel, true to its reputation for inverting nature's processes, 'plants' live cows (the members bury a live cow in the dead of each night) to ensure lasting ascendancy. And their harvest is a terrible harvest of evil directed against the people. Ultimately the aim of the Cartel is the unnatural mummification of the people: 'The means of this curse was however tangible, the end was the embalming of an entire people even as they breathed, deadening their nerve centres, willing the vital organs to malfunction, ending all co-ordination among the physical and thought processes' (p. 133).

The novel starts with the presentation of Aiyero society which is regarded by the rest of the country as an eccentric anomaly, simply because its quasi-communistic system ensures material prosperity, justice and equity and demonstrates concern for the welfare of every individual. It is most significant that while the descendants of other communities are lured by the attractions of the cities, the descendants of Aiyero, having experienced other values throughout the world, discover that what they left in Aiyero is superior to anything else and therefore always return. Aiyero society is vibrantly life affirming, the need for a commitment to truth and a better life having been the impulse behind the establishment of the community. Where the rest of human society seems to be defeated by life, the inhabitants of Aiyero affirm their vigorous commitment to life.

This is suggested by the nature of Aiyero's rituals. Even the funeral rites commemorating the death of the Custodian of the Grain are enacted in terms of regeneration, rebirth and fertility. The description of this ritual is one of the most powerful in the novel, reminding us of the magnificent presentation of Sekoni's dreams in *The Interpreters*.

> Ahime moved with feline balance, his hand poured back the drapes which fell away from his shoulder as he bent over the bull nearest the alcove. The cloth fell again so he caught it over the left arm and kept it there pressed against his waist. His knife-hand moved once, slashed deep and drew across the throat. The taut skin parted easily, opening to a layer of translucent membrane, yielding in turn the tendons and a commencement of red mists. Suddenly the white afternoon was showered in a crimson fountain, rising higher and higher, pumping ever upwards to a sun-scorched sky. Ahime stepped back quickly but not so far that the falling spray should not find him. His white vestments bloomed suddenly with red petals and a long sigh rose, fell and filled the air with whispers of wind and the opening of buds. He moved swiftly now, the sighs of relief were woven among the spreading mists, a thousand eyes followed the motions of the priest whose flutist blade was laid again and again to ivory pipes, tuned to invocations of renewal. Opening the vents of a rich elixir, he of the masseur's fingers stooped at each succeeding sluice-gate, a fountain-head covered in rime, his arms were supple streams in a knowing course through ridges bathed in a sun's downwash. He nudged the ridges' streams awake and they joined their tributaries to his fountain-head. A deep beneficence rested over the motions of his hands, opening red sluices for the land's replenishment.
>
> The jets climbed strongly, the springs seemed interminable. But at last even those cavernous hearts had no more to give; a last springlet of blood blossomed briefly, then the flood was dammed. A last gargle came through a blocked-up drain, a final shudder of love gave all to a passive earth. (pp. 16–17)

Ahime's association with blood here is quite different from Egbo's in *The Interpreters*. Where that symbolized destruction, this symbolizes reproduction and revitalization. The whole is shot through with suggestions of consummation, fertilization and joyful reproduction. Soyinka the poet is very much in evidence here as he conveys the potency with which Ahime unleashes the forces of regeneration and replenishment. The expressions 'he of the masseur's fingers stooped at each succeeding sluice-gate' and 'He nudged the ridges' streams awake', with their wealth of metaphor and pregnant turns of phrase, are surely reminiscent of Sekoni in *The Interpreters* harnessing the power of the waters and directing it to the improvement of a grateful land. The hard consonants in 'He nudged the ridges' streams awake' emphasize the power with which Ahime compels seemingly reluctant forces to join in the task of bringing nourishment and plenty to the land. The blood of the bulls is seen in terms of powerful nourishing streams and their final shudder is an orgasmic shudder, a final consummation in which the bull and the earth are wedded in love and the bull passes on the fertilizing agent to the passive earth as a result of which there will be replenishment and rebirth. Death in Aiyero is therefore linked with birth, both being parts of a continuing cycle. The dead Custodian is imbued with 'all the sympathetic potency, the healing and reproductive promise of the earth-bull union ...' (p. 18). The final song his people sing to him is not a dirge, but a prayer for regeneration.

> You dip your hand in the red clay bowl
> The gods eat from
> Lay your hand upon my earth
> Shower me with rain
>
> Lay your hand upon my roof
> Fill me with children
> Lay your hand upon my body
> Bless me with health ... (p.28)

The ideal community of Aiyero is clearly noted, then, for both its material prosperity and its spiritual and moral health. However, the fact that the head of this society is called 'Custodian of the Grain' suggests either that Aiyero wishes to conserve the grain for itself or that it is unaware that it could be disseminated to the world outside and thus become a powerful force for change. For, idealistic though this society is, it has limitations which Ofeyi is quick to observe and of which even its own leaders are becoming increasingly aware. Its much-vaunted virtue is too introspective. Its descendants are untouched not just by the world's corruption, but by the plight of mankind. In their view, to spread the message of Aiyero would be evangelism, evangelism is a form of aggression and they find no virtue in aggression. But Ofeyi points out to them that as a consequence of their refusal to evangelize a smell of mould and stagnation clings to the place. The Custodian's wish that a stranger should succeed him in his office is an indication of his own growing awareness of the need for Aiyero to move outwards. It is therefore essential to the very survival of Aiyero and its ideal of clean and decent living that it should abandon its self-regarding complacency and be prepared to evangelize. As Ofeyi puts it: 'The waters of Aiyero need to burst their banks. The grain must find new seminal grounds or it will atrophy and die' (p. 6).

The cocoa plant and the Cocoa Marketing Corporation also clearly have symbolic functions in the novel. Even in a very literal sense the cocoa plant is held to be the chief source of the country's prosperity. But the reference to it as the golden pod containing nectar and ambrosia suggests its association with the life of happiness enjoyed by the classical gods. The cocoa therefore symbolizes both material prosperity and happiness, healthy God-given luxuriance and contentment; in short, the good life that every Nigerian is entitled to. The idealistic Ofeyi's cocoa promotion campaign which he launches in his capacity as public relations officer for the Cocoa Marketing Board is therefore nothing less than the attempt to give every Nigerian a chance of a decent life, and to expose the greed of the rulers who have made that life impossible. The Cocoa Marketing Board should be the agent for making the good life available to every citizen. In practice, however, it falls short of this.

It is not too difficult to see the similarity between the cocoa drive and the Aiyero ideal. Both symbolize the good life. In fact, Aiyero represents a realization of the ideal good life which the cocoa plant is supposed to give to every Nigerian citizen. It is therefore perfectly natural for Ofeyi to think of the idea of linking Aiyero with his cocoa promotion campaign. The cocoa plant, like Aiyero, is also associated with images of germination, fertility and growth. In this corrupt society, however, the people are deprived of the good life which the cocoa plant should give them as of right, because the greedy authorities have sought to appropriate it all for themselves. They sell to the people, not the genuine thing, but a severely adulterated form: cocoa-wix, cocoa-bix and cocoa-flavoured sawdust.

During his visit to Aiyero, Ofeyi characteristically discovers that Aiyero soil is cocoa-earth; he thus thinks up the clever scheme of starting a model cocoa plantation within the communal where the seedlings would be nurtured to maturity but he also envisages the parallel progress of the new idea: 'the birth of the new man from the same germ as the cocoa seed, the Aiyero ideal disseminated with the same powerful propaganda machine of the Cartel throughout the land'. In becoming equated with the Aiyero ideal the cocoa-seed thus becomes the grain, which will eventually give rise to buds, tentacles, harvest and spores. The growth of the cocoa plant – the healthy virile shoot – suggests the nursing of pure vigorous ideals in Aiyero for export to the world outside, particularly to youth. The people of Aiyero are for once prepared to make a concession to outside ideas and set aside acres of virgin land for the scheme. The growth of the cocoa plant is also paralleled, of course, with the growth of the new man in Aiyero who will eventually carry the Aiyero message of a decent life to the outside world. The story of the Aiyero communal thus becomes not just the story of the cocoa plant from seed to ripening but also of the parallel life of the child (the child destined to become the ideal man) from seed to maturity.

Ofeyi's scheme to use the Cartel's own propaganda machine to develop a new type of man who would boost his crusade for a purer society means of course that he will have surreptitiously to attack the rulers responsible for the corruption and the erosion of what should be the good life. Most of the songs he composes to boost the campaign therefore have a double edge to them, exposing the Cartel's greed. Each contains a hidden dose of anarchy, for Ofeyi is really calling for a revolution.

> What's the might of the cocoa farmer?
> Matchet and hoe!
> What's the cure for weeds and nettles?
> Uproot entire!
> Root out the climbers and rotten creepers
> They don't-sow-nothing but ardent reapers
> Till harvest time they're heavy sleepers
> Root them out! (p. 60)

Thus in this modern rendering of the *Richard II* garden image the morally upright cocoa farmer becomes the cleaner of his stricken land, carefully pruning the corrupting weeds.

Ofeyi's cocoa promotion campaign linked with his crusade for a cleaner life is eminently successful initially because he himself is so resourceful, courageous, efficient and morally upright. He carries his crusade into another region, Cross-River, with Shage being the outpost for the new idea in this region. The Aiyero ideal is not just a moral idea; in Shage, as in Aiyero, it involves taking care of the people's material welfare. So there are also concrete schemes for improvement. We are told that 'Shage was central to the less obvious penetration of Aiyero through the land. Old villages had been uprooted, inundated and replanted making the concrete achievement visible, the marriage of the physical and the ideal. Even as the dam grew and the hydroelectric promise moved towards fulfilment, the men of Aiyero sowed their seeds in the soil of the new communal entity' (pp.87–8).

The ruling Cartel is typical of the system of government of a good number of independent African states; it is a dictatorial regime consisting of civilians backed by military might, the commandant-in-chief of the armed forces being one of its arms. Its realization that its power is not based on the will of the people makes the Cartel highly suspicious of anyone who shows the slightest signs of deviating from its wishes. The number of people that the Cartel bribes and corrupts into connivance is legion. Some are ordinary individuals who have to pay with their lives later; some are members of the judiciary. Nor are the police and the medical services exempt. When bribery fails bullying tactics are used. The Cartel will stop at nothing to achieve its dastardly ends and the kind of life it offers the people is one of unmitigated misery, fear and degradation.

Although this novel is less concerned with social corruption than *The Interpreters*, Soyinka does give some attention to social comment. This comes out especially in the lively scene describing the unveiling of the chairman of the corporation's new fountain. Soyinka very skilfully captures the chairman's thoughts revealing his stupidity, incompetence and vulgarity; in the new dispensation this is the kind of man who becomes chairman of an important corporation. As in *The Interpreters*, Soyinka concentrates attention on the stuffiness and artificiality of the gathering. The conversation between the journalist Spyhole and Zaccheus certainly brings out the stiff formality, and there is a distinct suggestion that in spite of this stiff exterior there is vulgarity simmering underneath.

Through Spyhole's reveries we get an insight into the chairman's tasteless extravagance. Like the managing director of Sagoe's newspaper company in *The Interpreters*, the chairman shows an unseemly anxiety to acquire the material artefacts that he feels are in keeping with a certain social position. It is an elaborate marble fountain with an effigy of St George and the dragon that is about to be unveiled, a monument to bad taste and extravagance.

> The Brigadier bowed, took the scissors, took her hand and implanted a kiss upon it to thundering applause and delight. He was a resplendent figure, the Brigadier, groomed it seemed from a nineteenth-century Venetian court – appropriately, it had to be

conceded, when the dust-sheet fell away and the glory of Italian marble was revealed to the benighted audience. Only the Chairman's running commentary jarred from time to time the viewer's contemplation of a florentine moment in the heart of a festering continent.

White-coated servants gathered up the dust-sheets and pulled them slowly backwards. The fountain pool, itself a fish-pond, was indeed scooped out in the shape of a cocoa-pod, floor and sides laid in tiny tiles of amber. From the centre of the pod rose a noble plinth, a marble arm from the enchanted lake, which for Excalibur upheld a blue marble platform upon which sat an armoured knight, equestrian. At the horse's feet writhed a monstrous dragon, scales of silver, tongue of bronze, fiery, fire-slashing eyes of onyx. It was transfixed by a ponderous silver spear and pounded by steel hooves of the noble steed.

'We all know the story of St George and the Dragon I think' the Chairman expounded as the applause rose and fell and the oh-ahs quietened. 'Well, you may not guess that what I have done here is to put it to symbolic use. Which is why I specially hoped that one of our new rulers would be able to unveil the masterpiece in person. St George seated on that horse there as you can see is representative of the new order which is battling the dragon which represents the forces of our greatest national enemy – corruption!' 'Hear, hear, hear, hear, hear hear...' (p. 44)

The criminal contrast between the rich treasures of this fountain and the degradation of a festering continent is unmistakable. When the resplendent figure of the brigadier kisses the hand of the chairman's wife to thunderous applause, he unwittingly emphasizes the society's lack of a proper order of priorities, the total unawareness that both Italian marble and the kissing of a woman's hand are completely out of place in a continent of people starving to death. The brigadier is an irrelevant anachronism – out of place in this century, out of place in this continent. The irony surrounding the extravagant fountain itself is obvious. It is a cocoa fountain, which in this novel should suggest that it is associated with the good life and the fight against corruption. But its use here is an empty facade since the chairman is one of the most corrupt people in the land. So also is the symbolism of St George and the dragon. The scene ends, of course, in general confusion due partly to Ofeyi's clever ruses. The cocoa-pod containing Iriyise, who is about to do one of her dances, refuses to open, while clouds gather overhead. Once more the symbolism is clear; because of the menace of corruption the cocoa-seed with its promise of the good life is not allowed to emerge.

Although the members of the Cartel inevitably impress the reader as a most unattractive quartet, Soyinka does not employ much depth and subtlety in their characterization. We know very little of Chief Biga, who hardly makes an appearance in the novel, except that he is a crude muscleman – the hatchet-man of the Cartel. This is also true of the commandant-in-chief who is little better than a caricature. It is a pity that Soyinka does not devote more attention to the presentation of the men from whom so much bestial evil springs. However, he is rather more conscientious with Batoki and the Zaki Amuri. The former's brutality and cynicism are obvious, and yet in a very powerful scene, the kind of scene that only Soyinka among African novelists can create, we see that Batoki who holds an entire nation in dread cannot keep order in his own household. Perhaps Soyinka intends his domestic disorderliness to be symbolic of his personal corruption; but he really gets underneath the skin of his virago of a wife as the latter defies Batoki. We meet this woman only once, and yet Soyinka's presentation is so sure that no one can deny that she is forcefully *there*.

If Batoki is the brains of the Cartel, the Zaki Amuri, the most deadly and sinister of the lot, is the real power, and the power is very forcefully enacted. Behind his taciturnity and apparent indifference lurks the most venomous malignity. The dominant impression conveyed at his court is of moral and social corruption and tyranny.

The *dongari* pushed his prisoner to the floor and the man cringed, his head between his arms to ward off expected blows. No sound came from him although spasms commenced around his jaws and his head bobbed up and down. On the raised floor at the opposite end of the hall, a seeming end of the world away from where the clerk had spoken, sat a turbanned figure at the sight of whom the prisoner had promptly lowered his eyes. Impassive and expressionless, permanent slits of boredom and disdain served for a pair of eyes. His figure filled a huge ornate chair ... Sprawled at his feet were a number of shapes in poses of seeming inattention. A young boy raised languid eyes from the comic strip paperback which had engrossed him until then, looked up at the turbanned figure, then across the vast expanse to the creature who still cringed against the *dongari*'s feet. The boy fluttered his long lashes, giggled and sent his voice lisping down the hall: 'Is the dog mute then!' ...

Pausing from time to time only to present the salutation fist of homage in the direction of the dais the man called Salau hastily began his journey to the throne in a strange combination of movements: sometimes he dragged on heels and buttocks, then sprinted a quick yard at a crouch, hands hung low to the ground so that his finger-tips retained a light contact with the marble floor, he slid a few more yards on one leg and half-buttock, his palm flat against the ground, then sprawled whining on all fours ... his movements were punctuated by a quick wringing of his hands, a trembling fist of homage and a quick gargle in his throat as he bobbed his head and saluted: 'Ranka dede, ranka dede.' (pp. 119–20)

Such is the degradation that the Zaki inflicts on his people. Because of his own moral corruption he encourages the most irresponsible and dangerous incompetence. There is a slight suggestion that he is a homosexual, and on his return from his Islamic pilgrimages he always brings back a minion whom he proceeds to instal in an important public position without regard to the individual's competence or qualifications. One of these, a mere hospital orderly from Pakistan, has been appointed senior medical officer in charge of a very important hospital. He has proceeded to carry out surgical operations and turn the surrounding mudflats into a cemetery for burying his victims. When Ofeyi's activities in Cross-River begin to have visible effect the Zaki gives orders for the most terrible reprisals, unleashing a war of genocide with the most inhuman consequences.

Ofeyi, the hero of the novel, is as courageous and idealistic as Sagoe and his friends in *The Interpreters* without possessing any of their unattractive qualities. He is significantly attracted to Aiyero from the very start, through an unconscious identification with the community's values. This is partly why the Custodian wishes to select him as his successor. Initially he is quite prepared to use peaceful methods to undermine the Cartel, the Aiyero idea being one such method. However, he is forced to change his views both by the failure of the Aiyero mission in the wake of the Zaki Amuri's onslaught and by his meeting and association with the dentist, whose symbolic name suggests that he advocates drastic action to remove the decayed portion of society before the whole is infected. The dentist sees violence as the only means of getting rid of a dictatorial regime and Ofeyi's development is in the direction of a gradual acceptance of the dentist's position. He is forced to accept that he and the dentist are kindred spirits: 'Violence is not what I want from here. Just the same, the sowing of any idea these days can no longer take place without accepting the need to protect the young seedling, even by violent means.' In a rapidly disintegrating situation such as that presented in the novel, even the most peaceloving are sometimes forced to abandon their principles and take refuge in violence, for violence breeds violence.

The dentist, for his part, is single-minded in his devotion to his philosophy of violence as the solution to the country's problems. It is right to talk of his 'philosophy of violence' for he is not simply a crude trained assassin. His conduct is backed by a carefully thought out and articulate rationale which is so impressive that Ofeyi often finds it unassailable: 'There is a pattern even to the most senseless killing. All that we must do is to take control of that violence and direct it with a constructive economy.' Soyinka skilfully demonstrates the dentist's cool, quiet professionalism, which comes out even in his tone of voice. He is neat and efficient in his methods and completely unsentimental. Even after the most sensational killing his voice betrays no touch of elation or of vindictiveness. He has just done a job of work well; he mentions it only in passing and goes on to other matters. Unlike some others, like Ofeyi, who waver under the influence of various dilemmas, the dentist derives strength from the unshakable conviction that his attitude and course of action are right.

Ofeyi's companion, Iriyise, undergoes a striking transformation in the novel from Lagos night-club girl to one of the society's real moral agents. The fact that she is immediately attracted to Aiyero during their first visit there is an indication of her own moral idealism. In the symbolic framework of the novel she is one of the forces dedicated to promoting the nation's moral and spiritual health. She responds to the vegetative, life-affirming rituals of Aiyero and in doing so becomes complete.

> She came in a white-and-ochre wrapper, antimony round her eyes, a solid bangle of ivory on her neck – how did they get those heavy things on a woman's neck! Ofeyi felt himself excluded by such transparent numinous excitement as flushed her face . . . how little I know of her, how very little after all. When they were at last alone she would only say, it filled me Ofe, it filled me completely where I had felt so empty. I know I am now complete. Who on earth, what on earth could have taught her to say that, whose only language of fulfilment till now had been the aftermath of love! (p. 7)

She is also, of course, the cocoa princess, the leading figure in Ofeyi's cocoa promotion campaign. Iriyise is associated with the images of vegetation, germination and fecundity associated with Aiyero and the cocoa plant, and after the establishment of the cocoa plantation in Aiyero she appropriately plays a prominent role in tending the young seedlings. 'Now she could even tell a blight on the young shoot apart from mere scorching by the sun. Her fingers spliced wounded saplings with the ease of a natural healer. Her presence, the women boasted, inspired the rains' (p. 20). An agent of healing, a source of inspiration who is in tune with the natural rhythms, she is also naturally a great vitalizing force.

One of the major consequences of the Cartel's manoeuvres in Cross-River is Iriyise's abduction and Ofeyi's subsequent quest in search of her. To link this more tightly with his theme Soyinka uses the parallel classical analogy of the abduction of Eurydice, the wife of Orpheus. It is quite clear that both Ofeyi and Iriyise are intended to be Nigerian variants of Orpheus and Eurydice.

The legend of Orpheus and Eurydice is about the high-handed rape of innocence by an immoral and irrational despot (Pluto) and also about the courage, determination and loyalty of the consort. Orpheus is an ideal figure who, because of the excellence of his artistry, has become the type of the accomplished musician. In certain variants of the legend Pluto is represented as a snake. The abducting agent is therefore associated with evil. Soyinka makes some alterations in his own adaptation of the legend to suit the demands of his theme. Thus, unlike Orpheus, Ofeyi's quest for his partner is successful, since he is able to rescue Iriyise and take her back to the realms of life, and he himself survives at the end. Otherwise Soyinka retains most of the details and attributes of the characters. Thus, the abducting agent here is the sinister Zaki Amuri – the all-powerful and corrupt despot of Cross-River – and he abducts Iriyise like Pluto in order to minister to his lust. Like Eurydice, Iriyise is a beautiful dancer and artistic performer, and Ofeyi like Orpheus is a musician, a determined and courageous idealist who refuses to be intimidated by the threats of the all-powerful seducer. The use of the Orpheus and Eurydice legend thus helps Soyinka to bring out the Cartel's villainy and Ofeyi's moral idealism.

As in most quest tales, Ofeyi's search takes him through a kind of waste land. The quest itself has a much greater significance than the mere search for Iriyise. As Ofeyi puts it: 'I am sure every man feels the need to seize for himself the enormity of what is happening, of the time in which it is happening. Perhaps deep down I realize that the search would immerse me in the meaning of the event, lead me to a new understanding of history' (p. 218). Ofeyi seeks then to see a pattern in the apparently chaotic jumble.

Soyinka skilfully ensures that every major event in Ofeyi's quest corresponds with some detail of the Orpheus legend. The landscape through which Ofeyi and his companion Zaccheus journey is bleak and forbidding in the extreme, possibly the harshest created in all literature. It is an arid, barren landscape of disease, death and devastation. As in the Orpheus legend, Ofeyi meets a number of people whom he asks for help in his quest. The beginning of what can be termed his descent into the 'underworld' is his meeting with Ahime on whose advice he looks for Iriyise in the mortuary. The mortuary is naturally a place of death, a real Hades; and the harrowing sight of bodies in drawers or on dissecting tables in various stages of post-mortem surgical mutilation is as scarifying as anything to be seen in Hades.

The local native Christian church, ironically named 'Tabernacle of Hope', where Ofeyi continues his search, also has suggestions of the underworld. Spooky, according to Zaccheus, it leaves on Taiila and the reader the impression of a subterranean camp. But the place which most resembles Hades is Temoko, the prison-cum-lunatic-asylum-cum-leprosy-camp, which is a veritable chamber of disease, death and horrors. The strong man, Suberu, whose major task is significantly to cow the inmates into submission and prevent them from escaping, is most probably meant to be a variant of Cerberus, the three-headed dog who guards the entrance into Hades. His original personality has been eroded, and he has been brainwashed and reduced to the level of an animal trained almost automatically to do his master's bidding.

In its presentation of violence and horror this novel possibly surpasses Ouologuem's *Bound to Violence*. It is possible that in the creation of some of these scenes Soyinka has in mind the turbulent events immediately preceding the first Nigerian coup. But there are also suggestions here of the state of the country under military rule. Certainly, the civilian rulers of the three regions – the Zaki Amuri, Chief Biga and Chief Batoki – are meant in a vague way to recall the three regional premiers of the northern, eastern and western regions of Nigeria before the coup. Zaki Amuri, like the emir, is a traditional Muslim ruler, and Cross-River suggests the North. But the dictatorial methods of the three rulers and the quasi-military discipline they impose suggest the post-coup situation, not just in Nigeria, but in many African countries. Then there are such glaring similarities between the massacre of Aiyero men and aliens in Cross-River and the massacre of Ibos in northern Nigeria which led to Biafra's declaration of independence and the Nigerian Civil War. Of course, Soyinka has written a novel and not a historical document, and he has quite legitimately altered some of the historical details and distorted some of the personalities to suit the needs of his work of art. Generally, the novel is meant to be a parable of the events in Nigeria both before the coups and during the miltary regime. Soyinka is expressing his detestation and horror at the cruelty and injustice that characterized the conduct of government in his country during both periods.

The worst atrocities in the novel are perpetrated in Cross-River itself where the Zaki has given orders for a campaign of genocide. The reader watches spellbound as helpless multitudes are massacred while the police, army and other forces of law and order stand idly by. Soyinka lays stress on the dehumanization and brutalization resulting from such lunactic acts. Men have become reduced to the level of animals in their hunt for others or in their attempt to escape. Both hunters and hunted are transformed into jackals, and Soyinka once more resorts to classical mythology for an image to illustrate man's growing bestiality. In a significant passage which is a blend of fantasy, classical legend and biblical lore and which is faintly reminiscent of Sagoe's hallucination in *The Interpreters*, Ofeyi imagines he is Anubis (An Egyptian god), the jackal-headed one, contemplating the ravage of the Egyptian people by the plagues of the God of the Old Testament.

The moth caress of Iriyise's scented room had not stopped the dreams of Anubis, the jackal-headed one, once he had absorbed the scope of the Cross-River event. He had fallen asleep thinking, this is the fifth face of the Apocalypse, the eighth plague that the Judaic sorcerer had omitted to include – the plague of rabid dogs. Cramped half-asleep between the bed and wall he watched the thousands and thousands of the slavering bare-fanged creatures emerge out of the corner of the floor and rush him. He turned and fled but his feet were trapped beneath a boulder. Struggling in vain to free himself he hit on the only salvation and bared his teeth, pronged and flaring just like the swarm whose spear-point snouts were aimed in unison at his throat. Miraculously he found that his teeth were no longer human, that his jowls dribbled the dirty-ash, crimson-blotched spittle of a recent bestial banquet. His neck grew warm at the back as hairs rose on them in defiance and, most wonderful of all, the sound that came from his throat was a perfected howl, fiercer than their prey-scenting wail. Kicking his leg furiously he woke and found it wedged between the bedpost and the wall. (pp. 159–60)

Contemporary Nigeria, like ancient Egypt, seems to be under the blight of a plague, specifically, the plague of dogs – human beings who in their rapacity and lust for human blood have been transformed into jackals. The human mind itself has undergone a bestial transformation. Soyinka also vividly demonstrates the human degradation, the absolute demoralization and collapse of the human will. The gruesome episode in which a group of villagers hunt down and ritualistically slaughter a helpless victim concentrates both the degradation and the mindless, almost purposeless cruelty.

A movement from the stunned creature, a stirring in the matted rags, a twig, a tubercular arm scrabbled on the tar ... again all was still. Only for an instant. The eyes of the watching group were suddenly alerted to the evidence that life still existed in him. Again the claw moved on as if it sought to smooth down the protruding pebbles. His elbow sought a feeble leverage on the ground and the head, a matted trap of seeds, berries, insect-life, pollen and earth, rose a little way from the ground. And only then was there animation in the eyes of his hunters who had waited, since their emergence it seemed, just for this moment. As if this flicker of life was a sign, a sanction and a command that must be fulfilled before it again petered out they swept him up, bore him onto the grass verge and held him by his wasted limbs to earth. The varnished skull of one – he seemed to be the oldest among them – rose above others and his mouth moved, shedding what seemed to be a brief devotional fragment on the scene. Then someone unsheathed a dagger, placed it in his hand. It rose, glinted briefly in the sun and the old man stooped and drew it across the throat of the prostrate figure.

His hand moved again, this time down the body, the knife-tip drew a swift practised circle on the crotch and his other hand held up the victim's genitals. He passed it to one of the many eager hands which also uselessly held open a jaw that had opened wide to thrust out pain. Into that mouth they thrust his penis with the testicles. Then they all stepped back and looked on the transformation they had wrought. (p. 164)

For a demonstration of sheer bestial inhumanity it is hard to beat. The episode is suffused with animal images: the victim looks like an animal covered with insect and plant life, his hand is referred to as a claw and his oppressors are hunters. Their activity takes the form of a ritual whose apparent mindlessness is reinforced by the striking absence of hate. The hunters set about their murderous mission with the dispassionate efficiency of people doing a job that has to be done. It is almost as though they have been conditioned to murder. Again and again Soyinka pauses to consider the psychology of mass murder and genocide. What is it that makes a populace engage in the mass slaughter of those against whom they could have no personal grudge? How is one to explain 'the unholy glee upon the faces of women, even of children' as they perpetrate these atrocities? Was the blood-lust just a legacy of the climate? Was the reason to be sought in the environment like other forms of pestilence like the tsetse-fly? 'Or was there a truly metaphysic condition called evil, present in epidemic proportions that made them so open to the manipulations of coldly unscrupulous men? There had to be a cause beyond mere differences in culture, beyond material envy ...' (p. 276).

A few spots of brightness enliven the almost unrelieved gloom of this bleak landscape, taking the form of the activities of a few morally upright individuals. Apart from Ofeyi himself there is the efficient and hospitable doctor, conscientiously carrying out his duties of proper healing in the midst of carnage and slaughter; there is the kindly guide Elihu, who takes Ofeyi and his companions through their tour of the Tabernacle of Hope in search of Iriyise; there is Aliyu the deformed watchman who impresses us with his tremendous courage and loyalty in the face of overwhelming odds even when his own life is at stake; and there is the courteous Lieutenant Sayi who gives Ofeyi vital help in his search. Above all there is the pure and idealistic Taiila. She originally intended to become a nun since she considered this a healing profession, a form of beauty and a refuge of peace. But realizing that a withdrawal from the complexities of the world into a life of peace would represent a stultification of her own potential as a healing agent, she postpones her decision to be a nun and comes to Nigeria where she achieves an actual realization of her healing potential in the tour of the Tabernacle of Hope with Ofeyi. Taiila and the dentist represent the two opposing forces in Ofeyi's nature – the pull towards peace and the pull towards violence which the search for Iriyise will inevitably involve. It is significant that Ofeyi meets both on the same day and they are all together at the end. Ofeyi is immediately drawn to Taiila because she represents this peaceful side of his nature, and she, for her part, thinks that they were destined to meet so that she can save him from the almost inevitable disaster that the quest involves. There are occasions when Ofeyi is tempted to give up the search and settle for a life of peace with Taiila. But she herself realizes later that to abandon the search would be to abandon all attempts at introducing some decency into an otherwise chaotic world. It is thus the dentist who wins in the end.

The novel moves towards a horrifying climax in the scenes at the prison/lunatic asylum of Temoko. In a sense, the prison is Hades from which Iriyise, like Eurydice, is eventually rescued. But it is also a microcosm of the society with which we have been presented. Here, in their most concentrated forms, are the criminal lunacy, unnatural diseases, plagues, deformities and inversions of the natural processes which afflict the world as a whole. The leper scenes suggest that blend of the grotesque, the pathetic and the comic which Soyinka can so admirably achieve.

The conclusion is one of the few question marks that one would like to place against this novel. In the general confusion of the leper fight, engineered, we are made to believe, by the dentist, Ofeyi is able to rescue Iriyise from the seemingly impregnable fortress of Temoko; they join some of the other refugees from Cross-River and trek back to Aiyero. This is a thriller-like end to a story which has hitherto left the impression that Temoko is impregnable, that it is virtually impossible to outmanoeuvre the Cartel because of their superior force, and that anyone who dares oppose them is doomed to destruction. The escape of Ofeyi and Iriyise is inherently improbable. Ofeyi is much too lucky to survive up to the end in the midst of all this vindictive carnage. However, Soyinka's motive, in altering both the conclusion of the classical legend and what should have been the logical outcome of the story, is clear. He wishes to hold out a ray of hope in an otherwise darkening atmosphere. The Aiyero idea has been checked but not defeated. In the escape, it is retreating back to source to reorganize itself and wait for a more favourable moment to strike again. The survival of the dentist, Iriyise and Ofeyi reinforces this hope. The impression left at the end is that they move upwards from the realms of death back to life: 'Temoko was sealed against the world till dawn. The street emptied at last as the walls and borders shed their hidden fruit. In the forests, life began to stir'. (p. 320)

NOTES

1 Wole Soyinka, 'The writer in a modern African state', in *The Writer in Modern Africa*, ed. P. Wastberg (Scandinavian Institute of African Studies, Uppsala, 1968), pp. 14–21.
2 See Eldred Jones, '*The Interpreters*: reading notes', *ALT*, no. 2 (1969), p. 42, and *The Writings of Wole Soyinka* (Heinemann, London, 1973), p. 155.

3 Derek Elders, Rev., 'James Ngugi: *A Grain of Wheat*', *ALT*, no. 1 (1968), p. 52; Eustace Palmer, *An Introduction to the African Novel* (Heinemann, London, 1972), pp. xiii–xiv.

4 All page references are to the Panther edition (Panther, London, 1967).

5 Eldred Jones, *The Writings of Wole Soyinka*, op. cit., p. 161.

6 Wole Soyinka, *Season of Anomy* (Rex Collings, London, 1973). All further page references are to this edition.

11. Ngugi wa Thiong'o

▼▼▼▼▼▼▼▼▼▼▼▼▼▼▼▼▼▼▼▼▼▼▼▼▼▼▼▼▼▼▼▼▼▼▼▼▼

Petals of Blood

James Ngugi's latest novel, *Petals of Blood*, is easily his most representative, for it incorporates all the major preoccupations of his novelistic career. Indeed it is not too much of an exaggeration to say that this most ambitious and comprehensive work incorporates all the major preoccupations of the African novel from its beginnings to the present day. Ngugi's first novel *The River Between* was concerned with the first phase of the historical processes consequent on the imperialist occupation and exploitation of Africa; it concentrated on the disruption caused within traditional society by the alien educational and religious systems. The second and third, *Weep Not, Child* and *A Grain of Wheat*, deal with the second phase, the Mau Mau struggle for liberation. *Petals of Blood* not only deals with these two phases, but also gives an extended treatment of the third phase. Of all African novels, it probably presents the most comprehensive analysis to date of the evils perpetrated in independent African society by black imperialists and capitalists. It subsumes several other aspects of Ngugi's earlier novels – the widespread and effective use of symbols and images, the concern with education and religion, the resourceful and morally courageous women and the indecisive young men who are called upon to play a major role in society but are unable to do so successfully because they are plagued by a sense of insecurity or guilt. Even the narrative technique seems to be a conglomerate of the methods of *A Grain of Wheat* on the one hand, and *The River Between* and *Weep Not, Child* on the other. The novel is constructed on grand epic proportions, but it is an epic, not just of the East African struggle, but of the entire African struggle. No wonder it has been described as the most ambitious novel yet realized by the pen of an African.[1]

The narrative technique of *Petals of Blood* is not as complex or as subtle as that of *A Grain of Wheat*. Most of it is told in the form of reminiscences rather than flashbacks. The story starts in the present with the four main characters – Wanja, Karega, Abdulla and Munira – in jail on suspicion of implication in the murder of the three African directors of the Theng'eta Brewery. It really takes the form of Munira's recollections as he sits in his cell, writing copious notes in order to clear his own mind about the significance of the events and satisfy the demands of the probing chief inspector, so that from the present the story goes back twelve years to Munira's recollections of his first arrival in Ilmorog. It periodically returns to the present and to Munira in his cell, and on one or two occasions goes even further back to his experiences while at school at Siriana in the 1940s, and the Mau Mau uprising in the 1950s. Otherwise it moves progressively forwards from Munira's first arrival in Ilmorog twelve years previously to the present, and to the resolution of the murder riddle. It would be inaccurate to say that *Petals of Blood* makes use of shifting chronology. The narrative method consists for the most part of reminiscences which none the less progress sequentially. Nor must we look in *Petals of Blood* for that subtle interrelationship between structure, narrative method and presentation of character which was one of the hallmarks of *A Grain of Wheat*. Here the narrative method is simply there to present the events of the story, not to help condition the reader's responses to the characters.

The novel's title, *Petals of Blood*, points to the centrality of the symbolism in the elucidation of the work's meaning. One dominant symbol cluster relates to flowers and other forms of vegetation. At times these suggest regeneration, fecundity and luxuriance; but more often, as in the poem by Derek Walcott with which Ngugi prefixes the novel, they suggest destruction, evil, the unnatural, corruption and death. It might seem from this poem that the petals of blood of the title are connected here with the 'potent ginger lily', one of the destructive, repulsive plants which give a scene, which should normally appear quite natural and beautiful, an eerie, unnatural and evil aura. The imagery therefore suggests the distortion of things in this society from the normal and natural to the abnormal and evil, and the introduction of chaos and destruction where there should be beauty and order. But in the novel itself we discover that the flower with the petals of blood belongs to a plant that grows wild in the plains.

> One child cried out:
> 'Look. A flower with petals of blood.'
> It was a solitary red beanflower in a field dominated by white,

blue and violet flowers. No matter how you looked at it, it gave you the impression of a flow of blood. Munira bent over it and with a trembling hand plucked it. It had probably been the light playing upon it, for now it was just a red flower. 'There is no colour called blood. What you mean is that it is red. You see? You must learn the names of the seven colours of the rainbow. Flowers are of different kinds, different colours. Now I want each one of you to pick a flower . . . Count the number of petals and pistils and show me its pollen . . .' He stood looking at the flower he had plucked and then threw the lifeless petals away. Yet another boy cried: 'I have found another. Petals of blood – I mean red . . . It has no stigma or pistils . . . nothing inside.'

He went to him and the others surrounded him:

'No, you are wrong,' he said, taking the flower. 'This colour is not even red . . . it does not have the fullness of colour of the other one. This one is yellowish red. Now you say it has nothing inside. Look at the stem from which you got it. You see anything?'

'Yes,' cried the boys. 'There is a worm – a green worm with several hands or legs.'

'Right. This is a worm-eaten flower . . . It cannot bear fruit. That's why we must always kill worms . . . A flower can also become this colour if it's prevented from reaching the light.'[2]

Unlike the flower in the prefix the flower with the petals of blood is itself the victim of evil. Its innocence, like that of Blake's sick rose, has been destroyed by the agents of corruption. The blood suggests suffering. The flower thus becomes a symbol of the entire society Ngugi is concerned with – potentially beautiful, healthy and productive; but its potential unrealized and itself destroyed by the agents of corruption and death.

The plant with the petals of blood is actually the Theng'eta plant which grows wild on the plains that are associated with luxuriance, vitality and vigour. It is also a plant that is associated with Ilmorog's pristine traditional splendour. 'Theng'eta is the plant that only the old will talk about. Why? It is simple. It is only they who will have heard of it or know of it . . . It was when they were drinking Theng'eta that the poets and singers composed their words for a season of Gichandi, and the seer voiced his prophecy' (p. 204). Theng'eta was the drink that Nyakinyua, that staunch upholder of traditional values, and her formidable husband brewed, and it is significant that it was stronger and much more efficacious than the impure adulterated variety now mass-produced by the greedy modern capitalists in their sophisticated distilleries. It also symbolized truth and purity for the flower with the four red petals was used to purify the drink and the purified drink itself had the remarkable quality of forcing people to confront the truth about themselves. The drink Theng'eta thus derives its name from the fact that the Theng'eta plant is used to purify the fermented stuff, which in Nyakinyua's words is nothing without it.

> 'This is only . . . this is nothing yet,' Nyakinyua explained. 'This can only poison your heads and intestines. Squeeze Theng'eta into it and you get your spirit. Theng'eta. It is a dream. It is a wish. It gives you sight, and for those favoured by God it can make them cross the river of time and talk with their ancestors. It has given seers their tongues; poets and Gichandi players their words; and it has made barren women mothers of many children. Only you must take it with faith and purity in your hearts.' (p. 210)

Therefore, when the people of Ilmorog, under the inspired leadership of Nyakinyua, decide to re-engage in the production of Theng'eta it symbolizes a decision to return to the purity of their traditional values; and the transformation of Theng'eta into a debased modern spirit by the capitalists suggests the erosion of those values and the destruction of traditional innocence by the corrupt and depraved agents of modernism.

The drought is another pervasive symbol in the novel. Here Ngugi has used an actual historical and ecological fact – the recent disastrous drought in most of Africa – for symbolic purposes with telling effect. For purposes of counterpoint it is often juxtaposed with rain symbolism suggesting the fecundity and luxuriance which the region, under normal circumstances, ought to enjoy. The telling descriptions of the people's suffering, the poverty of the harvest, the scarcity of food and the death of the animals ought to convince us that the drought is an actual physical fact. Yet there is no denying its symbolic significance as well. The drought is also emotional, spiritual, economic and political. It relates generally to the arid condition of the lives of the people – their general deprivation of all those things which should make life meaningful such as health, opportunities for the education of their children, gainful rewarding employment and freedom from exploitation. Again and again the people talk about the drought in their lives. Moreover, the physical drought accurately reflects emotional and spiritual aridity. Thus Wanja, yearning after a release from barrenness, grows more restless and moody, the more arid the environment becomes; and Munira, powerfully in the throes of love, is soon to discover that without Wanja Ilmorog has become a land of drought.

Then there is the symbol of maiming which also relates to the people's spiritual condition. The one-legged but very resourceful Abdulla, paralysed in one leg during the Mau Mau emergency, is the most concrete symbol in the novel of man's inhumanity to man. But the physical maiming, which the Ilmorogians almost extend to his donkey on one occasion, also relates to a spiritual condition, for the people all carry maimed souls. Abdulla's lame leg is therefore merely the physical manifestation of a general spiritual fact.

The scene of most of the events of the novel is the community of Ilmorog which grows from a small traditional village into a modern capitalist complex. But Ilmorog could easily have been any other Kenyan village. It is a microcosm of Kenyan society as a whole and its experiences are a paradigm of what has happened to a number of similar Kenyan communities. Ngugi's very compelling historical presentation gives us glimpses of the glory of Ilmorog's past. It was a purely traditional society untouched by western values, where the dignified, courageous peasants reckoned their wealth in land, cows and goats. Ngugi celebrates the valour of their warriors. The exemplary Nyakinyua, appropriately called 'Mother of men', is the living embodiment of the values of this society and the repository of its legends and its history. When she sings the admittedly bawdy traditional songs during the initiation ritual, she invests them with a dignity which exposes by comparison the obscenity of the modern rendition of them at the contemporary capitalist parties. At the start of Part Two, in a most impressive chapter called 'The Journey', Ngugi, making use of legend and oral lore, celebrates the valour of the first heroes of this community, showing the gradual change from a largely nomadic to an agrarian civilization; and presenting their prosperity, contentment and sense of community: 'It had had its days of glory: thriving villages with a huge population of sturdy peasants who had tamed nature's forests and, breaking the soil between their fingers, had brought forth every type of crop to nourish the sons and daughters of men' (p. 120). The imperialist intrusion which followed and the inhumanities perpetrated were the first blow to Ilmorog's pride, and the consequent disruption heralded the beginning of Ilmorog's decline.

Even before the period of the start of the novel, then, we see that the once-thriving community of Ilmorog has fallen on evil times. And at the start it appears a desolate, unprogressive place from which the young are only too happy to get away. It is significant that the only young people who come to Ilmorog and stay there have all been spiritually maimed in one way or another – Munira, looking for a place to hide away from the competitive adult world, Abdulla, para- lysed in the Mau Mau uprising and disillusioned by the results of independence, Wanja, disgusted by her life as a prostitute in the city and yearning for the fulfilment of motherhood, and Karega, expelled from school and unable to make headway in modern capitalist Kenya. For the first part of the novel Ilmorog is blighted by the drought and its suffering is enhanced by the neglect of the political authorities, in particular its Member of Parliament, Nderi, who having got the people's votes stays away in the city, concentrating instead on his capitalist enterprises. Eventually Karega, the bright young teacher in the community, puts forward the daring plan that they should march to the city, confront their Member of Parliament with their prob- lems and force him to acknowledge his responsibilities. With the imminence of the march the people of Ilmorog discover a new spirit. It is a community spirit inducing both men and women to pool their resources in preparation for the journey; but it is also a return of the pristine Ilmorog spirit when their warriors used to go out in pursuit of hostile nations who had stolen their goats and cattle and would not return until they had recovered their stolen wealth. The march reminds the reader of the similar exercise in Ousmane's *God's Bits of Wood*; and like that one it is an ordeal which tests the people's capacity for endurance and brings out the best in the leaders like Wanja, Karega and Abdulla. The success of the march in alerting the whole of Kenya to the plight of the people of Ilmorog is the turning point in the latter's fortunes.

Ilmorog is now earmarked for rapid development and there are visible signs of a revival in the small community. The revival is suggested by means of rain symbolism, the rain which falls immediately after the march being, in the elders' opinion, God's response to their sacrifice. Ngugi also suggests images of fecundity and fertilization to suggest the earth's response to the rain. 'This waiting earth: its readiness powered Wanja's wings of expectation and numerous desires. Feverishly she looked out for tomorrow, waiting like the other women, for earth to crack, earth to be thrust open by the naked shoots of life' (p. 196). Some of the images are taken directly from the oral tradition: 'The older folk told stories of how Rain, Sun and Wind went a-wooing Earth, Sister of Moon, and it was Rain who carried the day, and that was why Earth grew a swollen belly after being touched by Rain. Others said no, the raindrops were really the sperms of God and that even human beings sprang from the womb on mother earth soon after the original passionate downpour, torrential waters of the beginning' (p. 196). The spirit of rebirth finds a counterpart in the erstwhile arid souls of individuals: 'Wanja was possessed of the rain-spirit. She walked through it, clothes drenched, skirt-hem tight against her thighs, revelling in the waters from heaven' (p. 196). In Ngugi's novels, walking in the rain is always a good sign.

But the luxuriance which now pervades Ilmorog is different from earlier, similar times since it is punctuated by doubts. The people, with memories of their experiences in the city fresh in their minds, are uncomfortably aware of a more troubled world 'which could, any time, descend upon them breaking asunder their rain-filled sun-warmed calm'. The new birth is an unknown power bringing uncertainty in its wake and intimations of forces other than droughts threatening the security and tranquillity of their lives.

The people's doubts are justified. As the capitalists move in with their roads, banks, factories, distilleries and estate agencies, the old traditional Ilmorog is irreplaceably destroyed. The destruction of the hut of the mysterious spirit Mwathi by a giant bulldozer is the concrete symbol of the annihilation of a once-proud society by the forces of modernism. The reader watches with profound sympathy as the bewildered and deceived peasants, unable to match the business acumen and financial standing of the big men from the city, inevitably lose their lands and all their possessions and degenerate helplessly into labourers or worse. The courageous Nyakinyua is given real tragic stature when she decides, single-handed, to put up a determined fight against all those forces that have deprived her of her heritage. Her resolution constitutes the last flagging attempt of a once dignified and secure society to resist the encroachments of the new men. But it is doomed to failure, and the reluctance of others to support her suggests the demoralization that now pervades Ilmorog. It is soon transformed into a capitalist complex with all the attendant problems of prostitution, social inequalities and inadequate housing for the poor. It has twice been exploited and destroyed; once by the white imperialists, and now by their successors, the black imperialists.

The hero of the novel is Munira, the teacher who decides to settle in Ilmorog. Devotees of Ngugi cannot fail to recognize in him reminiscences of Ngugi's three earlier heroes – Njoroge in *Weep Not, Child* who pins his faith on education and refuses to face the world of adult responsibility; Waiyaki, who in spite of his admirable qualities fails to attain the stature of a manly hero through his indecision; and Mugo who is tortured by a sense of guilt and insecurity. Munira is an anti-hero, an ultra-sensitive young man whose life is a failure. Unlike Mugo, his sense of insecurity degenerates into an inferiority complex, a conviction of his irretrievable mediocrity. During his student days at Siriana he had been involved in a strike resulting in his expulsion, but where the other leaders, like Chui, were able to reorganize their lives by sheer determination and resilience, Munira, lacking the capacity to engage in the world of adult endeavour and experience, can only drift from one failure to another. He is a passive spectator hovering on the fringes of important actions, withdrawing from involvement, like Mugo. But where Mugo wishes to be left alone as an act of deliberate policy in order to guarantee success, Munira's desire for solitude is a concomitant of his character and personality. He recalls not just Ngugi's own Njoroge, who dreads the world of adult competition and struggle and is basically immature, but also Dostoyevsky's insecure, introspective heroes.

Ngugi's presentation of Munira unwittingly lends credibility to the adage 'He who can does; he who can't teaches'. His passionate desire being for a safe place in which to hide and do some work, Munira withdraws to the remote village of Ilmorog and settles down to the career of a teacher. There, safe from the competitive adult world, away from the glare of publicity, the intellectually timid Munira can create his own empire and at last become a leader and a success. He is therefore at his best in the classroom, although even there his ego takes a tremendous deflation whenever the students ask him difficult questions or when any of his brighter teachers prove more persuasive in argument. Ngugi uses significant images to define his character. First of all there is the image of the closed space – like the classroom. While the people of Ilmorog as a whole are associated with open spaces – the fields and the plains – Munira is associated with the four walls of a room: 'and they were all busy putting seeds in the soil, and he watched them from the safety of his classroom or of Abdulla's shop' (p. 24). This recalls Mugo's symbolic bolting of himself within the four walls of his hut in order to guarantee security against the encroachments of the outside world. Then there are images of darkness, shadows and twilight.

Munira relished twilight as a prelude to that awesome shadow. He looked forward to the unwilled immersion into darkness. He would then be part of everything: the plants, animals, people, huts, without consciously choosing the link. To choose involved effort, decision, preference of one possibility, and this could be painful. He had chosen not to choose, a freedom he daily celebrated walking between his house, Abdulla's place and of course Wanja's hut. (p. 71)

Ngugi's portrayal of Munira in the earlier sections of the novel shows keen psychological understanding. We have not only his thoughts and actions, but the forces which have conditioned him. His shrinking, introspective personality is an unconscious reaction partly to his overbearing, contemptuous and successful proprietor-father, and partly to his materialistic and no less successful brothers and sisters who have been able to carve niches for themselves in the highly competitive capitalist Kenyan society. But although Munira possesses a certain measure of idealism, it would be a mistake to suppose that his withdrawal from involvement is due to an idealistic revulsion against his competitive, materialistic and corrupt society. It is due more to cowardice than idealism. If we are looking for a man who deliberately rejects the materialistic ethos of his society, thus condemning himself to insignificance, it is Karega.

However, Munira succeeds in his career as a teacher and after some initial setbacks, becomes accepted and idolized by the people like Waiyaki in *The River Between* and Mugo in *A Grain of Wheat*. He thus achieves a sense of fulfilment at last and his love for Wanja pulls him also into involvement. The sexual prowess he demonstrates in his love making, both with Wanja and later with Lillian, helps give him that sense of mastery and masculinity which he has hitherto completely failed to manifest in the world of adult affairs. But it is the very association with Wanja which reveals the cracks in his personality and eventually leads to his disintegration; for when the young Karega arrives on the scene he deals the final blow to Munira's self-respect by winning Wanja's love. The section of the novel in which Ngugi analyses the rivalry between the two men for Wanja's love is compelling. His presentation of Munira, the basically immature man tortured by sexual jealousy, is very realistic. Munira takes every opportunity to find fault with Karega's work and finally engineers his dismissal on a most flimsy pretext. By this squalid manoeuvring he alienates whatever sympathy the reader may originally have been tempted to accord him. Mugo retains our sympathy right up to the end of *A Grain of Wheat* because of his basic honesty, integrity, humanity and willingness to acknowledge his faults; Munira on the other hand becomes a hypocrite, a liar and a destroyer whose conduct is hardly alleviated by any extenuating circumstances. He becomes no different from the other forces that have plagued and degraded the idealistic Karega.

Munira's transformation into a religious fanatic at the end is one of the novel's major weaknesses. A violent death seems to be a logical and well-deserved conclusion to the fortunes of the three African directors of the Theng'eta Brewery, but that it should be brought about by a fire started in a moment of inspiration by a religious fanatic seems a melodramatic contrivance which takes a remarkably serious work back to the level of the detective thriller. Munira's plunge into religious fanaticism when he sees his evangelistic one-time sweetheart, Lillian, is much too sudden for the reader to be convinced. The art here seems much cruder than we have come to associate with Ngugi. Munira's sudden decision to set fire to Wanja's 'whore-house which mocked God's work on earth' and save Karega from the clutches of a woman whom he now sees as Jezebel is no more convincing. From the events demonstrated Karega hardly seems to be in need of this kind of salvation both because Wanja's possessive hold over him is not shown explicitly and because he seems able to take care of himself in any case. Munira's decision can only be accepted as a sign of mental unbalance, but the process of derangement is not described. However, Munira the non-participator has at last acted: 'Munira had willed and acted, and he felt, as he knelt down to pray, that he was no longer an outsider...' (p. 333).

Wanja, the source of Munira's disintegration, is the most important woman in the novel. Unlike Munira, who is associated with closed spaces, Wanja's dynamism and vitality are suggested by her association with the fields and the plains. She belongs to that remarkable breed of Ngugi women – Mwihaki, Nyambura, Muthoni, Mumbi, Wambuku – all of them brave, resilient, resourceful and determined. There is an element of masculinity in all of Ngugi's major women, just as there is an element of femininity in all of his major men. Perhaps they have to be masculine to make up for their menfolk's indecision and lack of resolution. But there is no denying that it is the more masculine aspects of Wanja's character that are stressed. In spite of the assertions about and references to her beauty, Ngugi does not succeed in creating a sense of her physical appeal to the same extent that Ouologuem does with Tambira in *Bound to Violence* or Ekwensi with Jagua in *Jagua*

Nana. Apart from the comments about her make-up, hair-style and dress, there are hardly any detailed references to her physical features. Admittedly Ngugi is able to present Wanja's rapid changes of mood (not an exclusively feminine quality) but generally speaking he seems to be incapable of creating really feminine women without making them stupidly passive. Furthermore, he fails to present the kind of mesmerizing hold that a woman can exert over a man which Soyinka portrays so successfully in the character of Simi. Far from wishing to enslave men, Wanja's driving force throughout is the need to preserve her independence, and it is the energy, drive, courage, and resourcefulness that she uses to do this that impress us most. When she arrives at the village of Ilmorog she brings light and life to it and transforms it; and during the epic march to the city and its aftermath she develops a sense of purpose and social responsibility. It is her energy, initiative and inventiveness that begin the revival of Ilmorog.

Wanja is central to Ngugi's development of his theme of social disintegration. Her portrayal represents a thorough demonstration of the causes of prostitution in modern African societies. Seduced at an early age by an irresponsible married man old enough to be her father, she finds herself pregnant just as she is about to embark on higher education, and has to leave home and school rather than endure the taunts and cruelty of her parents. In desperation she murders her baby and is thrown, in the big city, on the mercies of even more unscrupulous men determined to exploit and degrade her. She is forced to play the tough city game in order to survive in that jungle and even after her regeneration in Ilmorog, when she discovers a new sense of purpose in helping to engineer that society's revival, she is thrown back into high-class prostitution through the intrigues of the new black imperialists. Wanja can be creative and imaginative, but she is also a practical realist who recognizes that in order to survive in this society one must use its weapons. Mere idealism will never do.

Kimeria, who made his fortune as a Home Guard transporting bodies of Mau Mau killed by the British, was still prospering ... Kimeria, who had ruined my life and later humiliated me by making me sleep with him during our journey to the city ... This same Kimeria was one of those who would benefit from the new economic progress of Ilmorog. Why? Why? I asked myself? Why? Why? Had he not sinned as much as me? That's how one night I fully realized this law. Eat or you are eaten ... I have had to be hard ... It is the only way ... the only way ... Look at Abdulla ... reduced to a fruit seller ... oranges ... sheepskins ... No, I will never return to the herd of victims ... Never ... never. (p. 293–4)

Like Karega, we may not agree with her methods, but we can certainly appreciate her reasons.

Wanja is associated throughout the novel with fire symbolism, being involved in at least four fires: the first gruesome one in which her aunt is killed and which breeds in her a neurotic dread of fires; another which occurs during her life of prostitution in the city and in which she is almost destroyed; one accidentally started by Munira soon after Wanja's arrival in Ilmorog; and the final murderous conflagration deliberately engineered by Munira. The fire is significant on several levels. First, it is literally an agent of destruction, a threat to Wanja's existence; in this sense all the various occurrences of fire are a prefiguration of Munira's destructive act at the end. But on another level the fire also represents a ritual – a ritual of baptism. She undergoes an ordeal by fire in the process of which she is exposed to the horrors of existence, her character is tested, and she emerges slightly tarnished, but toughened. On a third level the fire is a purifying agent, representing a kind of cleansing for Wanja. It reminds her 'of the water and the fire of the beginning and the water and the fire of the second coming to cleanse and bring purity to our earth of human cruelty and loneliness' (p. 65); and she adds: 'I have felt as if I could set myself on fire. And I would then run to the mountain top so that everyone can see me cleansed to my bones' (p. 65). Ironically, this is what Munira's arson unwittingly does for her.

> She wanted a new life ... clean ... she felt this was the meaning of her recent escape. Already she felt the stirrings of a new person ... she had after all been baptized by fire. And to think that it was Munira and Abdulla who were instrumental in her double narrow escapes, in her getting yet another chance to try out new paths, new possibilities? (p. 337)

Towards the end of *A Grain of Wheat* Ngugi gave a glimpse of the disillusionment that set in soon after Kenya's achievement of independence. *Petals of Blood* gives a most comprehensive picture of what the author sees as the evils pervasive in Kenya under black rule. The Member of Parliament whose corrupt activities were barely suggested in *A Grain of Wheat* appears as a real life-size character in his own person, demonstrating his incompetence, corruption and indifference to the people's suffering in a number of telling scenes. He converts the money he had collected from his constituents for a water project into security for loans, buying shares in companies and investing in land, housing and small businesses. He has become one of the country's wealthiest capitalists, a fitting illustration of a common phenomenon in Africa – the use of politics as a stepping-stone to material aggrandizement. The party in power also comes in for the most scathing denunciation because of its corruption, thuggery, sectionalism and indifference to the people's plight. In a grotesque parody of the Mau Mau oath the party forces people to swear an oath intended to perpetuate the complete dominance of a particular tribe. And all the time it blinds itself to the real problems of the country which are poverty, starvation, inadequate housing and educational provision.

Ngugi also shows tremendous concern about the clash between the old traditional values and the decadent values of a modern capitalist society. In particular, he exposes the tendency of the modern capitalists to debase those values, as when they convert the time-honoured songs of the initiation ritual into obscene entertainment at their parties, or pervert the custom of oath taking for the most sordid ends.

Ironically, it is those who almost sacrificed their lives during the Mau Mau struggle for liberation that are the most degraded and exploited in this independent Kenya. It is one of Abdulla's roles to emphasize this. Abdulla, who is potentially the most interesting character in the novel, ought to have been much further developed by Ngugi. He emerges as the most convincing moral spokesman, an idealist who joined the struggle in the hope of helping to bring about a better day. Originally a divided self because of his ambiguous racial origins, he is transformed into a man by the great struggle. His reminiscences give us as powerful glimpses of the suffering during the emergency as any to be found in the pages of *A Grain of Wheat*. His being maimed in the struggle is a concrete symbol of the sacrifice that had to be made. In this sense he is rather like his donkey with which he is closely associated. It is significant that Abdulla always refers to his donkey as his other leg, and when the people, in a desperate bid to propitiate the gods and end the drought, plan to use the donkey as a sacrificial victim and maim it, Abdulla correctly sees it as a maiming of his other leg. The donkey has always been a symbol of sacrifice, the scapegoat that takes the beatings on behalf of society. After independence Abdulla's disillusionment is total.

I waited for land reforms and redistribution.
I waited for a job.
I waited for a statue to Kimathi as a memorial to the fallen.
I waited. (p. 254)

During the march to the city Abdulla, like Ousmane's Maimouna, becomes the rallying force, sustaining the others, in spite of his lame leg, by sheer resourcefulness and leadership potential. But in the midst of the ensuing prosperity which could be said to be a direct result of his efforts he is degraded and ends up as the most abject peasant, forced to sell oranges and skins by the wayside for a living.

On the other hand it is the traitors of the people – Kimeria, Mzigo, Chui and Nderi – who prosper after independence. It is they who now ride the sleek Mercedes Benzes, own thousands of acres of land, housing estates and breweries, resort to golf clubs once frequented by the white imperialists where they clinch business deals, visit expensive nightclubs, exploit the women and hold frivolous parties. Ngugi spares no pain in exposing the cynicism and hypocrisy of it all, just as he forcefully registers his concern at the exploitation of the toiling masses. He also stresses the fact that the corruption of the system results in the under-utilization or destruction of potential. Wanja and Karega, both of them highly intelligent and resourceful young people who could have made a most significant contribution to their nation's life, are forced to drop out of school. And because of his integrity and idealism Karega is persecuted by this society and forced to drift from menial job to menial job. There could be no more powerful symbol of the destruction of potential than Karega in a drunken stupor in Munira's room having been rescued from a nightclub brawl: 'How, now, how could the young the bright and the hopeful deteriorate so? Was there no way of using their energies and dreams to a higher purpose than the bottle, the juke-box and sickness on a cement floor?' (p. 103).

Karega and the lawyer are the embodiments of Ngugi's moral positives in this novel. They are the spokesmen for his socialistic solution. But while the lawyer, like Armah's teacher in *The Beautyful Ones are Not Yet Born*, is an idealized symbol of perfection and purity, a mere voice who gives his views in lengthy speeches rather than a character playing a part in the drama, Karega is convincingly portrayed. Like Wanja he is a dynamic, vital individual who is also associated with the plains, and he brings to his vocation as a teacher a drive and an intellectual power which puts Munira's in the shade.

Together, he and Wanja act as forces of regeneration in Ilmorog, and it is significant that their love making is described in ritualistic terms. Images of vegetation abound in the scene, Karega and Wanja being associated with its luxuriance and freshness. There is even a suggestion that their mating heralds the dawn of a new day: ' "Wake up, Wanja," Karega called out to her ... "Wake up and see signs of dawn over Ilmorog" ' (p. 230). If there is any hope for the future, it is really Karega who holds it. It is Karega who confirms one's impression that Ngugi has been gradually leaning over to socialism as the solution to Africa's problems. But through his spokesman Karega he also seems to imply that socialism was a natural way of life in traditional African society. Appalled by the capitalism and materialism he sees around him, in a world 'built on a structure of inequality and injustice, in a world where some can eat while others can only toil, some can send their children to school and others cannot, in a world where a prince, a monarch, a businessman can sit on billions while people starve or hit their heads against church walls for divine deliverance from hunger, yes in a world where a man who has never set foot on this land can sit in a New York office and determine what I shall eat, read, think, do, only because he sits on a heap of billions taken from the world's poor' (p. 240), Karega comes to the conclusion that for a proper and equitable reorganization of society the people must go back to their African origins to learn lessons from the way in which African peoples produced and organized their wealth before colonialism. The implication is, of course, that it was colonialism that brought inequality, injustice and capitalism to Africa, and Karega feels that a thorough study of the African past would reveal systems which were fair and equitable, in which wealth was owned by those who produced it and where there was virtually no unemployment. In a bid to bring about this kind of socialist society in modern Kenya, Karega becomes a trade union agitator, tirelessly mobilizing the workers and the masses until a world can be created in which 'goodness and beauty and strength and courage would be seen, not in how cunning one can be, not in how much power to oppress one possessed, but only in one's contribution in creating a more humane world in which the inherited inventive genius of man in culture and science from all ages and climes would be not the monopoly of a few, but for the use of all ...' (p. 303). There is little doubt that Ngugi endorses Karega's socialist analysis and sees his solution – solidarity of the workers and the masses – as the hope for the future. But intelligent and idealistic though Karega is, his analysis involves oversimplifications and confusions. His view of the organization of African society in the past will probably not stand up to scrutiny. It is doubtful whether his creator has thought out the solutions to these problems more clearly than he. Perhaps this must not be expected of him. Ngugi is a novelist, not a political scientist. It is enough that he has presented the problems of his society as powerfully as anyone can.

The confusions become apparent when one considers Ngugi's treatment of the theme of education, which has always assumed a special importance in all his work. In this novel, as in the earlier ones, education is regarded by the people as the hope for the future, although those who pin their faith on it usually end in disillusionment since they have eventually to come face to face with political reality. In all these works also the leading teachers are usually lionized by the people and seen as both cultural and political heroes. But the theme of education gets a much more extended treatment in this novel than in the earlier ones. The purpose and content of imperialist education is thoroughly scrutinized and its relevance to the African situation questioned. It is presented as an oppressive, irrelevant and racialist system obviously geared towards perpetuating white domination and instilling into the pupils a respect for British institutions and attitudes. Cambridge Fraudsham, the eccentric headmaster who terrorizes his pupils and eventually provokes student riots, is the embodiment of this educational process. But his successor Chui, an African who in his student days has been victimized by the oppressive imperialist system and might therefore have been expected to effect changes, turns out to be more British in his attitudes and policies than Fraudsham himself. When Karega and his revolutionary contemporaries organize strikes first against the white Fraudsham and then against the black Chui they demand an African content to the education Africans are being given. They demand to be taught African literature and African history and to be taught to know themselves and their environment better; they object to a system which teaches them about white snow and spring flowers fluttering by icy lakes, and they demand an African headmaster and African teachers. Most reasonable readers would endorse these demands. But when they go on to call for an abolition of the prefectorial system and 'the knightly order of masters and menials', cry up black power, demand to elect their own leaders, call themselves African populists, and object to being taught world history and world literature, they surely reveal themselves as immature adolescents who are incable of making discriminations of value and have certainly not thought out their views on education clearly. They would throw out the baby with the bathwater. While emphasizing the need to increase the African content of education, there is nothing wrong in a headmaster telling his staff to teach his pupils good idiomatic English in a situation where the official language and therefore the passport to advancement remains English. There is nothing wrong with widening their horizons to include the world environment, either. The lawyer is right in asking Karega, 'What did you really want?' and, not surprisingly, Karega does not seem to know. But Ngugi ought to know. However, he has given no clear indication whether he endorses Karega's stand on education or not.

Organized religion also comes in for some savage satire in this novel. The Christian religion, which in the other novels was shown to exercise a firm hold over the lives of the people, is presented here as oppressive, unsympathetic and hypocritical. The portrayal of Munira's father is central to this exposure of religion. This man who is a patriarch of the church as well as a pillar of the state is actually a capitalist and black slaver of the most rabid sort. This determined opportunist who in his younger days turned his back on his traditional society and joined the white man, and in his later years supported the white oppressors against the Mau Mau freedom fighters, now participates wholeheartedly in the sordid exploitation of the masses. Like Joshua's in *The River Between*, his religion is a life-denying force which has stifled the life in Munira's wife and children. Essentially he is an irreligious and godless man who cannot see that his Christianity should preclude the taking of an oath geared towards the consolidation of tribalism; indeed he even ventures the opinion that God would throw his weight behind such a move. What astonishes the reader is not just the man's hypocrisy but his utter insensitivity. The behaviour of the Revs Kamau and Jerrod reinforces this impression of religious bankruptcy. The latter would rather read a sermon to starving itinerants about the need for industry than succour their wants and help a sick boy receive medical attention; and when Ilmorog attains prosperity he becomes a kind of society clergyman, the vicar of the most fashionable church in the neighbourhood. The church is, in fact, a great proprietor, its priests being no different from the other modern black capitalists and imperialists.

Ngugi has often been accused of not doing enough to impart an African flavour to the language of his novels. This charge could certainly not be laid against *Petals of Blood*, where Ngugi makes extensive use of legends, proverbs, songs and other aspects of the oral tradition, rendering them at times directly from the indigenous language. The use of the oral tradition – folk legends, celebrations and music – helps reinforce the sense of a society that used to be cohesive and dignified, and in most cases the relevance of the songs and legends can be demonstrated.

As in *A Grain of Wheat* a sense of the past pervades this novel. All the characters are continually discovering that their present fortunes are inextricably linked with their past, that they cannot avoid confrontation with their past actions which continue to haunt them. This is the main justification of the narrative technique which links present actions and comments with past reminiscences. The novel has been described by one reviewer as rambling.[3] This is unjust. Nevertheless, on putting it down the reader has the uneasy feeling that Ngugi has been too ambitious, that he has attempted to do too much within the compass of a single novel. There are both thematic and stylistic echoes here, not just of Ngugi's own earlier novels, but of Ousmane, Armah, Ouologuem, Achebe, Soyinka and others. Such a work is bound to be uneven in quality. There are brilliant scenes, superbly realized, alternating at times with rather more tedious ones. This is partly due to the fact that Ngugi's chosen method of narration – the use of reminiscences – involves much more telling than showing. There seems to be a preponderance of narration and assertion over detailed scenic demonstration. We hear people talking about their past experiences rather than see them enacted before our eyes. How much more effective it would have been to have seen Karega's trade union activities enacted than to be told about them by himself. It is also a pity that Ngugi decided to place at the centre of events a hero like Munira, who is not only spineless, but succeeds eventually in totally alienating the reader's sympathy. Mugo, in spite of his self-confessed treachery towards Kihika, never loses the reader's sympathy, because of his basic courage and honesty. There seems to be an uncertainty about Ngugi's attitude towards his hero. At the start he gives him a measure of idealism, but then goes on to suggest that his non-involvement is due not to idealism but to cowardice, and at the end he makes him a villain. This element of mistiness surrounding the hero seriously impairs the novel's impact on the reader. Nevertheless, no one can fail to acknowledge its importance and relevance. It is indeed a major publication.

NOTES

1 Angus Calder, in a review in The *New Statesman*.
2 Ngugi wa Thiong'o, *Petals of Blood* (Heinemann, London, 1977), pp. 21–2. All
  further page references are to this edition.
3 Homi Bhabda, *TLS*, 12 August 1971, p. 989.

12. Meja Mwangi

▼▼▼

Meja Mwangi is certainly one of the most exciting of the new East African writers who have made social comment and analysis the dominant trend in the contemporary African novel. *Going Down River Road* must surely rank as his most important work so far, but in the two earlier novels – *Kill Me Quick* and *Carcase for Hounds* – he had already shown his characteristic qualities: a touching compassion for the social or political underdog, a quietness of tone which emphasizes rather than obscures the very serious social problems being analysed, and a remarkably controlled though unpretentious prose-style.

Kill Me Quick presents with great pathos and commendable realism the fortunes of two adolescents in modern urban Kenya whose hopes and aspirations, buttressed by a successful secondary education, are eventually dashed by the nature of the Kenyan political, social and economic system. *Kill Me Quick* and *Going Down River Road* give a very detailed and convincing analysis of the causes of juvenile delinquency, prostitution and big-time as well as petty crime. In doing so Mwangi has staked his claim to a territory hitherto dominated by Ekwensi, and he carries out his analysis with greater depth of presentation, strength of characterization, psychological understanding and awareness of the implications of the issues he raises. The heroes of *Kill Me Quick* are two adolescents – Meja and Maina – both of whom have achieved very respectable school certificate passes, one a first and the other a second division, and so naturally expect that they will get jobs earning 600–700 shillings a month, thus ensuring a comfortable existence; but a combination of corruption, unfairness, nepotism and sheer bloody-mindedness ensures that their hopes remain unrealized. The experiences of Meja and Maina are thus a paradigm, not just of the Kenyan situation, but of that in the whole of Africa where hordes of youths educated up to the school certificate standard discover that in spite of their qualifications the economic and social situation ensures that they have to roam the streets unemployed for years. The consequence is not just tremendous waste of potential, but a loss of faith in the value of education. Maina states it cogently: 'So you see I am through with books. More than twelve years in school with fees to pay and then I go back home and just hang around: no not me, Meja. Imagine how my friends who never went to school and always stayed at home will laugh! I believe that I have a right to something better if only for the effort I put into those examination weeks' (p. 3).[1] This is a very savage indictment of the system. The complete absence of opportunity soon converts many such adolescents into delinquents.

> 'All my friends became thieves and robbers. I would have done the same too but I was too cowardly to break into houses at night. I had not done much practice in running at school and could never trust my speed for getting away with purse snatching. So my friends went into the main streets and snatched purses and they are almost all of them in prison now, for one reason or another. Me, I turned into the backstreets and thrived. There isn't much competition for existence here, except with the mongrels and mongrels do not know how to open closed back doors. And the food is not all that bad if you allow for the smell, and such minor things.' (p. 2)

The author tellingly presents the utter despair and hopelessness, the humiliation in going from employer to employer only to have the door slammed shut in one's face before one can shout out one's qualifications, the misery and degradation of having to live in dustbins and compete for food with stray dogs and cats.

> The hot season came, heralded by swarms of flies and a dry dust-carrying wind that swept down the backstreets choking everything. The two young men became dehydrated and their bodies were covered in scales. Food from the bins dwindled and the competition with mongrels increased. The stench of the gutters became almost unbearable and the office messengers no longer dared take their usual short cuts from backdoor to backdoor to deliver their never-ending messages. The backstreets were left to the boys and the beggars. Strangely enough, with the increase in the dust, heat and flies there was also an increase in the backstreet population, for some of Maina's old friends fresh from prison and determined to make a fresh start, came back to the old backyards. (p. 9)

The squalor in which the boys are forced to live is contrasted with the opulence of fat, lazy managers who deny them the jobs their qualifications demand. It almost seems as though the whole of society is against them. For a brief spell they find employment with a white farmer who exploits their labour and makes them live in the most deplorable conditions with bed-bugs and rats. Subsequently, however, the wicked foreman engineers their dismissal, and so desperate is their situation that they even miss the misery of the farm. Thrown again into the backstreets they can only drift further into degradation and ultimately into crime: Meja ends in prison and Maina on the gallows.

Mwangi presents the city, like Ekwensi, as a destructive force. But where Ekwensi uses images of eating, Mwangi uses images of accidents to show the city's destructive potential. And it is the young who are destroyed or mangled by irresponsible motorists. The city emerges as a most impersonal and unfriendly place where all the odds are heavily stacked against the boys. The presentation of the underworld is particularly powerful and convincing. Without resorting to melodramatics as Ekwensi often does, Mwangi gives a most realistic evocation of life among the gangster class. He shows their addiction to drugs and cheap drinks, their predisposition to violence leading eventually to murder, their dependence on the razor to maintain leadership of the gang, and their unashamed sexual indulgence. And he accurately captures the quality of their speech and the variety of temperaments among them. Mwangi is also convincing in his presentation of life in prison. The dialogue among the prisoners rings true, and he is able to persuade the reader that these men have become gradually hardened by their experiences.

In *Kill Me Quick* Mwangi displays not just great insight into social forces but also psychological understanding in the portrayal of his heroes. He is careful to distinguish between them. Thus Meja who, bearing the author's name, is probably idealized, is more compassionate, generous and respectful towards elders and authority than Maina. There is a basic softness, gentlemanliness and innocence about him which makes his experiences in the tough backstreets among the dustbins of Nairobi all the more pathetic. One feels that he simply was not made for this kind of life. Meja is understandably capable of a greater sense of shame than Maina. One of the most pathetic scenes in the whole novel is that in which Meja, having recovered from a disastrous accident which has left him crippled, decides to return home, but on arrival discovers he cannot face the accusations, disappointment and recriminations of his family, and therefore leaves without seeing them. We also admire the determination with which he later proves, against the odds, that, in spite of his crippled arm, he can undertake the onerous job of stone smasher. A boy like this, we feel, deserves a much better fate, a much better recognition of his abilities and moral quality than that Kenyan society is able to accord him.

On the other hand, Maina displays a flair for mischief and low cunning suggesting that he probably has criminal potential in him. He looks like the typical street-corner boy, displaying a capacity for violence and viciousness particularly in the scene where the old man Boi first meets them with a proposition. In a very real sense Maina seems to be Meja's evil angel, throwing all the blame for his own misdemeanours on the latter, luring him into all kinds of dubious practices culminating in the accident in which Meja is all but killed. We are astonished by the ease with which Maina succumbs to the temptations of the Razor and descends into big-time crime. If, on hearing the Razor's proposals, he goes through no process of soul searching but readily accepts the latter's invitation to join the gang, it is because his cast of mind is already fertile ground for Razor's suggestive seeds to sprout in; and once in the gang he readily uses his imaginative and inventive flair as the main contributory force to their temporary success. We may admire his tremendous sense of fun and feel compassion for his fortunes, especially when we experience his occasional moodiness as he withdraws to weep at the contemplation of the frustration of all his aspirations; but he connives much too readily in the process of his own deterioration.

The artistry of *Kill Me Quick* suggests miniature painting. Everything is done on a small scale but with such refinement, delicacy, accuracy and taste that one can only refer to the work as a minor masterpiece. Apart from the brilliant characterization, there is Mwangi's unquestioned ability at creating vivid realistic scenes. He achieves this partly by the flexibility of his prose and partly by his ability to concentrate on details of gestures and movements and give convincing dialogue. The scene in which Maina is caught stealing milk and that of Meja's disastrous accident are not likely to be forgotten.

Carcase for Hounds, like *Kill Me Quick*, is also a triumph of artistry. The author's powers of description here are possibly surer than in *Kill Me Quick* and the prose-style even more graceful and lucid. The following passage conveys its quality:

> Mist hung thick and low in the jungle. Visibility was reduced to only a few yards in any direction. The cold morning wind had died down and now a humid warmth enveloped the wet undergrowth. Birds twittered softly, timidly in their nests, afraid to venture yet into the

misty, late morning. And in the sleepy surroundings even the giant jungle trees seemed to have taken a nap.[2]

Mwangi certainly captures the quality of uncanny tranquillity. His powers of description and his ability to create suspense help give this novel a thriller-like quality; yet the reader also gets the impression that it is a deeply serious novel offering much more than the average thriller. There is a cinematic quality about the description and the evocation of scenes, as in this passage:

The little one was waiting, half concealed. The big one waved, and prepared to catch the Winchester. The little one pushed the bush to one side to make room. Then he looked up and down the river once more. Holding the rifle by the barrel, he swung it in a circling motion and sent it sailing across the river. The other one watched it come and lunged for it. The rifle slid through his hand. The sling caught on a small branch and held the rifle swaying above the frothing water for one breathless moment. Just as the branch gave under the weight one big hand grabbed the sling and retrieved the gun. The little man waded into the cold river and swam across. The big one was waiting for him, the rifle in his outstretched arm...

They approached the meeting-place slowly, warily. For a moment they lay concealed. They watched the vicinity of the giant fig. Then while the big one kept watch, the little one crept into the undergrowth under the fig. A big black bird, scared out of its sanctuary, went screaming to the west. The big watcher saw only a dark-grey shape hurtling away in the mist. Then his little companion materialized next to him. (pp. 3–4)

One can easily imagine this section of the novel's opening scene on the screen. Several other scenes can be similarly visualized. For instance, in a final desperate attempt to capture the Mau Mau terrorist Haraka, the English captain, Kingsley, throws a veritable drag-net around him forcing him to retreat into a cave in the jungle. But Haraka is dying, his men have been decimated and only a few of them are left half-asleep with him, waiting for the darkness to fall. A tired and careless soldier drifts past the hideout, 'his automatic rifle in hand, chewing gum and thinking of his girl back home in Liverpool. Only the humid jungle, the birds and the trees saw this tiny, gigantic slip and they would never tell. Never.'

Carcase for Hounds is about the activities of the Mau Mau during their struggle for the liberation of Kenya. Inevitably the novel has to concentrate on the presentation of life in the jungle. And Mwangi proves himself as much at home in the uncanny mysteriousness of the jungle as in the hustle and bustle of the city. Indeed, the powerful evocation of setting must surely rank among this novel's claims to attention. The jungle is unmistakably there – its power, its darkness, its mystery, its terror, its discomfort, and its luxuriance; and this evocation of setting is done not just to provide local colour, but meaningfully to reflect the characters' moods and circumstances. For instance, when General Haraka and his men, harassed by the English soldiers, have, on one occasion, to penetrate deeper into the jungle for safety, the setting looks suitably grim and uncomfortable.

> They hugged Likki river on their trek down the mountain. All the time the furious roar of the cold dirty floodwaters was in their ears. The jungle became colder. Darkness found them about two miles from Kangaita bridge. At the same time as the darkness a light rain started falling; a cold, silent drizzle that was only felt where the foliage thinned out or they came to a clearing. Kangaita bridge was overflowing. A thick smoggy raincloud hung low, shutting out even the meagre starlight. The forest as well as the bridge was pitch dark. Water could be heard lapping on the bridge railings and thus they were sure the bridge was still intact. (pp. 22–3)

On the other hand Captain Kingsley's exhilaration at the thought that he has put into operation the perfect plan for Haraka's capture confers on the usually forbidding vegetation a benevolent and beautiful aspect.

> Standing there, watching the scene below, the captain felt exhilarated. Watching the natural beauty of it all, the unmarred work of nature, he felt the way the Creator must have felt on the sixth day. The slopes, the jungle, the hot sun and the breeze were like a tonic. This below him was Africa, fresh uncontaminated Africa with its jungles, and he could not help thinking about the elephants and lions in Edgar Rice Burroughs' *Tarzan*. (p. 106)

Carcase for Hounds is a powerful presentation of the Mau Mau experience. Where novelists like Ngugi merely report the Mau Mau activities through reminiscences like those of Abdulla in *Petals of Blood*, Mwangi presents the Mau Mau from the inside, through the thoughts and activities of the freedom fighters themselves. The Mau Mau emerges as a necessarily ruthless organization, necessarily, because only by using ruthless methods can it be absolutely sure of the continued support of the people, who are themselves relentlessly terrorized by the British, and the solidarity of the fighters, many of whom are tempted to surrender when firm leadership is lacking. The people must be sworn to allegiance and secrecy and those fighters who disobey orders or fail in their appointed tasks must be eliminated. In the struggle for liberation no chances must be taken; and we are never allowed to forget the oppressiveness of the British administration or the vigilance of the British army in hounding the freedom fighters. The Mau Mau fighters themselves are aware that the odds are heavily stacked against them. At times they seem to be fighting in isolation, unable to identify their supporters, unable to establish contact with other groups, uncertain, in fact, whether other groups exist.

The hero is General Haraka, a veritable superman whose mysterious presence dominates the novel. Mwangi evokes a convincing impression of his imposing bulk, his tremendous physical strength and courage, and his mysteriousness. The very mention of his name is enough to make grown men wet their pants, and he easily becomes a legend, the man whom the English troops must get at all costs, dead or alive. It is significant that Haraka says comparatively little, much less than his arch-enemy Captain Kingsley, for instance, but there is no doubting that his presence, his force and his dynamism are superbly realized. This is done almost entirely through detailed descriptions of his activities and brilliant passages of introspection. In the scenes devoted to the freedom fighters we are kept close to Haraka's consciousness and we experience at first hand his doubts, his hopes and his despair.

The main interest of the novel is the running duel between, on the one hand, Haraka and the English captain, Kingsley, who has been detailed to capture him, and on the other, Haraka and the detested, effeminate, cowardly, traitor – Chief Kahuru Wamai. Captain Kingsley is also realistically presented. There is a love–hate relationship between him and Haraka, for the former respects Haraka's courage and abilities, really prefers him as chief to the cowardly Kahuru, and would have liked to have had him on his side. We also experience Kingsley's impatience and irritation with his superiors who are constantly urging him to produce results, completely oblivious of Haraka's skill and the difficulties involved in his capture. Kingsley emerges as a warm and thoroughly human individual and his presentation by Mwangi is very objective.

As the end of the novel approaches it becomes increasingly clear that it is the duel with Kahuru that is important for Haraka; hence his insistence, even during his final delirium, that his supporters should bring him the chief's head. Failure to get the chief's head looks like defeat for Haraka; and in a sense it is the worthless chief who defeats him, for under the mistaken assumption that Haraka is nowhere near the vicinity, he lays an ambush for some of his gang; Haraka is caught by a stray bullet and the wound leads to his death. But in another sense Haraka remains undefeated. Kingsley never succeeds in capturing him and there is no doubt that he is the moral victor.

Carcase for Hounds, like *Kill Me Quick*, leaves the impression of a minor masterpiece, with everything – characterization, dialogue, control of tone and narrative method, setting, description and exploration of themes – being extremely well done, though on a small scale. These two novels are a fitting prelude to the Mwangi who is revealed in *Going Down River Road*. Mwangi's latest novel subsumes all the characteristics of the two earlier ones. Set in Nairobi's seething brothel, pub and cheap nightclub area, the novel explores the harsh realities of city life to a much greater depth than *Kill Me Quick* and with a greater realism than Ekwensi's *Jagua Nana*. It is a novel which is also preoccupied with human relationships; indeed it presents with commendable power and detailed demonstration the fortunes of the hero, Ben, against the background of all those social evils which we have now come to associate with the growth of modern African cities. Mwangi does not flinch from details which would most tellingly present the squalor, degradation and misery that characterize the lives of most of his characters. First, there is the housing racket – an increasingly common feature of the new African conurbations. Sleek, well-fed landlords in Mercedes Benzes and other prestigious cars construct rickety flats with minimal conveniences and let them out to unfortunates in the lower income group at prohibitive prices. They have no hesitation in hiring thugs to throw the tenants' things into the street if the latter do not support them at elections or are reluctant to pay the most recent rent increase. The situation is worsened by the fact that for every flatlet thus vacated there are about ten prospective tenants eager to pay the new rate. Those in an even lower income group, who cannot afford the price of such a room, are forced to content themselves with the mushrooming shanty towns which are now an inevitable feature of most African cities, but are subject not just to the depredations of vermin, but to ravages by fire initiated by the health authorities. The following is the condition in which Ben finds their shared toilet one morning:

He wrapped a towel around his loins and went out into the misty morning. One hell of a Sunday morning. His nextdoor neighbour, a man he heard whistle every morning but rarely woke up early enough to see, shivered out of the shower room and called Good morning. Ben grunted a reply and walked into the toilet. He stood by the door and sent a jet of urine into the bowl. The stagnant mess splashed too much. He shifted the hose onto the wall and managed to keep his feet dry. Someone would have to do something about the toilet, either keep the shit flowing or demolish the goddam thing and dig a pit latrine. And then, he mused, what would the honourable roaches eat without their morning broth?[3]

The recurrent references to excreta and vomit underscore the pervasive squalor and degradation in the novel.

The sex market features just as prominently here as in the pages of Ekwensi. There are various gradations to suit every taste and financial situation – from the brothel/cattle market called 'Eden' through the 'Karara centre' to the more glorified 'Capricorn centre'. The author presents with great compassion the misery of prostitutes of various ages and temperaments who in their desperation for the next meal ogle at men whom in the normal way of business they would not bother to honour with a second glance; and inevitably cheapened sexuality goes with squalor and violence.

Mwangi presents the misery, squalor and degradation through case histories such as that of the daughter of a minister who got pregnant during her studies in America and had to return home to a life of prostitution. There is Wini, Ben's girlfriend, who had a child at the age of 14 and was forced into prostitution to keep herself and the fatherless child, but still possessed enough moral courage to see her through a secretarial course. She eventually gets a decent job, but is forced to abandon her baby and elope with her boss as a way out of the urban impasse. There is the 16-year-old prostitute who has sex with Ben in the same room in which her friend is simultaneously fornicating with another man while her month-old baby screams in the corner.

The bed groans some more. Bare feet approach and the door flies open. The room-mate stands at the door, stark naked.
'I thought it was those beasts again.' She indicates the waiting throng down the passage.
Susan shoves Ben into the stuffy, dim room and bolts the door. Her room-mate returns to her waiting partner. They resume their match. No ceremony. Just like that. Ben tries not to look ... A giant prize cockroach traverses the dirty floor leisurely relaxed. Places you find the bastards! Instinctively he gets up to do his duty. The beast proves too cunning. He chases it under the bed. The woman looks up at him. 'What is it?' 'A cockroach?' she chokes and her man does not

even know Ben is here yet ... The couple across the room start
arguing, first in whispers, then loudly.

'Enough,' the woman insists.

'Enough ... what?'

'I said enough, you have done me enough for your money.'

'Enough? I bought you ten beers,' he complains.

'You have to add money,' she informs him.

'But ...'

The woman gets out of bed and starts to dress.

'Get out,' she advises, cool and businesslike ... Faint whimpers
materialize out of a paper carton marked CORNED BEEF in the
corner across the room. The whimpers rise in volume into the
unmistakable cry of a tiny baby. The woman stands frozen, then
turns and points an accusing finger at the man:

'See what you have done, you ... you woke the baby!' ...

Susan holds her breath and watches Ben. He shrugs stupidly. She
climbs out of bed, patters to the makeshift cot and looks in. She
sticks a finger into the mass of rags in the carton. 'Stop it, boy,' she
soothes. 'Stop crying. Go back to sleep.' The baby goes into full
throttle and yells. The familiar sound grates on Ben's nerves. Slowly
he pulls on his pants and shoes.

'Whose it it?'

'Mine.'

'Yours?' he pauses in doing up his pants.

'Yes.'

'How old?'

'One month.'

He gets off the bed, grabs his coat. 'I must be going now ...' She
bites her lower lip, a little frightened and pitiful. (pp. 127–9)

Such scenes give convincing social motivations for conduct while
generating tremendous sympathy for the unfortunates who are
trapped in such situations. Far from being titillating, the sexual details
stamp unforgettably on the reader's mind the hopelessness of the
masses in the struggle to survive. The prostitutes are dogged by a basic
insecurity and the fear of hunger; the fun-loving girls who are hired
out by their boyfriends are vulnerable to the sadistic whims of
drunkards, thugs, and drug-addicts. Indeed the prostitutes of all ages
are liable to humiliation and violence. The following passage presents
the squalor and violence that go with this kind of sexuality.

Ben slides off the stool slowly, careful not to stagger. Nobody takes
any notice. The woman glares boldly back, her face screwed up in
distaste. His hand whips out, grabs and yanks. The bra and blouse
snap. The udders pour out, threatening to spill to the floor. A drunk
voice cheers as the woman unsuccessfully tries to contain her litre-

sized tits in pint-sized hands. She spits at him. He yanks at the skirt. The bastardly beast has nothing on underneath, nothing at all. Rolls of stomach flop loosely over her groin. She gives a scream that calls for everybody's attention, then snorting and blubbing drunkenly charges him. He steps back to take the shock, trips and falls over a table. She misses him and bulldozes into another table, smashing one of its legs and breaking drinks and glasses. She lies quite still in the rubble, her fat nude body as still as a basking hippo. As Ben gets up she starts to throw up in violent, retching movements that force out enormous chunks of unchewed whatever. (pp. 119–20)

Mwangi hits on the clever device of using the framework of the construction of the luxurious twenty-four-storey development building as a means of presenting the experiences of the ordinary workers whose life-styles are in such stark contrast to all that the building represents, but who must look forward to its completion with apprehension since it will mean unemployment. The building fittingly suggests that while 'development' goes on in one form, squalor and poverty still coexist with it. It symbolizes the indifference of the authorities to the sufferings of the masses, which the corruption of politicians and the police, the inequalities of the system and the high cost of living help to accentuate. In the meantime everyone is engaged in the 'get-rich-quick' syndrome: 'Everybody was scrambling for big money, and no-one cared how you made it. You could have sold the whole goddam country to eager buyers; a lot of those guys in the big cars on the avenue did just that' (p. 54).

Mwangi's city is remarkable for its display of violence which is never far from the surface, whether it be in the fleshpots among the prostitutes and pimps, or on a building site among workers, who suddenly become beasts charging into each other. The violence itself can easily degenerate into motiveless hatred and, as in the case of the maniac Onesmus, even into murder. We also see examples of blackmail, drug peddling and drug addiction and organized, big-time crime. The shady activities of the gangster Max and his group pale into insignificance when set beside the attempts by others to stage a hold-up or blow up the bank with explosives. The inhabitants of the River Road occasionally demonstrate a certain comradeship in adversity and the reader is made to experience the warmth of populist amusement spots like Eden or Karara centre, but he still senses the absence of real friendship which is ultimately attributable to the dehumanizing effect of the impersonal city where everyone is involved in the scramble to survive.

Mwangi's preoccupation with the social realities of the city does not prevent him from creating some interesting characters and exploring some significant relationships. The hero, Ben, is the most fascinating of them all. A central character through whose eyes almost all the events and the other characters are viewed, he survives in the mind of the reader as an anti-hero whose huge bulk and physical strength go oddly with his lack of resolution and real guts. Ben can pulverize the gangster Max and knock the terrible giant Onesmus senseless into the mud, but there is no doubt of a certain weakness at the core. There is even a slight hint of emasculation in this young man who, in spite of his sexual prowess, seems unable to father his own child or to have a lasting relationship with a woman, and at the end adopts a boy whom everyone knows is somebody else's. Indeed, the hint of some obscure psychological problem in Ben is seen particularly in his relationships with prostitutes. He seems unable to form a relationship with a girl who is not or has not been a prostitute, and he always behaves oddly towards them. At the start of the affair with Wini he is very much on his guard, cynical, non-committal, callous and hard, although Wini does her best to behave like a normal girl and not a prostitute. He is sadistic and vicious towards the pathetic 16-year-old prostitute Susan, although he himself is later forced to take pity on her plight; and he is not above mercilessly beating up others.

The central feature of the novel is, of course, Ben's relationship with Wini the prostitute/secretary whom he picked up in a nightclub and later goes to live with. There is no doubt that Wini is the dominant person in the household. In a sense it is she who has 'married' Ben, for he goes to live in her flat and is forced to accept her son. He eventually comes to love this girl tenderly, but he still apparently allows her to go out with other men when it suits her purposes. Eventually, she abandons both Ben and her baby with perfect nonchalance and elopes with her boss. It now turns out that the baby she is expecting is not Ben's, as he has fondly imagined, but her boss's. Ben is thus forced to realize that, far from loving him, Wini does not even estimate him highly, and he is now plunged into a total disillusionment with women: 'Bitches. All women are dogs. They will lay with anybody for anything. Bitches, bitches...' (p. 115). From now on his attitude and behaviour towards women are highly coloured by Wini's infidelity.

The portrayal of Wini is probably one of the few lapses in this book. Certainly Mwangi is able to evoke her sheer physical appeal; indeed, he is even more adept at evoking sensual, feminine appeal than Ekwensi.

> She was stretched full length, eyes closed, breathing softly. Her flat belly lay placid like the cool gentle waters of a quiet bay. Her right hand covered her navel, the chocolate body expanse exaggerating the large blue-green tanzanite. Her bust thrust up invitingly, tapered down to the smooth goddess neck and the smooth curved shoulders, interrupted only by the thin gold chain. Just below the bust her heart beat fast and hard. Her legs sprouted thick and soft at the base, then flowed gently down his bed to the small feet. (p. 20)

Thus we get a very good impression of Wini's body, but a very hazy one of her personality. The problem is partly that Wini is kept very much in the shade and the reader is seldom taken into her mind or made to see events from her point of view. We would really have liked to see some of the motives of Wini's conduct – such as the decision to abandon Ben and the baby. Mwangi does not really succeed in convincing us that Wini, who has seemed to be such a devoted mother, who has idolized her baby and seemed to live only for him, can suddenly become so callous as to abandon him nonchalantly with the directive to Ben that he is to be sent to a charity home. It is neither natural nor psychologically plausible. We must face the real possibility that Mwangi is incapable of creating realistic and convincing women. Very few women appear in the pages of his books. There are only three in *Kill Me Quick* – the white farmer's wife, Maina's shanty-town girlfriend and the Razor's girlfriend; the first is only mentioned, and the other two only make brief appearances. There are hardly any in *Carcase for Hounds* (though the chief's wife is mentioned), and although several appear briefly in *Going Down River Road*, they are no more than sex objects and all of them, including Wini, are inadequately realized. Mwangi's world is very much a man's world.

Ben's story is one of progressive deterioration; there is the initial disgrace when he succumbs very easily and without much thought to a gangster's temptation, and is expelled from his position as first lieutenant in the army. The same offence later costs him his cosy insurance job. It is that first easy drift into crime which warns us that in spite of his physical strength Ben is hollow at the core. Robbed thus of self-respect and strength of will, he merely drifts from one temporary job to another until the educated, one-time lieutenant ends up as a casual labourer on a building site. He is soon kicked out of his lodgings in Grogan Road and has to move in with Wini. We later see him indulging even in drug pushing in order to ingratiate himself with the foreman, Yussuf, and in order to accomplish this to his own advantage he is even prepared to take tips from his arch-enemy, the murderous crook Onesmus. On being abandoned by Wini we see him indulging in the most animalistic lechery as a kind of consolation; his personality has visibly begun to disintegrate. Ben is now forced to take responsibility for Baby as though he were the mother and Wini the father. Subsequently the landlord ejects him from the flat on the pretext that it had been rented not to him but to Wini. He is thus forced to move into his friend's Ocholla's makeshift shanty hut with all the squalor and degradation that that involves. And when Ocholla's enormous family turns up unexpectedly from the provinces all the signs suggest that Ben and Baby will be turned out homeless once more, though it is possible that they will now build a shanty hut for themselves.

Yet for all his weakness we are always aware of Ben's compassion for his fellow-sufferers. He is largely redeemed by this compassion as well as by the ever-widening circle of relationships he acquires in the course of the novel. His relationships with Ocholla and little Baby are touching and fascinating. Some of the most intriguing scenes in the novel are those in which Ben shows his concern for Baby and his determination to care for him. Thus when he discovers one day that Max and his gang have lured the boy into their den with the intention of introducing him to drugs, Ben almost murders Max in his rage. At the start Ben had been repelled by Baby's unfortunate habits, but when Wini absconds the reader watches fascinated as Ben gradually comes to accept responsibility for the boy and to care for him, effectively playing the roles of both mother and father. A stage even arrives when he can refer to Baby as 'My Baby', and this acceptance of responsibility for the boy marks the restoration of his dignity. At the end of the novel, both Ocholla and Ben, who have been rather aimless drifters for most of it, come to accept the lessons of responsibility. Just as Ben accepts responsibility for Baby, so Ocholla accepts responsibility for his large family whom he had completely neglected in the provinces. This acquisition of wider relationships is perhaps the most convincing ray of hope held out in the novel; for with it both men begin to regain their self-respect. As Ben, now playing the role of the responsible father, begins to tell Baby, who has been playing truant, of the difference between right and wrong and the need for decent living, the real man in him emerges and we conclude that he more than deserves his promotion to the post of foreman.

The most significant development between the first two novels and *Going Down River Road* is in the manipulation of language. The grace and lucidity of the earlier novels give way in this latest one to a tough earthiness which admirably matches the status, occupations and circumstances of Mwangi's characters. It is sometimes realistic, coarse, workers' language, abounding in four-letter words. But it is surely inexcusable for Mwangi to lapse into it himself for his own narration of events as in: 'Kanji Bhai stirs awake, scrambles from under the lorry, and makes his way through the lunchtime inertness to the latrine at the further corner of the site. He never eats anything for lunch, but he is always shitting' (p. 53). It must be said, however, that Mwangi is adept in capturing the speech registers of the various classes, including the Europeans. His mimicry of the Indian Kanji Bhai is particularly adroit. Mwangi uses the past tense when describing scenes that have occurred in the past, but for most of his narrative uses the present tense, thus creating a sense of immediacy and drama. With the exception of Wini's portrayal almost everything in this novel is extremely well done, thus making it a most accomplished achievement.

NOTES

1 Meja Mwangi, *Kill Me Quick* (Heinemann, London, 1973). All further page references are to this edition.
2 Meja Mwangi, *Carcase for Hounds* (Heinemann, London, 1974), p. 1. All further page references are to this edition.
3 Meja Mwangi, *Going Down River Road* (Heinemann, London, 1976), p. 22. All further page references are to this edition.

Select Bibliography

▼▼

List of Abbreviations

ALT	*African Literature Today*
ASB	*African Studies Bulletin*
BA	*Books Abroad*
BO	*Black Orpheus*
BAALE	*Bulletin of the Association of African Literature in English*
CLAJ	*Commonwealth Languages Association Journal*
CUP	Cambridge University Press
JCL	*Journal of Commonwealth Literature*
JMAS	*Journal of Modern African Studies*
JNESA	*Journal of the Nigerian English Studies Association*
JNALA	*Journal of the New African Literature and the Arts*
OUP	Oxford University Press
Pres. Afr.	*Présence Africaine*
REL	*Review of English Literature*

Books

Barker, W. and Sinclair, C., *West African Stories* (Harrap, London, 1917).

Beier, Ulli, ed., *Introduction to African Literature* (Longman, London, 1967).

Brench, A. C., *The Novelists' Inheritance in French Africa* (OUP, London, 1967).

Carroll, David, *Chinua Achebe* (Twayne, New York, 1970).

Cartey, Wilfred, *Whispers from a Continent* (Heinemann, London, 1971).

Collins, Harold, *Amos Tutuola* (Twayne, New York, 1969).

Cook, M. and Henderson, S. E., *The Militant Black Writer in Africa and the United States* (University of Wisconsin Press, Madison, Wisconsin, 1969).

Dathorne, O. R., *African Literature in the Twentieth Century* (Heinemann, London, 1975).

Dayrell, Elphinstone, *Folk Stories of Southern Nigeria* (Longman, London, 1910).

Duerden, Dennis and Pieterse, Cosmo, eds, *African Writers Talking* (Heinemann, London, 1972).

Emenyonu, Ernest, *Cyprian Ekwensi* (Evans, London, 1974).

Gakwandi, A. S., *The Novel and Contemporary Experience in Africa* (Heinemann, London, 1977).

Gleason, Judith, *This Africa: Novels by West Africans in English and French* (University of Illinois Press, Evanston, Ill., 1965).

Iyatemi, P. and Currey, P., eds, *Folk Tales and Fables* (Penguin, Harmondsworth, 1953).

Jablow, Alta, *Yes and No! The Intimate Folk-Lore of Africa* (Horizon Press, New York, 1961).

Jahn, Janheinz, *A History of Neo-African Literature* (Faber, London, 1966).

Jahn Janheinz, *Muntu: An Outline of Neo-African Culture* (Faber, London, 1961).

Jones, Eldred, *The Writing of Wole Soyinka* (Heinemann, London, 1973).

Heywood, Christopher, ed., *Perspectives on African Literature* (Heinemann, London, 1971).

Kesteloot, Lilyan, *Les Ecrivains noirs de language française* (Université Libre de Bruxelles, Institute de Sociologie, Brussels, 1965).

Killam, G. D., *The Novels of Chinua Achebe* (Heinemann, London, 1969).

Killam, G. D., ed., *African Writers on African Writing* (Heinemann, London, 1973).

King, Bruce, ed., *Introduction to Nigerian Literature* (University of Lagos and Evans, London and Lagos, 1971).

King, Bruce and Ogungbesan, Kolawole, *A Celebration of Black and African Writing* (Ahmadu Bello University Press and Oxford University Press, Zaria and Oxford, 1975).

Larson, Charles, *The Emergence of African Fiction* (Indiana University Press, London and Bloomington, Ind., 1971).

Laurence, Margaret, *Long Drums and Cannons* (Macmillan, London, 1968).

Lindfors, Bernth, *Amos Tutuola and His Critics* (African Studies Centre, UCLA, Los Angeles, Calif., 1969).

Lo Liyong, Taban, *The Last Word: Cultural Synthesism* (East African Publishing House, Nairobi, 1969).

Makward, Edris, *Is There an African Approach to African Literature?* (African Studies Centre, UCLA, Los Angeles, Calif., 1969).

Moore, Gerald, *Seven African Writers* (OUP, London, 1962).

Moore, Gerald, ed., *African Literature and the Universities* (Ibadan University Press, Ibadan, 1965).

Moore, Gerald, *The Chosen Tongue* (Longman, London, 1971).

Moore, Gerald, *Wole Soyinka* (Evans, London, 1971).

Mphahlele, Ezekiel, *The African Image* (Faber, London, 1962).

Nazareth, Peter, *Literature and Society in Modern Africa* (East African Literature Bureau, Nairobi, 1973).

Ngugi wa Thiong'o, *Homecoming* (Heinemann, London, 1972).

Obiechina, Emmanuel, *An African Popular Literature* (CUP, London, 1973).

Obiechina, Emmanuel, *Culture, Tradition and Society in the West African Novel* (CUP, Cambridge, 1975).

Ogumetun, M. I., *Yoruba Legends* (Sheldon Press, London, 1951).

Palmer, Eustace, *An Introduction to the African Novel* (Heinemann, London, 1972).

Press, John, ed., *Commonwealth Literature: Unity and Diversity in a Common Culture* (Heinemann, London, 1965).

Ramsaran, J. A. and Jahn, J., *Approaches to African Literature* (Ibadan University Press, Ibadan, 1959).

Ravenscroft, Arthur, *Chinua Achebe* (Longman, London, 1969).

Roscoe, Adrian A., *Mother Is Gold* (CUP, London, 1971).

Rotberg, R. and Mazrui, Ali (eds), *Protest and Power in Black Africa* (OUP, New York, 1970).

Soyinka, Wole, *Myth, Literature and the African World* (CUP, Cambridge, 1976).

Taiwo, O., *An Introduction to West African Literature* (Nelson, London, 1967).

Taiwo, O., *Culture and the Nigerian Novel* (Macmillan, London, 1976).

Tibble, Anne, *African-English Literature* (Peter Owen, London, 1965).

Walsh, William, *A Manifold Voice: Studies in Commonwealth Literature* (Chatto and Windus, London, 1969).

Wanjala, Chris, ed., *Standpoints on African Literature* (East African Literature Bureau, Nairobi, 1973).

Wastberg, P., ed., *The Writer in Modern Africa* (Almquist & Wiksell, Uppsala, 1968).

Wauthier, Claude, *The Literature and Thought of Modern Africa* (Pall Mall Press, London, 1966).

Wright, Edgar, ed., *The Critical Evaluation of African Literature* (Heinemann, London, 1973).

Articles

Achebe, Chinua, 'The novelist as teacher', *African Writers on African Writing*, ed. G. D. Killam (Heinemann, London, 1973), pp. 1–14.

Achebe, Chinua, 'Where angels fear to tread', *African Writers on African Writing*, in Killam (ed.), op. cit., pp. 4–7.

Achebe, Chinua, 'The role of the writer in a new nation', *African Writers on African Writing*, in Killam (ed.), op. cit., pp. 7–13.

Ackley, D., 'Wole Soyinka's *The Interpreters*', *BO*, vol. II, nos 5 and 6 (1971), pp. 50–7.

Afolayan, A., 'Language and sources of Amos Tutuola', in *Perspectives on African Literature*, ed. Christopher Heywood (Heinemann, London, 1971), pp. 49–63.

Anozie, S. O., 'Structure and utopia in Tutuola's *Palm-Wine Drinkard*', *The Conch*, vol. II, no. 2 (1970).

Banham, M. J., 'The beginnings of a Nigerian literature in English', *REL*, vol III (1962), pp. 88–9.

Banham, M. J. and Ramsaran, J., 'West African writing', *BA*, 36 (1962), pp. 371–4.

Banjo, Ayo, 'Language in Aluko: the use of colloquialisms, Nigerianisms', *Ba Shiru*, vol. V, no. 1 (Fall, 1973), pp. 59–70.

Bestman, Martin T., 'Sembène Ousmane: social commitment and the search for an African identity, in *A Celebration of Black and African Writing*, ed. Bruce King and Kolawale Ogungbesan (Ahmadu Bello University Press and Oxford University Press, Zaria and Oxford, 1975), pp. 139–49.

Blair, D. S., 'Background to a literature', *English Studies in Africa*, vol. XIV, no. 2 (1971), pp. 147–59.

Bradley, S., 'African fiction and the future', *Cimarron Review*, 14 (1972), pp. 46–53.

Brench, A. C., 'The novelist's background in French colonial Africa', *African Forum*, 1 (Summer 1967), pp. 34–41.

Brown, Lloyd W., 'Culture norms and modes of perception in Achebe's fiction', *Research in African Literatures*, vol. III, no. 1 (Spring 1972), pp. 21–35.

Chukwukere, B. I., 'African novelists and social change', *Phylon*, vol. XXVI, no. 3 (1965), pp. 228–39.

Chukwukere, B. I., 'The problem of language in African creative writing', *ALT*, no. 3 (1969), pp. 15–26.

Clark, J. P., 'Our literary critics', *Nigeria Magazine*, 74 (December 1962), p. 80.

Collins, H. R., 'Founding a new national literature: the "ghost novels" of Amos Tutuola', *Critique*, 4 (1960), pp. 24–30.

Crowder, Michael, 'Tradition and change in Nigerian literature', *BAALE*, 3 (1965), pp. 1–17.

Dathorne, O. R., 'The African novel: document to experiment', *BAALE*, 3 (November 1965), pp. 18–39.

Dathorne, O. R., 'The beginnings of the West African novel', *Nigeria Magazine*, 93 (June 1967), pp. 168–70.

Dathorne, O. R., 'Amos Tutuola: the nightmare of the tribe', in *Introduction to Nigerian Literature*, ed. Bruce King (Lagos University Press and Evans, Lagos and London, 1971), pp. 113–34.

Davis, Charles, 'Whose mission to Kala? A study of the problems of translation', *Ba Shiru*, vol. IV, no. 2 (Spring 1973), pp. 25–33.

Deloney, J. D., 'Yambo Ouologuem: conceptualising the African past', *African Studies Review*, vol. XIV, no. 1 (1971), pp. 147–9.

Drayton, Arthur, 'The return to the past in the Nigerian novel', *Ibadan*, 10 (1960), p. 29.

Echeruo, M. J. C., 'Chinua Achebe', in King and Ogungbesan (eds), *A Celebration of Black and African Writing*, op. cit., pp. 150–63.

Edwards, P., 'The novel in West Africa', *Overseas Quarterly*, 3 (June 1963), pp. 176–7.

Edwards, P., 'Polemics: the dead end of African literature', *Transition*, vol. III, no. 12 (1964), pp. 7–8.

Edwards, P. and Carrol, D. R., 'Approaches to the novel in West Africa', *Phylon*, 23 (Winter 1962),

Emenyonu, E., 'African literature: what does it take to be its critic?', *ALT*, no. 5 (1971), pp. 1–11.

Folarin, Margaret, 'An additional comment on Ayi Kwei Armah's *The Beautyful Ones Are Not Yet Born*', *ALT*, no. 5 (1971), pp. 116–29.

George, Robert A., 'Towards an understanding of story-telling events', *Journal of American Folk-lore*, vol. LXXXII, no. 326 (Austin, Texas, 1969),

Gleason, Judith, 'Out of the irony of words', *Transition*, 18 (1965–6).

Gleason, Judith, 'The African novel in French', *African Forum*, vol. I, no. 4 (Spring 1966), pp. 75–92.

Griffiths, Gareth, 'Language and action in the novels of Chinua Achebe', *ALT*, no. 5 (1971), pp. 88–105.

Hanshell, D., 'African writing today', *Month*, XXXII (November 1964), pp. 246–54.

Heywood, Christopher, 'Surface and symbol in *Things Fall Apart*', *JNESA*, 2 (November 1967), pp. 41–6.

Ikiddeh, Ime, 'Ngugi wa Thiong'o; the novelist as historian', in King and Ogungbesan (eds), *A Celebration of Black and African Writing*, op. cit., pp. 204–15.

Irele, Abiola, 'In defence of Negritude', *Transition*, vol. III, no. 33 (1964), pp. 9–11.

Irele, Abiola, 'Negritude or black cultural nationalism', *JMAS*, vol. III, no. 3 (October 1965), pp. 321–48.

Irele, Abiola, 'The criticism of modern African literature', *JNESA*, vol. II, no. 2 (1968), pp. 146–8.

Irele, Abiola, 'The tragic conflict in Achebe's novels', *BO*, 17 (1965), pp. 24–32.

Irele, Abiola, 'The criticism of modern African literature', in Heywood (ed.), *Perspectives on African Literature*, op. cit., pp. 9–24.

Iyasere, Solomon, 'The liberation of African literature: a revaluation of the socio-cultural approach', *Prés. Afr.*, 90 (1974), pp. 215–25.

Iyasere, Solomon, 'African critics on African literature: A study in misplaced hostility', *ALT*, no. 7 (1975), pp. 20–7.

Izevbaye, D. S., 'The relationship of criticism to literature in Africa', *JNESA*, vol. II, no. 2 (1968), pp. 148–9.

Izevbaye, D. S., 'African literature defined: the record of a controversy', *Ibadan Studies in English*, vol. I, no. 7 (May 1969)

Izevbaye, D. S., 'Criticism and literature in Africa', in Heywood (ed.), *Perspectives on African Literature*, op. cit., pp. 33–48.

Izevbaye, D. S., 'Ayi Kwei Armah and the 'I' of the beholder', in King and Ogungbesan (eds), *A Celebration of Black and African Writing*, op. cit., pp. 232–44.

Izevbaye, D. S., 'The state of criticism in African literature', *ALT*, no. 7 (1975), pp. 1–19.

Jahn, Janheinz, 'African literature', *Prés. Afr.*, vol. XXXX, no. 48 (1963), pp. 47–57.

James, Adeola, review, 'Eustace Palmer: *An Introduction to the African Novel*', *ALT*, no. 7 (1975), pp. 147–52.

Jones, E. D., 'Language and theme in *Things Fall Apart*', *REL*, vol. V, no. 4 (October 1964), pp. 39–43.

Jones, E. D., 'Interpreting *The Interpreters*', *BAALE*, 4 (1966), pp. 13–18.

Jones, E. D., 'Turning Back the Pages: *The Palm-Wine Drinkard* 14 Years On', *BAALE*, 4 (March 1966), pp. 24–30.

Jones, E. D., 'Jungle drums and wailing piano: West African fiction and poetry in English', *African Forum*, vol. I, no. 4 (Spring 1966), pp. 93–106.

Jones, E. D., 'Locale and universe: three Nigerian novels', *JCL*, 3 (July 1967), pp. 127–31.

Jones, E. D., '*The Interpreters*: reading notes', *ALT*, no. 2 (1969), pp. 42–50.

Jones, E. D., 'The essential Soyinka', in *Introduction to Nigerian Literature*, ed. Bruce King (Lagos University Press and Evans, Lagos and London, 1971), pp. 113–34.

Jones, E. D., 'Wole Soyinka: critical approaches', in *The Critical Evaluation of African Literature*, ed. Edgar Wright (Heinemann, London, 1973), pp. 51–72.

Jordan, A. C. 'Towards an African literature', *Africa South*, vol. I, no. 4 (1957), pp. 90–8.

Jordan, J. O., 'Culture, conflict and social change in Achebe's *Arrow of God*', *Studies in Modern Fiction*, vol. XIII, no. 1 (1970), pp. 66–82.

July, R. W., 'African literature and the African personality', *BO*, 4 (February 1964), pp. 33–45.

Kamara, Jeanette, review, 'Ferdinand Oyono: *The Old Man and the Medal*', *ALT*, no. 3 (1969), pp. 50–2.

Kane, M., 'The African writer and his public', *Prés. Afr.*, vol. XXX, no. 58 (1966), pp. 8–32.

Kesteloot, L., 'The problems of the literary critic in Africa', *Abbia*, 8 (1965), pp. 29–44.

Killam, G. D., 'Recent African fiction', *BAALE*, no. 2 (October 1964), pp. 1–10.

Killam, G. D., 'Cyprian Ekwensi', in King (ed.), *Introduction to Nigerian Literature*, op. cit., pp. 77–96.

Leslie, Omolara, '*The Palm-Wine Drinkard*: A reassessment of Amos Tutuola', *JCL*, 9 (July 1970), 48–56.

Leslie, Omolara, 'Chinua Achebe: his vision and his craft', *BO*, vol. II, no. 7 (1972), pp. 34–41.

Leslie, Omolara, 'Nigeria, alienation and the novels of Chinua Achebe', *Prés. Afr.*, 84 (1972), pp. 99–108.

Leslie, Omolara, 'The trial of Christopher Okigbo', *Ba Shiru*, vol. IV, no. 2 (Spring 1973), pp. 81–6.

Lienhardt, Peter, 'Tribesmen and cosmopolitans: on African literature', *Encounter*, vol. XXV, no. 5 (November 1969), pp. 54–67.

Lindfors, Bernth, 'Five Nigerian novels', *BA*, vol. XXXIX, no. 4 (Autumn 1965), pp. 411–13.

Lindfors, Bernth, 'African vernacular styles in Nigerian fiction', *CLAJ*, vol. IX, no. 3 (March 1966), pp. 265–73.

Lindfors, Bernth, 'Amos Tutuola and his critics', *Abbia*, 3 (May 1966), pp. 109–18.

Lindfors, Bernth, 'Achebe's African parable', *Prés. Afr.*, 66 (1968), pp. 130–6.

Lindfors, Bernth, 'The palm-oil with which Achebe's words are eaten', *ALT*, no. 1 (1968), pp. 3–18.

Lindfors, Bernth, 'Cyprian Ekwensi: an African popular novelist', *ALT*, no. 3 (1969), pp. 2–14.

Lindfors, Bernth, 'Amos Tutuola and D. O. Fagunwa', *JCL*, 9 (December 1970), pp. 57–65.

Lindfors, Bernth, 'Amos Tutuola: debts and assets', *Cahiers d'études Africaines*, X (1970), pp. 306–34.

Lindfors, Bernth, 'Approaches to folk-lore in African literature', *The Conch*, vol. II, no. 2 (September 1970), 102–11.

Lindfors, Bernth, 'Chinua Achebe and the Nigerian novel', in *Studies in Modern Black African Literature*, ed. P. Paricsy (Centre for Afro-Asian Research, Budapest, 1970), pp. 29–49.

Lindfors, Bernth, 'T. M. Aluko: Nigerian satirist', *ALT*, no. 5 (1971), pp. 41–53.

Lindfors, Bernth, 'Ambiguity and intention in *Arrow of God*', *Ba Shiru*, vol. V, no. 1 (Fall 1973), pp. 43–8.

Lindfors, Bernth, 'The blind men and the elephant', *ALT*, no. 7 (1975), pp. 34–52.

Lindfors, Bernth, 'Amos Tutuola's *The Palm-Wine Drinkard* and the oral tradition', *Critique*, vol. XI, no. 1, pp. 42–50.

Makward, E., 'Negritude and the new African novel in French', *Ibadan*, 22, pp. 37–45.

Maes-Jelinek, Hena, review, 'Yambo Omologuem: *Le Devoir de violence*', *ALT*, no. 4 (1970), pp. 54–5.

Mazrui, Molly, 'Religion in African fiction: a consideration', *East African Journal* (January 1968), pp. 32–6.

McDonald, R., '*Bound to Violence*; a case of plagiarism', *Transition*, 41 (1972), pp. 64–8.

McDowell, R. E., 'Four Ghanaian novels', *JNALA*, 4 (1967), pp. 22–7.

Melamu, M. J., 'The quest for power in Achebe's *Arrow of God*', *English Studies in Africa*, vol. XIV, no. 2 (1971), pp. 225–40.

Michelman, F., 'The beginnings of French-African fiction', *Research in African Literatures*, vol. II, no. 1 (Spring 1971), pp. 3–17.

Moore, G. M., 'Amos Tutuola: a Nigerian visionary', *BO*, 1 (September 1957), pp. 27–35.

Nance, C., 'Cosmology in the novels of Chinua Achebe', *The Conch*, vol. III, no. 2 (1971), pp. 121–36.

Nkosi, Lewis, 'African literature: part II – English-speaking West Africa', *Africa Report*, vol. VII, no. 11 (December 1962), pp. 15–17 and 31.

Nkosi, Lewis, 'Some conversations with African writers', *Africa Report*, vol. IX, no. 7 (July 1965), pp. 7–21.

Nkosi, Lewis, 'Where does African literature go from here?', *Africa Report*, vol. XI, no. 9 (December 1966), pp. 7–11.

Nnolim, C. E., 'Jungian archetypes and the main characters in Oyono's *Une Vie de Boy*,' *ALT*, no. 7 (1975), pp. 117–27.

Obiechina, E. N., 'Modern African literature and tradition', *African Affairs* (July 1967), pp. 246–7.

Obiechina, E. N., 'Growth of a written literature in English-speaking West Africa', *Prés. Afr.*, 66 (1968), pp. 58–78.

Obiechina, E. N., 'Cultural nationalism in modern African creative literature', *ALT*, no. 1 (1968), pp. 24–35.

Obiechina, E. N., 'Transition from oral to literary tradition', *Prés. Afr.*, 63 (1967), pp. 140–61.

Obiechina, E. N., 'Tutuola and the oral tradition', *Prés. Afr.*, 65 (1968), pp. 85–105.

Obiechina, E. N., 'Ekwensi as novelist', *Prés. Afr.*, 86 (1973), pp. 152–64.

O'Flinn, J. P., 'Towards a sociology of the Nigerian novel', *ALT*, no. 7 (1975), pp. 34–52.

Odundipe, Abiodun, 'Some aspects of the technique of Chinua Achebe', *JNESA* (1969), pp. 160–2.

Ogungbesan, Kolawole, 'Symbol and meaning in *The Beautyful Ones Are Not Yet Born*', *ALT*, no. 7 (1975), pp. 93–110.

Ogungbesan, Kolawole, 'Wole Soyinka: the past and the visionary writer', in King and Ogungbesan (eds), *A Celebration of Black and African Writing*, op. cit., pp. 175–88.

Ogundipe, Molara, '*The Palm-Wine Drinkard:* a reassessment of Amos Tutuola', *Prés. Afr.*, 71 (1969), pp. 99–108.

Ohaebgu, A. U., 'Literature for the people: two novels by Sembène Ousmane', *Prés. Afr.*, 91 (1974), pp. 116–31.

Okpaku, Joseph, 'Tradition, culture and criticism', *Prés. Afr.*, 70 (1969), pp. 137–46.

Olney, J., 'The Nigerian novel in transition', *South Atlantic Quarterly*, vol. LXX, no. 3 (1971), pp. 199–316.

Palmer, Eustace, 'Mongo Beti's *Mission to Kala:* an interpretation', *ALT*, no. 3 (1969), pp. 27–43.

Palmer, Eustace, 'Social comment in the West African Novel', *Studies in the Novel*, vol. IV, no. 2 (Summer 1972), pp. 218–30.

Palmer, Eustace, 'The criticism of the African novel', *Africana Research Bulletin*, vol. II, no. 4 (July 1972), pp. 52–69.

Palmer, Eustace, 'Vox populi, vox sembène: a preliminary look at the art of Sembène Ousmane', *Ba Shiru*, vol. V, no. 1 (1973), pp. 3–13.

Palmer, Eustace, 'The criticism of African fiction: its nature and function', *International Fiction Review* (Spring 1974), 112–19.

Palmer, Eustace, 'A plea for objectivity: a reply to Adeola James', *ALT*, no. 7 (1975), pp. 123–7.

Palmer, Eustace, 'Development and change in the novels of T.M. Aluko', *World Literature Written in English*, vol. XV, no. 2 (1976), pp. 279–96.

Palmer, Eustace, 'Twenty-five years of Amos Tutuola', *International Fiction Review*, vol. V, no. 1 (1978), pp. 15–24.

Palmer, Eustace, 'Two views of urban life: Meja Mwangi, *Going Down River Road*, Nuruddin Farah, *A Naked Needle*', *ALT*, no. 9 (1978), pp. 104–8.

Palmer, Eustace, 'Wole Soyinka's *Season of Anomy*', *World Literature Written in English*, vol. XVII, no. 2 (1978), 435–49.

Parry, John, 'Nigerian novelists', *Contemporary Review*, 200 (1961), pp. 377–381.

Passmore, D. R., 'Camp style in the novels of Cyprian O. D. Ekwensi', *Journal of Popular Culture*, IV (1971), pp. 705–16.

Povey, John, 'Cyprian Ekwensi and *Beautiful Feathers*', *Critique*, vol. VIII, no. 1 (1965), pp. 63–9.

Povey, John, 'Changing themes in the Nigerian novel', *Journal of the New African Literature*, 1 (Spring 1966), pp. 3–11.

Povey, John, 'Contemporary West African writing in English', *BA*, vol. XL, no. 3 (Summer 1966), pp. 3–11.

Povey, John, 'The quality of African writing today', *The Literary Review*, 4 (1968), pp. 403–21.

Povey, John, 'Political protest in the African novel in English', in *Protest and Power in Black Africa*, eds R. Rotberg and Ali Mazrui (OUP, New York, 1970), pp. 823–53.

Povey, John, 'The novels of Chinua Achebe', in King (ed.), *Introduction to Nigerian Literature*, op. cit., pp. 97–112.

Povey, John, 'Cyprian Ekwensi: the novelist and the pressures of the city', in Wright (ed.), *The Critical Evaluation of African Literature*, op. cit., pp. 73–94.

Ravenscroft, A., 'African literature V: novels of disillusionment', *JCL*, 6 (January 1969), pp. 120–37.

Ravenscroft, A., 'An introduction to West African novels in English', *The Literary Criterion*, vol. X, no. 2 (1972), pp. 38–56.

Redding, Saunders, 'Modern African literature', *CLAJ*, vol. VII, no. 3 (March 1964), pp. 191–201.

Reed, John, 'Between two worlds: some notes on the presentation by African novelists of the individual in modern African society', *Makerere Journal*, 7 (1963), pp. 1–14.

Riddy, Felicity, 'Language as theme in *No Longer at Ease*', *JCL*, 9 (December 1970), pp. 38–74.

Rugyendo, Mukotani, 'Ferdinand Oyono: a dissenting view', *ALT*, no. 6 (1973), pp. 152–6.

Schmidt, Nancy, 'Nigerian fiction and the African oral tradition', *JNALA*, 5/6 (Spring/Autumn 1968), pp. 10–19.

Schorer, Mark, 'Technique as discovery', in *The Novel: Modern Essays in Criticism*, ed. Robert Murray Davis (Prentice-Hall, Englewood Cliffs, NJ, 1969), pp. 75–93.

Sellin, Eric, 'Ouologuem's blueprint for *Le Devoir de violence*', *Research in African Literatures*, vol. II, no. 2 (Fall 1971), pp. 117–20.

Sesay, K., 'Ekwensi and Okpewho on the Nigerian Civil War', *ALT*, no. 9 (1978), pp. 99–103.

Shelton, Austin, 'The articulation of traditional and modern in Igbo culture', *The Conch*, vol. I, no. 1 (March 1969),   .

Shelton, Austin, 'The offended chi in Achebe's novels', *Transition*, vol. III, no. 13 (1964), pp. 36–7.

Shelton, Austin, ' "Rebushing" or ontological recession to Africanism: Jagua's return to the village', *Prés. Afr.*, vol. XVIII, no. 46 (1963), pp. 49–58.

Soyinka, Wole, 'From a common backcloth: a reassessment of the African literary image', *American Scholar*, vol. XXXII, no. 3 (Summer 1963), pp. 387–96.

Soyinka, Wole, 'The writer in a modern African state', in *The Writer in*

Modern Africa, ed. P. Wastberg (Scandinavian Institute of African Studies, Uppsala, 1968), pp. 14–21.

Sterling, T., 'Africa's black writers', *Holiday Magazine*, vol. XLI, no. 2 (February 1967), pp. 131–40.

Stewart, Daniele, 'Ghanaian writing in prose: a critical survey', *Prés. Afr.*, 91 (1974), pp. 73–105.

Stock, A. G., 'Yeats and Achebe', *JCL*, 5 (July 1968), pp. 105–11.

Stuart, Donald, 'African literature III: the modern writer in his context', *JCL* 4 (December 1967), pp. 113–29.

Taiwo, Oladele, 'T. M. Aluko: the novelist and his imagination', *Prés. Afr.*, 91 (1974), pp. 225–46.

Wake, Clive, 'African literary criticism', *Comparative Literary Studies*, vol. 1, no. 3 (1964), pp. 197–205.

Wali, O., 'The African novelists', *Freedomways*, vol. VI, no. 2, pp. 163–71.

Wali, O., 'The individual and the novel in Africa', *Transition*, vol. IV, no. 18 (1965), pp. 31–3.

Waterhouse, K., review, 'Achebe's *No Longer at Ease*', *New Statesman*, LX (17 September 1960), p. 398.

Wright, Edgar, 'African literature I: problems of criticism', *JCL*, 2 (December 1966), pp. 103–12.

Wright, Edgar, 'Critical procedures and the evaluation of African literature', in Wright (ed.), *The Critical Evaluation of African Literature*, op. cit., pp. 1–22.

K. W., 'In Defence of Yambo Ouologuem', *West Africa*, 2850 (28 January 1972), pp. 939–41.

Index

▼▼▼

The names in the bibliography (on pp. 323–33) have not been included and additional information may be found there.